Barney White-Spunner has commanded British and allied troops at every level from troop to the Field Army, including the elite 16 Air Assault Brigade whom he took into Kabul in the immediate aftermath of 9/11. He has also led operations in the Balkans and Iraq, as well as in Africa and Asia. A noted military historian, his previous books include *Horse Guards*, the story of The Household Cavalry. He was knighted in 2011, is an Honorary Legionnaire in the French Foreign Legion and holds the US Legion of Merit.

Praise for *Of Living Valour*

'A glorious book. The personal narratives work brilliantly' Peter Oborne, *Daily Mail*

'Of all the many Waterloo books, this is the one that will endure' Alistair Bunkall, Sky News Defence Correspondent

'The former Household Cavalry General ... really brings to life what it was like for the common soldiers, many of whom were weavers and country boys who had signed up for the campaign. Lying in the open in torrential rain the night before, they spent the day of the battle being blasted by cannonballs, charged by fearsome cavalry and regularly engaged in desperate hand-to-hand fighting' Rupert Uloth, *Country Life*

'An intimate account of the Battle of Waterloo drawing on extensive unpublished letters and diaries of the ordinary soldiers who took part' *The British Sporting Art Trust*

'A lucid account of the battle itself seen from British eyes, as well as the days and weeks leading up to it, and a particularly good section on the aftermath which graphically describes the sight of thousands of dead and dying men on the battlefield' *Who Do You Think You Are? Magazine*

Also by Barney White-Spunner:

HORSE GUARDS

OF LIVING VALOUR

The story of the
soldiers of Waterloo

BARNEY
WHITE-SPUNNER

**SIMON &
SCHUSTER**

London · New York · Sydney · Toronto · New Delhi

A CBS COMPANY

First published in Great Britain by Simon & Schuster UK Ltd, 2015
This paperback edition published in Great Britain
by Simon & Schuster UK Ltd, 2016
A CBS COMPANY

Maps © ML Design

1 3 5 7 9 10 8 6 4 2

Simon & Schuster UK Ltd
1st Floor
222 Gray's Inn Road
London WC1X 8HB

www.simonandschuster.co.uk

Simon & Schuster Australia, Sydney
Simon & Schuster India, New Delhi

A CIP catalogue record for this book
is available from the British Library

Paperback ISBN: 978-1-4711-0293-6
eBook: 978-1-4711-0294-3

The author and publishers have made all reasonable efforts
to contact copyright-holders for permission, and apologise
for any omissions or errors in the form of credits given.
Corrections may be made to future printings.

Typeset in the UK by M Rules
Printed and bound by CPI Group (UK) Ltd, Croydon, CR0 4YY

MIX
Paper from
responsible sources
FSC® C020471

Simon & Schuster UK Ltd are committed to sourcing paper
that is made from wood grown in sustainable forests and supports the Forest
Stewardship Council, the leading international forest certification organisation.
Our books displaying the FSC logo are printed on FSC certified paper.

This book is dedicated to those who fell

And Ardennes waves above them her green leaves,
Dewy with nature's tear-drops, as they pass,
Grieving, if aught inanimate e'er grieves,
Over the unreturning brave, – alas!
Ere evening to be trodden like the grass
Which now beneath them, but above shall grow
In its next verdure, when this fiery mass
Of living valour, rolling on the foe
And burning with high hope, shall moulder cold and low.

LORD BYRON,
Childe Harold's Pilgrimage

CONTENTS

LIST OF MAPS AND ILLUSTRATIONS

MAPS

PLATE SECTION ONE

1. Captain Rees Gronow: frontispiece to *The Reminiscences and Recollections of Captain Gronow* (The Bodley Head, 1964).
2. Lieutenant Edmund Wheatley: frontispiece to *The Wheatley Diary* (Longmans, 1964).
3. Corporal John Shaw: private collection.
4. Captain Cavalié Mercer: provenance unknown.
5. The prevailing patriotic spirit: *Buonaparte 48 hours after landing,* by James Gillray; published by Hannah Humphrey, hand-coloured etching, published 26 July 1803 © National Portrait Gallery, London.
6. Gillray's portrayal of the Volunteers: *Supplementary-militia, turning-out for twenty-days amusement*, by James Gillray; published

by Hannah Humphrey, hand-coloured etching, published 25 November 1796 © National Portrait Gallery, London.

7. Light Cavalry: by kind permission of the Queens Royal Hussars.

8. Heavy Cavalry: *1st King's Dragoon Guards at Waterloo*, by R. Caton Woodville, frontispiece to *And They Rode On* (Michael Russell, 1984).

9. Lieutenant Colonel Henry Murray, by kind permission of Vicountess Stormont.

10. Emily Murray, by kind permission of Vicountess Stormont.

11. Henry, Earl of Uxbridge: *Lieut-Colonel Of The 7th Light Dragoons (Hussars)* by John Hoppner © National Trust.

12. Dr Haddy James: frontispiece to *Surgeon James's Journal 1815* (Cassell, 1964).

13. The weapons of Waterloo: © Mark Adkin, *The Waterloo Companion* (Aurum, 2001).

14. Wellington: Arthur Wellesley, 1st Duke of Wellington, c.1815 (oil on canvas), Lawrence, Sir Thomas (1769–1830)/Apsley House, The Wellington Museum, London, UK/© English Heritage Photo Library/Bridgeman Images.

15. Colonel de Lancey: drawing c.1813, *A Week at Waterloo in 1815* (John Murray, 1908)(Wikimedia Commons).

16. Field Marshal Prince von Blücher: Field Marshal Prince von Blücher (1742–1819) c.1816 (oil on canvas), Dawe, George (1781–1829)/Apsley House, The Wellington Museum, London, UK/Bridgeman Images.

17. August von Gneisenau: Field-Marshal August Neidhardt, Count of Gneisenau, 1818 (oil on canvas), Dawe, George (1781–1829)/Apsley House, The Wellington Museum, London, UK/© English Heritage Photo Library/Bridgeman Images.

18. Napoleon: Napoleon Bonaparte in His Study at the Tuileries, 1812 (oil on canvas), David, Jacques Louis (1748–1825)/Private Collection/Bridgeman Images.

19. Marshal Soult: Jean-de-Dieu Soult (1769–1851), Duke of

PLATE SECTION TWO

PROLOGUE

The Day After

Mrs Tidy, whose husband Colonel Frank Tidy commanded a battalion of the 14th Regiment of Foot, received news of the great victory at Waterloo when a coach passed the gate of her cottage on the Isle of Wight, 'streaming with gilded flags that bore the words "Wellington! Victory! Waterloo!"' Her children saw them and rushed in to tell their mother. 'There has been a battle,' they said, 'they have been fighting the French and *we* have beaten them.' But Mrs Tidy's concerns were more immediate. Was her husband still alive? Had he survived the battle uninjured? And, if not, how was she now to raise the son and daughter who crowded round her? Her priority was to get to the post town and find out. She was to be one of the lucky ones. There was a short letter from her husband waiting for her, saying that his favourite mare had been shot from under him but otherwise he was safe. Her daughter remembers her sitting that evening on a low hall chair in the porch of their cottage, Carisbrooke Castle in the distance, her husband's letter in her hand, and she reading it aloud. 'The golden sun streamed up the garden-walk, and shed its light upon our little group: bees murmured in the jasmined porch, and the perfume of June flowers came floating through the open door.'

Others were to be less fortunate. About 55,000 men were killed or wounded at Waterloo. Sergeant Thomas Howell of the Highland Light Infantry noted prosaically of an artillery barrage, 'The young man I lately spoke of lost both his legs by a shot at this time. They were cut very close; he soon bled to death. "Tom," he said, "remember your charge: my mother wept sore when my brother died; if she saw me thus, it would break her heart. Farewell! God bless my parents!" He said no more, his lips quivered and he ceased to breathe.' Many of the wounded lay where they had fallen. 'I went to visit the field of battle,' wrote Major Frye four days afterwards, 'but the sight was too horrible to behold. The multitude of carcasses, the heaps of wounded men with mangled limbs unable to move, and perishing from not having their wounds dressed or from hunger.' The dead were tipped into 'large square holes ... thirty or forty fine fellows stripped to their skins were thrown into each pell mell, and then covered in so slovenly a manner that sometimes a hand or foot peeped through the earth'. Some Russian Jews were assisting in this spoliation of the dead, by chiselling out their teeth, 'an operation they performed with the most brutal indifference'.[1] Local Belgians went out to shoot the hundreds of wounded horses so they could eat them.

Major Cavalié Mercer was woken early in his bloody bivouac on the day after the battle. One of his sergeants asked him whether he might bury Driver Crammond. 'And why Driver Crammond?' asked Mercer. 'Because he looks frightful, sir; many of us have not had a wink of sleep for him,' replied the sergeant. Mercer went to look. 'A cannon shot had carried away the whole head except barely the visage, which still remained attached to the torn and bloody neck. The men said they had been prevented sleeping by seeing his eyes fixed on them all night; and thus one dreadful object had super-seded all the other horrors by which they were surrounded.'[2] The British army's sang-froid was in evidence. A short dis-tance away, Mercer found two light-infantrymen, one who had lost his leg and the other who had had his thigh smashed by a cannon shot. But they were 'sending forth such howling and wailings, and oaths and execrations', which Mercer con-trasted disapprovingly with the 'quiet resolute bearing of hundreds' of both English and French wounded lying around them. They could easily see where 'G' Troop of the Royal Horse Artillery had been, as their carcasses formed 'a dark mass which, even from that distance, formed a remarkable fea-ture in the field'.

The bodies lay on the battlefield 'like sheaves cut down by the hand of the reaper'. Captain Frederick Pattison was struck by their 'diversity of expression. From the distortion of their faces many of them must have had a terrible struggle with "the king of terrors"; others, from the placidity of their expression, seemed as if they had sunk into refreshing slumber. The separation between body and soul in their case must have been instantaneous.'[3] Major Harry Smith, a veteran of Spain and the terrible siege at Badajoz, 'had never seen anything compared with what I saw ... the *whole* field from right to left was a mass of dead bodies. In one spot, to the right of La Haye Sainte, the French Cuirassiers were literally piled on each other; many soldiers not wounded lying under their horses; others, fearfully wounded, occasionally with their horses struggling upon their wounded bodies. The sight was sicken-ing.'[4]

The Battle of Waterloo is arguably the British Army's most

famous victory and certainly one of the most significant it has ever fought. It took place only 200 years ago, which is not quite as distant a memory as we generally suppose. There are people still alive whose grandparents fought there, although they were born too late actually to have talked to them about their experiences, and the last veterans lived until the 1890s. The last English person to witness the battle, Elizabeth Watkins, died only in 1903. Her father, Daniel Gale, was one of the many who joined up in March 1815 and took his wife and child with him to Belgium, as was common practice. She remembered cutting up lint and seeing many dead. Thérèse Roland, a local Belgian, was still mourning Napoleon's defeat in 1904 when she was 103 years old. She remembered the sound of the battle, 'like a rough sea breaking against the rocks', and she recalled 'one woman of Gotarville cut off the fingers of a Prussian officer, sorely hurt but still living, to secure the jewelled rings that he wore'.[5]

There are two main reasons why the battle still exercises such a hold on our imagination. First, it finally ended the Napoleonic Wars, which everyone except Napoleon had assumed had finished in 1814 with his first exile. There is a tendency today to regard Napoleon's wars as in some way glamorous and chivalric but the reality for early-nineteenth-century Europe was very different. Seven million Europeans were killed as a direct result of warfare in the 23 years between 1792 and Waterloo in June 1815,[6] and a fifth of all European battles fought between 1490 and Waterloo took place in that very short period. Societies were mobilised and nations broken up, economies ruined and families devastated in a manner similar to that which Europe experienced between 1939 and 1945. Britain escaped invasion then, as it did in 1940, but the impact of the wars on people at home was in many ways as far-reaching. Napoleon's image, as a brilliant general, a great romantic, an inventive lover and an exceptional administrator, has outlived the brutal reality of what his political and military ambition meant both for Europe in general and France in particular. By 1815 at least one and a half million Frenchmen had lost their lives, a figure that rises to nearer 3 million if you include all the territory which could be counted part of the Empire. He left France hated and feared throughout Europe. Some contemporaries were as entranced by Napoleon as many people are today, confusing Napoleonic militarism and conquest with the early liberal principles of revolutionary France. They were, though, in a minority, and heartily detested by those who actually had to fight the French in the field or on the sea. Waterloo was so important because it put an end to that Napoleonic menace, brought peace to a generation who had known little but constant warfare, and allowed Europe to start to assimilate the revolutions in agriculture and industry that would transform her economically rather more successfully than Napoleon had attempted to do with violence.

The second reason it is such a famous battle is because of the extraordinary heroism of the British soldiers who fought there, and that is what this story is about. Much has been written about Napoleon and Wellington but not enough about the young ploughboys and weavers who stood on that bloody ridge and whose bravery and sacrifice saved Europe. That is not to say that soldiers of other nations did not fight as well or as courageously, particularly the French, whose conduct, at least in combat, earned the grudging respect of the British. It was, though, the obstinate determination of those British infantry battalions, those decimated cavalry regiments and mauled artillery batteries which stopped the French

advance, allowed the Prussians to join the battle and ultimately defeated Napoleon. Who were they? Why were they
soldiers? Why did they fight so bravely?

This is also the story of the British Army. Waterloo came at
the end of the Napoleonic Wars, which meant that the British
Army had already corrected the mistakes with which it habitually starts any campaign. It had competent generals and some
inspirational leadership; it had good weapons and sound if
basic tactics and, most importantly it had a core of professional
officers and non-commissioned officers (whom we will refer
to as NCOs) who had recent operational experience fighting
the French in the Iberian Peninsula. But this was not the
Peninsular Army. That had been disbanded and dispersed in
1814 after Napoleon's first exile when the British government
had, equally habitually, decided prematurely that it could
severely reduce it. The officers and NCOs might have been
experienced, but Waterloo was the first battle in which most
of the young private soldiers had fought. They were volunteers who had joined the Army of their own free will. They
may have joined for a variety of reasons, not all from sheer
patriotism as we will see, but the idea that they were the
'scum of the earth', flogged into battle by an authoritarian
duke, is as false an image as that which suggests the French
army they were fighting took the field for love of their
emperor. The British Army at Waterloo had more in
common with that which deployed to France in 1914 or
stood on the beaches at Dunkirk than it did with its eigh-
teenth-century predecessors. The soldiers who fought in 1815
served for the same reasons as British soldiers serve today and
the ethos and pride which bound them recently in Iraq and
Afghanistan was the same that held their forebears in the
squares against Napoleon's cavalry.

They were also remarkably literate. Improvements in education, particularly village church schools, meant that approximately half those who fought at Waterloo could read and write, which was considerably more than at the start of the Napoleonic Wars. There are few letters or diaries from the battles of the 1790s, more from the Peninsular Campaign of 1808–14 but hundreds from Waterloo. Some of these are written by men who joined in the months before the battle, as many did, particularly from the militia, but most are by career soldiers. This means that Waterloo is the first major battle about which we know a great deal of detail from the first-hand accounts of the men who fought in the ranks rather than, as was more common before, from the politicians and generals who were often trying retrospectively to justify their actions. It is these letters, diaries and memoirs that I have used to write this book. My problem has not been to find enough materials but rather to decide what to ignore.

I have quoted their words literally wherever possible, resisting the temptation to tidy them into what we would consider more grammatically correct modern English. This can occasionally make them a bit difficult to understand, and you may have to read the odd piece two or three times to understand its full meaning, but the authenticity of the language is, I think, more important.

No single person had a complete view of what happened at Waterloo. There were too many people involved in actions on different parts of the battlefield for anyone to know the exact sequence of events with authority. Those who had watches understandably had other priorities than regularly consulting them.

Lastly, what is most difficult to understand about Waterloo is just how many soldiers were crammed into the very restricted space that comprised the battlefield. It should not surprise us, given the limited firing range of the weapons they used but it can be confusing that so much seemed to be happening in such close proximity. It may be helpful to remember as you read that the great British cavalry charges took place over a distance of only about the length of a football pitch, and that an infantry battalion could only effectively influence the distance of a 100-metre running track.

THE BRITISH ARMY IN 1815

The British Army at Waterloo was made up of three distinct parts or 'arms' as soldiers refer to them:

The **cavalry**, who fought on horseback. It was divided into two parts. First, the heavy cavalry, big men on heavy horses whose role was shock action, to charge and overpower the enemy by sheer weight and mass. They carried carbines and pistols but only for patrolling duties and in battle always fought with swords. Secondly, the light cavalry, whose duties included reconnaissance, patrolling, escorts and guarding the army's flanks, but who in battle were also used en masse to charge and destroy enemy formations. All the cavalry was organised in regiments, which varied in size between 300 and 600 strong, and which were commanded by a lieutenant-colonel. They were subdivided into troops in peacetime and when in barracks, usually of about 60, and commanded by a lieutenant. However, once deployed on operations, two to three troops were teamed up to form a squadron commanded by a captain or occasionally a major. Rank in the early-nineteenth-century Army was less rigidly tied to age and regimental appointment than it has since become, and although most lieutenants tended to be in their twenties, the vagaries of the British promotion system meant that it was quite common to find them in their fifties.

The **infantry** fought on their feet with muskets and bayonets. It too was divided into regiments, who were either one of the three élite Guards regiments or numbered (since 1752, before which they had been known by the name of their colonel) from 1 to 104. Each regiment was then divided into a series of battalions, usually two but sometimes three or only one depending largely on how good its recruiting was. Each battalion, of about 1,000 men, was sub-divided into ten companies of about 100 soldiers, commanded by a captain. Two of these were flank companies, in other words those that stood on the right and left flanks of the battalion when it was drawn up in line. The right-flank company was usually the grenadier company, so called from when they were once armed with grenades (one of Charles II's less successful military experiments) but by Waterloo tended to have the tallest men. The left-flank company was the light company, with smaller, more active soldiers, as they were often used for skirmishing, which effectively meant acting as a screen in front of the main position. The remaining eight companies were known as the line companies, which accurately described their role. By Waterloo there was one regiment of rifles, which was to play a very active role in the battle.

The **artillery** served larger-calibre guns, either cannon, which were known by the size of the solid iron shot they fired (either six- or nine-pounders at Waterloo) or the modern howitzer, which fired an explosive shell at a higher trajectory. Rockets were also used at Waterloo, although the British generals were not at all sure they trusted them not to do more damage to their own soldiers than the enemy. The artillery was grouped either into batteries of foot artillery, who supported the infantry although the guns and ammunition wagons were horse-drawn, or troops of horse artillery, who drew six-pounders behind teams of eight horses (although one troop actually used nine-pounders at Waterloo), allowing them to move quickly so they could operate with the cavalry. Each battery or troop consisted of about 200 soldiers, who were either artillerymen who actually served the guns (usually five to each gun), or drivers who were recruited separately and who drove the gun trains and ammunition carts.

The other parts of the Army were a very small **Corps of Royal Engineers**, being about 250 specialist officers who advised the generals on mapping, bridging, defensive works and routes. Only eleven were present at Waterloo. There was also a corps of **Royal Sappers and Miners**, which was present in Belgium, working, slightly redundantly, on defences along the Belgian–French border, and an enormous pontoon or bridging train, capable of crossing a river of 100 metres, although it was not involved in the battle.

Lastly there were the **staff officers**. These were officers seconded from their regiments to form the headquarters of senior officers. They can be roughly divided into executive officers and aides-de-camp. The executive officers were either responsible for manning and discipline, and known as variations of Adjutant Generals (Deputy or Assistant), or for movement and operations, known as Quartermaster Generals of some description. Aides-de-camp, or ADCs, were younger officers whose role was to carry orders and messages from the general to his regiments during a battle. This was dangerous work, and many were to fall on 18 June. In addition larger headquarters like Wellington's had a skeleton medical staff, an artillery staff, a Royal Engineer and a section for foreign military representatives, but the total was still only about 40 officers. Below that level, the headquarters were small, down to a brigade commander, who would have one executive officer, a brigade major, and some ADCs.

The supply system was civilian, divided into two parts. The Commissariat, responsible for acquiring supplies, and the Royal Waggon Train, responsible for delivering them. Regiments were critical of their commissaries, as soldiers always are of those responsible for supplying them, but generally they didn't do a bad job.

When the British Army was deployed on an operation, such as the Waterloo campaign, the regiments and battalions were grouped together to form bigger units to make it easier to exercise command and control on the battlefield. Four battalions of infantry were brought together as a brigade, commanded by a major-general, and three or four brigades formed a division under a lieutenant-general, who, in the occasionally confusing British rank structure, ranks higher than a major-general. Divisions were in turn grouped into corps, of which there were three at Waterloo, commanded by the Prince of Orange, Lord Hill and Wellington himself. The artillery tended to be commanded at the divisional level. The cavalry were also grouped into brigades, there being two heavy brigades at Waterloo and five light brigades, each of three regiments.

1

JANUARY–MARCH 1815

The Royal Dragoons had been longing to get home. They had been fighting for five hard years in Portugal, Spain and more recently France as part of Wellington's Peninsular Army and were looking forward to a heroes' return. As with many British armies fighting overseas, home always seemed more attractive when they were missing it, and the thought of English food, English beer and English women sustained them through the last battles in south-western France around Toulouse and as they made the long ride north to the Channel ports. They arrived back in Dover on 19 July 1814, before being quickly despatched to Bristol, where they celebrated by going on a 'bender'* that lasted four days, helped by the issue of five months' back pay. But once the initial celebrations were over, and the hangovers cured, they began to find that home life was not quite all they had imagined.

Lord Liverpool's government thought the threat from Napoleon was over. The French emperor's disastrous 1812

---

* A traditional British Army term for soldiers going on a drunken spree.

campaign in Russia had left France severely weakened militarily, so that – as Wellington closed on Paris from south-west France – the Russians, Austrians and Prussians, advancing from the east, defeated Napoleon decisively at Leipzig in October 1813. It was the bloodiest battle in the Napoleonic Wars, with the French losing a further 81,000 men to the Allies 54,000. By March 1814 the Allied armies had entered Paris and on 6 April Napoleon had abdicated. Louis XVIII was 'restored' on 11 April, and the victorious allies met at the Congress of Vienna to carve up the extraordinary European empire Napoleon had spent the last fifteen years creating. As always happens after major wars, the British government's first and usually premature priority is to reduce the size and hence the cost of the armed forces, and in August 1814 the experienced and professional force that Wellington had commanded with such distinction was reduced by 20 per cent from its Peninsular peak of 287,000. Cavalry regiments like the Royal Dragoons were cut by a quarter, to six troops of 60 men, whilst the infantry lost 35 battalions, each of about 1,000 men, and the artillery was cut by 7,000.[1] By the end of 1814 a total of 47,000 soldiers had been discharged.

These reductions were not surprising, nor unwelcome to the taxpayer, but they came as an unexpected shock to the soldiers themselves, not least because mechanisation was depressing the living standards of the industrialised working class from which most of them came and to which those discharged now had to return.[2] This made jobs difficult to come by. Whilst their erstwhile commander-in-chief negotiated the future of monarchies and nations at the Congress of Vienna, many of the troops he had until so recently led felt the chill of being no longer wanted. Regiments took the opportunity to get rid of 'old and worn out men and bad subjects'. The Royal Dragoons, or 'the Royals' as they were always known, were not sorry to see the back of their Provost Marshal, Sergeant Else, whom the regiment thought so stiff 'that it seemed as if he had swallowed a poker',[3] and who had been responsible for discipline. Within a month he had been convicted of theft in Birmingham and hanged; those soldiers whose backs still bore the marks of the lashes inflicted by the cat o' nine tails must have permitted themselves a satisfied smile. A few older soldiers were keen to go, particularly those whose service carried a pension, and the combined effect of taking these volunteers together with those that the regiment no longer thought fit was that there was an influx of younger private soldiers. They were sad though to lose nine young officers, most of whom had just joined, and they departed to 'their fathers' homes with heavy hearts at the thought of quitting a service of which they had only tasted the sweets'.[4] This was a serious blow to a small regiment which needed new blood, but the cutbacks meant that there were just not the commissions available unless some of the older officers decided to sell their positions, which they did not.

Soldiers' dreams of a hero's homecoming were also rudely interrupted by the realisation that the government would require them to serve in altogether less exciting places than the Peninsula. The recent trouble in Ireland meant that there was now to be a regular garrison of 30,000 troops there,[5] and there were 75,000 posted in overseas garrisons like the West Indies, particularly unpopular because it was so unhealthy, the Mediterranean and in Africa. The most dreaded news, though, was a posting to North America, where Britain had been at war with the United States since June 1812. The Royals were warned for service in Canada, at that time threatened with invasion by the United States, which caused considerable gloom. 'Was the repose of barely five months in

England to be considered as too great a blessing, only to be expiated by an immediate embarkation to the frozen lakes and black forests of Canada?' bemoaned Lieutenant Sigismund Trafford.[6] In the end they were stood down, but others were less fortunate. The end of hostilities in Europe allowed Britain to send three major deployments to America, so that by late 1814 there were 48,000 regular troops fighting there. Peace was finally negotiated in December 1814, but news of it reached the army besieging New Orleans too late to save them from a bloody and unsuccessful attack under Wellington's brother-in-law General Packenham. Twenty-eight per cent of the soldiers who fought there became casualties.

But the most persistent complaint of these returning warriors was that they were bored. This was a young, aggressive army, most of whom had only known active service. The Napoleonic Wars had been going on, intermittently, since 1793, and anyone who had joined before then, when soldiers still powdered and tied their hair in queues and wore breeches and gaiters, was now well into their forties or dead. Then the British Army had been something of a joke. It had never 'shown itself on the continent but to be beaten, chased, forced to re-embark or forced to capitulate', Macaulay commented, unkindly but truthfully.[7] Its equipment was poor, its soldiers badly trained and its tactics unaltered since the Seven Years War 30 years earlier. The defeats and embarrassments of the 1790s had been hard lessons, but, as Wellington remarked, they taught the Army 'what not to do, which is always something',[8] and they had been learned. The reforms introduced by the Grand Old Duke of York, much maligned as commander-in-chief because of his private life and later by nursery rhymers, had proved remarkably effective and, once they were honed by Wellington in Spain, had produced, for its day, one of the most efficient and well-equipped armies that Britain has ever fielded. Weapons, tactics and training had been comprehensively improved and updated, and new techniques were introduced. The horse artillery, with its fast gun teams that could operate with the cavalry, was expanded, and the Baker rifle was introduced into specialist 'rifle' regiments, who wore green as opposed to the regulation red. From 1801 specific battalions were trained as light infantry under the new 'Shorncliffe' system, pioneered by Sir John Moore; by 1815 there were ten of these battalions of 'light bobs'. They trained their soldiers to operate in small teams making use of the ground rather than in the line formation of the traditional infantry. From the fortified lines of Torres Vedras, outside Lisbon, where Wellington had turned back Massena in 1810, to Toulouse, which they took in April 1814, this 'infamous' army had been never lost a major engagement. They were an army used to combat, and peacetime soldiering in barracks was something new to them. They were not at all sure that they liked it.

The Royals certainly did not much like their new home in Bristol. Trafford thought the people there were 'Jacobinically inclined' and 'omitted nothing to induce the men to desert'.[9] This was possibly because they had been outraged at a particularly severe flogging the regiment had inflicted on one of its soldiers, something which, although unusual in a cavalry regiment, usually caused public revulsion. In December 1814 the Royals were moved to the West Country to help the excise men catch smugglers, but they found Exeter even worse. 'Barrack life is everywhere and always the same,' Trafford complained, 'uniformly dull and uninteresting. It is precisely the same thing whether the regiment is quartered in Exeter or

Ipswich or Canterbury or Birmingham or where you please in the United Kingdom, the same routine invariably takes place. The barrack Chaplin regularly attends the Riding School on a Sunday at twelve o'clock. Riding School drills and squad parades at 4 pm on Monday. Tuesday a parade under arms, every man off duty to attend. A parade in marching order and inspection of necessities the other two days in the week.'[10]

William Hay of the 12th Light Dragoons was even ruder about Dorchester. 'It was the most horrid, dull, stupid inland town I had ever known. I may say that, until then, I never knew what it was to lead, what is commonly termed, a barrack yard life. We had hunting, it is true, of an indifferent kind; and an old fellow, a yeoman farmer, who at the time was an Army contractor to supply the cavalry regiments with forage, gave us some amusement in his meadows, where we used to hunt rats to pass the dull hours.'[11]

Part of the problem was women, or the lack of 'society', as female companionship was politely known. Soldiers then, as now, suffer from conflicting emotions. They love the excitement and comradeship of active service but equally they worry that army life will stop them forming relationships. After five years in the Peninsula, one of the things they were looking forward to most about coming home was the chance to find girls. The reluctance to deploy to the USA and Canada was not so much fear of fighting again, which offered the opportunity for promotion, although Major Phil Dorville did say when he was drunk in the mess one night that he didn't want to 'cock-up upon a bank of snow in the middle of a dark wood and perhaps find the arrow of some damn'd copper coloured Indian sticking in one's arse'.[12] It was more a fear of missing out once again on the opportunities to which they had looked forward for so long.

The Royals found Exeter distinctly unfriendly. 'The society of the town is rarely open to the military and when it is, after a length of time, a change of squadrons or of quarters puts an end to the little visiting that may have commenced. The billiard tables, the pastry cook, the fruitier or the oyster shop is the general resort of the barrack officer. To him the joys of love are never known',[13] Trafford continued. He and his brother officers mercilessly teased poor Lieutenant Ralph Heathcote, one of those 'certain number of men found in every regiment who are incapable of dancing and of frivolity',[14] whose rather clumsy efforts to find a wife ended in ridicule. Heathcote 'was a clever, studious man but very retired in his ways and besides very plain in his person and apparently the last man to attempt to make himself agreeable to women'.[15] He had purchased a commission in 1806, and he had fought through the Peninsula, writing a series of rather priggish letters to his parents in (what was to become) Germany, where his father was George III's minister in Hesse-Kassel. His friends were therefore somewhat surprised that he should choose to go to the Exeter Ball, a monthly gathering of the great and the good. There he met a Miss Dickenson, 'a young innocent girl, who was fond of flirting, handsome, well made and perfectly adapted by nature to inspire the softer passion'. They exchanged half a dozen words and parted. Heathcote then took himself to the next monthly ball, and found Miss Dickenson during the few spare minutes when she happened to be unengaged to dance. He told her that he had something important to say to her in private. The bewildered girl asked what it could possibly be that could not be said in public, but Heathcote insisted it was 'of particular consequence' and begged her to follow him into the card room.

'Hereupon Heathcote put on a grave face, took out his

snuff box and taking a large dose between his fingers, applied it abundantly to his nostrils by way of making himself more lovely. He then informed the young trembling girl that she was the object of his heart, that he was persuaded she had a mutual passion for him, and proposed an immediate marriage with her. The poor girl began to stammer and hesitate. This Heathcote argued favourably to himself. Then taking an additional pinch of snuff he added "well then I will immediately mention the thing to your father and I doubt not that it will be settled immediately".' It was not until Miss Dickenson had made it abundantly plain that she entertained no affection whatever for Heathcote and that her father would be extremely offended by any such approach that he desisted. It could all have remained private had Heathcote not called for silence in the hackney coach taking the officers back to the barracks where 'he began rubbing his hands and having obtained silence, exclaimed how happy he was to have got so well out of the scrape'.

Otherwise 'Servant girls, the very refuse of footmen and ostlers, whores, that prostitute themselves for a glass of liquor, are the officers' most obedient attendants',[16] bemoaned Trafford, who was reflecting a general view prevailing throughout the Army that the victors of the Peninsular Campaign had somehow been ignored by women since they had got home. The only female company poor clumsy Heathcote had known was to be found in Spanish prostitutes, and they regarded the British as inferior performers to the French, much to the fury of Trafford. He and his friend Captain Micklethwaite had found one of his officers, Lewis Gasquet, drunk and completely naked in a Spanish house with 'the females extremely mirthful upon the smallness of poor Lewis' male instrument at the same time exclaiming that all the English were made alike, children in their genital parts. This accusation incensed Micklethwaite to such a degree that he instantly pulled forth his own well proportioned instrument and placed it upon the shoulders of one of the girls. This frightened all the ladies, who locked themselves up for the night in their rooms.'[17]

During the war, when regiments had fought and suffered alongside each other, and been closely grouped in brigades (a combination of three or four regiments or battalions under a general, usually assembled for a particular battle or operation),[18] the distinct social hierarchy that normally differentiated them had become less relevant. Now they were back home, in a Britain very aware of position and income, and with ambitious mothers and wives, it became more important. At the top of this hierarchy were the cavalry and Guards regiments. All the cavalry were considered smart, but some more so than others. The very smartest were the two regiments of Life Guards, who constituted the Household Cavalry, and who were now back in London once again guarding the monarch, together with the Royal Horse Guards, always known as the Blues, with whom they alternated between Knightsbridge, Regent's Park and Windsor. The accepted stereotype was that all their officers were very rich and joined as much for the social life of London as for soldiering, but, as so often with stereotypes, this masks a more complicated reality. There were certainly very rich officers throughout the ranks of both the Life Guards and the Blues, men such as Robert Hill, who commanded the Blues, and who had large estates in Shropshire, or George Sulivan, a young lieutenant in 1st Life Guards whose father had made a fortune in India and who had bought him a lieutenancy at the huge cost of £1,600 (£120,000 today).[19] Yet there were also men like Captain Edward Kelly, for whom life was a protracted struggle to support a wife and daughters whose social ambition rather overmatched his means. He saw himself very much as the professional soldier, perhaps rather more than his contemporaries did, and he had been one of the first instructors at the new military academy. For Kelly, soldiering was more a method of advancement and paying his bills than it was a social pleasure.

The Household Cavalry was 'heavy cavalry' – big men riding strong horses, whose role was to shatter enemy formations in the charge, as they had done very effectively in the Peninsula. After them in terms of regimental seniority came the rest of the heavy cavalry, dragoon or dragoon-guard regiments such as the Royals. A dragoon was originally a soldier who would ride a horse but dismount to fight. However, that role had gradually disappeared during the previous century and all such regiments were now cavalry who would fight on horseback. There were 15 of them in total. Next in seniority to the Household Cavalry came the King's Dragoon Guards, then the remainder of the dragoon-guard regiments, and after them the five regiments of dragoons. There was no actual difference in role between a dragoon guard or a simple dragoon; they all did the same thing.

Francis Kinchant, whose father managed in late 1814 to purchase a 'cornetcy' for him in the 2nd Dragoons, the famous Scots Greys, so called because they always rode grey horses, was fairly typical of those who served as a junior cavalry officer. A cornet was the most junior commissioned rank in a cavalry regiment, equating to a second lieutenant or ensign in the infantry. Kinchant was full of enthusiasm for his regiment and for life in general and thought his regiment 'the most crack cavalry corps in the service. I don't think there is a private [soldier] under 5 feet 11 inches and the officers are a fine gentlemanly set of fellows, there being only three Scotchmen among the officers' although, he added, the majority of the private soldiers were 'Scotch'. He was very keen to get himself passed out of riding school, where he was being made to ride without stirrups to develop a more secure 'seat' and where he found that 'the method of riding is altogether different to that of the country squire'. He wanted to join his troop and take his full place in the regiment but his concerns were as much about money and girlfriends. He did not greatly rate his father, whom he referred to as 'the old goat', and with whom his main communication seemed to be to extract money for horses and uniform, which were certainly expensive. The 'most dashing appearance' of the regiment came at a cost, such as their best dress coats at 40 guineas, which would be about £3,150 today. He also spent quite a bit of his time chasing 'that beautiful creature Letitia', on whom he seems to have set his heart. 'Amongst the innumerable collection of pieces at this place I have met with no one half so enchanting, nor have I had a *real relish* since I left her' he wrote to his friend John Hall from Bristol, where his regiment were stationed.[20]

It was, however, the 'light' cavalry who were seen as the more fashionable regiments and several of them had distinguished themselves on operational service in the Peninsula. One of the best known was the 7th Light Dragoons, the famous 'Saucy Seventh' as they were nicknamed, whose colonel was Henry Paget, Lord Uxbridge. The 7th prided themselves on their rather rakish image. Their recruiting posters declared that they wanted 'young fellows whose hearts beat high to tread the paths of glory' and had an enticing 'NB' at the bottom, designed to appeal to high-spirited young men, and which read 'The Regiment is mounted on Blood Horses, and being lately returned from Spain, and the Horses Young, the Men will not be allowed to HUNT during the next season more than once a week'.[21] In 1807 the 7th had been allowed by the Prince Regent to style themselves unofficially as hussars, after the famous Hungarian light cavalry, and had adopted the hussar uniform of fur capes and imposing if impractical tall caps; but, as with dragoons and dragoon guards, there was no actual difference in role between hussars and light dragoons.

Lieutenant Standish O'Grady found life in Brighton, where the 7th was guarding the Prince Regent, rather more agreeable than Sigismund Trafford found Exeter. After returning from the Peninsular War he had gone home on leave to Limerick, where his family had large estates, and was not really sure that he wanted to return to the regiment. 'Dear Chief', he wrote to his father, who would become Lord Chief Justice in Ireland, 'I never left home with more regret than last time, we had so delightful a party and all seemed so sorry to part.'[22] Yet once he was back with his old friends from the regiment he seemed to cheer up. 'I go out with the fox-hounds tomorrow in a capital country', he wrote, proving there was some truth in what the recruiters had said, and 'I intend going to every ball, party, drum, humdrum and alarm that is given – this is a very neat little place' and, he added, reflecting no love for his future monarch, 'likely to be pleasant when our nuisance goes to Carlton House, which I am sorry to say will not be for a month'.

Romance was as dominant in the lives of the officers of the 7th Light Dragoons as it was with the Royals, but they seemed to be more successful. 'Pipon is to be married at the beginning of next month to Miss Ommany, rather a rum one, by whom he gets five hundred a year. It is said he expected 2,000 but he may think himself well off if that is his only complaint', O'Grady told his parents, and later 'My friend Bob Uniacke is, I am much afraid, to be married to a Miss Dashwood, daughter of Lady Dashwood who is rather a tiger; he is more changed than any young man I ever heard or read of; from being a fine rattling noisy fellow he has now not a word to say for himself ... Wildman is certainly to be married; if she'll accept him to a Miss Lieth, a daughter of Lady Augusta Lieth; she is not quite fifteen and the joke is Wildman's only reason to us for being such a fool is that it has ever been his opinion that the first love insures happiness – forgetting that this girl was near hanging herself for Synge of the old 10th who is at least six feet 4. I did not think we had so many fools in the 7th.'

O'Grady was an intelligent and articulate man, and a competent and brave soldier, and although his letters could be dismissed as mere gossip, they tell us much about regimental officers' priorities that winter. O'Grady himself was in something of a quandary. His socially ambitious mother wanted him to marry a certain Kitty. He undoubtedly liked Kitty very much, but never quite seems to have been in love with her. He was only 22, and not the sort of man to marry just because his parents wanted him to. His correspondence over the months ahead would be full of teasing for his mother's matrimonial ambition.

Such apparent flippancy is understandable, given what the regiment had been through in the Peninsula, and if Standish O'Grady appeared to be focusing on all the wrong things, then Captain Rees Gronow of the 1st Foot Guards, the son of a wealthy Welsh landowner and close friend of Shelley, would appear to have drifted further astray. The Foot Guards were

very much the smartest of the infantry, and were, like the Life
Guards and the Blues, now back in London. Gronow's battalion returned from Bordeaux in 1814 to its old quarters in
Portman Street where, whilst his soldiers mounted guard in
London much as the Foot Guards still do today, Gronow and
his friends became preoccupied with London society. 'At the
present time one can hardly conceive the importance which
was attached to getting admission to Almack's, the seventh
heaven of the fashionable world. Of the three hundred officers
of the Foot Guards, not more than half a dozen were honoured with vouchers of admission to this exclusive temple of
the beau monde, the gates of which were guarded by lady
patronesses whose smile or frowns consigned men and women
to happiness or despair.'[23] Yet Gronow had been campaigning
with his battalion since leaving Eton, aged 18, in 1812 and
had fought in all the major actions since. He described 'the
sensation of being made a target to a large body of men' as
'not particularly pleasant' and noted that 'the first man I ever
saw killed was a Spanish soldier, who was cut in two by a
cannon ball'.[24] We can, therefore, perhaps forgive him for
wanting to live a little.

After the Foot Guards, ranked the line infantry regiments.
They were known by their number, from 1st to 104th, and
about half of them had two battalions, each of about 1,000
men. They were the backbone of the Army, the men who
had trudged across Portugal, Spain and France, withstanding
the best Napoleon could throw at them. They were not
county regiments as such, that connection only being formalised much later in the Cardwell Reforms of 1871, but
tended to have strong local links, to recruit from a particular
area and to be listed in the Army List as, for example, '14th or
Buckinghamshire Regiment of Foot'.

This regional recruiting was more marked in regiments with a definite local identity, such as those raised in Scotland, like the 42nd (the Black Watch), the 73rd (Highland) and the 92nd (Gordons) from the Highlands. The 27th Foot were an Irish regiment, confusingly called 'Inniskilling' like the 6th Dragoons, which was an Irish cavalry regiment of whom we will be hearing much, and had a majority of Irish soldiers. But even in these regiments with clearly defined geographical links there were many soldiers from all over the British Isles and, as Kinchant noted, the officers did not necessarily go for commissions in their local regiment, but went instead where there were vacancies or they could establish some link through family or friends. There was one regiment of riflemen, the 95th, of whom we will also be hearing much more, and the ten battalions officially designated as 'light infantry', who had developed a reputation for particular skill and fitness in the Peninsula that gave them a certain *esprit*.

None of these officers actually needed to stay in the Army. Trafford's family had a productive estate at Wroxham Hall in Norfolk, and both O'Grady and Gronow had family money behind them. They stayed for much the same reasons that they had originally joined. First, they had a genuine desire to serve the country, a sort of social reimbursement by those for whom the agricultural and industrial revolutions had provided ample funds and time. They hated what Napoleonic France stood for, threatening what they regarded as British liberty, their 'property' in the widest sense and their right to acquire it and enjoy it. It was no coincidence that the Yeomanry, who were created by Pitt as a sort of mounted Home Guard, adopted as their motto 'For King, Liberty and Property'.

For some officers the hatred of France was deep and personal, such as for Thomas Graham, a Scottish landowner whose young wife died whilst being treated in the south of France. As Graham was bringing her coffin back for burial in Scotland, it was waylaid by a party of drunken French Revolutionary soldiers who molested the body, so enraging Graham that he immediately enrolled as a volunteer. Secondly, officers stayed because the Army gave them position and a role in life when such things were even more important than they are today; the Army was a route to social advancement. Thirdly, they stayed because they liked what they were doing and did not want to leave their regiments, their brother officers and their soldiers. That has not changed to this day.

Trafford, Kinchant, O'Grady and Gronow had all purchased their commissions, which had been common practice in the cavalry and infantry since the Restoration of 1660. The most expensive was Gronow's; it cost his father £3,500 (£262,500 today)[25] for him to become a captain in the First Guards, whilst Trafford paid £2,782 (£209,000 today) for the same rank in the Royals, and O'Grady paid £997 (£75,000 today) to purchase his lieutenancy in the 7th Light Dragoons.[26] They could have sold these valuable positions easily in 1815, the army reductions having created a shortage of vacancies and many young men who had hoped to join their regiments being turned away.

Life as an officer was hardly remunerative. Once they had purchased their commission, young officers then had to buy their uniform and, in the case of Trafford and O'Grady, mount themselves. In return they were all paid about £300 per annum (about £22,500 today), from which deductions were made by both the government for food and lodging, and by the regiment for membership of the mess, where officers collectively ate, and for extras such as paying for the regimental bands, which were then privately raised. Once they had paid for their own servants, there was very little left and all three, being in what were termed fashionable regiments, needed a private income to survive. Yet except for a very few particularly rich young men, army pay formed the main source of income for the majority of officers and it was what allowed them to live. Seniority and promotion, with its accompanying increase in pay, was therefore jealously guarded, and although many of the letters home from Waterloo were requests for extra parental funds, these tended to be to help with the extras rather than the basics.

Commissions themselves were seen as an investment, which were sold on when an officer was promoted or when he left, so the initial outlay was recouped. Officers could also elect to go on 'half pay', which meant that they stayed in the Army and kept their commission but did not actually have a job with their regiment. This was a useful way of maintaining a sort of regimental reserve, which was to prove critical in 1815, although it remained unpopular with many politicians and commentators, who saw it as an unjustified use of public money. Not all commissions were purchased, and officers could also be promoted to vacancies caused by death on active service – brevet rank as it was known – or just by seniority if there was no one available to purchase an appointment that needed filling. The casualties in the Peninsula, and the fact that campaigning did not appeal to everyone, meant that by 1811 there was a serious shortage of candidates to purchase; between 1810 and 1815, on average only 12 per cent of commissions were purchased in regiments of foot and 42 per cent in the cavalry.[27] But by 1815 the reductions meant that commissions had become difficult to get and purchase was consequently once again becoming more frequent.

In the artillery, which had become an increasingly important part of the Army during the war, and in the small corps of Royal Engineers, officers were appointed to commissions rather than buying them and then promoted according to seniority. Artillery and engineer officers were also the first to be professionally trained, at the Royal Military Academy at Woolwich, which meant that they were often a source of wise advice, although Wellington, who did not much care for 'gunners', as the artillery were called, initially made a point of ignoring it in the Peninsula.[28] Both the artillery and the engineers answered to the Master-General of the Ordnance rather than to the commander-in-chief as the cavalry and infantry did, although once mobilised they were firmly under the operational orders of the field commander. Alexander Mercer, who commanded 'G' Troop Royal Horse Artillery in Colchester, was a typical artillery officer. Thirty-two in 1815, he had fought in America but not Spain, and his father had been an army officer before him. Professional, not particularly rich, and technically competent, he and his soldiers will play a major part in our story.

Something of a myth has developed which holds that all British army officers during the Napoleonic Wars were remote and separated by some huge social gulf from the soldiers they led. There were, certainly, a few very rich officers; for example, 206 peers or sons of peers were serving in 1815.[29] They were mostly, but by no means exclusively, in the Guards or cavalry, or on the staff, as Wellington and his senior officers rather liked having the 'sprigs of the aristocracy' as their ADCs. Wellington seems to have had something of an obsession with having Foot Guards officers on his staff, prompting the Duke of York, as commander-in-chief, and Colonel of 1st Guards, to complain to him before Waterloo that he was taking so many that the actual battalions were in danger of being weakened.[30] But most officers were the sons of the landed gentry, churchmen or businessmen, and, although not poor, were certainly not grand.

Several routes were also open to young men who wanted a commission but couldn't afford one. They could join on the 'volunteer system',[31] not to be confused with the county volunteer regiments that Pitt raised against possible French invasion, who were also called volunteers. Under this individual volunteer system, which predominantly applied to the infantry, young men joined as potential officers. They fought in the ranks but lived and ate with the officers, the idea being that the commanding officer would eventually appoint them to a vacant position as an ensign when one became available. They were unpaid but received rations and carried a musket and bayonet, as opposed to the sword and pistols with which officers were usually armed, although in practice on the battlefield most young officers would use a musket like their men. Edward Macready joined the 30th Foot under this system as a 16-year-old in 1814. His father was an Irish actor-manager who came over to England to start a theatre; but it went bust and purchasing a commission was beyond their means. With his elder brother William, who would later become a well-known tragedy actor, already following his father onto the stage, Edward joined the Army. He served in Holland with the regiment and was duly made an ensign, in which rank he would fight at Waterloo.[32]

Young men could also purchase quartermasters' commissions, which were cheaper and which meant they didn't have to live in the officers' mess, which could be a significant additional expense, especially in peacetime. John Elley's father ran a pub called the Furnival Inn in Leeds. He initially apprenticed his son to a tanner, but Elley soon got bored of tanning and, aged 17, persuaded him to buy him a quartermasters' commission in the Blues, one of the grandest and most efficient regiments in the Army. Elley did so well that he was 'gazetted' as a troop cornet and by 1808 was a lieutenant-colonel commanding the regiment, having progressed entirely on merit. At Waterloo he was Uxbridge's deputy, commanding the cavalry,[33] and Wellington would have had him commanding the Household Brigade had the Duke of York, as commander-in-chief, not already given it to Somerset.[34] His is a remarkable story but he was by no means unique in a world where social mobility was sometimes easier to achieve than it has been in 21st-century Britain.

Commissioning soldiers from the ranks was also quite normal, even in the cavalry and regiments of foot. During the Peninsular War 803 non-commissioned officers (NCOs) were given commissions. Two hundred and seventy-one became quartermasters, and 139 became adjutants, the positions in a regiment responsible for food and accommodation, and daily administration, respectively. A further 392 were given what were known as 'combatant' commands, leading fighting troops on a par with those who had purchased commissions.[35] More common was to give NCOs commissions in regiments which were stationed overseas in places that conventional officers did not want to serve, partly because they were unhealthy and partly because they were away from the action. This was to cause some issues after Waterloo. Generally, commissioned NCOs were quickly accepted by both their brother officers and their soldiers, although there were the odd exceptions. Lord Hill, one of Wellington's most senior and trusted generals, congratulated a sergeant on being commissioned, asking him 'How do you feel in your new character? You are a gentleman now, you know'; to which Sergeant Macbride replied,

'Thank you, my lord, for myself I feels perfectly comfortable, but I trembles for Mrs Macbride.'[36]

Thomas Morris, of the 73rd Regiment and a bit of a barrack-room lawyer, whose journal bristles with indignation at the severe corporal punishment often inflicted, was a more discordant voice. He hated the purchase system. 'Should this country again be involved in war, it is to be hoped the army will be placed on a different footing to what it has been, and that commissions will not be bestowed on individuals simply because they belong to this or that noble family. Then we may expect to have an efficient set of officers.'[37] His unusually strong opinion may be partly because he would fight at Waterloo under a very old company commander who had never been in action before and whom he despised, yet he did have considerable respect for the lieutenant-colonel in overall command of his battalion.

Despite what Thomas Morris thought, most soldiers felt that the officers were rather closer to their men than is generally supposed. Although officers would naturally bond with and 'mess' with each other both in barracks and on active service, they also bonded with the unit for which they were responsible, whether it was a troop of 60 cavalrymen or an infantry company of around 100. Regiments were close-knit groups, with soldiers and officers mutually dependent, and with a shared sense of coherence and pride. Even the 1814 reductions, hard as they were, had not seriously weakened the sense of camaraderie developed in Portugal and Spain. There are several reports of soldiers found guilty of an offence choosing to be flogged rather than transferred to another regiment when given the option. The majority of soldiers regarded their regiment as their home and family and were intensely jealous of its reputation and of their part in it; the opinion of their comrades was often the most important thing to them. William Wheeler, a private in the 51st Regiment of Foot, just missed having his head blown off by a round shot at Badajoz. 'I thought I was wounded', he wrote, 'my head ached violently. I felt the pain a long time and it was with difficulty I could perform my duty. Had I been working in a place where there was no danger I certainly should have given up, but here I was ashamed to complain, lest any of my comrades laugh at me.'[38] Wheeler was later offered the chance of being invalided home but didn't take it, preferring to 'rejoin my regiment again and take my chance with it. Then when this protracted war is over ... I should have the proud satisfaction of landing on my native shores with many a brave and gallant comrade, with whom I braved the dangers of many a hard fought battle.'[39]

The 200,000-odd soldiers serving in the British Army in 1815 represented a considerable cross-section of society. The average age for joining was 18, although some joined at 16, which was technically the minimum. Men signed up either for unlimited service, which meant as long as the Army needed them, after which they would be discharged with a pension, or alternatively they could choose to sign for seven years without a pension. It might be supposed that this would lead to quite an old army but, in reality, a combination of an annual attrition rate from disease and battle of about 10 per cent in the Peninsula, together with the 1814 reductions, meant the average age for those serving in early 1815 was 22. The oldest man in the Blues at Waterloo was Joseph Holdsworth, who at forty-two was one of the very few still serving who had fought in the Revolutionary Wars in Flanders in the 1790s. From 1811 the practice of recruiting boys under 16, usually as drummers or trumpeters, was formalised and the limit was set at ten per company. Many of these were in fact 'children of the regiment', whose father was serving or had been killed, and who regarded the regiment as their home. Not all drummers and trumpeters were boys, their function being vital to communicating orders.[40]

About half the soldiers could probably read and write, and the increasing number of letters and journals from the 1790s onwards shows how educational reforms were beginning to take effect. Those who were literate tended to be promoted to NCO more quickly, given the increasing amount of administration an NCO had to deal with, and able men could advance rapidly. Thomas Bell, a well-educated man and a silversmith who joined the Blues in 1806 aged 22, was a corporal-major, the most senior NCO position in the regiment, at Waterloo aged 31.

The idea that there were lots of ex-criminals in the ranks is without foundation. Recruits had to swear on 'attestation' when they signed up that they had no criminal record, and had to provide character witnesses, although in practice petty crimes were probably overlooked.[41] Many joined because they were running away from family problems, a refuge that armies have traditionally provided, but men would not be accepted if they were already apprenticed in another trade. Crime within the Army itself was low, especially when compared with civilian life, with theft from one another rare, although on campaign more looting went on than was generally acknowledged, despite officers' attempts to stop it. There had, in particular, been one or two major breakdowns in discipline in Spain after the terrible sieges of 1812, which have had a disproportionate effect on the Peninsular Army's reputation. This has contributed to the false idea that the British Army in the

Napoleonic Wars was a group of ruffians who fought from fear of the lash; they were no saints but they certainly conducted themselves better than their later image suggests. All soldiers joined the Army of their own free will, unlike many of their European counterparts and their French enemies. They joined for a variety of reasons; as far as one can generalise such a commitment, it was a mixture of patriotism combined with a motivation to achieve more than their current circumstances offered.

Thomas Playford joined the Army because he wanted more out of life than labouring on his father's small farm in Yorkshire. He had attended the village school until he was 15, where he asked about everything and was nicknamed 'the unbelieving Jew'[42]. He was very fond of reading and 'seldom joined the village boys in their sports, but on holidays I was often to be seen alone on the banks of the river [Dun] angling'. The Life Guards, whom his mother had heard were respectable, 'had more pay than the wages of a farm labourer, attended the King and Queen on public occasions and never went abroad', or so he thought. He joined in September 1810, aged just 16 but very tall at six foot two, fought in the Peninsula, returning to London in July 1814. He found London quite dull but was struck by the opulence of Carlton House, the Prince Regent's London residence, where he 'looked on in bewildered amazement as if I was in an enchanted region. A stream of water flowed along the centre of the tables, with fish of a golden and silver kind swimming' in it. His duties, 'performing guard at Whitehall, attending the royal family on public occasions, suppressing riotous assemblages of the populace, with attending field exercises and taking care of my horse and appointments, were not things of difficult performance even for a youth in his teens'. Bored, he took a walk-on part in *Timour the Tartar*, then playing in Covent Garden.

Another Life Guard was John Shaw, something of a national celebrity by January 1815. From Wollaston in Nottinghamshire, Shaw was a boxer, both bare-fisted and with gloves. Aged 16 he had challenged a 'strongly built man, at least three stone heavier than himself'. Shaw 'stripped, and, heedless of the disparaging remarks from all quarters about himself, walked confidently into the ring, and formally defied his adversary by throwing up his hat'. The fight went badly, and Shaw was getting severely mauled, when a 'powerful looking man elbowed his way into the ring, and, tapping the lad on the shoulder, encouraged him with the words "Youngster, don't you give it up. The big un won't get the better of you after all; he's hitting too wildly, and's a deal too cheeky. Take my advice, back away from him, and fight slow, and you'll lick him, as sure as my name's Jem Belcher."'[43] Shaw took the advice of the all-England champion and duly won his fight. He joined the Life Guards in 1807 and continued his boxing career, training at the famous Fives Court gymnasium, and building up his strength so that by 1812 he was over six foot and weighed 15 stone. He won a series of fights, including beating the celebrated West Countryman Burrows in just 17 minutes, which resulted in Burrows being led blind and bleeding from the ring. He also developed something of a reputation as a ladies' man, making himself available for a very wide variety of services to fashionable women, including posing nude as an artist's model. He was described by a contemporary as 'large and rather coarse, his countenance indicated a measure of good nature as well as of determined purpose. His broad chest, muscular arms, and large bony hands, denoted a powerful antagonist.' He was as good a swordsman as he was a pugilist and 'a blow from his sword would have been dangerous and disabling if not fatal to an armed man, and a stroke of his clenched fist dreadful to a weak man'.[44]

John Bingley was more of the *Boy's Own* hero type who longed to get away from the drudgery of rural Leicestershire. He had seen a troop of the Blues in the local area and was immediately taken with them. The newspapers were full of Wellington's success in pushing Massena back into Spain and the victory of Fuentes de Oñoro. Having promised his father to be home in good time from Blaby market, he instead took a stagecoach to London, walked to Windsor, and just outside the barrack gates met 'the Corporal Major and asked him if he wanted a jolly recruit. He replied I was joking him, I said I was not come 130 miles for a joke but was serious and sober – so after going through different examinations he engaged me.'[45] Bingley was 26 when he joined, much older than normal, and he started something of a craze in Leicestershire with 20 more recruits following him in the next few weeks. Their motivation was partly patriotic and partly the need to do something more with their lives than cart vegetables. They would soon have all the excitement they needed.

Then were those who had rows with their parents and just wanted to get away from home. William Lawrence, from Briantspuddle in Dorset, joined to get away from the builder to whom he was apprenticed and who beat him. One of seven children, uneducated, and with unsympathetic parents, he first tried to join the artillery, but they found out he was an apprentice, and he had to go as far as Taunton, where he would not be recognised, before he was accepted by the 40th Regiment.[46] There were many similar stories in Ireland, which then, before the Great Famine, made up a quarter of the population of the United Kingdom but provided a greater proportion of recruits. They joined not just the official Irish regiments, of which there were three cavalry and eight infantry, but were also recruited by English regiments which were stationed for so long in Ireland. About 30 per cent of the Army in 1815 was Irish, and they predominantly served in the infantry as opposed to the cavalry and artillery.[47]

About a third of recruits listed their previous profession as labourer, and about a quarter of the remainder had been weavers, a proportion which held good for both English and Irish recruits. The large number of weavers joining the Army had been the case for the last decade, as mechanisation in the textile industry had gradually made the old village hand looms redundant. The decline in these village looms was one of the most significant aspects of the Industrial Revolution and one which would have as great an effect on rural English life as enclosures. Whereas in the eighteenth century manufacturers would distribute their yarn around villages to be spun into cloth in so many homes, it was now cheaper and more efficient to spin it centrally, using new technology. A spinning jenny required only a quarter of the labour force of the hand looms and a water frame replaced several hundred. It was very good work if you could get it, paying 44s. (£165) per week, but it came at the cost of the 3–4s. a family could have earned from their hand loom, which, with bread at about 1s. a loaf (£3.75 today) had meant the difference between young men staying in their village or having to find work elsewhere such as in the Army. This was particularly true in the North of England, Scotland and in Ireland, where village weaving had been prolific, and where the parallel industrialisation of the linen industry was putting additional pressure on rural life.[48] Mathew Clay, a framework knitter from Mansfield in

Nottinghamshire, joined the 3rd Foot Guards in London in December 1813. He had 'a fresh complexion, with grey eyes and light hair' and was only five foot seven inches tall so he was assigned to the Light Company of the 2nd Battalion. It was to prove a rather more significant posting than he realised. Weavers also joined the cavalry as well as the infantry, and it was a myth that cavalry regiments were full of farm boys who had grown up with horses. Most had to be taught to ride from scratch, and part of the Duke of York's army reforms after the Revolutionary Wars in the 1790s was a three-month basic plan for riding school.

Poverty and lack of opportunity of a rather different kind was what drove Thomas Howell to join the 71st Highlanders. He came from an educated Edinburgh family, and his parents had intended him to be a 'clergyman or writer' but his father's ill health meant he had to give up work so that there was little money for Thomas to continue studying. By 1815 the family income was 11s. per week (about £40 today), of which half came from his two brothers and half from a parish benefit society; parish contributions were not untypical in many families. Howell first tried to be an actor, despite his parents' entreaties, and actually appeared in a play in Edinburgh, but once on stage his confidence deserted him and he 'shrank unseen from the theatre bewildered and in a state of despair'. He joined up for seven years in July 1806, aged 16, without realising that his seven years would only start from his eighteenth birthday.

Soldiers also joined from either the Volunteer Force or the militia. The Volunteer Force, as opposed to the volunteer system by which men who could not afford commissions could join regiments as potential officers, had been originally created by Pitt in response to a possible threat of invasion by France and was an early sort of Home Guard. Locally raised, volunteers were part time but were compensated for lost wages, consequently making it rather popular. Over 200,000 had joined in 1803, growing to 400,000 as the threat of French invasion seemed very real before Nelson put a stop to it at Trafalgar. It was never perhaps the most effective military force, and its standard of training was low, as cartoonists like Gillray regularly pointed out, but its numbers showed a concerned patriotism. Thomas Morris, the barrack-room lawyer who despised the purchase system, and who later joined the 73rd Regiment, started life as a volunteer in Middlesex. 'I was particularly fond of reading the heart-stirring accounts of sieges and battles, and the glorious achievements of the British troops in Spain ... which created in me an irrepressible desire for military service; so, as the first step towards it, I became a Volunteer, and oh! How proud did I feel when having gone through my course of drill, I was permitted to join the ranks.'[49] After 1805 the volunteers were slowly reduced, the government finding it rather expensive and difficult to control, but many of the volunteers found their way into the Regular Army, including quite a few boys. The Yeomanry cavalry regiments, which would later play such an important part in the British Army, were founded as part of the volunteer system,[50] and their officers spent many happy hours designing splendid uniforms which would show just how fierce and patriotic they were and which would come to rival even Napoleon's gorgeously arrayed light cavalry for the amount of gold lace and various parts of animals they incorporated.

The militia were a different and distinct organisation who produced better-trained recruits and on a more regular system. They were county-based and an ancient part of local British life which has no readily identifiable modern equivalent. They were unique in that they were allowed to conscript if they could not recruit enough volunteers to fill their ranks. This was done by a ballot amongst the able-bodied men of the county, although in practice there were many exemptions, such as apprentices, and if selected you could opt to pay for a substitute, which meant that the poor or unemployed tended to end up being the ones who joined. Most, though, were volunteers, and the militia as a whole represented a wide cross-section of British life. They were not originally allowed to serve overseas and their role was largely home defence, which in reality meant maintaining law and order at a time when there was considerable civil unrest and no police force. However, as the need for regular army manpower increased, from 1805 the government introduced a system whereby 10 per cent of the militia were encouraged to enlist in the Regular Army and were paid a bounty of between £11 and £14 (£825 and £1,050 today) for doing so, depending on how long they elected to serve. Militiamen could choose their own regiment, and often responded directly to appeals for recruits. When a particular regiment like the 95th Rifles badly needed volunteers to make up their losses after Corunna, 1,282 militiamen came forward immediately,[51] and in 1814 Parliament sanctioned the transfer of whole companies from the militia to the Regular Army, many of whom fought with distinction in Spain and France and were still serving in 1815. Indeed by 1815 about 40 per cent of the Regular Army had come via the militia and about 20 per cent of the officers, who were given a commission if they could bring over 40 men with them. It was the militia to whom the Regular Army regiments would turn again in March 1815 when they had quickly to rebuild their numbers.

James Anton, the son of a poor widow in Aberdeenshire, and his friend Huntly, the son of the village schoolmistress and who was due to become apprenticed to a weaver, both joined the militia in Aberdeen in 1803. Anton's 'inclination was bent upon the army' and he thought it was his duty to join whilst Huntly was simply determined to avoid being a village weaver, something he realised had little future, despite his mother wanting him to stay at home. Anton and Huntly both served all over Scotland except in Aberdeenshire itself, militia regiments never being deployed in their own counties in case they sympathised with any local troublemakers. In 1813 they transferred into the 42nd Regiment, the Black Watch, with whom they fought in Spain. Anton's logic was that he served 'at present secure of life and limb, but with no prospect of future benefit in old age, which I may attain; it is better to hazard both in the regular service, than have poverty and hard labour accompanying me to a peaceful grave at home',[52] which in other words meant that he thought that if he was going to serve then he might as well get the pension. Moved directly from France to Ireland after Napoleon's fall in 1814, Anton found himself in early 1815 running a small detachment of six soldiers quartered in a village outside Kilkenny. Another soldier who joined via the militia was Edward Costello, one of the many Irishmen to do so. He was bored of being a shoemaker, so applied for the Dublin Militia, from which he transferred to the 95th Rifles, with whom he had a distinguished career in Spain, serving in a company commanded by a captain who had been promoted from the ranks for his bravery. Returning to Dover from France in 1814, he soon found himself 'panting for fresh exploits'.[53] He would not be disappointed.

Military life also offered a certain security in a world that was, for many, changing and unpredictable. The Army was certainly tough, excessively so at times, but then so had been the lives soldiers had previously been leading as labourers or

weavers. Soldiers were not well paid, with an infantry sergeant earning 11s. (£40 today) a week, and a private soldier 7s.
(about £26 today), although the cavalry were paid slightly
more; but they were not badly paid either and their food and
accommodation were provided, despite deductions being
made from their pay for that. Other deductions were also made
for equipment and a subscription to Chelsea Hospital should
they need its services in old age. This meant that the lower
ranks had very little left at the end of the week, but this was an
age when saving was the privilege of very few and most
people's priority was to feed themselves and provide a roof over
their heads. Given that the Army also provided pensions, albeit
not very generous ones, most soldiers looked at the world
outside and felt adequately provided for if not comfortable.

For both the officers and the soldiers, much depended on
their commanding officer, the colonel, the man who ran the
cavalry regiment or infantry battalion, and who was a
demigod in that slightly closed world. They had much more
influence on the everyday lives of their soldiers than did the
very senior commanders, like Wellington, who were nicknamed 'the Wigs' and who, whilst they may have been
glimpsed on a parade or inspection, to most soldiers were
remote and known only by reputation. The colonel, on the
other hand, was seen every day and held huge power, particularly over appointments and discipline. Although he was
always referred to as 'the colonel', in a typically confusing bit
of British Army nomenclature these commanding officers
usually held the rank of lieutenant-colonel. A lieutenant-
colonelcy could be purchased, and the step up from major, the
rank below, was very expensive, costing £3,500 (£262,500
today) for a line infantry battalion as opposed to £2,600

(£195,000 today) for a major. However, to purchase into a lieutenant-colonel's position an officer had to have served for nine years, and reforms introduced successively in 1801 and 1809 effectively meant that they also had to have served for at least two years in every junior rank. Many, though, of the commanding officers in 1815 were brevet appointments, usually given to experienced Peninsular veterans in recognition of their service. The average age of commanding officers at Waterloo was 37, much the same as in the British Army today.

The colonel and his character effectively made a regiment what it was; a fair and competent man – such as Frank Tidy, who commanded a battalion of the 14th Regiment – created an efficient unit and a happy atmosphere and was greatly respected by his officers and soldiers. The son of a clergyman, Tidy was a very experienced soldier and a typical commanding officer of a line infantry battalion. He had joined the Army as a volunteer aged 16, and his first overseas service was in the West Indies, where his regiment lost 13 men a day from disease. Eventually the rump surrendered to the French on Guadeloupe, reduced to two officers and 20 men. Tidy was imprisoned on a French hulk, a prison ship, in appalling conditions for 15 months before being paroled, leaving him with a particular hatred of Napoleonic France. He fought in Spain and took command of the very young 3rd Battalion of the 14th Foot in 1813, being appointed to the lieutenant-colonelcy, not purchasing it. The 3rd Battalion were typical of many battalions in the winter of 1814–15. First they were told they were being sent to Canada. Those orders were subsequently cancelled and they were told they were to be disbanded. They were then reprieved, although by that stage they had lost most of their older men. They would end up on the ridge at Waterloo.[54]

A rather different character was Ben (actually Arthur) Clifton, who commanded the Royals. He had taken over in the Peninsula, transferring from 3rd Dragoons over the head of Jervoise, the popular major. Immediately nicknamed 'Ben the Ruler' by Trafford and the Club because they found him humourless, a strict disciplinarian and bad-tempered, he was to command for 19 years.[55] In the Peninsula he earned the regiment's grudging respect because he was a competent horseman and an efficient soldier, but once back in barracks in the West Country he was a nightmare, endlessly picking up the officers for alleged neglect of duty, making them retrain in the riding school, and generally showing no capacity to relax.

More typical was Sir Henry Ellis, who commanded the 23rd Foot, the Royal Welch, and whose long career in the regiment had seen him serve in Holland, Egypt, America, the West Indies, Spain, Portugal and France. He was to be mortally wounded at Waterloo, shot by a French cuirassier with a carbine. He tried to take himself to the rear, but fell from his horse as it jumped a ditch. His men left their square to rescue him, carrying him into an outhouse near Braine-l'Alleud, where he later died. He was buried near by on 23 June. His last words, which may seem almost hackneyed to us now having seen so many Hollywood films, were 'I am happy, I am content, I have done my duty'. One of the men who buried him was a well-known bad character in the 23rd who had been flogged several times on Ellis's orders. Someone asked him why he should mind that the colonel was now dead. '"Sir," he replied, "I deserved the punishment, else he would never have punished me." With these words, he turned his head a little from me, and burst into tears.'[56]

*

This victorious Peninsular Army had returned to a Great Britain that had changed much since many of them had last seen it. During the five years they had been away the economy had grown, and the agricultural and industrial revolutions meant that productivity was increasing, but the benefits were not evenly spread and with growth came higher prices; a 25-year-old soldier in 1815 had seen prices rise by 150 per cent in his lifetime.[57]

The changes in weaving and manufacturing were mirrored in agriculture. The war had diminished the supply of foreign corn just when an increasing population needed it. This had been a boon to British farmers, who had seen the price of their home-grown corn rise, and who were also able to take advantage of the new agricultural techniques available to them. 'Every gentleman's conversation was taken up with turnips, clover, enclosures and drains,' complained the French traveller Louis Simon.[58] Before the war many of Britain's ancient open fields and much common land had been 'enclosed', in other words hedged off under the control of one landowner; but wartime price increases meant that now every available acre was taken, including barely productive land which, with wheat at 107s. a quarter (£400 today) by 1813, would still turn in a profit. Although wages for those producing this corn, and operating the new devices like threshing machines, rose roughly in line with the cost of living, particularly in the North, driven by competition for skilled labour from the new industrial towns, fewer farm labourers were needed and life was not easy for those made redundant.

The end of the war meant that cheap foreign corn could be imported once again and this threatened farm incomes. Landowners lobbied for a 'Corn Law' which would give them a guaranteed price, and in 1815 a bill was passed prohibiting the import of foreign corn until the British price was 80s. (£300 today) a quarter. This meant that marginal farms could stay in production, and farmers who had taken out large wartime mortgages would not go bankrupt, but at the cost of higher food prices. Actually 80s. was less than the current market price, and much less than the 120s. (£450 today) those farmers had been demanding, but the perception was that the government was favouring the landowners over the agricultural poor. Coupled with existing unemployment and grievance at mechanisation, the first few months of 1815 saw considerable civil unrest, and the main job of those regiments left in Great Britain in the early months of 1815 was to control it.

It is never a duty the British Army warms to, often being more in sympathy with those they were supposed to be policing than with the authorities, and it was no different in 1815. It was, after all, a duty for which the militia were better suited. The Life Guards were particularly busy in London. Thomas Playford, who kept a very honest, if at times slightly confused, diary, found he had rather less time to be a theatre extra and was frequently deployed on crowd-control duties. He resented 'supporting might against right', and wondered whether 'a retainer of the crown might not be a supporter of the tyranny of a class in the legislature'.[59] But the disorder was such that even William Hay's 12th Light Dragoons were warned to deploy to London, the prospect of which delighted him as it meant he could leave the detested Dorchester.[60]

The affluence which offended Playford was especially abundant in London where, isolated from the poverty and unemployment in the Home Counties, those who were making money from all this increased productivity enjoyed it. This was the London of the Prince Regent and Beau Brummell, when huge sums and estates passed hands at the gambling tables in clubs like White's and Brooke's, Boodle's and Wattier's. General Scott, who, sensibly if perhaps unsportingly, took the precaution of learning the rules of whist thoroughly and dining off a boiled chicken with toast and water whilst others at White's Club enjoyed rather too good a dinner, won £200,000 in a single evening, equivalent to £15 million today. Men's reputations were made by how many bottles of port they could drink after dinner, with Lords Panmure, Dufferin and Blayney being 'six-bottle men', which, Gronow tells us, possibly with a degree of understatement, rendered them fit only for bed.[61] Men who had made fortunes were determined to flaunt them. One such was Edmund Boehm, who had made his money trading with Russia, and whose wife's ambition was to have the Prince Regent to dinner in her splendid house in St James's Square. She succeeded, but it did not quite work out as she had hoped, as we shall see. This was the high society which caused Byron to write *Childe Harold's Pilgrimage*, which 'epitomised an age of exuberance, vice and social whirl'.[62] It was a flippant society, and Childe Harold had not, at this stage in Byron's epic poem, heard the 'sound of revelry by night' nor stood on this 'place of skulls'.[63]

Apart from smarting at being used as an instrument of this affluence, both officers and soldiers also objected to the fact that quite a few of the beau monde retained considerable sympathy for Napoleon and what he stood for. This was particularly galling after what they had been through in Spain and not unlike the Army's annoyance at Communist sympathisers in the 1960s and 1970s. This 'Napoleonist syndrome'[64] was not as prevalent by 1815 as it had been a decade earlier, when even quite sensible people enthusiastically supported a movement that would lead to the deaths of millions of Europeans, but there were still those who would regret Napoleon's defeat. Alongside the butchery and destruction he had brought, those who could afford the luxury of such whims applauded much of what they assumed he stood for.

This then was the British Army and the world it inhabited in the winter of 1814–15. The great majority of its soldiers were decent, honest and ambitious. They had joined for much the same reasons that young people join the Army today, driven by a sense of adventure, a feeling that life should offer more than the rather boring circumstances in which they found themselves and, in some cases, to make a clean break when things were difficult. They were also patriotic, reacting to a genuine hatred of what Napoleon had done to Europe and a fear of what a British version of the French Revolution would do to their country. They were proud to be free-born Britons, compared to the French, whom they saw as slaves of Napoleon's totalitarian regime. Cartoonists showed them as John Bull or Jack Tar fighting 'against a pygmy with an enormous nose'.[65] They sang songs like 'Britons Strike Home', which had been the Army's battle cry in the Seven Years' War; its chorus of:

> Britons strike home! Avenge your country's cause,
> Protect your King, your liberties, and laws!

summed up for many why they were serving. They also sang 'Rule Britannia', the patriotic naval song which first came to popularity in the 1740s, and laughed at cartoons such as Gillray's entitled 'Buonaparte 48 hours after landing!', which depicted John Bull holding Napoleon's severed head on a pike.

It was, however, a very different army to that fit and coherent

force, trained to perfection by Wellington in Portugal and
Spain, which had returned so victoriously only nine months
before. Its most experienced regiments were now overseas,
many of its veterans discharged, and the majority of its soldiers
were young men most of whom had never seen the sea let
alone crossed it. It still had though, particularly in its officers
and NCOs, that hard core of Peninsular veterans who served
on, slightly bored, wondering what to do about life, and finding policing duties distasteful. Their thoughts in the cold of
January and February were far from fighting. Apart from anything else, they were preoccupied with keeping warm, it being
a bitterly cold winter with the Thames in London freezing
over on 5 February. People enjoyed a four-day 'Frost Fair' with
a booming market on the ice. An elephant was led over the
river below Blackfriars Bridge. Much of the world was following a predictable pattern around them. Jane Austen was
finishing a novel, *Persuasion*, which would be her last; Shelley
was on the run from his creditors; Caroline, the Princess of
Wales, was causing a scandal in Naples; London's traffic was
becoming unmanageable; and Edmund Kean, the celebrity of
the day, was fighting with his managers. Some things were
new: in Australia the colonists had finally broken through the
Blue Mountains, opening Sydney to its hinterland; and Byron
had just got married. In Ceylon the last king, Vikrama
Rajasinha, was capitulating to the British; 378 of the British soldiers who had been wounded in the campaign were being
loaded onto the transport ship *Arniston*, which would sink,
drowning all but six of them. But no one expected the news
that Napoleon had escaped from exile on Elba and had landed
on the south coast of France on 1 March. All their lives would
soon be very different.

*

The Royals' rather dull routine of barrack life and anti-smuggling patrols on the south coast was interrupted by this altogether more exciting news, which pleased Ralph Heathcote as the officers finally had something else to think about and stopped teasing him about Miss Dickenson. Initially the regiment thought that Napoleon would be easily defeated. The French papers reported the 'arch-rogue surrounded on all sides and inevitably destined to be made prisoner and doubtless to be publicly executed',[66] but he confounded their expectations, entering Paris on 20 March after King Louis XVIII fled to Belgium and the majority of the Bourbon army came over to him. It was clear that the British Army would have to fight again. This was something they had not been expecting to do.

Most of them were elated. It was not so much the prospect of fighting as such, although that was certainly important for many, but more that it meant a break in the peacetime routine which they were finding both boring and disagreeable. The reaction of the 51st Foot in Portsmouth shows just how little they had been enjoying life. The Bugle Major had just dropped off the newspapers in the officers' mess and someone opened one, glancing carelessly over its contents when 'suddenly his countenance brightened up, and flinging the newspaper into the air like a madman, he shouted out, "Glorious news! Nap's landed again in France! Hurrah!" In an instant we were all wild . . . the men turned out and cheered – nay, that night at mess, the President rose and drank success to old Nap with three times three – our joy was unbounded, and few, I believe, went to bed sober.'[67] The 40th Regiment heard the news on the ship bringing them back from the West Indies and 'the young officers, ravenous for promotion, rejoiced and treated all the men to an extra glass of grog in order to make everyone as lively as themselves'.[68] William Hay was similarly delighted, now sure that he would see the back of Dorchester for good and because, as he wrote summing up the attitude of many, 'I had no liking for the life of a soldier in idleness'.[69]

Others were more sanguine. James Gardiner of the 95th had been planning to visit his father in Augusta, Georgia. The 95th had originally been warned that they were heading for duty in the American War, which was causing his father, a planter, considerable difficulty locally. He was consequently relieved when the December 1814 peace treaty was signed and their orders cancelled. He was amongst the few who did not celebrate the prospect of fighting again so soon. 'This cursed war has knocked all my plans in the head', he complained to his father from Dover in April. 'I thought a month ago that by this time I should have been on my way to see you, but this scoundrel Bonaparte, to the astonishment of the world, as it were by magic, re-seated himself without spilling a drop of blood on that throne which it cost Europe just twelve months ago so much blood and treasure to pull him down from.'[70] Outside the Army, reactions were more mixed. The media were mostly against Napoleon, but the Napoleonista syndrome lived on, with the *Statesman,* true to its long history of contrarianism, arguing that Napoleon was the legitimate ruler of France, having been recalled by the 'universal voice of the people'.

Napoleon's coup caused something quite close to panic in Whitehall, where the British government had only the week before been agreeably and leisurely corresponding over the boundaries of the new Europe with Wellington in Vienna, he having just assumed the lead of the British delegation from Castlereagh. The issue that faced Lord Liverpool, as prime minister, and Lord Bathurst, as Secretary for War, was to become a familiar one for generations of politicians, but a very particular one for them at the time. Having cut back and dispersed the victorious Peninsular Army, how did they now quickly assemble a force capable of taking on an apparently reinvigorated Napoleonic France? 'What a fatal event this invasion of Buonoparte's is', lamented General Torrens, who, as Military Secretary to the commander-in-chief, the Duke of York, was responsible for coordinating the work at the War Office. He referred to Napoleon just by his surname, as the British government always rather scornfully did, 'and', he continued, 'it is truly provoking to reflect the little precautions which might have saved the world the infliction of such a misfortune'.[71]

In the early days of March the British government was worried that Napoleon would make a rapid move into Belgium, or Brabant as it was known, the lower French-speaking part of the recently created Kingdom of the Netherlands. There was already a small British force there under General Clinton, along with some of the King's German Legion, 15,000 Hanoverian militiamen, and a Prussian contingent, to ensure that there was no resurgence of violence whilst terms were being thrashed out in Vienna, the whole force being commanded by the Prince of Orange. This was rapidly reinforced by moving seven battalions from Ireland. Plans were also drawn up to despatch two brigades of cavalry and one of Foot Guards 'and', Torrens continued to Clinton, 'this is all we can do for you until the arrival of the army from America'. However, within a couple of weeks it was clear that Napoleon would take a little longer to move: 'it is not supposed that Buonaparte would advance with a handful of men' risking 'the heart of France without positive and general assurances of support. So,' Torrens wrote, 'the orders for the cavalry and Guards have been suspended until it shall be seen whether this formidable brigand can gain a military and political ascendancy in France and, I may add, the delay is likewise occasioned by the agitated state of the public affairs here regarding the Corn Bill etc.'[72] But within a week they realised that Napoleon was 'turning his immediate attention to the Netherlands, and it forms a considerable feature in the present and embarrassing state of affairs that our Force is not of a description to afford an efficient resistance'.[73] They had to assemble an army, and to do so quickly.

The effect of the various decisions made during the autumn of 1814 was that the more experienced infantry battalions were already overseas. An infantry regiment was divided into a series of battalions, the number generally depending on how many soldiers it could recruit, a system that has endured in much the same way to the present day. The idea was that the older and more experienced soldiers would form the first battalion, which would be sent overseas on operations whilst the second and third battalions, if they had one, would stay at home recruiting young soldiers, volunteers and militiamen, and training them until it was ready to deploy itself. It would take over from its sister first battalion, which would come home and recover. The system worked quite well until 1812 when Wellington started refusing to release his experienced first battalions from the Peninsula, even though they were short of soldiers, arguing that he could not operate with inexperienced replacements when the war was at such a crucial stage. Instead drafts of men were sent out to fill gaps created by battle casualties and disease, but the majority of experienced men remained in Spain and then France throughout the whole war. Consequently the second battalions became a sort of sausage machine, feeding reinforcements to their first battalions; but this meant that by mid 1814 the British Army was unbalanced. The first battalions were generally experienced and battle-hardened, with a majority of older men, albeit some of them were badly under strength, whilst the second battalions were untried.[74]

No sooner had the best-manned first battalions returned from the Peninsula than they were sent abroad, deploying in the autumn of 1814 to Canada, the USA, India, the Mediterranean, the West Indies and even Cape Colony.[75] No one in the War Office had thought to reverse the traditional pattern and, with Wellington absent at the Congress of Vienna, process took precedence over ingenuity, possibly not for the last time in the history of that particular department. This was not at all popular with many of the first battalions' soldiers. Even some of those who were nearing their discharge points were sent. Thomas Howell was particularly bitter. He thought he was about to be discharged after his seven years' service, and only now realised that because he had been only 16 when he signed on he still had 18 months to go, the Army dating service from a soldier's eighteenth birthday as it still does today. En route to America with the 71st, he 'lamented becoming a soldier at this time more than I had done' at any time, even 'on the retreat or upon the Pyrenees. To be so near home and free and yet sent across the Atlantic was very galling. I knew not what to do' but he 'kept [his] honour and embarked'.[76] In the end he was saved from America. A fast schooner intercepted his troop ship and diverted it to Deal. 'Freedom! Freedom!' Howell rejoiced, but within a week he was being landed by a fishing smack in Antwerp.

The problem that the War Office now faced was twofold.

First, they had to find enough infantry battalions. Only 25 line battalions of the 163 in the Army were judged to be available, meaning based in Britain or Ireland or, like Thomas Howell's 71st, able to be diverted from America. Of these 25, only 18 had served in the Peninsula and 11 were second or third battalions. Secondly, they had to address the urgent issue of how to make up their numbers. All regular units were under strength by about a quarter from the size they should have been to operate effectively in battle, and on average an infantry battalion needed an extra 200 men.

Those that were up to strength were also very young. Colonel Frank Tidy's 3rd Battalion 14th Foot, for example, had 14 officers and 300 soldiers under 20, having lost its older soldiers when it was under threat of disbandment. When William Wheeler did finally rejoin his 51st Regiment at Portsmouth on 25 September 1814, he found 'The battlefield, fatigue, privations and sickness has made sad havock in the ranks of as fine a set of young fellows as ever belonged to the service'. But, he added, 'the blanks are filled up and the Regiment is fit for any service the country should require'.[77]

It was different for the cavalry regiments, very few of whom had been posted overseas, despite the nasty shock that the Royals had received when they were warned for service in Canada. In the end only two cavalry regiments were sent, partly due to the expense of shipping horses and partly because it was decided, as the Royals had correctly predicted, that the forests of Canada and the swamps of the Mississippi Delta were not good cavalry country. With three regiments in India and one each in the Mediterranean and Cape Colony, most of the experienced cavalry, like the Life Guards, the Royals, and the 7th Light Dragoons, were available in Great Britain, together with other regiments who had never actually served in the Peninsula. In the event 16 British cavalry regiments would serve at Waterloo, only five of which had served in the Peninsula and three in southern France. Cavalry regiments, though, were also under strength after the 1814 reductions, and needed about 120 men, or two troops each, to be effective. They also had a large proportion of young soldiers.

It was also different for the Foot Guards, who had been required for ceremonial and guard duties in London and consequently been kept more up to strength and who not been redeployed overseas. Since their return they had reverted to their traditional company organisation but they were now quickly reorganised into four deployable battalions, two from 1st Foot Guards and one each from the Coldstream and 3rd Foot Guards. Both the cavalry and the Foot Guards would consequently form a major part of the army that would soon deploy to the Netherlands; as would the artillery, which, despite having suffered such a severe reduction in 1814, could produce 17 batteries in Britain which could be got into a deployable state.

Some of the manpower gaps could be filled by bringing forward recruits in the various depots where their training had been proceeding without much urgency, but otherwise it meant an appeal to the militia, being the only source of at least partly trained men. The end of the war in 1814 had led to strong opposition calls for the militia to start disbanding, which it had, but there were still 17,000 militiamen serving; the government considered bringing in a new Militia Act, given that they were now at war again, but decided, wisely, that it would be quicker and more efficient to get those still serving to transfer into regular infantry battalions. James Gairdner of the 95th thought the militia preferred joining his regiment because 'there was less trouble with the dress in keeping it clean; as they have when in our regiment no facings, or white belts to keep coloured with pipe clay',[78] but with only one regiment of riflemen to choose from, most militiamen volunteering found themselves making up the numbers in the line infantry. It is a remarkable tribute both to Pitt's foresight and to the patriotism of the volunteers that by the time the regiments and battalions arrived in the Netherlands they were mostly up to strength. Ploughboys, artisans, craftsmen and labourers would soon stand in the squares on that bloody ridge alongside professional soldiers.

Many men also came forward to join in March and April as volunteers with no military experience. William Leeke was a 17-year-old from a naval family who lived on the Isle of Wight. He had already lost his elder brother in the war – he had been killed off Cadiz in 1810. Leeke did what many would do, which was to use what family connections he had to get a place. His mother's family were married into the Colborne family, and Sir John Colborne commanded the 5nd Light Infantry. Leeke got himself taken on as a volunteer. In the rush to field battalions it was not always possible to get hold of all known candidates for commissions so Leeke was lucky and as he was with the battalion he was almost immediately made an ensign, although he had precious little formal training.[79] In Dorset Daniel Gale, from Beaminster, signed up as well, but as a private soldier. He took his wife and five-year-old daughter with him to 40th Foot and on to the Netherlands.

The War Office's normally rather sedate style of correspondence, which until the end of February 1815 had been taken up with somewhat mundane issues like pensions and allowances, such as those Sir Thomas Maitland thought his

due as Governor of Malta, assumes from March a tone as near
urgent as it is possible for that department of state to sound.
The rapid reorganisation as the army was cobbled together
from recruits, the militia and re-enlistments meant that there
was an inevitable degree of chaos. In early April, for example,
reinforcements for 1st Battalion of the 15th Foot were still
loaded on to a ship to join their battalion in the West Indies,
until someone realised the error and disembarked them. They
were then joined up with a detachment of troops on the Isle
of Wight to form a new 2nd Battalion but had no officers. An
order went out to the captains and subalterns of the recently
disbanded 2nd Battalion to rejoin, but by the time the whole
new battalion was ready the battle had been fought. The 2nd
Battalion of the 69th was still despatched to India, where it
was due to relieve the 1st Battalion, although they were
recalled just in time and redirected to Brabant. It was to prove
a fateful decision for many of them.

As well as making up the numbers in regiments due to
deploy to fight Napoleon, the War Office was also ever
mindful of 'the state of public affairs' at home, and the
Prince Regent reminded them frequently lest they forgot.
Consequently the process of augmentation and reinforcement
was extended to all units, giving some sort of reserve for policing duties, although this process was far from complete even by
mid summer. Bounties for recruits, which had been slashed by
75 per cent in 1814, were reinstated at the rate of £19 12s. for
the cavalry (about £1,460 today) and £23 for the infantry
(about £1,700 today). In May the period of service for those
on seven-year contracts was extended indefinitely.

In between all this activity the War Office was still bom-
barded by Maitland about his allowances, and dealt with the
normal correspondence from nutcases with brilliant war-

winning ideas. 'I should be wanting both to my country and myself', James Sadler wrote to the Prince Regent in May, 'were I to withhold the great advantages that would necessarily accrue to the general interest of Europe from dispersing proclamations and momentous papers through France by the means of improvised small balloons' which, he added, he could provide at the 'most trifling expense'.[80]

Throughout all this, the British government also had to consider the rather tricky issue as to whom they were actually at war with, and this would soon cause the Army considerable problems. Were they at war with France? Well, not exactly, as they recognised Louis XVIII's regime as the legitimate government of France and he was now in exile in Belgium. Were they at war with Napoleon? Yes, but it was not at all clear what Napoleon actually represented, and his propaganda machine was already busy declaring his peaceful intentions, eagerly seized upon by his apologists both in Parliament and the media. Were they then at war with the French army? Possibly, but nations cannot declare wars on armies. This apparent sophism was part of the reason that the government could not call out the militia *per se*, and would lead to Wellington being unable to send troops across the Belgium– French border to reconnoitre Napoleon's intentions. Opponents of the government in Parliament, of whom there were many, maintained that the militia could not be used to replace troops in garrisons, 'saying it is contrary to the act to apply the assembly of this description of force to Garrison Duty', much to the War Office's extreme frustration.[81]

In addition to the British regiments, the Army also retained the King's German Legion. Although completely integrated with the Regular Army, the Legion had its own cavalry, infantry, artillery and engineers and at its peak was over 28,000 strong. It had been created in 1803 after the French annexation of Hanover, of which George III was king as much as he was king of Great Britain, and was manned by volunteers who loathed the French. Most of these were German but there were quite a few from the rest of occupied Europe, and some of the officers were English. It was one of those curious heterogeneous forces that the British Army is so good at assembling, and it had earned an excellent reputation in the Peninsula. Two of its battalions were riflemen. If Englishmen joined the Army for fear of what Napoleon might do to Great Britain, then men like Frederick Lindau signed up with the Legion because of what Bonaparte had already done to Hanover. It was a brutal occupation; somewhere the concept of the Napoleonic armies as apostles of the new liberty they had created in France had gone very badly wrong.

Lindau lived in Hameln on the River Weser, anglicised as the Hamlin of Pied Piper fame, which the French sacked on 20 November 1806. Initially Napoleon had given the Hanoverian territories to Prussia, which had garrisoned strategically important towns like Hameln. However, alarmed at Napoleon's growing power, Friedrich Wilhelm III of Prussia bravely issued an ultimatum on 1 October 1806 that all French forces should withdraw west of the Rhine. The result was a second French invasion, resulting in the Prussians' catastrophic defeat at the twin battles of Jena and Auerstädt, after which Napoleon systematically reduced the remaining Prussian garrisons. Sickened by French atrocities, particularly in the hospital where he was working as an orderly, Lindau managed to slip out of the city and made his way to England, where he joined the King's German Legion (KGL) infantry stationed at Bexhill. Tough, independent, and not very susceptible to military discipline, Lindau fought with the Legion all through Spain, where he distinguished himself, although not without being frequently in trouble.[82] He would soon be distinguishing himself again.

Lieutenant Edmund Wheatley was one of the Legion's British officers. Twenty-two years old and from Hammersmith, he had fought in the latter stages of the Peninsular War. It is not clear why he joined the Legion, but it is apparent from his letters and his diary that he was fond of his German soldiers and took good care of them, although he detested his German company commander, Nötting. He served in the 5th battalion of the KGL infantry, and admired his colonel, Baron Ompteda, a distinguished soldier who had originally been in the Hanoverian Guards. Wheatley's real love, though, was Eliza Brookes, who was seldom far from his thoughts. It was a difficult relationship as her family disapproved of Wheatley, who had no money and who had been fairly headstrong in his youth, fighting a duel whilst he was still at school and getting himself arrested after going on a 'bender' in Brighton. He was also unaccountably fond of his army cap, from which he hated to be separated. He would soon find it very difficult to keep hold of.

The conversation around the messes, the barrack rooms and the stable yards throughout March now turned to who would be called and who would stay behind. The decision to send all the available infantry was taken quickly, there being few battalions in Britain to choose from. The issue was with the cavalry, of which more was available but which was expensive to ship to the Netherlands. Wellington was also known to be a little cynical about their effectiveness, preferring to include more infantry and artillery; much as he may have disliked gunners he did not doubt that arm's effectiveness. For the Royals this meant that they spent the last weeks of March and early April in a state of agonising indecision. At first it seemed very unlikely that they would go. Ben the Ruler had written to the Adjutant General, the officer responsible for assembling and deploying the Army, 'intreating that the Royals might have the honour of forming part of the army in Belgium', only to receive the reply that 'in consequence of the great importance of the excise duty on the coast ... it was impossible that the Royal Dragoons could form part of the army in the Netherlands'. Trafford and the young officers were furious. 'This at once put an end of all hopes to the Royals. Thus were the veteran Royals whose conduct during five years in the Peninsula had been irreproachable, condemned to linger out an inglorious existence in performing the part of excise officers and constables.'[83] Ralph Heathcote threatened to resign his commission in disgust, but did not actually leave; later he would wish that he had. Ben the Ruler became increasingly impossible. 'As a laughing stock Ben did very well. His red face, the volubility of his tongue, after the rum ration was turned out, his bad grammar and vulgar wit, furnished an unnecessary amusement', complained Trafford.[84]

Then, on 21 April, after twelve other cavalry regiments had been mobilised, whilst Ben 'had retired sulkily from the mess and was in the act of venting his spleen upon Tucker and Philip for some neglect of duty, some one tapped on the door, Ben Cook walks in and presents an Adjutant General's letter ordering the Royal Dragoons to proceed to Canterbury and prepare for immediate embarkation'. The two troops which had been disbanded the previous summer were reinstated, and Lieutenants Ommaney, Blois, Goodenough, Sanders and

Arnold, the officers who had been turned away as there were no vacancies, were contacted to rejoin. Captains Methuen and Webb were called back from half pay. All this happened remarkably quickly, so that by the time the regiment had marched to Kent via Salisbury, arriving on 13 May, they were back to their full strength.

Gronow found himself not selected to deploy. Some of the Coldstream Guards companies had been grouped into a deployable battalion, two of which were to go, but Gronow's was left behind to continue to mount guard in London. This was very painful to a man like Gronow. It was not so much that he was an enthusiastic soldier, more that he could not bear the thought of not 'taking part in the great events which were about to take place on the continent'.[85] For a man about town, a gossip and a diarist, the thought of missing out was intolerable. He contrived to be invited to dinner with the fiery Lieutenant-General Sir Thomas Picton, a neighbour of his brother in Wales and who was to command a division, and let it be known how mortified he was at being left behind. Picton rose agreeably to the challenge: 'Is the lad really anxious to go out?' he demanded of his aide-de-camp, who confirmed that indeed he was. He then asked if all the appointments on his staff were full, adding with a grim smile 'If Tyler [an existing aide-de-camp] is killed, which is not at all unlikely, I do not know why I should not take my young countryman; he may go over with me if he can get leave'. Gronow was 'overjoyed at this ... thanking the general a thousand times'. His priority then, in typical Gronow style, was how to equip himself so that he should be able to 'appear at Brussels in a manner worthy of the aide-de-camp of the great general'. He was very short of money but managed to borrow £200 (£15,000 today) from his regimental agents, which he promptly took to 'a gambling house in St James's Square, where I managed by some wonderful accident to win £600 (£45,000 today) and, having thus obtained the sinews of war, I made numerous purchases, amongst others two first rate horses at Tattersalls'. Given that Picton was to eventually arrive in Belgium late, and to fight in civilian clothes as his baggage had not caught up with him, Gronow need not really have worried.

Corporal John Shaw of the Life Guards had other priorities. The Life Guards had been as concerned as the Royals that they might not be selected. The Prince Regent liked to have them in London, partly to maintain law and order but also to escort him, and it had been a protracted battle for both regiments to be allowed to send a detachment to the Peninsula. However, Wellington's arrival in Brussels on 5 April and the dawning realisation that there was an urgent need for heavy cavalry, meant that the Life Guards and the Blues were warned for duty the same week as the Royals. But Shaw had an important engagement to complete before he deployed. He was to fight Ned Painter for the chance to challenge Tom Cribb as the champion of England, and the fight was to take place at Hounslow Heath on 18 April. 'All the roads leading to the destined battle-field were thronged from early morning by strings of carriages of every description – men on carts, men on horseback, and men on foot, flocking to see the Life Guardsman display his prowess.'[86]

Shaw was in his prime, 'his naturally fine form ... so magnificently developed, that he used to sit as a model to Haydon the sculptor', whereas Painter had been doing a spell in the Fleet Prison for debt and had only been released that morning. However he 'set to work' on Shaw 'with great gaiety, at first holding his own very fairly, and gave and received terrific hits'. Shaw's reach and weight, however, soon began to tell and it became 'piteous to witness the punishment' he meted out. Eventually Shaw gave Painter ten knockdown blows in succession and after 28 minutes he was unable to get up. Shaw was now the challenger and the money was on him to beat Cribb, who had, perhaps unwisely, acted as Painter's second. But the next week 2nd Life Guards marched out of London bound for Ramsgate, and Shaw would soon be engaged in an even more lethal fight.

For Friedrich Lindau the call to arms came just in time. He was on leave in Lemgo in Germany, where he became involved in a drunken brawl. He had stabbed a man with his bayonet, which, as always, was not his fault. He was arrested and marched in front of the local commandant, escorted by six soldiers with loaded muskets. 'If I looked to run away, the six bullets would be sent after me', he was told, to which he scornfully replied that 'I did not think much of six bullets, many had already whistled past my ears'.[87] He was despatched back to his battalion, the 2nd Light, who were in Antwerp, where he met the adjutant, Riefkugel, who greeted him with the cheerful news that he would be hanged the next morning. Lindau replied, with remarkable self-possession, 'The rope will not be made by then.' His commanding officer, Colonel Halkett, now intervened, and, aware that they would soon need every experienced man they could, spared him after extracting a promise of good behaviour, which may not have been totally sincere given that two thalers' worth of wine were drunk by his company when they heard that he was to be spared. Very soon that wine would be a distant memory and the hangman's rope may have been something of a deliverance. Edmund Wheatley had been on garrison duty in Tournai, where he had found the winter months 'the most

pleasing, the most instructive and the most amusing of any I
ever enjoyed when absent from her' but what upset him now
was that there was no opportunity to see Eliza before they
marched.[88]

For William De Lancey, whom we have not yet met, the
only thing on his mind was his brand-new wife, Magdalene
Hall, whom he had married on 4 April after a whirlwind
romance. De Lancey, already a distinguished general and
knighted despite only being in his late thirties, had been
Wellington's Deputy Quartermaster-General in the Peninsula,
and enjoyed his complete confidence. A Huguenot, originally
from New York, he had been a soldier since he was 14, serving with both the cavalry and the infantry until he was
attached to Wellington's staff in 1809. He happened to get
married the day before Wellington arrived in Brussels, and his
honeymoon on his parents-in-law's estate at Dunglass was
predictably cut short by orders to join the duke in the
Netherlands. This was rather embarrassing, as he was to
assume the position of Quartermaster-General, a position
effectively equal to the chief of staff in a contemporary army
headquarters, after Wellington had sacked the incumbent, Sir
Hudson Lowe, who happened to be married to Magdalene's
sister. The job was an enormous one, being responsible for the
supply, quartering and movement of the rapidly assembling
army in the Netherlands, and given that no one really knew
what was going to happen, the newly-weds decided that
Magdalene should accompany him. She arrived in Brussels on
8 June.[89]

The mobilisation process also affected those many civilians
without whom a military force cannot operate. George
Guthrie had been a surgeon with the Army in Spain but was
put on half pay in September 1814 as part of the overall army

reductions. This had put him in an awkward financial position, his salary being cut from £456 per annum (£34,200 today) to £228 (£17,100 today). He tried to set up in private practice in Jermyn Street but by early 1815 he had only attracted two patients; his specialisation, gunshot wounds to the extremities, was probably felt to have limited use in peacetime despite the violence of early nineteenth-century London. With a wife and young daughter to support, and having just established the routine of family life, it was with mixed emotions that he heard the entreaties of generals like Rowland Hill and Thomas Picton to join their staff as medical adviser. He declined an administrative role, but took himself to the Netherlands as a surgeon, in case his expertise could be of use.[90]

John Haddy James was Assistant Surgeon to 1st Life Guards. He had been contemplating establishing a quiet country practice in Exeter, but decided that duty called and deployed with his regiment, showing 'the love of adventure inherent in every man of parts'.[91] He seems to have had a better sense of what was to come than many, actually writing a long letter to his mother before he left, instructing her what to do with his possessions if he didn't return. 'Trifling as they are', he wrote, 'they are yours, and I wish they were a thousand times more valuable' and, he continued, 'Would to God I had it in my power to make you some return for the unexampled kindness and affection you have shown me, and which was never exceeded by any mother'.

Officers employed servants, as did everyone else of their standing, and hundreds of these now also found their lives taking an unexpected turn. Sir George Scovell, an Assistant Quartermaster-General, in other words a senior staff officer, who worked with De Lancey, had been in the 4th Dragoons;

when he was warned to deploy he sought out an old soldier from his regiment called Heeley to come as his head groom, a general then requiring several horses both as chargers and to carry his baggage. Heeley asked to take his 14-year-old son Edward with him. Scovell asked what the boy was doing. 'Nothing, only going to school,' Heeley replied, so Scovell agreed. Edward wasn't consulted and 'could not help now and then think that it must be dreadfull to go where there was war – and half wished myself at home again' but 'on our arrival at Ramsgate ... I had to begin grooming in reality, without being allowed even to grumble'.[92] Once deployed with the Army, civilians became subject to military law (as they still can be) and were provided with rations and supplies just as soldiers were.

During April and May the Army converged on the Channel ports, on Dover, Deal, Folkestone, Ramsgate and also Harwich and Felixstowe, and in Ireland on Cork. They were cheered out of their garrison towns, cheered as they passed through the villages of Kent and Essex and cheered on arrival, not least by the innkeepers who would do very nicely out of their trade whilst they waited for shipping. 'The weather was fine, the scenery as we skirted the beautiful banks of the Stour, charming and the occasion exhilarating,' Mercer remembered.[93] The Peninsular veterans had done it all before but most of the new recruits had never even seen the sea, let alone sailed on it, and the journey itself was some-thing of an adventure. It was an adventure not without its frustrations – military moves never are – and the Transport Board, who were responsible for coordinating troops with boats, came in for the same criticism then as the Army some-what unfairly directs at its movements staff today. Lieutenant Johnston of 6th Dragoon Guards thought 'the thing has been shamefully mismanaged and we have been much annoyed. We are detained here till we have been obliged to re-sell some of the gold intended for foreign parts, everything here is dear, small, dirty and uncomfortable';[94] this may have been a slightly unfair criticism of Gravesend and probably said more about the regiment's desire just to get on with it. James Anton's Black Watch boarded five 'small vessels with miserable accommodation' in Cork, 'with not a single cot or hammock on board'.[95]

However frustrating the journey, there was a sense that they were all departing on some great adventure; but such had been the rush to mobilise, to recruit new soldiers, to acquire equipment and purchase 'necessities', to stock up on comforts and to be on the march to embark that few had time to ponder what was likely to happen once they arrived. They knew they were bound for the Netherlands, where the Allied armies were assembling, but they knew very little beyond that.

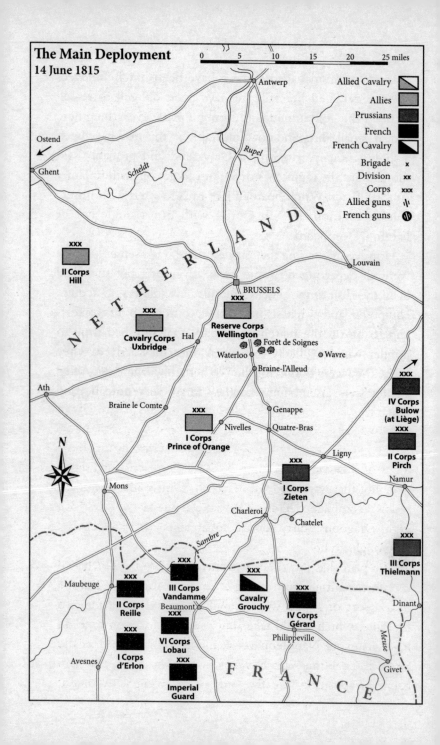

The Main Deployment
14 June 1815

0   5   10   15   20   25 miles

Allied Cavalry
Allies
Prussians
French
French Cavalry

Brigade   x
Division   xx
Corps   xxx
Allied guns   ⑂
French guns   ◍

Antwerp

Ostend

Ghent

Scheldt

Rupel

N E T H E R L A N D S

Louvain

BRUSSELS

xxx
Reserve Corps
Wellington

Forêt de Soignes

Waterloo   Wavre

Braine-l'Alleud

xxx
II Corps
Hill

xxx
Cavalry Corps
Uxbridge

Hal

xxx
IV Corps
Bulow
(at Liège)

Ath

Braine le Comte

Genappe

xxx
I Corps
Prince of Orange

Nivelles   Quatre-Bras

Ligny

xxx
II Corps
Pirch

N

Mons

xxx
I Corps
Zieten

Namur

Charleroi   Chatelet

Sambre

xxx
III Corps
Thielmann

Maubeuge

xxx
II Corps
Reille

xxx
III Corps
Vandamme

xxx
Cavalry
Grouchy

Beaumont

xxx
IV Corps
Gérard

Dinant

Avesnes

xxx
I Corps
d'Erlon

xxx
VI Corps
Lobau

Philippeville

Meuse

xxx
Imperial
Guard

F R A N C E

Givet

2

APRIL–JUNE 1815

'We arrived here this evening at 5 o'clock. The whole town was in confusion from the number of English troops lately disembarked, all of whom, true to their English nature, were wandering about with their hands in their pockets, and their eyes and mouths wide open, staring at the sight of a few dozen heavy stupid Flemings', wrote Captain Digby Mackworth, who was serving as an ADC to Lord Hill, of his arrival in Ostend, and the same story would be repeated hundreds of times in the coming weeks. The troops themselves were not that impressed with Ostend. 'This is like all foreign towns', complained Hussey Packe, a lieutenant in the 13th Light Dragoons, 'dirty and the inhabitants are not so civil as they ought to be'.[1]

The plan that the Allies had made at Vienna, which had transformed itself from being a congress to remap Europe into a sort of Allied war council, was for their armies to mobilise, which would take time, and then to converge on Paris to expel Napoleon once and for all. Known as the Seventh Coalition, which shows how many times they had been threatened by the Emperor of the French, the major allies were Russia, Prussia and Austria, the European powers who had defeated Napoleon at Leipzig, together with Great Britain, the Netherlands, which now included Belgium, and the German states of Hanover and Brunswick. The mobilisation plan put four armies into the field. The Austrians started to assemble an Army of the Upper Rhine, 285,000 men from Austria, Bavaria, Württemberg and Baden under Schwarzenberg. The Russians promised 150,000 under the splendidly named and occasionally able Barclay de Tolly, one of the heroes of Napoleon's defeat in 1812, whilst Prussia would lead the Army of the Lower Rhine, 130,000 men under Blücher drawn primarily from Prussia and Saxony. The efficient Prussian staff system ensured that this army mobilised first, despite the Prussian army being in some chaos as it was in the middle of a major reorganisation. Blücher started to move westwards on 23 March to join up with the Prussian garrison already present in the southern Netherlands.

The fourth army was the Army of Flanders, planned to be 155,000 soldiers from Britain, the Netherlands, Hanover and Brunswick, commanded by William, the Prince of Orange, which was to assemble in Belgium with Wellington commanding his right wing. This caused considerable concern in London. 'To have supposed, or expected, The Prince of Orange capable of making arrangements calculated to meet the difficulties of such a crisis would have been doing HRH an infinite injustice', wrote Torrens, the Military Secretary in Horse Guards, to Clinton on 28 March, 'and whatever might have been the policy of placing him originally in the situation, it was of course never supposed that any event could have prayed upon him the responsibility for which his inexperience renders him so unfit' and, he continued, '[we] now feel the fatal error of making him a General'.[2] Luckily common sense prevailed and he was quickly replaced by Wellington, who assumed overall command, with the prince commanding a corps. This was a wise decision both for the prince, who was a brave if rudimentary soldier, and for Europe.

The army of which Wellington assumed command on 5 April, and which was now slowly building centred on the Belgian capital in Brussels, would eventually number only 112,000. Of these just over one-third (36 per cent) were British; 10 per cent were the King's German Legion; 10 per cent came from Nassau; 8 per cent, from Brunswick; 17 per cent, from Hanover; 13 per cent were Dutch; and 6 per cent, Belgian. Almost a half of them spoke German as a first language. 'This army is not unlike a French pack of hounds,' wrote Sir Henry Hardinge, 'pointers, poodles, turnspits, all mixed up together and running in sad confusion.'[3] This was really quite an insult, French hounds naturally being considered very inferior to British ones, and even Wellington wrote, 'To tell you the truth, I am not very well pleased . . . It will be admitted that the army is not a very good one.'[4] Later, walking across the battlefield, he confided, 'I had only 35,000 men on whom I could thoroughly rely; the remainder were but too likely to run away.'[5] Given that only half of his British troops had been in the Peninsula, and that the rest were mostly in their late teens or early twenties, he was expecting quite a lot even from those he thought he could trust.

Napoleon, consolidating his new regime in Paris, did not, of course, fail to notice this. He was also mobilising his army and seeking a way of defeating the powerful coalition that was now preparing to attack him for a second time. The French army had been severely weakened by its defeats in Russia in 1812, and at Leipzig in 1813, since when it had been largely neglected in the nine months it served Louis XVIII. Looking at the armies totalling three-quarters of a million men who were gathering to destroy him, Napoleon realised that he needed to defeat them individually if he was to have any chance of success; if the Allies were allowed to join together they would tactically overwhelm the weakened French forces however strong his generalship.

He therefore determined to go on the offensive, to concentrate his available forces in Northern France, to invade Belgium and capture Brussels, defeating the Anglo-Dutch and Prussian armies in the process and before he had to face the Austrians and the Russians, neither of whose commanders he rated as highly as Wellington or Blücher. This, he reasoned, would 're-establish the ascendancy of his genius, and justify the rashness of his enterprise'.[6] It would also mean that he could deal with the Allied armies in detail. A successful campaign would also encourage the French-speaking Belgians to come over to him and could cause the collapse of the government in London. This plan was not evident to the British troops marching and sailing to their concentration areas, and many thought it more likely that they would be invading France as they had done in 1813, rather than defending the Netherlands. However, what was very clear was that they would almost certainly have to fight and that they would be fighting a French army which would most likely be commanded by Napoleon himself. From the moment they landed, an air of expectation, almost menace, overshadowed their preparations.

Their first challenge, though, was to disembark from their requisitioned ships and move to their designated concentration areas. Of the three corps in the army, the Prince of Orange's 1st Corps was to gather around Genappe and Mons, south of Brussels, whilst Hill's 2nd Corps would concentrate on Ath and Ghent, leaving Wellington's 3rd Corps to the area around Brussels itself. The principal port was Ostend but it became so crowded that most ships beached on the sand and put the men over the side. Cavalié Mercer was incensed that his troop horses and all their saddlery and effects were simply hoisted into the sea. When he complained to the naval officer in charge he was firmly told it was Wellington's order and that no delay was to be permitted; the ships had to turn around as quickly as possible and return for the next load. The poor horses had to swim to the shore as best they could, and his soldiers wait until the tide had gone out before they could retrieve their now-soaking equipment. The same thing happened to the Royals, whose horses all contracted bad colds as a result and were unable to do much for a week except walk. Mercer did manage to persuade the Navy to leave his guns and ammunition on board, but his men spent a wretched night fishing around in the rising tide, with a violent storm blowing, searching for what they could retrieve. It was, all agreed, a fairly miserable way of going to war.

Once they were ashore, and dried out, morale began to improve. The plan in the concentration areas was for the cavalry and artillery to be billeted in the villages and farms, with space for their horses, whilst the infantry would be put in the towns. The soldiers were billeted with local families where possible, which meant they lived in their houses and ate with them, for which the family was recompensed. Where there was not enough room, tents were used instead. This in itself was quite an adventure for those young men who had rarely been beyond their own local town let alone across the sea. They liked the neat, well farmed Belgian countryside, and the farmers' boys appreciated the healthy-looking crops and farm

animals. 'There is no part of England so entirely under culti-
vation. The rye is now standing 7 feet high, the barley up to
my chin',[7] wrote Samuel Ferrior. They also liked travelling by
barge along the canals, not least because it saved them marching. They were generally well treated by the Belgians, and
although there were the inevitable accusations of overcharg-
ing, most enjoyed Belgian hospitality and cooking. Sometimes
this was a bit overwhelming. 'Some of us poor soldiers found
a strange contrast when sitting at table with and by the side of
the most wealthy gentlemen ... in the Netherlands; and the
same time surrounded by the most fashionable and the greatest blaze of female pride and beauty ... and where the strictest
etiquette of field discipline was maintained. Thus surrounded
by such a brilliant blaze of beauty and fashion stood the untu-
tored and rustic British soldier', wrote Private Thomas
Jeremiah, possibly exaggerating the refinement of his billet,
but who became much attached to his hosts who 'never tired
of administering comfort to the British soldier'.[8] He was
greatly irritated when Napoleon finally disturbed his luxurious new lifestyle.

For many British soldiers, used to hardship at home, those
weeks of good living and Belgian food were amongst the
most comfortable they had experienced. When Cavalié
Mercer finally got his troops safely to their billets in the village
of Saint-Gilles, he went round his men, whom he found 'scattered by threes and fours all over the commune amongst the
farmers and with these good and simple people I found them
already quite at home. In most houses I found them seated to
dinner with the family.'[9] Lieutenant John Macdonald was positively lyrical about it all. 'We are in a delightful country here
covered with towns and villages and appearing much more
like a garden or gentleman's pleasure grounds in England than

the whole face of a country . . . I am billeted in a house with an uncommon nice family. I feel myself quite at home. We rise every morning at five to exercise the men for the campaign, at eight come home and breakfast, after breakfast take a book from a very good little library in the house and stroll into the garden, here we romp among the groves and banks till you choose to sit and eat fruit, of which there is the greatest abundance, about two, lounge about, pay your visits and return at four for dinner at the mess, at seven we generally ride out in the country for an hour or two, from nine to eleven always with the family.'[10]

Some of the cavalry were less impressed, irritated at being relatively cut off in their villages. James Johnston was still complaining, now moaning that 'our people have an idea that even after having entirely put down Boney we shall keep a large force in this country; this is not a particularly pleasant prospect to me, as the cavalry on account of forage and stabling are sure to be always scattered about in little villages; if we stood a chance of being quartered in towns that would be delightful, not the Lord preserve us from such villages as these for winter quarters.' And, he added, rather smugly, 'My landlord's wife votes herself desperately in love with me, which is a bore as she is neither young nor pretty.'

Once their immediate concerns of food and shelter were taken care of, and their commanding officers had instituted a routine of drills and training, they had time to think about what might happen. Waiting before action is always the part of a military operation that soldiers find the most difficult, particularly if that period is drawn out over several weeks; and as those weeks turned into months, men's thoughts focused on the two things that always preoccupy them, the battle ahead and their families. Some of those families were actually accompanying them. It may seem rather strange to the modern reader that a soldier should take his wife and children on active service, but in 1815 it was a long-standing British military custom, cherished by soldiers who felt they could care better for their families if they had them with them, although it was unpopular with some generals, who thought it distracting and an added complication. It was also unpopular with the War Office, which begrudged the expense.

The War Office regulation was that six wives were permitted for every 100 soldiers and Wellington insisted on this being rigorously enforced despite the demand greatly exceeding the places available. Regiments used different methods to allocate spaces, quite frequently resorting to drawing lots or shaking dice. Some would only allow wives with no children. Colonel Sir Andrew Barnard of the 95th refused to allow any wives at all. He was consequently rather surprised at seeing Corporal Pitt on the docks at Ostend with his wife on his arm. He remonstrated with Pitt, who said, 'Sir, my wife was separated from me when I went to the Peninsular War and I had rather die than be parted from her again.' 'Very well, then. Take the consequences,' replied Barnard. Mrs Pitt was forcibly put back on board the ship and Corporal Pitt was sentenced to 300 lashes and reduced to the rank of private soldier.[11] This was seen as harsh, even for a soldier disobeying a direct order, and Pitt's punishment was stopped after 120 lashes; but Barnard was considered a competent and decent commanding officer whose insistence on his orders being obeyed was respected by his battalion.

The issue most soldiers had was how to care for their wives and children whilst they were abroad. The War Office line was simple. Soldiers were not intended to marry; and, if they did, then care of their families was their own concern. There were no married quarters and in barracks wives simply lived in a curtained-off part of the barrack rooms. Those left behind when their husbands deployed were given 2d. per mile (about £1 today) and told to go back to wherever they came from.[12] This caused considerable annoyance to senior NCOs, like Sergeant-Major James Page of the King's Dragoon Guards, who brought his wife to Dover to embark but had to send her away. 'I am so fond of being in the army in some respects that I should be sorry to leave it,' he wrote, 'but you see what troubles I am exposed to. In regard to my wife and family, I could support them in a very comfortable manner, but cannot get them to me, but have to support them to so much disadvantage where the necessaries of life are so very dear.'[13] And of course no one knew for how long they would be away. It could be for a few months, or it could be for years, as it had been in the Peninsula.

During those long and unusually wet months of the spring, soldiers' thoughts therefore dwelled as much on their families and girlfriends at home as they did on Napoleon. Standish O'Grady very much liked Belgium: 'it is a very fine cavalry country, we have not even seen anything like a hill since we landed and the inhabitants do everything in their power to oblige us – the cottages are uncommonly clean and in every respect I think this country exactly the reverse of Spain so I look forward to the campaign as a most delightful excursion to Paris.' But what annoyed him was that he had heard nothing, not even from Kitty. 'I have not had a line from anyone – you must have had a most delightful season in Dublin to have made you all forget me. However it is still in your powers to make amends and whilst I am here you must make a point of getting someone to write to me as I don't want to think I am in another country … P.S. my horses looking uncommonly well.'[14] O'Grady was not sure what his real feelings were for Kitty; she was certainly the girl his mother thought most suitable and he was undoubtedly very fond of her, but was that all? Would she be in his thoughts after the battle if he were to survive it?

Captain Courtney Ilbert, of the Artillery, reassured his wife that, although she 'would be a little jealous' were she 'to see what a pretty girl the fille de maison where we lodge is' he would not look at her, given that he had sworn to be constant.[15] Inevitably, though, three months in close proximity to Belgian families meant that some soldiers did develop relationships. There was a well known ditty, one of those rather trite rhymes which armies love, which went: 'In my dear country, Women are delightful. None here I've seen as yet, but what are frightful'.[16] But that did not stop many of them trying their luck.

Predictably one of these was Francis Kinchant. He was missing his divine Letitia, and often thought of her in his surprisingly miserable billet near Grammont. 'Oh how much I wish the lovely Letitia was here, she would surpass even the most beautiful, depend on it, there is no greater luxury in life than to have an angelic creature such as Letitia to keep one warm at night and dispel the damp air and fogs so prevalent in this country. Some of our lads have pieces and I wish I was of their number.' Instead he had to make do with what girls he could pick up locally. 'I asked a girl one day if she would let me *manoeuvre* her', he wrote to John Hall, with whom he shared most intimate details. 'She answered, "Yaw, Yaw",' which he took to mean 'Yes, Yes'. However, 'I proceeded to action when lo! To my astonishment she kicked up such a row in Dutch that I never before heard, & ran away as fast as she could. There are however,' he continued, 'excellent pieces to be had at Brussels and Ghent and other large towns at regular licensed bawdy houses. When you enter one of these houses you are ushered into a room adapted for the purpose and immediately 10 or 12 girls present themselves so that anyone that may be a good judge of that species of biped may have an opportunity of selecting a capital goer.' And, he added reassuringly, 'All the girls are examined three or four times a week by a surgeon and before I was allowed to perform, the girl just examined his worship.'[17]

Others, like Digby Mackworth, regretted that suddenly leaving England again had ruined the progress he had been making with girlfriends since his return from Spain. 'At this moment I should perhaps have been dancing at our Farnham Ball', he recorded in his diary, 'and enjoying all the delights which for many days I had promised myself but I must be content with imagination, where I might have enjoyed the reality. I do think the greatest drawback on the pleasure of a military life is that a man is so continually liable, just as he has formed connexions and acquaintances, the most delightful to him, to receive an order, without the slightest previous notice, to quit them, to go heaven knows where.'[18]

Courtney Ilbert would have been an unlikely love rat, writing to his adored wife Anne every few days. 'I kissed your dear picture fifty times before I went to sleep last night and it was my first occupation this morning', he wrote on 13 May, and he was equally attached to his children. 'I assure you', he told Anne, 'my dearest love that I never cease to think of and pray for my darlings.' Most correspondence between husbands and wives was, though, as it always is, about the more mundane issues of life – predominantly money but also children, health, prospects, horses (especially in letters from the cavalry), who could be helpful in advancing their careers and endless speculation about what would happen in the coming months. Lieutenant-Colonel Henry Murray was still trying to sort out his wife Emily's obsession with moving house even as Napoleon was massing to cross the frontier. Emily was from a Portuguese family, and although theirs was a happy marriage, she could go through periods of being particularly tiresome and emotional. 'You are depriving yourself of the opportunity of learning to ride, which you have now and will not have again. You have a cheap house, which you will not have again, you know the inconvenience of dragging quantities of baggage of all description there is about the country. I see it as absurd in the highest degree and without rational object', he wrote crossly to her on 7 June, adding, sensitively, 'Therefore if you mean to throw yourself out of the window, don't.'[19]

Captain Edward Kelly, for one, was pleased to be back on active service, but for rather different reasons. He had been finding life in the Life Guards 'fatal to our pecuniary affairs', and thought that whatever should happen in Belgium it must be 'more advantageous than remaining in London'. He had already concluded that he could not afford to stay in the Life Guards. His adored wife, Maria, was living in Marlow, and she and her two daughters seemed to have an insatiable demand for money which poor Kelly was ill equipped to provide. He was an able officer, respected by his men, but his lack of money made him desperate for advancement, and led to a rather unattractive campaign of self-promotion. He had approached Wellington for a place on his staff and, although refused, was at least honoured with a reply. He even sold a horse to a brother officer for £54 despite knowing that it had been injured on the ship to Ostend and was going blind. Maria does not seem to have been very sympathetic, her demands for cash growing shriller and probably driving Kelly further than he would have gone, as we shall shortly see.

Whereas the post was carried out from Belgium quite efficiently, it was more haphazard coming in, and there were frequent outbursts of annoyance that letters weren't being answered. Surviving return letters from wives and girlfriends are less frequent, not least because those sent to men who fell at Waterloo were mostly lost, and many were also in the army's baggage, which was comprehensively plundered. One wife who was a faithful correspondent was Ann Tennant, married to Sergeant Billy Tennant of the 1st Foot Guards. She was pregnant as her husband left, and went home to her parents in Radnorshire to have her baby. Theirs is one of the most touching correspondences, both writing regularly, excited about the baby, who was to be called William or Ann after them, but, despite starting his letters 'My dear and loving wife', Billy still signs off very formally as 'William Tennant, Sergeant 1st Guards'. She is very worried about him going. 'My suffering was more than I can describe, I had a heart for nothing but to love you and grieve for the loss of so dear an object as you will ever be to me.' He tried to reassure her, writing that 'There is great talk here that this disturbance will be settled without any fighting' but both seem to have known that was unlikely.[20]

In between the training and the drilling, the Army still found plenty of time to enjoy life in Belgium. They were compulsive tourists, visiting all the sights, particularly in Ghent and Brussels, and writing long descriptions of the churches and museums to their families. Given that this was the age of the Grand Tour, it is not altogether surprising that they would take advantage of the cultural opportunities on offer, but boredom played a part and visiting was something to take their minds off the waiting. There were also frequent regimental sports, and, for the cavalry, race meetings, at which large amounts of money were inevitably lost, and then subsequently requested from forbearing fathers at home. Sometimes the celebrations after these meetings went too far. By June they were taking place weekly, and were followed by 'Race dinners where people get very drunk and ride across the country, killing their horses, and getting half drowned themselves', Henry Murray complained to Emily, adding, 'I don't partake of the late festivities of the day and retire early after only a few tumblers of champagne.'[21]

Drink played an important part in their lives, as it always has done with the British Army. Rum was issued as part of the rations. Local wine was expensive and generally considered pretty filthy – 'an inferior kind of hock'[22] – and cost four local franks a bottle (about 40p today),[23] although the exchange rate went up considerably after Waterloo, which made it more agreeably priced. Gin, or Hollands as it was suitably called, was cheaper at around 3d. a pint, about £1.50 today, which was the same price as they paid for small beer in England. This was the soldiers' favoured drink; they particularly liked the locals' advice that the best way to ward off a cold was to drink a glass first thing in the morning. In these months of waiting, drink certainly helped relieve boredom and keep soldiers cheerful, although a pint of gin was quite an amount of spirits. There were the inevitable incidents of excess and rowdiness, with consequent punishment, but less than there would have been had they been at home and there were few complaints from the locals, who were keen to keep British troops in their area lest they have Prussians billeted on them; Prussians had a terrible reputation and their military authorities were reluctant payers. Pipe tobacco, another staple of the Army, was equally reasonable at 4d. per pound, or £2 today.

It was smoked in small, disposable clay pipes and was very much the contemporary equivalent of cigarettes for soldiers in the twentieth century.

For the officers there was some 'society' in Brussels, where hostesses like the Duchess of Richmond, wife of the British ambassador, entertained regularly. Standish O'Grady much enjoyed her parties. He thought he 'had never passed a more agreeable afternoon. Lord Apsley was there who is to be married to Lady Sarah; he is all for love and [he added] a little for the bottle.' O'Grady enjoyed himself too, and 'felt rather unsteady the next morning and had such a tremble in my hand that in shaving I absolutely cut off one of my whiskers'.[24] The exiled Louis XVIII also kept a sort of court in Ghent and officers billeted locally were expected to be received. George Simmons of the 95th couldn't take his eyes off the vast monarch. 'I was quite astonished at his enormous dimensions', he noted in his diary, 'they were marvellous, he was really a moving mountain of flesh.'[25] Frederick Johnston was similarly dismissive. 'I saw him go to church in a coach and six with some Garde du Corps and with magnificent coats and helmets but dirty breeches and boots and miserable horses . . . all a mixture of dirt and finery',[26] he wrote to his mother but she, as mothers will, thought she should arrange an introduction for her son to the exiled king. This got poor Frederick very worried. 'I would not give a fig to be led up with a dozen others like a flock of sheep and in fact do not wish to be presented [to] the poor old fat king. In a town crammed full of military, where every damned tinker's son has an ensigncy given him, must needs go and be presented.'

But for all the racing and socialising and drinking and visiting, much of their time was, understandably, given over to preparing for what they were about. The brigades, those groups of three to four regiments or battalions into which they had been formed since their arrival, exercised together three times each week, and in between commanding officers conducted their own training in the fields around their concentration areas. There was a lot to teach the many young soldiers. They had been taught the basics of their individual skills, such as how to care for their horses and weapons, whilst they were undergoing their initial training in their depots. However, they would not have done much training as to how to fight together in a company or troop, and these few months were now a welcome opportunity to rectify that and to drill them alongside the Peninsular veterans. There was also the question of how to train up men like William Leeke and Daniel Gale, and all the thousands of others who had joined up in the last few weeks. Men also had to get fit. This did not mean going on runs or doing PT, as it has tended to become in modern armies – PT was not introduced into the British Army until later in the nineteenth century – but it did mean being fit to march and carry the standard infantryman's load of at least 60 pounds. It also meant being strong enough to hold and fire unsupported a musket, which weighed 14 pounds with a bayonet.

Horses also had to be fit, and much of the cavalry's time was spent feeding and exercising so that they were. Waterloo was not the first battle in which the fitness of horses decided the fate of Europe, although it was arguably the last. Many men would soon lose their lives because their horses became exhausted, but that was as much a factor of the exceptionally wet spring that year, which waterlogged the ground, and because of the extraordinary amount they were asked to do. The British cavalry were well mounted, there being plenty of good horses available in the British Isles, unlike France where Napoleon's continual wars, and particularly the Russian campaign, had used up the better-quality animals. Most colonels preferred geldings to mares, and certainly insisted that officers rode geldings as their 'first chargers', there being a long-held but possibly unfair cavalry view that mares were less reliable; troop horses were mixed but soldiers again preferred geldings if they had a choice.

Cavalry saddles looked much like a more uncomfortable version of a modern riding saddle, with a large flat seat. They were usually covered with sheepskins to make them more bearable to sit in. They were not particularly efficient at evenly distributing the heavy weight a horse had to carry across its back, which meant that sore backs and saddle sores, raw patches under the saddles, were common and could put a horse off the road for several weeks. Seawater was considered very good for them, the salt hardening the skin, as was urine, and the standard British cavalry treatment was for the soldiers to pee on them.

Where there were insufficient stables the horses were picketed, which meant being tied to a long rope stretched between two trees in a field; the issue bridle, or 'head kit' as it was called, allowed for this, having a detachable bit (the metal bar which goes in the horse's mouth), leaving a head-collar and rope which was coiled away under the horse's neck and clipped back to the front of the saddle when not in use. Their bits would be considered severe today, having long side-pieces and a curb chain to give more control. Soldiers rode with two reins, partly for safety if one got cut and also again to give more control. A chain, called a bright chain as in barracks it was tossed in bran to keep it sparkling, was attached to the bit and back to the saddle as a last resort if both reins got cut through. In most regiments the horses' tails were 'docked', cut back to the hard tissue at the top, so as to stop them getting clogged with dirt, although this practice was never followed in the Household Cavalry as it was felt to look strange on parade in London.

Cavalry training was, in effect, a series of marches and drills. Cavalry tactics had evolved in the Peninsula and were quite simple. They were, for the most part, an adaptation of French cavalry tactics which had been perfected for Napoleon by inspirational if eccentric commanders like Murat. On an advance or retreat, they went ahead of the army or covered its rear. This job was normally given to the light-cavalry regiments, particularly if the role required scouting or screening, but occasionally they were not strong enough if the enemy was close by, in which case they needed heavy-cavalry support. In a pitched battle, the light cavalry tended to be placed on the flanks, slightly out of harm's way and so that it could be used in a pursuit of a defeated enemy. The heavy cavalry was used differently, being kept back to be unleashed in a massed charge to destroy enemy formations. They hadn't done this very often in the Peninsula, but when they had, such as at Fuentes de Oñoro and at Salamanca, it had had a devastating effect.

On operations, two to three troops were put together to form a squadron, so typically there were three to four squadrons in each regiment, commanded by the senior captains. Squadrons moved in 'sections' of three men whilst they were marching, but prior to going into action would form into lines, usually two, and were closely packed together so that their effect was concentrated. Officers rode at the side of their lines, not in front, as artists would have us believe. This was less suicidal, but made it more difficult for them to control their men. When it was formed up like this a cavalry regiment only occupied 200–300 yards. This tight formation also encouraged the horses. It is actually quite difficult to get a horse to trot or canter into a mass of men or other horses, particularly if they are doing disagreeable things like pointing bayonets at you; anyone who has taken part in equestrian sport will know how determined a horse that doesn't want to do something can be. Being packed tightly together gave the horses the encouragement of the herd, and meant that they, like the men, found it more difficult to duck out. It also encouraged them when they were being shelled. 'The horses are very unwilling to go into battle', Frederick Ponsonby, who commanded the 12th Light Dragoons wrote, 'and they cower and hang down their heads when balls are whistling about them',[27] but being formed into close ranks meant that they were less likely to break away.

The term 'cavalry charge' is something of a misnomer. The problem with using cavalry in a battle was maintaining control, and the British cavalry in particular had earned the unenviable reputation of being a one-shot weapon who, once unleashed, went galloping off as if they were enjoying a hunt and deaf to their officers' efforts to regroup them; in fact the officers were considered to be the worst culprits. This was not a new problem. Charles I had blamed Prince Rupert and his dashing Cavalier horse for losing him battles in the Civil War because they had done the same thing. Wellington was especially caustic about it, and throughout the Peninsular campaign reforming cavalry generals like Le Marchant and Stapleton Cotton had been trying to instil greater discipline. The reason that the issue bits were so severe, with their longside pieces and curbs, was an attempt to solve this. Ideally the charge was delivered at the trot, at which pace horses will stay close to each other and there was a decent chance of a regiment maintaining its formation, thus being able to deliver a concentrated effect at the right place. As soon as they broke into a canter the space between the ranks widened and it became impossible to maintain any formation for more than 100 yards or so. Cavalry charges were also over much shorter distances than we may imagine. The idea was to get as close to your target as you could so as to keep your tight formation as long as possible; the enemy were, after all, going to be engaged in hand-to-hand fighting with swords so range was not an issue. The charge was only sounded at the last safe moment or when the colonel's nerves got the better of him.

The Royals had bitter experience of being asked to charge over too long a distance in the Peninsula. Under the command of a General Slade, whom they heartily detested, they had been unleashed in pursuit of the able French General Lallemand, who would reappear at Waterloo, during a minor action near Maguilla, in Andalusia, in 1812. Slade had ordered them to charge the retreating French at what eventually turned out to be over twelve miles. This 'ridiculous, impossible and dangerous order'[28] had catastrophic results. The regiment became spread out in ones and twos, the horses got blown, and by the time they reached the enemy, the French were able to round on them and pick them off individually. Seventy-nine men were lost, either killed, wounded or taken prisoner, and 150 horses, making it one of the worst cavalry defeats of the whole campaign. Slade was sacked by Wellington but that had not made the losses any easier to bear and some of the prisoners were not released until 1814.

Although cavalry regiments were issued with carbines, a sort of shortened musket easier to handle on a horse, and pistols, these were rarely used in a battle, when they relied instead on swords. The completely useless British cavalry sword of the 1790s, which bent and broke, had been replaced in the Duke of York's reforms by ones that were marginally less useless. The heavy cavalry now carried a long, straight sword with a point, which they were meant to direct at the enemy when they charged. It was stronger than its predecessor, although still thought likely to break in combat; it also rattled in its scabbard and rusted easily. French heavy-cavalry swords were longer, which was a serious advantage if you were trying to run your sword point into an opponent armed with one. Instead the British heavy cavalry developed a slashing technique. They preferred the light-cavalry sword for this, a curved sabre that was better made, weighted towards the point and an effective slashing weapon.

No British cavalry wore any armoured protection. This had been the subject of an endless and heated debate, particularly amongst retired cavalry colonels, who argued that a good breastplate and backplate, called 'cuirasses' after the French, would protect the wearer from both sword strokes and musket balls, as would a steel helmet of some sort. Yet there had been few incidents in the Peninsula to prove this, and the regiments there had valued their mobility more than protection. Nothing was done, but then they had not yet met Napoleon's feared élite heavy cavalry, the cuirassiers, who took their name from their effective armour. A private in the heavy-cavalry regiments just wore a short red or blue jacket, long overall trousers not unlike modern jodhpurs, and a leather helmet. When on the march he also carried everything he and his horse needed for the immediate future, including forage and hay nets, although before going into action as much as possible was ground-dumped. The exact and organised Frederick Johnston told his mother in great detail what he carried with him. In his little valise 'which we all have behind our saddle, which is another very convenient thing, I carry the writing roll, two shirts, one flannel waistcoat, a night cap, pair of stockings, a leather roll containing comb, toothbrush, razor etc., a knife, and a pair of pantaloons, so that even if I am in advance of the heavy baggage, I have some little comforts with me'.[29]

There was nothing very glamorous about their appearance, which was more utilitarian than showy, more threatening than exotic. Tall men on heavy horses, with docked tails, simple uniforms and long swords looked frightening, which was exactly the effect intended. They did not look anything like the Household Cavalry do when on parade in London today, and who wear a uniform designed rather later by Prince Albert specifically for ceremonial duties.

The light-cavalry approach was a little different. Their reputation for style and hard riding, for speed and dash, meant that they dressed more elaborately. Their uniforms were more close-fitting, embroidered with gold and silver lace; they rode on glossy sheepskins over their saddles and carried elaborate embroidered sabretaches, pouches that hung from their saddles. They wore tall hats, often made of fur. However, after a few days in the field all cavalrymen looked very unlike the immaculate apparitions we may have become accustomed to from the work of war artists, and more like walking haystacks.

General Lord Uxbridge, the Colonel of Standish O'Grady's 7th Light Dragoons, commanded the Allied cavalry. He was not Wellington's first choice; he did not much care for Uxbridge, partly because he lacked recent Peninsular experience and partly because he had eloped with his sister-in-law. He had in fact already asked Stapleton Cotton to command his cavalry, much to the Duke of York's annoyance. He did, however, respect Uxbridge's ability and, grumpy as he would be with Horse Guards, Wellington was nothing if not a political realist. When ultimately forced by the Duke of York to make a choice between keeping him or sending him home, Wellington decided he should stay.[30] Uxbridge divided the cavalry into two heavy brigades, the Household and Union brigades, and five light brigades, which included the four light-cavalry regiments of the King's German Legion. There was also a Netherlands cavalry division, which came under Uxbridge's command, and a Hanoverian cavalry brigade, which was to be the source of some embarrassment. Robert Hill, Edward Kelly, George Sulivan, James Page, John Shaw, Thomas Playford and John Bingley were all in the Household Brigade, so called because it contained the Life Guards and the Blues, together with the King's Dragoon Guards. Ben the Ruler, Sigismund Trafford and the Royals, and Francis Kinchant were in what was known as the Union Brigade because it had three regiments from different parts of the United Kingdom – the Royals from England, the Scots Greys and the Inniskillings from Ireland. Henry Murray, Standish O'Grady and William Hay were in the light-cavalry brigades.

Whatever the private feelings between Wellington and Uxbridge, it was clear to the former that the cavalry now formed a substantial part, almost a third, of his British troops; and to the latter that his reputation would depend on their performance. Uxbridge knew he owed his position to the Duke of York, although it must have been with mixed feelings that he received a package from his patron in late May enclosing a short pamphlet on Spanish cavalry tactics, in case he should find it useful; the Spanish cavalry was not noted as being amongst the finest in Europe! Uxbridge therefore determined to show his men and horses off to their best advantage before any fighting took place, and arranged a mass review of all his regiments, including the horse artillery, for Wellington to inspect on 29 May in a large flat field at Meerbeck between Ghent and Brussels. Private Thomas Jeremiah was decidedly grumpy about this as his battalion along with two others were employed for three days beforehand 'filling up holes and levelling the hills',[31] the poor infantry doing the hard work for the cavalry to enjoy themselves.

A review was, however, more than just a parade and inspection and it served several useful training purposes. It practised the deployment of the regiments from their billets, what the Army today calls its 'crash out' procedure. It allowed them to practise forming up together, as they would soon have to do on the battlefield, and of manoeuvring en masse, and there was also something in the impression of their appearance. This was an age when soldiers were still meant to overawe their enemy physically. The size and grim uniformity of the heavy cavalry, and the bright, showy uniforms of the light cavalry, were designed to make them both look more impressive and terrifying. Camouflage only became relevant when weapons had developed so that they could be fired accurately at long ranges; the whole point of a cavalry regiment was that, once committed, it should shock and overpower the enemy and its appearance was an important part of that. Even the military genius of Napoleon dressed his cavalry in elaborate and showy uniforms and Marshal Joachim Murat, his most talented cavalry commander in his early campaigns, rivalled Göring in his choice of outlandish forms of dress.

Most of them much enjoyed the great review. 'At twelve precisely, The Earl of Uxbridge appeared on the field arrayed in the richest uniform, and took command of the most

numerous and precise body of British cavalry that was ever
assembled in a body in the annals of history,' wrote Trafford
approvingly. 'Eight and forty squadrons of cavalry exclusive of
the artillery were drawn up in review order.'[32] Mercer was
equally impressed, contrasting the first rank of the light-cavalry regiments in their 'fanciful yet picturesque costume' to
the second rank, 'the far more imposing line of heavy dragoons, like a wall of red brick'.[33] Wellington was late, probably
to annoy Uxbridge, not arriving until 2.30 p.m., when he was
greeted with a 21-gun salute. He was escorted through the
ranks by Uxbridge and was genuinely impressed. The horses
had recovered well from being dumped into the sea off
Ostend, and looked fit, a most important factor in their pre-
paredness. Trafford was amused to see Marshal Marmont,
who had deserted Napoleon, amongst Wellington's retinue,
'distinguishable by a white Arabian horse and the same he
rode at Salamanca and which form'd a singular contrast with
his black face', he wrote, highlighting Marmont's dark skin.
The Royals did not like Marmont, whom they blamed for
some of their Peninsular casualties, and much later the whole
regiment broke out into uncontrolled cheering when he was
bucked off at a similar review. 'As Wellington passed The
Royals, he gave Ben The Ruler a very friendly nod and ask'd
him how he did. The Ruler dropped his sword in reply, and
cock'd his ugly face in the air and look'd wonderfully happy
for a minute or two.'[34]

After the review the squadrons wheeled and trotted and
cantered past and it was all considered to have been a great
success. 'Nothing could be more brilliant', thought Henry
Murray, and Blücher, who had accompanied Wellington, said
that he could not look at his own cavalry for a fortnight afterwards, or so Murray believed. This intelligence was reported

to him by General Dörnberg, who did not speak a word of English so Murray couldn't be sure. The infantry battalions billeted round about also came to watch, and swallowed their indignation at having to prepare the ground, even Jeremiah admitting that the scene was 'truly affecting'. He particularly noticed 'fathers and sons belonging to different regiments embracing each other ... the last it happened to many, yes they little thought that in 26 days more their worldly affairs would be all over'. Many fathers and sons and brothers in fact served not only in the same regiments but in the same squadrons or companies, with terrible consequences for families should their unit take heavy casualties, but it would not be until the terrible losses of World War One that the British Army introduced a policy that brothers should serve separately. A rumour went round that Napoleon was there to watch, disguised as a fruit seller, and some of the spectating troops amused themselves by accosting innocent local hawkers to see if they really were the arch rogue. The review was followed by a dinner, always an important part of contemporary military inspections, which was 'sumptious without being ostentatious, not even servants in livery', noted Murray, who sat next to Dörnberg. They had a long conversation about Napoleon's intentions, or at least Murray thought they did, but he didn't understand a word.[35]

By the beginning of June the cavalry were feeling as ready as they could be. Their horses were fit enough, or so they thought, and the waiting was getting on their nerves. The infantry were less ready, largely because reinforcements kept arriving throughout May and into June, and were still being unloaded at Ostend as Napoleon made his move. Under his three corps, Wellington divided his infantry into six 'divisions', numbered from one to six, with the First, the most senior, being the Guards Division, in other words made up entirely of British Foot Guards, although they had artillery attached. In the remaining five divisions he mixed British, King's German Legion and Hanoverian infantry brigades together. He did this because he thought the more reliable British troops would encourage the possibly less reliable Hanoverians to stand firm, although he had few such doubts about the King's German Legion. He did not mix the brigades themselves, thinking this would cause confusion in language and tactics, and each brigade consisted of three to four battalions of either British or German infantrymen.[36] In addition there were two Dutch infantry divisions, a Brunswick division commanded by their charismatic duke, and an independent brigade of Nassauers. The divisions varied greatly in size, but they consisted of about 6,000 men, with a brigade being 2,000 and a battalion, by the time it actually arrived on the battlefield, about 600.[37]

The British infantry battalions were then subdivided into ten companies of roughly 60–100 men each. One of these companies was the grenadier company, which stood on the right when the battalion was in line; and one was a light company, which tended to have the fitter men and the better shots. It traditionally stood on the left but in practice they were often deployed as skirmishers, well forward of the main position, to warn of an attack and, particularly those which were armed with rifles, to pick off the enemy officers. The remaining eight companies were line companies, who stood in the middle.

The basic infantry weapon was the Brown Bess musket. The version used at Waterloo was known as the India Pattern simply because the government had bought quantities of them from the East India Company at the outset of the Napoleonic Wars. It was a fairly basic smoothbore weapon (which meant that the barrel was smooth not twisted or 'rifled'), which had been in service for 80 years by Waterloo, and fired a round ball propelled by black powder ignited by a flintlock. It was not very accurate – even experienced infantrymen would only hit a target at 100 yards every three shots – but, used at closer ranges and in volleys, it was devastating. A lead musket ball weighed about an ounce and would flatten on impact, smashing bones and causing horrific injuries to tissue and muscle. It was propelled by a five-dram cartridge, there being 16 drams to the ounce, so about twice as much powder as the normal load in a modern sporting shotgun. This gave it considerable penetrative power. A bullet fired recently from a Waterloo-era musket passed straight through a wall of railway sleepers at 50 yards.[38]

By modern standards it was slow to load, with a good battalion being able to get off four shots a minute, something infantry tactics addressed by firing in alternate ranks. Loading was a complicated procedure, starting with biting the top off a paper cartridge, which soldiers carried made up and wrapped in greased paper in a leather pouch, whilst holding the bullet in their mouth. The cartridges were well made by 1815, and proved reliable and fairly resilient to the weather. The hammer of the flintlock mechanism was then pulled halfway back, and a little powder was poured on to the priming pan, whilst the rest was poured down the barrel. The shot was then spat down the barrel and the paper case of the cartridge rammed down on top to form a wad, using the ramrod which was stored under the barrel. This was an awkward process, which led to numerous cuts and bruises, although the bayonet was fitted at an angle away from the muzzle so that it didn't get in the way. However, this meant that the bayonet was more likely to bend in action; it was not until the advent of the percussion cap that the British Army enjoyed the luxury of straight bayonets. The musket was then brought to the horizontal, aimed using a small bead foresight, which was also the bayonet lug. Before firing, a line of infantry would take a quarter turn to the left, a deliberate move that signified the imminent discharge of a volley and which the French found most unnerving. The musket's barrel was 39 inches, so about 9 inches longer than the average modern shotgun, and, at 14 pounds, it needed considerable strength to hold steady and fire. The vast majority of the infantry at Waterloo carried the Brown Bess, although about 4,000 were equipped with the relatively new Baker Rifle. This looked similar to a musket, and was also fired by a flintlock, but it had a shorter barrel, which was 'rifled' with seven turns that made the ball it fired spin and gave it greater range and accuracy. It was slower to load, so that even experienced riflemen could only get off two shots a minute, but they could hit targets at 200 yards.[39]

Muskets quickly became clogged up in an intensive action, with deposits of gunpowder accumulating in the barrel, and when quick reloading was at a premium, as it would be at Waterloo, soldiers didn't bother with the ramrod, simply tapping the butt of the musket on the ground to shake the ball down the barrel. Consequently the shot lost much of its effect, and its accuracy; the more carefully a weapon was loaded the more accurately it fired. The priming pan also got clogged with old powder, as did the touch hole (which connected the priming pan to the powder in the barrel), and every infantrymen carried a small wire brush and picker tied to his cross belts so that he could clear them, although this required cool nerves in the thick of an attack. The flint in the hammer which struck the priming pan also became less reliable after ten shots or so, and few would do more than 30. Changing one in action was something to be avoided. The physical effects of repeated volley fire could be severe. Tearing off the cartridges with their teeth gave soldiers a terrible thirst, and their faces soon became blackened from the powder. The musket gave a heavy recoil, so that after an action their shoulders were black, as was their trigger finger. A common mistake in action was to lose concentration and put too many cartridges down the barrel, or too much powder on the priming pan, leading to flashbacks or exploding barrels. The French musket was a little better, being slightly more refined and built to a predictably finer design but it was less robust. Despite these drawbacks, the British infantry firing volleys in line was deadly, and, not unlike their longbow-firing forebears, acquired a reputation for determined defence during the Napoleonic Wars which the French rarely succeeded in breaking.

Infantry training was mostly about loading and firing muskets and the drills necessary to achieve this, what has been known for many years as 'fire and movement'. There were effectively three formations that battalions used. They were either in columns, when they were marching or moving across the battlefield, or line, which usually meant that they were in a defensive position. The drill book specified that in line they should be in three ranks, the front rank kneeling whilst the rear two ranks fired over their heads, the theory being that by the time the rear rank had fired its volley the front rank would have reloaded. In the Peninsula, and after the early British victory at Maida in southern Italy in 1806,[40] where the two-rank line worked particularly well, the infantry were more normally deployed in two ranks, as they were to be at Waterloo. Wellington and his generals liked this as they could cover more ground, effectively increasing their firepower by 50 per cent, and the soldiers liked it because it meant those in the front rank were less likely to be shot by tired men in the third rank. Interestingly several of Wellington's brigade commanders at Waterloo had been present as more junior officers at Maida.

The majority of Wellington's victories in the Peninsula had resulted from choosing a good defensive position which suited this line formation and then waiting for the French to attack in dense columns, which they obligingly did, and would again. There were three rules for employing this linear defence. The first was that the line must not be exposed until it was about to fire, something which could be achieved by skilful choice of ground. Secondly, it must be protected by a screen of skirmishers, the role of the light companies, so that the enemy were not sure exactly where the line was; and, thirdly, its flanks must be secured by cavalry or artillery, or ground, so that it could not be outflanked. All three principles would be put into practice at Waterloo. The British infantry would have to wait until the French were within 100 yards, protected by a rise or ridge, then pour musket fire into their columns, the line formation allowing them to bring every musket to bear. Napoleon insisted on continuing to use columns, despite remonstrations from his marshals that it was dangerous when facing well-trained opponents, as he believed that any disadvantage in their restricted ability to fire (effectively only the front and outside ranks could use their muskets) was outweighed by the mass they produced to smash through a thin enemy line. On most occasions he had been correct. It was the formation that had brought him victory in the majority of his 60-odd battles and, when well coordinated with artillery, could be devastating. The alternative, attacking in line, was difficult to control, and meant that you could not easily mass enough men in one place to achieve a break-through.

The third major infantry formation was the square, when the battalion formed from line or column into a hollow square, presenting a wall of bayonets to an enemy. This was used predominantly to protect against enemy cavalry. Their greater height and speed meant that cavalry could quickly cut an infantry battalion caught in column or line to pieces, but they could not break into a square which presented a wall of fire or bayonet points to them. Even the most obliging horse will not ride into a wall of men pointing long spikes at it, and one of the few examples where a horse did this at Waterloo was because it was blind in one eye. The speed with which an infantry battalion could form square was key to its survival, and at Waterloo the most frequent moves were from line into square and vice versa. The story of the British squares on that bloody afternoon is one of the most frightening and exciting of the battle.

The British infantrymen wore a red tunic, sometimes with coloured regimental facings, grey trousers, except for the Coldstream Guards, who wore impractical white ones, and shoes, roughly made so that they fitted either foot. Veterans would swop them over daily so that they wore evenly. On their heads they wore a strangely shaped tall leather shako, not unlike a top hat with a peak, and on which was a brass regimental badge. Hair had been cut short for many years by the time of Waterloo, the old-fashioned queues being finally forbidden in 1808. Over their tunics they wore two broad cross belts, one for carrying their bayonet in a scabbard and the other for their cartouche box in which were 60 cartridges in a wooden frame; where these two belts crossed on their chest they wore a brass regimental badge. They then carried a wooden water canteen and a cloth haversack for rations. Each man had 60 musket balls, usually carried in their pockets from where they could quickly transfer them to their mouths when loading. Their less immediate possessions were carried in an uncomfortable canvas knapsack, painted black and stretched over a wooden frame. These were unpopular and Peninsular veterans carried the more convenient French ones if they had been lucky enough to pick one up on a past battlefield.

Greatcoats were rolled and strapped above the knapsack, but at Waterloo these were all sent back to Ostend as the staff thought they wouldn't be needed in the summer. They were replaced by rather good blankets which, 'for quality and size, were such as an army had never received before',[41] and which were designed to double up as temporary tents. So good were they that each fetched 20s. in Brussels, about £75 today, and inevitably a few of the worst characters sold theirs. The most unpopular item of the infantrymen's dress was a leather stock, which they wore around their neck, but which was tight-fitting and restrictive, more like a ligature, and quickly discarded once in action, although the more old-fashioned colonels would soon insist on them being worn again. Soldiers hated them, regularly claiming that they throttled them on long marches, but they were still being issued nearly 50 years after Waterloo. The total weight came to anything up to 70 pounds, and the loads were cumbersome so that running was difficult. The usual action was to dump knapsacks, and just keep cartouche boxes, haversack, water bottle and weapons, but that meant that you might never see your kit again, which soldiers never like; for many of them everything they owned in this world was carried in that knapsack. No army has ever effectively solved this problem of allowing the infantry soldier to carry everything he needs without making him carry so much weight that he can't move around the battlefield, and it taxed commanders even in Afghanistan recently.

The third of the three main parts of the Army was the artillery. This was divided into the horse artillery, who drew lighter six-pounder guns behind teams of eight horses so that they could operate with the cavalry, and the field artillery, who supported the infantry although their guns and ammunition wagons were also horse-drawn. There were three types of British guns used at Waterloo. The first two, and by far the most common, were the six-pounders and nine-pounders, effectively smooth-bore cannon, so called because of the weight of the solid iron shot they fired. Although this had been in use for hundreds of years by Waterloo, being little different to the medieval cannon ball, it was still very effective. The third type was the more modern howitzer, which fired a high-explosive shell. Both the guns and howitzers could also fire canister, also called case-shot, a cartridge filled with small pieces of metal which was deadly at short ranges, and which would be much used at Waterloo. All the guns were mounted on wooden frames with high wooden wheels. The artillery was organised in batteries of six guns, typically five six- or nine-pounders and one howitzer; the horse-artillery batteries were, in the British Army's persistently confusing nomenclature, usually referred to as troops. There was also a rocket troop in the Army, commanded by Captain Whinyates, but he didn't find much favour with Wellington, who thought rockets were a useless invention. He instructed the troop to replace its rockets with guns, prompting Sir George Wood, his artillery commander, to comment that this would break poor

Whinyates's heart. Wellington's caustic reply can be imagined, but Whinyates seems to have got the better of him as he
did have his rockets with him on the battlefield, where they
were just as useless as Wellington had predicted.[42]

An artillery battery, or troop, was a large and complicated
organisation. Mercer's totalled 200 men and 226 horses. Each
gun had a crew of five men to manhandle and fire it and then
four drivers who rode one horse in the eight-horse team that
pulled it and controlled a second; they were not actually
artillerymen but belonged to a separate organisation. Each
gun also had an ammunition wagon, and the battery had a
forge, a wheelwright, a wagon for spare wheels (critical to
keeping the guns in action) and harness makers as well as the
usual collection of baggage vehicles. It was a large number of
soldiers and horses, but well used artillery was quickly becoming a battle winner, and it would prove crucial at Waterloo.
Napoleon had initially trained as an artillery officer, and the
French artillery was known and feared as very effective.
Would the British be equal to it?

The artillery spent the weeks of waiting training and per-
fecting their drills, Mercer using a 'scrubby common near
Denderhout' which he was irritated to have to share with the
Duke de Berri, Louis XVIII's brother, and his Bourbon cavalry.[43] The way the artillery operated was for the horse teams
to drop the guns off in the position from which they were
going to fire, and then pull back to a slightly safer distance.
Gunners had to be able to see their target, and once they had
acquired it, the guns were actually aimed by being manhandled into position by their crew. Ranges were short; the
six-pounder was most effective at only 600 yards; and the
nine-pounder at 800. Howitzers had a higher elevation and
could be fired at unseen targets, although their range was not

that much greater. At Waterloo the distances were so close that most targets were easily visible. Canister was really only effective at under 400 yards.

An efficient gun crew could get off two to three rounds a minute, and the loading procedure was as convoluted as that for the musket. The NCO in charge, called the detachment commander, aimed the gun and controlled the crew. A second man was responsible for sponging out the barrel after every shot to clear out the debris of cartridge and powder, and any remaining burning fragments which could cause the next round to go off prematurely. The third was the loader, who then placed a cartridge followed by the ball in the barrel and rammed it home. The fourth, and least popular job, was the ventsman. His job was to put his thumb over the small vent, or hole, in the top of the barrel as the loader was ramming home the cartridge and shot. This was to prevent the air rushing back down the barrel as the cartridge was rammed home, which could ignite any remaining glowing fragments. If the ventsman was slow, the cartridge could detonate prematurely, taking off the loader's hands. It also meant that the ventsmen frequently lost their thumbs, and by Waterloo they wore a leather thumb sleeve. Relations between loaders and ventsmen were understandably often strained. Once the gun was loaded, the ventsman pushed a pricker through the vent to pierce the cartridge, and then inserted a firing tube, effectively a small tube of gunpowder in a quill or paper. The fifth man, who had the easiest job and tended to be the most senior, then touched the top of the firing tube with a burning match to ignite it and fire the gun. The effect of firing meant the gun jumped back, and it had to be hauled and dragged back into its firing position before it could be loaded again.

Serving the guns was tiring and dangerous and, like all

complicated drills, could be rushed or forgotten in action. Accidents were common. The vent holes became so hot after repeated rounds that the firing tube would cook off, meaning that the gun could not be used. The large quantities of gunpowder, carried in combustible wooden limbers and wagons, was easily ignited, and gunners firing in exposed positions were vulnerable to being cut down by cavalry. The infantry thought the gunners, with all their horses and wagons to carry their kit, had a soft life compared to them but the reality was that their role was equally hard and dangerous.

Throughout May and early June, as the regiments and battalions drilled and practised, and as they sorted and packed their equipment in the unaccustomed comfort of their Belgian billets, their thoughts were increasingly on the fighting ahead. Soldiers preparing for battle have two fears. The first is the most obvious fear of being killed, being hit by that unfortunate shot or shell or, and soldiers sometimes worry more about this, being wounded, of losing a limb or their eyesight, or being emasculated as so often happened with upper-leg and abdominal injuries. Their second fear, and possibly the greater, was that they would not do the right thing and that they would let down their comrades or their regiment. The younger soldiers, those who had not been in action before, worried whether their nerve would hold up and whether they would be able to remember their drills when they were frightened. Part of the British Army's success over the centuries is that it has always based its training on a series of drills, which, however mind-numbingly boring they may be to learn, are designed to become so familiar to soldiers that they can remember them even in the most terrifying parts of an engagement.

Cavalrymen were also worried that they would not be able to retain control of their horses, and that they would bolt, particularly in the wrong direction, something that happened regularly in mounted engagements. The fear for the officers and NCOs was a little more complicated. It was would they do the right thing at the right time? Would they give the correct order, do what their colonels expected and emerge with honour, or would they get it wrong and end up in disgrace or possibly worse? Decisions in battle are more difficult than historians sometimes imagine. What might be very clear in the aftermath can be anything but for a young officer half deafened by the noise of gunfire and half blinded by smoke from volleys of musket fire. A tactical opportunity is less easy to spot when it confronts you in the heat of the moment than when you are thinking about what you wished you had done afterwards.

The British Army has never been much given either to pre-battle speeches or exhortations from its commanders, correctly believing them often to be delivered more for an external audience than for the combatants themselves. There is also something in the British soldier's quiet sense of resilience which bridles at the assumption that he needs to be reminded to do his duty or how to behave. The most famous example of this was the fury of Nelson's captains at his signal before battle was joined at Trafalgar that 'England expects that every man will do his duty'. The cavalry were not impressed when Uxbridge put out a message in early June which read 'His Lordship expects everything from discipline, bravery, and a high sense of honour', and that was not just because of his grammar. Soldiers' loyalty was certainly to king and country, but this was an unquestioned, assumed and slightly remote idea for many. More important and immediate was their loyalty to their unit, which in so many cases had come to replace their family as the body to which they saw themselves belonging. Such was the commitment to this 'family' that on the morning of Waterloo there were 933 men 'present sick' with their battalions (in other words wounded soldiers present for duty) mostly from Quatre Bras, who could have taken themselves behind the lines for treatment but who would not leave their comrades.[44]

The focus of this regimental loyalty was the battalion's Colours, two flags on poles carried by young officers and placed in the centre when the battalion was drawn up in line. One was a King's Colour, a large Union Flag with regimental badges, representing loyalty to the sovereign. The second was the Regimental Colour, emblazoned with the names of the previous battles in which the battalion had fought and which represented loyalty to that tradition of service. It was meant to be a great honour for a young officer to carry the Colours, but it was a slightly double-edged one during a battle as the enemy would always concentrate on capturing them. Not only was a Colour important symbolically but also practically as its seizure would generally mean that the battalion's centre had collapsed. Twenty-eight men had been killed defending the Colours of the 40th when William Lawrence was ordered to take them over at Waterloo, and a further 26 would die before the battle was over.[45] Eleven British and King's German Legion infantry battalions lost their Colours in the Napoleonic Wars, three at Waterloo.[46] Cavalry regiments had Standards or Guidons instead of Colours, which were as important as symbols of the regiment's service but which were not treated with quite the same veneration. They were carried by senior NCOs rather than an officer, and were often left with the baggage, as taking part in a cavalry charge carrying a heavy flag on a pole was not considered very effective. The artillery did not have colours at all, regarding their guns as symbolic enough of their service. Every soldier saluted the Colours, the Standards or the guns whenever they passed them, a tradition which is fiercely maintained in the British Army today.

Despite the inevitable nerves, morale was generally high throughout the Army, helped by the abundant food and good quarters, the absence of which is usually the first thing that makes soldiers complain. It was also helped by a general trust between the soldiers and their commanders, that Peninsular spirit which had fairly quickly re-established itself. It started with Wellington, who was almost universally respected if not liked, and it ran through to the companies and troops, although obviously there were exceptions. Thomas Morris, predictably, had no time for his company commander, a Captain Robinson, who had 30 years' service but who had never been in action, and whom he accused, fairly, of nearly getting them all killed at Quatre Bras; he would cease to bother Morris after Waterloo.[47] Most of the officers and NCOs had previous combat experience, and when 'the young soldiers begun to smell powder and talk of the cannon fever which, however, by the cheerful and undaunted advice of our old and tried soldiers, the young ones soon learned to dispel those tremendous fears and soon showed that they were as great a set of fire eaters as their more fired veterans', thought Thomas Jeremiah.[48]

That trust was not threatened by the strict discipline that prevailed throughout the Army. Much has been made of the widespread use of flogging with the cat o' nine tails, but this needs to be judged in the context of contemporary attitudes to punishment. Corporal punishment was frequent both in homes and at school and was considered both desirable and necessary for the proper development of children. In an age when religion dictated the moral compass, corporal punishment was seen as a means of expiating the original sin with which they had been born. The novelist Samuel Butler 'beat his children viciously in order to subdue unregenerate flesh',[49] whilst others thought it essential to instil a proper respect for authority. Ensign George Keppel, who joined Frank Tidy's 14th Foot at the age of 16, had been birched at Westminster four months before he fought at Waterloo.[50] The Army did not resent it quite as much as others, such as the radical MP Sir Francis Burdett, did on their behalf. Even Thomas Morris, who objected to most established military practices, exonerated his colonel, 'the worthy Lord Harris', who 'always considered himself the father of his regiment, and behaved towards the men with the utmost kindness': even though 'he ordered and superintended a great number of corporal punishments, yet I verily believe that nothing but an imperative sense of duty made him do it'.[51] Soldiers were the first to want transgressors punished – if they were not, it cheapened their own good behaviour – and flogging was seen as an effective method of doing so and one which was accepted and familiar in civilian life; this was after all an age when children were still executed for petty theft, and men and women transported for stealing apples from a garden. Imprisonment was very difficult, and almost impossible on prolonged mobile campaigns such as in the Peninsula, and the lash had come to be seen as the harsh but most practical means of instilling discipline. What soldiers objected to was when flogging was overdone, either imposed too frequently or when the number of lashes was thought excessive, and incidences of both of these occurred regularly.

Flogging was most prevalent in the infantry and artillery, less so in the cavalry. A soldier accused of an offence was tried by a military court. This was either a general court martial with a panel of 13 officers for a major crime such as murder or desertion, and where he could receive the death penalty; or, more commonly, an offender was tried by a regimental court martial, which dealt with less serious offences. The definition of what constituted an offence was widespread, but the most common were: theft either of government property or from a comrade; temporary absence (in other words when the soldier returned rather than deserted, when it was necessary to prove he had no intention of doing so); insubordination; and drunkenness. Drunkenness was not usually punished *per se* but only if it led to some other offence such as unfitness for duty or assault. The use of flogging to punish what might now seem relatively trivial offences was at its height in the first decade of the nineteenth century, but became more restricted thereafter, partly because of public anger at its overuse by one or two tyrannical colonels. In 1813 Colonel Archdall of the 40th Foot was dismissed the service for having men flogged without establishing a proper regimental court and for 'piling up' sentences on soldiers for trivial offences so as to inflict several separate punishments at the same time.[52] When the respected commanding officer of the 94th was sent away on sick leave, command reverted to his major, an ex-'ranker' (i.e. promoted from being a private soldier rather than being directly commissioned). He seemed to have some grievance to work off, as he instituted flogging for every minor offence and 'invented disgraceful and torturing modes of inflicting the lash'. He ordered his men to wear a yellow patch sewn onto their sleeve, in which a hole was cut for every time the wearer was punished, which quickly destroyed any self-respect in what had been a first-class battalion. There were also occasional excessive sentences such as in 1807 when a private in the 54th had suffered 1,500 lashes, which was in effect a death sentence.[53]

From 1813 the maximum sentence a regimental court could award was reduced to 300 lashes. But in practice these punishments were rarely carried out in full, culprits either being pardoned by their commanding officer or taken down after receiving only a part of their sentence. Regimental courts could award other punishments instead, and these gradually came to be used more, with flogging being reserved for more serious offences. Edward Costello recorded that during his full six years in the Peninsula, only six men were flogged in the 95th, and yet 'he could not brag of our fellows being the honestest branch in the army'.[54] Flogging remained, however, a major part of regimental life, and was used on many occasions during those anxious weeks in the Belgian countryside. It was carried out with grim circumstance. The whole regiment or battalion was paraded to witness the punishment, forming a hollow square around a tripod of halberds, the long spiked poles the sergeants carried. The victim was brought out, the charges read, and he was then stripped to the waist and tied to the tripod. The lashes were inflicted by the battalion drummers in an infantry battalion or by the farriers in the cavalry and artillery. The cat consisted of 'nine small cords, twisted very hard, and having three knots on each cord; sometimes the ends are bound with wire. The whip is usually about eighteen inches long and the handle fifteen.'[55] The lashes were administered in time to the drum, usually one stroke on every tenth beat, which sound, added to the victim's screams, made the whole occasion all the more terrible.

The physical damage the cat did to its victims was severe,

particularly for any sentence over 100 lashes, leaving 'the blood running down into their shoes and their backs flayed like raw, red, chopped sausage meat'.[56] Heavy sentences would strip away the flesh completely, leaving the bones exposed, requiring the victim to be hospitalised, but those who received lighter punishments were able to return to duty immediately afterwards. The psychological damage was probably as serious. It did not seem to have much effect on the 'King's hard bargains', those habitual offenders who were frequently in trouble, the records showing many repeat punishments, and yet it could destroy the self-respect of a keen man who just happened to have been unlucky. It depended very much on the regiment; decent commanding officers would pardon a first-time offender or a man with a good record of service whereas others would be more capricious. William Wheeler quoted his first commanding officer as being fond of saying that flogging a young soldier would 'do him good, make him grow and make him know better for the future' and that for an old soldier 'he is old enough to know better'.[57] Morris, predictably alternative, thought that flogging 'made a tolerably good man bad and a bad man infinitely worse'.[58]

The local Belgians, however, made it very clear that they detested this form of punishment, which was alien and barbaric to them. A couple of commanding officers had ordered floggings to be held in public places, from the sensible if misplaced notion that being seen to punish offenders severely would encourage the locals that the Army would not tolerate any form of theft or drunkenness. This principle had worked well in the Peninsula but proved to have the opposite effect around Brussels, with the local townspeople demonstrating noisily on one occasion. Colonel Ellis, the much loved commanding officer of the 23rd, whom we saw being so mourned earlier on, was not a particularly harsh commanding officer. Private Thomas Jeremiah thought very highly of him, being 'respected by his superiors ... loved by his officers and loved and feared by his men, so that the whole regiment lived in harmony under his mild administration', but in the weeks leading up to Waterloo he had decided that two men had to be punished. He marched his whole battalion two miles out of town and found a suitable tree to which the men could be tied for their flogging. The first of the men was 'one of those hardy Welsh mountaineers who generally have more courage than judgement' and he received a full 300 lashes 'without one sigh from this hardy Briton'. But 'the next man was of more delicate feeling for he shouted loud before the lash had touched him'. This was seen as very cowardly by his fellow Welshmen, and 'caused us all to blush to think that the Irish and English should ridicule us because that one Welsh could not stand the lash, but to prove them wrong, the man who had already received his punishment volunteered to take this fellows punishment so he should not disgrace the hardy Welsh'. Colonel Ellis sensibly decided that the spectacle had already had a salutary effect on the 'young Welsh lads' and 'took the man by the ear and gave him such a kick as became a coward who could not stand his punishment without disgracing his country'. As soon as the battalion had marched off, the local farmer came and cut down the tree and burnt it to show his aversion to the bloody spectacle he had just witnessed.[59]

Most armies used some form of flogging in the Napoleonic Wars and for a long time afterwards. The British Army's practices were mild when compared to the Russians or Prussians and there is a widespread myth that the French army never had to revert to physical punishment, a concept which apologists seem to identify with Napoleon's qualities as a leader. They may not have used flogging as a routine punishment, but they certainly used equivalent corporal punishment on operations, witnessed by some of the excesses of the 1812 campaign.[60] Discipline is vital to the operational effectiveness of any army, and particularly so to one like Wellington's which relied on rapid and absolute adherence to shouted words of command and drills. Flogging was a sanction which even the best commanding officers employed when soldiers transgressed beyond what were acceptable limits, and was a way of ensuring that their orders on the battlefield would be obeyed.

Many soldiers also found themselves becoming more religious in those long weeks of May and June. It is a common and very understandable trait in armies facing the prospect of action; contemporary British Army religious services were always much better attended in Iraq and Afghanistan than they ever were in barracks. Many of that half of Wellington's British troops who could read and write had been educated in village church schools, so it may not be surprising that their letters home frequently mention God, although it is sometimes hard to decide whether this is more from habit than from a genuine belief. Thomas Bingley certainly seemed genuine enough when he wrote to his father on 17 May from 'a village near Brussels'. 'Dear Father', he wrote, 'God only knows the event that will take place, but may He protect the efforts of the British Army and its allies against the common enemy Napoleon whose soldiers are daily deserting and we are thankfully informed that the bold Russians have arrived with a forcible army on the opposite side of Mr Boney when an advance on either side takes place if it should please God that I shall survive the conflict I will give you the most speedy information.' Bingley's brother had already been killed in 1812, so his next few lines are poignant. 'Dear father I earnestly hope you will not grieve for me. I throw myself wholly on the mercy of the Lord who is all sufficient to deliver and save me from the hands of the enemy and to restore one safe back to you.'[61]

Those like Bingley, who did believe, as most would certainly think they did, received little help from the Church. Chaplains were but few, which is strange in an age when religion was so consuming, and those who did serve were not well thought of. William Wheeler, when he had been lying ill in a Peninsular hospital, complained that 'the people of England little think how her soldiers are neglected respecting spiritual aid . . . If they could but hear or see the agony of the dying, their prayers, their despair and the horrid oaths uttered by some in their exit from this world, I am sure this most of wants would be attended to.' He acknowledged that 'there are chaplains with the army who sometimes perform divine service, but what use are they, the service they perform has no effect, for their mode of living do not agree with the doctrine they preach'. The general consensus was that 'the chaplain is no more use . . . than a town pump without a handle' and that they preferred following their regiments with their 'brace of dogs and gun' than performing a useful service at the hospitals.[62] One exception to the rule was the splendid Edward Frith, known as the 'fighting parson', who preached stirring sermons on the battlefield, and would shortly do so again.

Until 1796 each regiment was meant to have its own dedicated chaplain, but they had proved difficult to find, and in that year the Army Chaplains' Department was established, which was intended to provide civilian clergy for services in barracks and a small pool for deployment abroad. But it remained a very small pool indeed, with only 37 on the books in 1814 and a mere six deployed to Belgium.[63] They were all, predictably, Church of England, no Roman Catholic priests being allowed despite the large number of Irish Catholics in the Army; Wellington was not in favour of providing for Catholics, remarking that he had not seen a single act of worship by his Catholic soldiery in Spain save 'them making the Sign of the Cross to induce local people to give them wine'.[64] There was also a concern that Methodism, which was growing in popularity in some regiments, could prove subversive, especially as it made use of NCOs to lead religious services and preach sermons. Very few officers were members of the Reformed Church. Freemasonry was an equally growing force, which did involve all ranks, and which started to exercise an influence on the Army which it has retained ever since.

The medical profession, by way of contrast, reacted commendably to the Army's requirements that spring; the lack of chaplains is in direct contrast to the number of professional medical men who volunteered. The majority of regiments deployed with their full complement of one surgeon and two assistants, the numbers made up by volunteers like George Guthrie and John Haddy James. The medical services, which had been appalling in the Revolutionary Wars of the 1790s, had become rudimentary after the Duke of York's reforms and were again overhauled in 1806. They could never be described as good but they were certainly better, even more so after a commission in 1807 established a proper supervisory Medical Board which appointed the able James McGrigor to review and improve the medical arrangements in the Peninsula. After 1803 regimental surgeons, who ranked and were paid as captains, were selected by a board having satisfied it as to their qualifications rather than just being appointed by the colonel. From 1806 their assistants, who were originally more medical orderlies than surgeons, had to have a qualification from Surgeons' Hall, responsible for professional medical standards, before they could apply. They ranked as lieutenants and their position became more of a first step towards becoming a full surgeon.

The administration of regimental hospitals was also overhauled in 1806, and an infantry battalion was required to be able to handle 60 casualties, although only equipped with bedding for twelve and 24 stretchers. Their standards of hygiene and medical efficiency were usually not that bad, given that they were under the direct control of commanding officers. Above the regimental level was an army-level system of surgeons who advised senior officers and inspected hospitals. It was also responsible for the general hospitals, to which more serious and long-term cases were referred by the regimental hospitals, which necessarily had to remain mobile and restrict themselves to more immediate cases. It was these general hospitals which had acquired such a bad reputation in the Peninsula, the one in Plymouth being where it was found that 'the bedding belonging to some wards had never been changed for a series of years',[65] but they gradually became better after McGrigor's appointment.

Although there were inevitably a small number of malingerers who feigned illness to avoid duty, soldiers did not relish going into hospital and many feared wounding more than death. However, they were rather better cared for under the basic military system than they would have been in civilian life, where they may not have been able to afford or access any medical services at all. Those deploying to Waterloo were all also inoculated with Dr Jenner's new serum against smallpox, something of a revolutionary development. Although there were no antibiotics and no anaesthetics, judged by contemporary standards it was an adequate system, and a surprisingly high number of soldiers who would be operated on for wounds received at Waterloo would not only survive but make a full recovery even from traumatic procedures such as amputation. The issue, though, was whether they would actually get to the surgeons' tables, and where the system failed badly was in the collecting and processing of casualties off the battlefield.

Much of the talk around the billets was inevitably of their allies, for whom the Army did not have a particularly high regard, with the exception of the King's German Legion and the Brunswickers, with whom they had already fought in Spain. The Black Brunswickers, so called after the colour of their uniforms, were similar in origin to the Legion, being men from Brunswick and Prussia who had followed their duke, Frederick William, who was George III's nephew, in his patriotic insurrection against Jérôme Bonaparte's Kingdom of Westphalia. Escaping to England, his corps became part of the British Army, but, now short of recruits, went through rather a difficult period when they were forced to recruit any non-French from the prisoner-of-war camps – Poles, Swiss, Danes, Dutch and Croats were all signed on with consequent problems of discipline and motivation.

By 1815 the Duke was able to use the corps as the basis of a new national army, a strong detachment from which he had now offered to the Allies, under his personal command. It amounted to about 6,000 men, roughly a division, providing two infantry brigades, a hussar regiment, an independent cavalry squadron of feared Uhlans, and some guns. Its problem was that, after the manpower depredations of the past decade, its soldiers were even younger than the British but, given the circumstances, they would fight bravely when the time came.[66] One problem that did develop, though, was that they ate dogs, something of which the British troops, who were as sentimental about dogs then as they are now, strongly disapproved. Edward Costello, who had previously rather respected their soldierly qualities, could not say a civil word about them after they were rumoured to have captured and eaten the 95th's pet dog, predictably called 'Rifle', who went into action with them and 'dashed about barking though it was all a great game' and survived the bullets only to end up barbecued by the Brunswickers.[67]

Much as they enjoyed Netherlands hospitality, they had less time for their soldiers, particularly the Belgian regiments, whose uniforms were confusingly similar to the French. There was a lingering suspicion that many Belgians rather preferred Napoleon to their own government, and their military qualities would be found rather wanting in the days ahead. This was not altogether surprising. The whole of the Netherlands had been controlled by France throughout the Napoleonic Wars, and Napoleon's brother Louis had been made king of Holland. From 1810, when Louis resigned, the country was absorbed into France and it wasn't until after Leipzig that it re-emerged as a separate kingdom, which united the northern Dutch-speaking and Protestant part of the Netherlands with, reluctantly, the southern French-speaking and Catholic Belgium. The Belgians had hoped for independence from Vienna and were not very happy at this arrangement, and many individual sympathies did indeed lie with Napoleon, part of whose strategic plan was to invade Belgium to persuade them to join him once again. Two out of the three Netherlands divisional commanders and all their cavalry brigade commanders had fought for France. Wellington and the Prince of Orange ensured that the Dutch and Belgian battalions were deployed in mixed brigades so that the more reliable Dutch could bolster any Belgian doubts. The Prussian army was unfamiliar, and known mostly for its unenviable reputation as being given to treating the local inhabitants badly, not paying for food and generally stealing and plundering. This would soon become a major problem for them, not least because it was adopted as official Prussian policy.

There was also much talk about the enemy and how they rated the French. There was a deep respect for the fighting qualities of French troops, and some, like the cuirassiers, whom they had not fought in Spain, had almost mythical status, supposed to be giants encased in impregnable armour. Yet none of them thought they would fail to beat them, despite it being the first time the British Army had fought a major pitched battle against Napoleon, for whom they thought Wellington was more than a match. There was also a feeling that Napoleon was past his best, and that his return was not really that welcome in France. Thomas Playford wrote, in a very well informed piece, that the 'French nation did not espouse the cause of the Emperor with all the zeal he had hoped; yet he had a body of veteran troops fully devoted to his interest, which he believed was more than a match for any of the armies preparing to attack him: but not capable of contending with the whole united'.[68]

Private Charles Stanley, of the King's Dragoon Guards, was more forthright, even if his English was not quite as polished. 'We are only 15 miles from Mr Boney Part Harmey wish we expect to have a rap at him exerry day', he wrote to his cousin in mid May. 'There is no doubt of us beting the confounded rascal – it ma cost me my life and a meaney more that will onley be the forting of war – my life I set no store by at all – this is the finiest country exer is so far before England – the peepel is so sivel.'[69] They were seeing the French newspapers fairly regularly, which exasperated them. 'It is an extraordinary age we live in', James Gairdner complained to his father, 'the preparations for war going on here with wonderful activity and the French papers wish to persuade the nation that all the world are delighted with the return of Bonaparte.'[70] They were quietly confident that they were right to stop Napoleon and all he stood for, that they were better than his army and that they would win. They now just wanted to get on with it. 'Although', as Thomas Morris noted, 'we were so pleasantly situated here, we began to tire of the monotony, and there was a restlessness and an anxiety to know what the French were about.'[71]

The answer to which was that they knew very little, and life in Brussels had assumed an air of brittle normality. The 14-year-old Edward Heeley had moved there with his father and Sir George Scovell, and the four good chargers, two baggage animals, pony and the fine Spanish mule for which they were responsible. Edward was to have a love/hate relationship with the mule, but for now it was behaving. They were very well billeted, Sir George in a house belonging to the Count de St Louis, whoever he may have been, and the Heeley family with the horses in a butcher's near by. 'The town was very gay and bustling, all day long soldiers were parading, music playing and the streets continually full of all sorts of uniforms. There were balls every night and plenty of amusement for those who wanted it. It appeared more like troops assembling to be reviewed than to fight, for no one seemed to think of

fighting . . . in a general way things were going on as if nothing was the matter.'[72] Visitors had started arriving from
England to join in the temporary and rather exciting 'society'
that was forming, and were making a nuisance of themselves
by visiting the outlying billets, much to Wellington's annoyance. But on 16 June many wished they had stayed safely at
home.

3

12–17 JUNE 1815

Napoleon left Paris very early on 12 June. His army had been assembling on the French side of the Belgian border since 5 June, and all the five corps of his Army of the North, his main fighting force, and the Imperial Guard were ready, centred on Phillipeville, by 14 June. It was a classic Napoleonic move, efficiently planned and executed in strict secrecy, with all communications with Belgium closed down, all shipping embargoed, even fishing boats, and National Guard soldiers, the French equivalent of the militia, replacing regular troops when they moved so it looked as if nothing was amiss. The French media, under Napoleon's tight control, reported him to be in several different places at once. These moves were consequently largely blind to Wellington and Blücher, who were unable to push any reconnaissance force across the French border as they were still not actually at war, a point made with tiresome regularity by the more awkward parliamentarians in London. Napoleon, with typical masterly use of spin, denounced the British seizure of a French frigate in the Mediterranean on 7 June as 'bloodshed during peace'.[1] Although the allies had a general notion that the French army was gathering, they had received conflicting and vague reports since early June and they had no hard intelligence against which to plan. Their own armies remained widely dispersed in their comfortable billets, and both commanders felt that their most likely course of action was to wait until the remaining Allied armies were ready and then invade France.

In the mean time Wellington had to protect his line of communications and supply back to the Channel ports, and particularly Ostend. Blücher, or General Gneisenau, his chief of staff, who, under the Prussian system, took many of the decisions on deployments, likewise had to protect their communications, which lay along the River Meuse back towards Liège. This meant that their armies were spread out over a line 150 miles long, stretching from Ostend to Liège, although with the majority of Wellington's force centred on Brussels and Blücher's on Namur. Although neither commander thought they would be attacked, believing themselves with a combined force of around 175,000 men to be too strong for Napoleon to risk such a move, they nevertheless had to guard against such an eventuality, and this extended deployment left them vulnerable. Wellington was particularly concerned at the possibility of Napoleon doing a 'left hook' via Lille, severing his communications and taking Brussels from the west, as many French armies had done over the centuries. For Blücher it meant guarding against a move further east, via Liège. He had a Prussian cavalry screen on the border, provided by the non-English-speaking General Dörnberg, and the border fortresses had been repaired and garrisoned, but their armies overall remained postured to invade France not to defend Belgium.

Napoleon had taken over an army of 200,000 when he reached Paris in March, and in the following two months he had increased this, largely by conscription, to 300,000. He had also called up 150,000 of the National Guard. Yet he could not afford to concentrate his whole force to invade Belgium. He needed to guard France's long frontiers, and once he had allocated troops to the Alps, Pyrenees and the Rhine as well as put down uprisings such as that in the staunchly royalist Vendée, he could only allocate 124,000 men to the Army of the North under his personal command. Yet although this army was his main strike force, and contained the famous regiments and names that had brought terror to Europe and victory for him at Austerlitz and Jena, it was a much weaker force than those he had commanded at the height of his imperial power. The defeats of 1812 and 1813, and especially the huge losses in Russia and at Leipzig, had drained France of many of its experienced soldiers.

Horses, moreover, were in very short supply, France having been stripped of all those available in 1812. Napoleon had crossed the Niemen into Russia with close on 100,000 cavalrymen and 155,333 horses, and received a further 24,569 from France that winter. He returned with 1,600. It was his lack of cavalry that had contributed so much to his defeats in 1813, and when he returned to Paris in March he found only 35,629 horses in the army, many of which had been let out to farmers to save the cost of their keep. To mount the Army of the North he had to requisition the Gendarmerie's horses, but that only produced 4,250, albeit of just adequate quality. They were issued to the cuirassiers and dragoons. Otherwise it was a matter of seeing what more could be squeezed out of reluctant farmers, and by June there were still only 30,000 available to support the invasion.

That, once the essential artillery and commissariat functions had been taken care of, was only enough to allow him to mount about 15,000 cavalrymen, and most of them not very well. These were divided roughly equally into light and heavy regiments, of which half the latter were cuirassiers, so about a quarter of his total cavalry force. The remainder were either carabiniers, who wore armour like the cuirassiers, or dragoons. All carried long straight swords, pistols and an efficient carbine, from which the carabiniers took their title, but, like the British cavalry, in effect all French heavy cavalry by 1815 had a similar role, which was to charge and overawe the enemy by weight and mass. There was also a regiment of Grenadiers à Cheval, part of the Imperial Guard and who were very much an élite, enjoying all the privileges reserved for that body. It was the cuirassiers, though, who were the most talked about in the Allied lines and who had the more frightening reputation. Napoleon had created them in his early reorganisation of the French army, when he found he had no heavy cavalry who could overmatch the Austrian cuirassiers, although their individual regimental histories went back much further. They were heavily armoured, with steel front and backplates (the actual cuirasses) and steel helmets with face guards. They were classed as élite troops, which gave them a rather bizarre set of privileges. Apart from higher pay, an extra five centimes per day, they were permitted to grow moustaches from December to March and incorporate a flaming grenade badge in their uniform. What really distinguished them, however, was their size. They were all very tall and big men who, when mounted as they should have been on big horses, were considered almost impossible to stop.

The light cavalry were *chasseurs à cheval*, hussars and lancers. The *chasseurs* and hussars performed much the same role as their British counterparts, scouting, gathering intelligence, acting as the advance and rear guards of the army as it

Captain Rees Gronow, diarist, socialite and brave field soldier, who had been campaigning in Spain since leaving school.

Lieutenant Edmund Wheatley, a British officer in the King's German Legion, whose thoughts during the battle were mostly of his dearest Eliza. He would endure a horrific captivity.

Corporal John Shaw, 2nd Life Guards, prize fighter, artist's model and ladies man. Napoleon's return from Elba would rob him of the opportunity to challenge for the All England title.

Captain Cavalié Mercer, the professional artillery officer, who would go to his grave bitter that his contribution to the victory remained unrewarded.

The prevailing patriotic spirit. *Buonaparte 48 hours after landing*. John Bull carries Napoleon's severed head on a pitchfork.

Gillray's unkind but not necessarily inaccurate portrayal of the Volunteers. In fact, many would go on to join the regular army.

Light Cavalry. A blood horse and private of Standish O'Grady's 7th Light Dragoons, considered one of the most fashionable regiments in the army.

Heavy Cavalry. A Private of the King's Dragoon Guards, one of those who made up the 'lines of brick red menace'.

Lieutenant Colonel The Hon. Henry Murray, who commanded 18th Light Dragoons, and his beautiful and highly strung Portuguese wife, Emily, with whom he kept up a lively correspondence. Murray disliked Wellington and felt he did not do justice to his light cavalry.

Emily Murray, painted by Raeburn. She had a predilection for moving house.

Henry, Earl of Uxbridge, commander of the Allied cavalry, in his uniform as Colonel of 7th Light Dragoons.

Assistant Surgeon John Haddy James, 1st Life Guards. James was one of many medical men who volunteered to serve with the allied army, and whose skill was to save many lives.

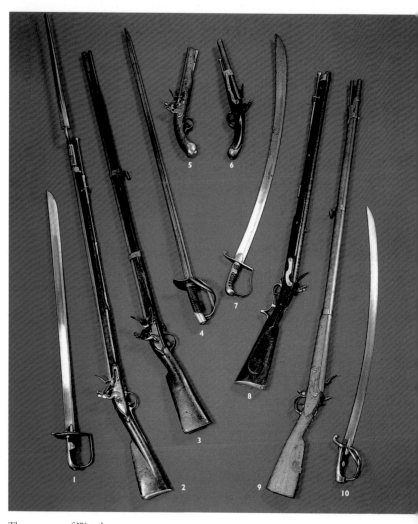

The weapons of Waterloo:

1. British Heavy Cavalry sword, which soldiers did not trust.
2. The 'Brown Bess', the standard British infantry musket with its rather flimsy bayonet, fitted at an angle to allow rounds to be rammed down the barrel.
3. Prussian musket.
4. French Heavy Cavalry sword, longer and stronger than its British equivalent, putting the British heavy cavalry regiments at a disadvantage in hand to hand fighting.
5. British cavalry pistol, hardly used in the battle.
6. French cavalry pistol; the British thought the French cavalry were dreadful shots.
7. British Light Cavalry sabre, the weapon of choice.
8. British Baker Rifle, as slow to load as the musket but accurate at a much greater distance.
9. French infantry musket; those of the Imperial Guard had brass fittings.
10. The effective French Light Cavalry sabre.

Wellington. Respected, but not liked by all, he remained a remote figure to the ordinary soldiers.

Colonel Sir William De Lancey, Wellington's Deputy Quartermaster General, effectively his chief of staff.

Field Marshal Prince von Blücher, the charismatic, brave and enigmatic Prussian commander.

August von Gneisenau, Blücher's Chief of Staff, whom the British found difficult to work with.

Napoleon, who fascinated and disgusted British soldiers in equal measure.

Marshal Jean Soult, Napoleon's Chief of Staff at Waterloo, but not considered the equal of his predecessor, Berthier.

Jean Baptiste Drouet, Comte d'Erlon, whom the British had thought an unimpressive commander in the Peninsular.

Marshal Ney, in tactical command of the French at Quatre Bras and at Waterloo. Undoubtedly brave, but his operational judgement was questionable.

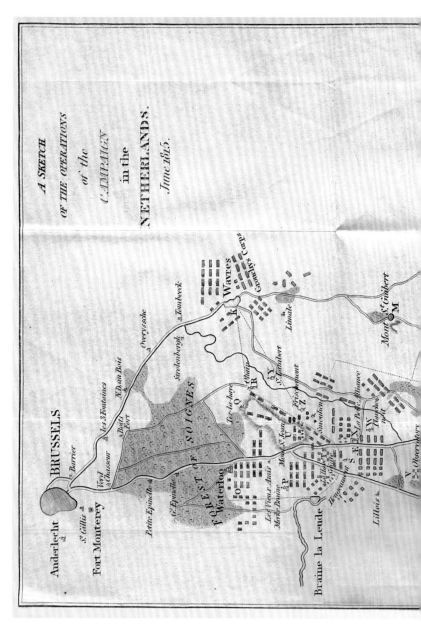

A SKETCH
OF THE OPERATIONS
of the
CAMPAIGN
in the
NETHERLANDS.
June 1815.

BRUSSELS

Anderlecht
St Gillis
Fort Monterey
Barrier
Verd Chasseur
les 3 Fontaines
N.D. au Bois
Boits Fort
Petite Epinette
G.te Epinette
FOREST OF SOIGNES
Waterloo
Les Vieux Amis
Merbe Braine
Mont St Jean
P.
Q
Maison du Roi
Hougoumont
Smohain
Lillois
La Belle Alliance
La Haye Sainte
Planchenoit
N.º Observatory
Braine la Leude

Ter-la-haye
R
Phap.
A Y
G.t Lambert
Frischemont
Z
Limale
Mont St Guibert
M

Wavres
K
Grouchy's Corps
Sovenberghe
Overyssche
a.Tombeek

A contemporary map showing the French invasion of the Netherlands, the Allied
deployment and how the armies manoeuvered to fight the main battle at Waterloo.

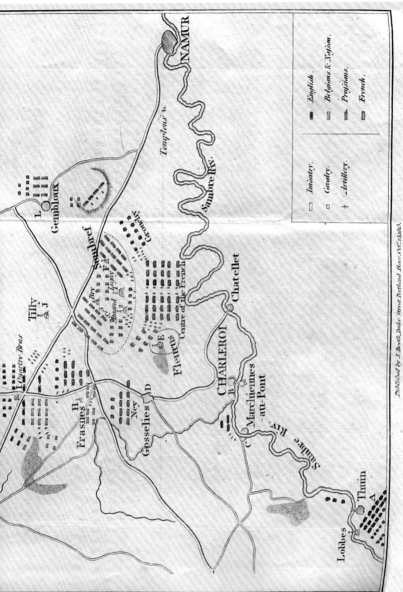

NAMUR

Sambre Rv.

Templeux a.

Gembloux

L

Sombref

Brye

(Girard)

Ligny

3 4 3 2 1

Ligny

Fleurus

Centre of the French

E

CHARLEROI

Chatellet

B

Marchiennes-au-Pont

C

Sambre Riv.

Tilly

J

Quatre Bras

Ney

H

Frasnes

Gosselies

D

Lobbes

Thuin

A

English

Belgians & Nassau.

Prussians.

French.

Infantry.

Cavalry.

Artillery.

Published by J.Booth, Duke Street Portland Place, 1816.

British Infantry in a 'square' at Quatre Bras, being attacked by French cavalry. Once formed into squares, infantry were difficult to break but, if caught in the open, they were easily destroyed, as the 69th would discover.

A British Gun Crew. Artillery formed 7 per cent of Wellington's army. Although he professed to have little regard for his gunners, who were mostly professionally trained, his gun batteries played a major part in his victory.

marched, and on the flanks in battle. The lancers also carried the fearsome lance, which the Allies were to find so unpleasant.

Napoleon had also found that the army had plenty of artillery, but not much ammunition; clothing and other equipment were also lacking. Only someone with his organisational genius could have turned the ramshackle Bourbon army he inherited into an army fit to fight within two months, but even he could not eradicate all these shortcomings, nor could he get the soldiers and in particular the horses as hard and as fit as they should have been. Nor was his return universally popular. France knew that it meant war, and they had already suffered too much of that, but as his return gathered pace so the public mood began to change. One popular French newspaper's headlines ran on 6 March: 'The Corsican Ogre, having escaped from his lair, is again preparing to devastate France and deluge Europe in blood'. By 12 March they were writing that 'The Tyrant is again seeking to grind France under his iron heel'; by 14 March he had become 'Bonaparte' who 'is striving in vain to seduce the population and soldiers from their legitimate monarch'. As Napoleon neared Paris, their tone began to change more markedly. On 15 March we hear that 'Napoleon entered Lyons, where he was enthusiastically received by the soldiers but coldly by the people'. However, by 18 March we hear that 'The Emperor is anxiously expected at Fontainebleau', and by 20 March 'His Imperial Majesty the Emperor Napoleon entered the Tuileries at 9 p.m. last night, amid the frenzied acclamations of his loyal and devoted subjects'.[2]

The Army of the North was grouped in five corps, each of about 20,000 men. Napoleon had effectively originated the concept of creating 'corps', subdivisions of an army, with their own cavalry and artillery, which could operate and fight on their own. Drouet, now Comte d'Erlon, commanded the 'First Corps d'Armée'. A pre-Revolutionary soldier, who had been elected to be an officer by his soldiers, and a veteran of many of Napoleon's battles, he had fought as a corps commander against the British throughout the Peninsular campaign, where he had been thought of as rather 'a laggard'.[3] He had thrown in his lot with Louis XVIII in 1814, and been made Governor of Lille, one of the more important garrisons in France, but as soon as he heard of Napoleon's landing, he reverted and tried to march his troops on Paris. Temporarily frustrated by Royalists, he was nevertheless in Paris in time to welcome the Emperor on 21 March. Reille commanded the Second Corps, another hugely experienced soldier who had fought under Napoleon in Italy and central Europe. He had then served in the Peninsula, where he had not done so well, being routed by Wellington at Vitoria, giving him a healthy respect for the British infantry.

The Third and Fourth Corps, commanded respectively by Vandamme and Gerard, will not concern us so much as they were to be primarily engaged against the Prussians, but we will be seeing much of the Sixth Corps under Mouton, Comte de Lobau. One of Napoleon's most battle-hardened veterans, Mouton was one of 14 children of a baker who had joined the army as an escape from the drudgery of the bread oven early in the Revolution. He had fought and been badly wounded in Italy, fought at Marengo, Jena, Eylau and Friedland, where he was wounded again and after which he was given command of a division. At Landshut in 1809 he had taken a bridge by drawing his sword and marching his men straight over it without firing, and in the same campaign had retaken a village where another division was in danger of being cut off, for which feat he was made Comte de Lobau (the name of the island on the Danube where the action was fought).

Although each of these corps had its own cavalry division, Napoleon also had four reserve cavalry corps, each of about 3,500 horses. Two of these, under Pajol and Exelmans, will concern us only peripherally, but those commanded by Kellerman and Milhaud were to be fully engaged at Waterloo. The French, matching the Allies, had a high proportion of cavalry in the Army of the North, and hence Waterloo would be very much a cavalry action. Kellerman, also Duc de Valmy, was not considered a natural soldier, being sickly as a child, and had hoped to enter the diplomatic service. However, he followed his father, a marshal, into the cavalry, and distinguished himself in Italy, at Austerlitz and in Spain, where he was accused of organised plundering. He missed Russia in 1812 because of ill health, but served in Germany in 1813. He quickly became a Royalist on Napoleon's first abdication, and had the distinction of being known as the ugliest man in the army.

Milhaud had one of the most prestigious commands in the army as his corps consisted entirely of 3,000 cuirassiers. He was an ardent Revolutionary, who had been a deputy in the Convention, where he had argued passionately for Louis XVI's execution. Later he would play a major role in Napoleon's *coup d'état*, and was rewarded by senior cavalry commands in Italy, at Austerlitz and in Spain. He fought in Russia and Germany in 1813 and, in what must have been one of the most hypocritical moves by any Napoleonic general, declared his loyalty to the Bourbons in 1814 and became inspector general of the cavalry. Quickly returning to Napoleon, the Allies would soon be seeing rather too much of his feared cuirassiers.

Then there was the Imperial Guard, Napoleon's élite formation of 21,000 men under Drouot, and in effect a corps with its integral cavalry and artillery. The infantry were divided into three parts – the Old Guard, and the Middle Guard formed regiments of grenadiers and *chasseurs*, whilst the Young Guard were *tirailleurs* and *voltigeurs*. The cavalry had a heavy brigade, commanded by Count Claude-Étienne Guyot, an ex-heavy-cavalry trooper and Napoleonic loyalist, which consisted of the Grenadiers à Cheval, and the Empress's Dragoons, and a light brigade commanded by Count Charles Lefèbvre-Desnouëttes, another long-term Napoleon loyalist. The son of a Paris draper, he had risen through the ranks to become a general by the age of 35. He was captured in Spain and sent as a prisoner to Cheltenham, where his good looks and dashing personality caused something of a stir. He persuaded Napoleon to allow his wife and son to join him and, posing as a Russian count, escaped in 1811 and joined Napoleon in Russia. He had Napoleon's allegedly favourite regiment under his command, over 1,000 *chasseurs à cheval*, organised originally around Napoleon's guides from Italy and Egypt, and who had habitually escorted him as emperor. They called themselves 'the Invincibles', whilst others referred to them as 'the Pet Children', not without a heavy hint of sarcasm. He also had the Red Lancers, who likewise would play a major part in the coming battle.

The Imperial Guard served several purposes for Napoleon. First, it helped his own reputation and mystique, having an élite fighting formation dedicated to him personally, in a way that monarchs have used their household troops for centuries. Secondly, it was a method of patronage and preferment and of rewarding successful soldiers, who would be transferred into it. Thirdly, it gave him a reliable battlefield reserve which he retained under his own command, and whom he could deploy at critical moments in the fighting. The Imperial Guard had become part of the Napoleonic legend, seen as the epitome of the awesome fighting power of the French army, and a powerful example of Napoleon's belief that psychologically overwhelming your enemy was as important as overmatching him physically. Yet in June 1815 the Imperial Guard was not all it should have been and this would soon have serious consequences.

The artillery too was an essential part of how Napoleon fought his army. An artilleryman himself, being one of his artillery commanders cannot have been a particularly satisfying job as Napoleon would inevitably interfere with quite low-level decisions as to how the guns were positioned. Napoleon believed that artillery should be massed so that its firepower could be concentrated on the decisive point on the battlefield, and this would happen at Waterloo with the deployment of 'the Grand Battery'. His insistence on this may have seriously weakened the various attacks his corps were to make. The French had 246 guns in the battle, 68 howitzers and 142 six-pounders, which were both similar to the British counterparts, but they also had 36 twelve-pounders, which Napoleon called his 'beautiful daughters'. They were the heaviest and most effective gun on the battlefield and one which Wellington had being trying unsuccessfully to get the British government to acquire. There would be 18 of these firing from the Grand Battery. Napoleon thought the Army of the North was short of artillery, despite his having one gun for every 315 men versus Wellington's one for every 466, but this was a poorer ratio than he had enjoyed in previous campaigns and was a reflection of how much administrative disorder existed within the French army.[4]

It was, though, as with the British Army, the French infantry, the 'poor bloody infantry', who would do much of the fighting in the coming campaign. There were 77,000 infantrymen in the Army of the North, organised either in *ligne* (line) or *légère* (light) regiments, the equivalent of the British line and light infantry. Each regiment was intended to have six battalions, one which stayed in their depot recruiting and training young soldiers and five combat battalions, organised, since 1813, into six line companies with, again similar to the British system, a grenadier company who took position on the right of the battalion line and a *voltigeur* company on the left, whose role resembled that of the British light company. In practice the hurried mobilisation meant that the infantry regiments started the campaign with widely differing strengths; one regiment had four battalions at Waterloo but most had two or three, and few battalions mustered their full complement. Two regiments formed a brigade, so each brigade had between four and six battalions, and two brigades formed an infantry division, making a French division about 4,000 men, roughly a third smaller than its British equivalent.

Napoleon also had three other senior officers with him. First was Soult, his chief of staff, the general who ran the Imperial Headquarters, the Quartier-Général, and performed a role equivalent to De Lancey's for Wellington. Soult, now marvellously titled Duc de Dalmatia, was new to the post, and, great field commander as he undoubtedly was, not the equal in operational staff work to Napoleon's old chief of staff, Berthier. Berthier had fallen out of a window in Bamberg en route back to Paris to join Napoleon, apparently by accident, and his loss would have profound consequences. Soult was also unpopular in the army and not trusted by the generals, who thought him indolent.[5] Neither did he have the practised staff who had served Berthier so well over countless campaigns and who understood the workings of both the army and Napoleon's mind. It is sometimes difficult for civilians to appreciate the importance to a commander like Napoleon of having someone who can take ideas and orders and translate them into detailed instructions to the different units of an army, ensuring that they all do roughly what is intended at the right time, in the correct place, and with adequate supplies and support. Many of Napoleon's victories had been due to his and Berthier's ability to mass troops rapidly at a particular point to overpower an enemy, and this was the basis of his current campaign plan; he aimed to do precisely that so that he could defeat Wellington and Blücher one after the other, but it would only work if Soult got it right. Things had already got off to a bad start. Soult forgot to send preliminary orders to the cavalry to mobilise for the invasion of Belgium, so that they had to move by forced marches and arrived exhausted for the start of the campaign.[6]

Two other senior commanders would also play a major part in the campaign. Grouchy, nominally commander of the cavalry, would take command of the right wing of the army, the force Napoleon sent to pursue the Prussians after Ligny. Grouchy would become something of a French scapegoat for what was about to happen. He was undoubtedly a very competent field cavalry officer, but his record of independent command was not good and he had made a comprehensive muddle of the French expedition to Ireland in 1796. Soult warned Napoleon not to trust him with the right wing but was ignored.[7] The second was Marshal Ney. Ney, called correctly 'the bravest of the brave', was an inspired tactical commander whose disregard for his own safety was legendary. Starting life as a private soldier in the cavalry, he rose to be a sergeant-major after four years and to command a division within eleven. He was a marshal of France within 17 years of joining up. He had commanded the rearguard on the retreat from Moscow, which must rank as possibly one of the most challenging military roles in history, and had discharged it as well as anyone could have. He had been created Prince de la Moskowa in recognition of his conduct in Russia and his leadership at Borodino in particular. He commanded the left wing of Napoleon's army, the main part of the French force and the one that would attack Wellington. At Waterloo he therefore assumed tactical control of the battle and would have five horses shot from under him. His bravery would be proved once again, but his operational direction of the battle was to be more questionable.

Napoleon's army was not therefore the equal of its great forebears. It had been assembled in a rush, and although its ranks were filled with generally experienced soldiers, they were fighting in new regiments alongside men they did not know. There were also many recently recruited, some of whom did not really want to be there. It was poorly equipped when compared to previous Napoleonic armies, being short of horses and those horses it had were unfit. It had experienced and dedicated generals, but they were not all the equal of their more famous predecessors and the great Napoleonic staff system was not working as it should, which would mean that their talents could not be best employed. But if the French army was not at its best, then neither was Wellington's nor Blücher's. What was about to happen was far from being the final clash of the titans; rather it was to be a meeting of hastily assembled and partially trained armies, none of which was to equal its reputation.

*

Napoleon's plan was to attack the Allies at the junction of the British and Prussian armies, at Charleroi on the River Sambre. He had made this decision because he thought that, taken by surprise, Wellington would fall back west towards Ostend and the Channel, protecting his communications and supply lines, and that Blücher would do the same thing to the east. Having split their armies he would then be strong enough to defeat each in turn before taking Brussels and facing the gathering Austrian and Russian forces, both of which he had beaten in the recent past. His army numbered 124,000 men, dangerously small if it had to face the combined Allied and Prussian strength of close to 175,000, but adequate, under his leadership, to overmatch their respective 74,000 and 99,000 individually. What his intelligence had not discovered was that Wellington had agreed with Blücher that, if attacked, they would move to keep their two armies together, realising the danger of either being caught on its own.

On 14 June, the anniversary of Marengo and Friedland, Napoleon issued a stirring 'Order of the Day', urging his troops to victory. At half-past three in the morning of 15 June, the Army of the North started to move towards the border of the Kingdom of the Netherlands and to invade Belgium. The order in which they moved would, unintentionally, dictate who would fight the Allies, and who would fight the Prussians. D'Erlon's and Reille's corps moved on the left, on the British and Allied side. In the centre were Vandamme and Lobau, with the Imperial Guard and the cavalry reserve. Gérard's corps moved on the right. The move did not go smoothly. D'Erlon's corps moved an hour and a half late, and Vandamme never received his orders. General Bourmont, who commanded a division in Gérard's Fourth Corps, deserted to the Allies with his entire staff, although he does not appear to have been that helpful in developing the Allied plan. Things were not proceeding with quite the expected Napoleonic precision, but nevertheless by nine o'clock that morning the centre and left of the French forces had reached Charleroi, where they started to engage the Prussians. The Waterloo campaign had begun.

Blücher's reaction was initially lethargic, the Prussian head-quarters being equally unpractised, and it was slow to receive reports from the frontier and to react to them. Blücher and Gneisenau started to concentrate their army around Sombreffe, a crossroads on the Namur–Nivelles road close to the village of Ligny. Word was sent back to Wellington, asking him to con-firm his intentions. Wellington at this stage felt he did not know enough about Napoleon's plan to start to move. He was concerned that what the Prussians were seeing might just be part of the French force, and that a second part would attempt to outflank him by attacking via Mons and approaching Brussels from the south-west. He would remain concerned by this possibility for the next three days. The Prussian reports to his headquarters during the day were fairly sporadic and did not help him much, Gneisenau not being as assiduous as he should have been at keeping his allies informed, and it wasn't until later that evening that Wellington was able to give defi-nite orders. Gneisenau was later said to have tasked the fattest man in the Prussian army with taking his reports, which may explain why it took him over eight hours to cover 40 miles; a second officer subsequently took six hours to cover 34 miles.

For much of 15 June Wellington was not well informed as to what was going on around Charleroi and it was not until ten o'clock that evening, when a report from Dörnberg con-firmed that there was no enemy activity around Mons, that he felt it safe to conclude that what the Prussians were seeing was the main French force. He therefore issued orders to concentrate his army to conform to the Prussian position at Sombreffe and Ligny. He despatched his reserve to a crossroads south of Brussels at Mont St Jean, where the Charleroi road crossed a significant ridgeline just before it entered the Forest of Soignes. Hill's Second Corps was to concentrate at Braine-le-Comte, just to the west of Mont St Jean, whilst the cavalry and the remainder of the Army were to march on Nivelles. The Second Netherlands Infantry Division, which had been billeted near Nivelles, concentrated around a crossroads just east of the town, where the Charleroi–Brussels road crossed that from Nivelles to Namur. It was called Quatre Bras after the four roads that met there.

Once Wellington had given his orders he went with his senior officers to a ball given by the Duchess of Richmond, wife of the British ambassador. This has entered legend as the way that the British army spent the night before the battle, which is untrue both because it was three days before Waterloo and because very few officers attended. It was also not a very jolly affair. 'It was', in fact, 'a dreadful evening, taking leave of friends and acquaintances, many never to be seen again', wrote the Duchess of Richmond's daughter, who later spent the evening helping her brother, who was serving as ADC to the Prince of Orange, to pack and who was shocked when she returned to find 'some energetic and heartless young ladies still dancing'.[8] Standish O'Grady went, as did a group of other officers who had come into Brussels for the evening, but he found a vehicle and returned to his regiment as soon as he heard the news. He did not even mention the ball in his letters home.

In fact people in Brussels had been alerted at three o'clock

that afternoon that something was happening by distant
artillery fire, a 'rumbling noise in the air. Some said it was distant thunder, others that it was cannonading', and they had
gathered on the ramparts nearest Waterloo to listen.[9] Harry
Ross-Lewin had been dining with his brigade commander,
Sir James Kempt, when Kempt received his orders to move.
On his way back Ross-Lewin found a group of his officers sitting in a coffee house who seemed at first to think he was
joking but soon 'the most incredulous would have been thoroughly undeceived, for the drums began to beat, bugles to
sound and Highland pipes to squeal in all quarters of the city;
such was the excitement of the inhabitants, the buzz of
tongues, the repeated words of command, the hurrying of the
soldiers through the streets, the clattering of horses' hoofs, the
clash of arms, the rattling of the wheels of wagons and gun-
carriages, and the sounds of warlike music'.[10]

Brussels in fact quickly became chaotic. Edward Heeley
saddled Sir George Scovell's best charger at midnight and
witnessed 'a scene that baffles all description. Drums, trumpets, bugles, all kicking up the finest discord that ever was
heard. The inhabitants all rose from their beds, and the soldiers were collecting in the streets, such shouting, swearing,
crying, arms rattling, dragoons and officers galloping about,
in short I should think the confusion at Babel was a fool to it.
What caused the confusion to be worse than it need have
been was that everybody thought the French were close at the
gates. This dreadful state of things continued till about half
past one o'clock, and then it was astonishing to see the order
at that time as if by magic. All the troops were on parade and
ready to march. The park was full and all the streets round it,
and in a very few minutes the order was given to march.'[11] It
was the sound of the drums and trumpets that people would

remember long afterwards. 'It is impossible', wrote John Whale, an ADC to Lord Edward Somerset who commanded the Household Brigade, 'to describe the effect of those sounds, heard in the silence of the night.'[12]

Things were more relaxed outside the city, where Thomas Morris and the officers and soldiers of the 73rd were playing football when they received their orders from an orderly dragoon at four p.m. By six p.m. they had all paraded in marching order. The cavalry didn't receive orders until later that evening. Dr Haddy James had walked back to his quarters with 1st Life Guards 'replete with my friends' excellent dinner and vintage wine on that fine warm night'. He may have drunk rather too much of it as he was woken two hours later by Edward Kelly telling him the trumpeters had been sounding 'To Horse' for an hour. 'It was a lovely morning, the sun about to rise and our trumpets sounding in every direction – a tremendous air of bustle, clatter and indeed confusion.' He bumped into 'two hussars, staggering down the street very drunk and unconscious of the call to action around them. One said to his companion "I don't think I shall go to bed now". One of our lads who heard him laughed and called over, "Belike you will be put to bed with a shroud this night, and know nothing about it."'

The Life Guards were eventually ready by four a.m. on 16 June, but James's horse then lost a shoe, starting what was to be a frustrating day for him.[13] George Farmer had paraded with his troop of 11th Light Dragoons ready for routine exercise that same morning when their orders came. They were told that the Prussians had been defeated and that Napoleon was in 'full march to attack the positions of the English'. The regiment quickly mustered in full marching order, but not before Farmer had, like the old soldier he was, taken care not to move without a stock of provisions for himself as well as his charger. 'All the men carried their nose-bags filled with corn, and a supply of hay behind them ... but the young hands forgot that men, as well as horses, are little fit for work when they are starving. I had a lump of bacon and a loaf of bread in my haversack, of which not many hours elapsed ere I experienced the great benefit.'[14] Ensign George Keppel, in Colonel Frank Tidy's 14th Foot, arrived rather late for parade on the morning of 16 June. He found the regiment parading, also in full marching order. He rushed back to his billet, 'swallowed a few mouthfuls of food, and with the assistance of my weeping hostesses packed up my baggage', which he placed on his 'bat horse' and consigned to the regimental baggage guard, which would follow on behind. 'Thus when I entered the Waterloo campaign, all my worldly goods consisted of the clothes on my back. As we passed through the village our drums and fifes played "The Girl I Left Behind Me".'[15]

Poor Mercer received his orders when he was asleep in bed, a note 'which might have been an invitation to dinner' until he opened it and found he was to proceed with 'utmost diligence' to Enghien. This was difficult. All his officers were absent, as were his supply wagons and one-third of his troop. Gathering them took until seven o'clock, which at least allowed them all to cook breakfast, and when 'Turn Out' was finally blown on the trumpets, his dog, Bal, increased the confusion by performing his party trick of running down the lines barking and trying to bite the horses' noses.[16] Some regiments, like Thomas Lawrence's 40th Foot, who were not ordered to Nivelles, did not move until 17 June, and were annoyed by the locals shouting at them as they passed through Brussels that they would be slaughtered like bullocks. 'We laughed and said that was nothing new' but 'some of the younger recruits were very frightened at the thought of fight-ing'.[17]

After the initial panic had died down, many were relieved finally to be going into action. Like Morris, they 'tired of the monotony, and there was a restlessness and anxiety to know what the French were about as it was universally believed that Napoleon would make a desperate attempt to drive the Anglo-Prussian armies from Belgium',[18] which is a perceptive observation given that Wellington and Blücher both believed until mid June that they would be invading France. There was very little time to say goodbye to families and farewells were short but sad. 'The worst part of the business was to see the officers' and soldiers' wives hanging onto them, almost broken hearted and wanting to go with them',[19] noted Edward Heeley. 'One poor fellow immediately under our windows, turned back again and again to bid his wife farewell, and take his baby once more in his arms; and I saw him hastily brush away a tear with the sleeve of his coat, as he gave her back the child for the last time, wrung her hand, and ran off to join his company', wrote Charlotte Waldie, one of those tourists who had just arrived in Brussels from England.[20] Madeleine De Lancey had been supremely happy in Brussels, very much in love with her new husband. 'I continued musing on my happy fate; I thought over all that had passed, and how grateful I felt! I had no wish but that this might continue; I saw my husband loved and respected by everyone, my life gliding on, like a gay dream, in his care.' But shortly after she had helped him dress in all his finery, and pin his decorations on his coat before he went off to dine, an ADC arrived to find out where Sir William was. She did not like 'this appearance but tried not to be afraid'. Her bliss would soon come to a most unhappy end. 'Shall I ever', she wrote later, 'forget the tunes played by the shrill fifes and the buglehorns which disturbed that night?'[21]

There was also no time in those frantic hours of packing and parading to write a last letter home, although many correctly suspected that that is exactly what they would have been. What 'last letters' there are from Waterloo were written some weeks before, whilst the men were still waiting comfortable, bored and nervous in their Belgian billets. Most of the declarations of everlasting love had been made in the early days, in April and May when men had had time to adjust after their sudden departure from England. Some of those written in late May and early June are rather more down to earth. Edward Staveley had got so bored that even by 31 May he was writing to his mother that 'I have seldom been so idle as in this place, and consequently have nothing to write about'.[22] On 15 June, the day Napoleon invaded Belgium, Ensign Samuel Barrington of 1st Foot Guards wrote to his mother asking her to send out his shotguns so that he could go shooting to kill the time. Twenty-four hours later he would have no more use for them.[23]

Courtenay Ilbert, the affectionate officer in the Reserve Artillery, found time to write to Anne every day throughout the crisis. On 15 June he was reassuring her that 'there is no chance of my being immediately in the way of danger', which, as a Reserve Artillery officer, was probably true, and he never made it onto the battlefield until the day after Waterloo, but for most there was no time and no way of finding a post.[24] There is, in many of these letters, a hint of apology for being a soldier – for exposing family and friends to the worry and hurt. Some families, like Edward Kelly's, would rather unhelpfully agree, make it plain that they thought he would have been better employed doing something more peaceful and remunerative. Many soldiers, before and since, have experienced the same feelings and a similar reaction.

Friday 16 June was, as Haddy James had remarked, a beautiful day, unusually in that soggy summer, and it soon became stiflingly hot. The older soldiers were cheerful, glad to be on the move. The 95th saw 'the sun slowly rising above the horizon and peeping through the trees, while our men were as merry as crickets, laughing and joking with each other, and at times pondered in their minds what all the fuss, as they called it, could be about; for even the old soldiers could not believe the enemy were so near'.[25] The narrow Belgian roads quickly became blocked and many commanding officers felt their blood pressure rise as they tried to force their way through the seemingly endless stream of marching troops, guns, supply wagons and 'a long procession of carts coming quietly in as usual to market filled with old Flemish women seated among their piles of cabbage, peas and strawberries, totally ignorant of the cause of all these warlike preparations'.[26] Haddy James, who had to stay behind to get his horse shod, now tried to catch up with the 1st Life Guards. He soon ran into the back of a German regiment, 'which had marched a weary way already that day, and were continually obliged to halt, and lie reclining on their mighty packs to procure some rest in the shade'. As they went they were singing 'a hymn like music'. No sooner had James got past them than he ran into 'baggage and artillery of every description and without end'. Now desperate to get to his regiment before they went into action he put his horse into a trot and barged his way forwards, shouting '"Bridle hand right!" Or "Bridle hand left!" Or "Make way if you please" at the top of my voice'.

Sixteen miles later James began to get clear of the blockages in that afternoon of 'clear blue sky, but in the south there were some clouds. These in one part assumed the form of a pyramid, whose base was a line, straight as if drawn by a ruler. It was the canopy which the combatants had formed for themselves.' He reined in his horse and listened to the deep grumbling of the distant artillery, 'a music which constantly serenaded' him.[27] He, like most others caught in that moving mass, had very little idea what was actually happening to their front. George Farmer and his 11th Light Dragoons had followed a less congested road, and had been able to trot for 14 miles before resting their horses. They heard what 'the excessive heat of the weather induced us to believe was the rolling of thunder at a distance. Another half-hour's progress, however, set that notion aside; for then we could distinguish the smoke as it curled over the woods of Quatre Bras.' Soon they passed 'groups of persons whom, on nearing one another, we recognised to be the wounded. Poor fellows, they drew to one side that we may pass, and cheered lustily. "Push on, push on", was their cry, "you are very much wanted". We had ridden about forty miles, when the red flashes of musketry and cannon greeted us. "Halt!" was the word given, "cut away forage, and draw swords". The hay was cut loose, our swords flashed in the air, and at the signal "Quick Trot", away we went again.'[28]

Lieutenant Edmund Wheatley had heard very loud cannonading all afternoon as he marched. 'A thick wood at a distance was envelop'd in smoke, and at intervals a strong flash of light could be caught in the dusky hue. The sound was at times close, sometimes receded – so uncertain is war. The suspense and anxiety of our situation was indescribable, for none but those who have experienced the uneasiness of mind a soldier endures when standing for orders to move in sound of battle, can conceive the astonishing length to which the moments are stretched on so critical an occasion. We marched nearly three hours unknowing our destination, until three or four wounded passing convinced us that every step was bringing us nearer and nearer to the scene of slaughter.'[29]

What was happening to their front was that Napoleon's left-hand column, commanded by Ney, had been attempting to push north up the Charleroi–Brussels road when it had run into the Allies at the crossroads of Quatre Bras. Napoleon had been satisfied with the events of 15 June. He had pushed the Prussians back from Charleroi and got his army safely across the Sambre. He had faced little serious resistance and reckoned that he had successfully divided the Allies from the Prussians, both whose armies he fancied had retreated at the surprise of his rapid advance. He therefore determined to put the next phase of his plan into effect on 16 June, which would see him defeating first the Prussians, whose strength he thought was about 40,000, before turning on the Allies. His main effort would therefore first be on the right, against Blücher. Grouchy and the right wing, with Gérard's and Vandamme's corps, and with Napoleon and the Imperial Guard, would attack the Prussians, of whose exact whereabouts he remained unsure, whilst Ney would take Reille's and d'Erlon's infantry corps, and Kellerman's cavalry corps, on the left. Ney's orders were to occupy the village of Genappe, about halfway to Brussels, and push out reconnaissance parties towards Brussels itself, which Napoleon wanted to occupy by 17 June.

The expectation seemed to be that Wellington would have fallen back westwards, and that the left wing would have a relatively easy passage as Napoleon had predicted, and Ney's initial moves were certainly not very urgent. He did not move his force off before eleven a.m. on 16 June, about the same time as Grouchy commenced his attack on the Prussians at Ligny, and they only reached Frasnes, the village just south of Quatre Bras by 1.30 p.m. At two p.m. Reille himself, with Husson's brigade of infantry, met Ney with a light cavalry force on the high ground between Frasnes and Quatre Bras and immediately south of Hutte Wood. Ney reckoned Quatre Bras was only lightly held, and was all for pushing on, but Reille, with his experience in the Peninsula, thought he had seen red coats in the wood and wanted to bring up another brigade before advancing. There was therefore a short pause as extra troops came up, and the force was divided into four columns.

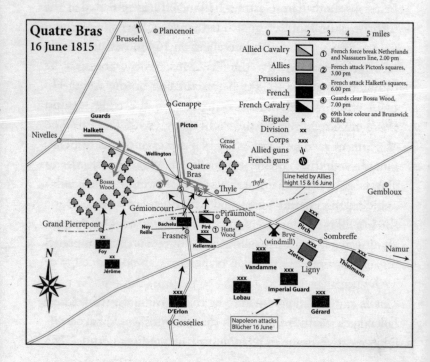

Quatre Bras is best understood by looking at the plan opposite. It is a straightforward battle to follow in outline but more
difficult in detail. The Allies were defending the hamlet on the
crossroads at Quatre Bras from the north, trying to stop Ney
advancing up the Brussels road from the south. Quatre Bras
consisted then, as it still does, of a series of farm buildings
clustered around the crossroads itself. South of it, in other
words on the side from which the French were advancing, are
two woods. On the right, from the Allied perspective (so, on
the French left) is Bossu Wood, which was then very thick
with high trees and criss-crossed with wide rides or breaks. It
ran south for nearly a mile, about halfway to Frasnes, and it
gradually widened from 500 yards at Quatre Bras to being
nearly a mile wide at its southern end, near which was the
farm of Grand Pierrepont. On the other side of the road but
further south was Hutte Wood, about two miles long and a
mile wide. On the same side as Hutte Wood and north of it, so
in effect between the French and the Allies and where most of
the fighting would take place, were two other farm complexes,
Gémioncourt, a few hundred yards south of Quatre Bras on
the main road, and Piraumont, about half a mile east of
Gémioncourt. The country here was more open cornfields
interspersed with copses and a sizeable lake. The hamlet of
Thyle, about three-quarters of a mile east of Quatre Bras crossroads on the Namur road, marked the eastern extent of the
battlefield. North of the Namur road, and east of the Brussels
road, were two other smaller woods, both of which are much
bigger today.

What makes the detail of the battle more difficult for us to
follow, and which also made it very confusing for the soldiers
fighting, is that the country is rolling and hilly so that it is difficult to see more than a few hundred yards at any time. The

Thyle, dignified with the title of river but in effect a large stream, rises in Bossu and Hutte woods, flowing north-west, creating rivulets. The Namur–Nivelles road, in other words the one that ran east–west, had to cut through this undulating country so ran from embankment to cutting to embankment, giving a good natural line of defence. The fields were all planted with rye, which stood about five foot high – old-fashioned corn had longer stalks and smaller heads than modern varieties, which have been developed to produce more grain and less straw – so troops lying down or kneeling were invisible. It also meant that, although well suited for defence, the French could approach the crossroads unseen through the two woods and by making skilful use of the ground.

Wellington had, as we have seen and he would later admit, been wrongfooted by Napoleon's move and Quatre Bras was consequently a battle to which British and Allied troops were committed piecemeal and as they arrived. Fortunately one of the more reliable Netherlands divisions, the 2nd Division, commanded by the competent Baron Perponcher, had been billeted around Nivelles. One of its brigades was Prince Bernhard of Saxe-Weimar's brigade of Nassauers, who happened to be billeted at Frasnes. On the evening of 15 June, French light cavalry reconnoitring in front of Ney's force had run into them. The Nassauers had quickly defended the village, and fired on the French, who tried to cut round to their eastern flank. The Nassauers then withdrew into Bossu Wood, and, it now being nearly dark, the French withdrew. With remarkable initiative, and in advance of any orders from Wellington or his corps commander, the Prince of Orange, Perponcher reinforced Quatre Bras from Nivelles so that by first light on 16 June he had 6,500 men there and eight guns, although no cavalry.

The Prince of Orange, who had been in Brussels, arrived at six a.m., and quickly agreed Perponcher's plan, as did Wellington who got there at nine a.m., confident that the rest of the British and Allied troops would arrive by midday. The Prince of Orange and Perponcher decided to extend their line, so that it ran for about two miles from the hamlet of Thyle across to the west of Bossu Wood, the idea being to give a greater impression of strength but in fact leaving it dangerously thin in places. Wellington then rode over to Ligny to meet Blücher, leaving the Prince of Orange in command. At this stage Wellington thought that the French were not intending to attack Quatre Bras in strength and that it was more of a feint. His view was confirmed when he saw the great columns of Napoleon's army manoeuvring to attack the Prussians at Ligny, and he promised an anxious Blücher and Gneisenau that he would march to their assistance if not attacked himself. He would, in effect, be attacking the left flank of Napoleon's army. But by the time he got back to Quatre Bras he realised that Ney's attack was very much more than a feint. Ney had 35,000 infantry, 7,000 cavalry and 92 guns at his disposal, and he opened his first assault, late in the day as it was, with 6,000 infantry and 2,000 cavalry, and six guns. Ney's problem was that he had delayed so long that he had given Wellington's army time to arrive.

Only a part of Wellington's force was to fight at Quatre Bras, effectively those divisions which formed the Prince of Orange's corps. This included two British divisions, Cooke's First Guards and Alten's Third together with Perponcher's Second Netherlands Division. Wellington also called forward Picton's Fifth Division as a reserve and the Brunswickers, both of whom would be heavily engaged. Hill's corps, and the rest of the Army remained back around Mont St Jean, further north up the Brussels road. The cavalry, although they were all called forward, with George Farmer and his comrades in a state of nervous excitement, did not actually fight until the next day.

Ney's attack finally began at around two p.m. when Reille had brought up his additional troops; timings during the battle and later at Waterloo are always approximate given that the few people who had watches rarely found time to consult them. The right hand of his four columns consisted of Piré's cavalry. Next, astride the main road were two brigades of Bachelu's 5th Division, with Foy's 9th. Division on the far left opposite Bossu Wood. Jérôme Bonaparte's 6th Division was in reserve together with Lefèbvre-Desnouettes' Light Cavalry of the Imperial Guard, temporarily attached to Ney's force. Kellerman's 3rd Cavalry Corps were spread out to the rear, with 800 cuirassiers of Guiton's brigade forward at Frasnes but the rest two miles away at Liberchies. At this stage Ney also knew he could count on d'Erlon's corps, which Napoleon had detached to him, and whose 19,000 men would give him a decisive advantage, the comfort of which may have contributed to his otherwise somewhat dilatory approach.

As the drums of Bachelu's and Foy's divisions beat the *pas de charge*, that stirring rhythm that still inspires French troops today (it is well worth playing it on YouTube as you read this), the Dutch skirmishing line began to fall back so that Foy took Gémioncourt and Piré's cavalry and Bachelu's infantry closed towards the Namur Road. On the left Jérôme's division came up and started slowly to push the Netherlanders back, taking Pierrepont Farm and beginning to clear through Bossu Wood. It seemed as if Napoleon might have been right and that any resistance would soon be brushed aside, leaving the Brussels road open. Once he had defeated the Prussians,

Napoleon could occupy the capital on 17 June and his brief but glorious campaign would be over.

It was at that moment that Wellington returned from his meeting with Blücher. At the same time 1st Battalion 95th Rifles appeared, leading Picton's Fifth Division, which had made a forced march of 27 miles in the baking heat. Edward Costello was in the leading company. They halted briefly at Quatre Bras whilst Wellington gave orders. Picton's British battalions were to line the Namur road east of the crossroads, with his Hanoverian brigade forming a second rank, securing his essential line of communication to the Prussians should he have to go to their assistance. A brigade of Netherlands cavalry came up too, and was despatched to retake Gémioncourt. Prince Bernhard was deployed to reinforce the Netherlanders in Bossu Wood, to which the Brunswick contingent, who arrived just after Picton, were also committed. The 95th were placed on the far left, between Piraumont Farm and Thyle. As they moved into position, Costello could see the French emerging from Hutte Wood, 'which was rather on a hill, with a clear plain between us'. Soon their skirmishers, in an extended line, came up and started a 'very brisk fire on us'. The Rifles occupied the few houses of the hamlet and immediately a 'blaze of fires' developed around their positions and on the open ground to their right towards Quatre Bras where Picton's other battalions were moving into position.

The French brought up artillery, positioning it on the rising ground by Gémioncourt and also around Piraumont Farm, from where it began firing round shot into the house Costello was occupying. He asked a 'young woman in the place for a little water, which she was handing me, when a ball passed through the building, knocking the dust about our ears; strange to say, the girl appeared less alarmed than myself'.[30] He had so far been lucky, as casualties began to mount, particularly amongst the inexperienced men. 'Recruits in action are generally more unfortunate than the old soldiers. We had many fine fellows, who joined us on the eve of leaving England, who were killed here. An old rifleman will seek shelter, while the inexperienced recruit appears as if petrified to the spot by the whizzing balls, and unnecessarily exposes himself to the enemy's fire.' His luck was not to hold much longer. Wellington ordered the battalions lining the Namur road to advance to clear Bachelu's men from the open ground to their south. The fields of rye obstructed Costello's view as he moved, and the French surprised them from the low ground along the Thyle. Just as he was taking aim at a French skirmisher, 'a ball struck my trigger finger, tearing it off, and turning the trigger aside; while a second shot passed through the mess-tin on my knapsack'. Costello was moved to the rear with his lieutenant, James Gardiner, 'a worthy little officer severely wounded in the lower part of the leg'. Poor James Gardiner; his plans to visit his father in America would now have to wait even longer.[31]

As always in battles, the soldiers actually doing the fighting often have no idea what is happening elsewhere on the battlefield, being preoccupied with their own immediate actions. Lieutenant George Simmons, also of the 95th, was one of those competent but perhaps rather irritating officers who was always making hearty jokes. As his company arrived on the Namur road they were engaged by the French, who, confusingly, was then referred to as 'Johnny'. 'Ah! My boys, you are now opening the ball in good earnest,' he joked and, when his sergeant, Underwood, found it difficult to get through the hedge, saying the pricks were very sharp, Simmons said to him, 'Why, man, you are like a fine lady.' He then took a few steps back, ran forward and physically knocked the unfortunate Underwood through the hedge. 'Who the hell sent me through the hedge in that manner?' demanded the enraged Underwood. 'I did, Sir! We must have no fine ladies here.'

The French withdrew in front of them, ultimately taking up position behind some houses, north of Piraumont Farm. One French sharpshooter wounded Lieutenant Layton in the arm. Simmons told him to go to the rear but Layton refused until the Frenchman had been killed. Simmons bent over a sergeant to direct his fire but 'at this moment a round shot struck the sergeant in the face, dashing his head into long shreds or ribbons, throwing him backwards a distance of 10 yards. It was quite marvellous, his smashed head did not touch me, only a little sprinkling of blood. In my excitement I said "men look at that glorious fellow, our comrade and brother soldier, he now knows the grand secret. He has died nobly for his country and without a pang of suffering."'[32] It is not clear how this rather pious advice was received by his somewhat cynical riflemen.

The 95th and Kempt's men succeeded in holding the right-hand side of the French advance but Ney's men made rather more progress on their left, having some success in pushing the Netherlanders back through Bossu Wood. The Brunswickers, in the open ground between Bossu Wood and the road, were also being forced back by Foy's and Jérôme's men. The Duke of Brunswick led a charge of one of his cavalry squadrons in person, which was beaten back, and as he was trying to reorganise his battered force just south of the Quatre Bras crossroads he was killed by a French sharpshooter. The French followed up their success by launching four regiments of Piré's cavalry, two of *chasseurs* and two of lancers.

The *chasseurs* came thundering down the main Brussels road, now seemingly with nothing to stop them. Again luck was on Wellington's side as the 92nd Highlanders, the last of Picton's battalions, had just arrived, and had been sheltering from the French artillery by taking refuge in the ditch alongside the Namur road immediately adjacent to the crossroads. Wellington, who had been watching events a little to their front, suddenly realised that he was in danger of being cut off. Turning round, he galloped at the men lying in the ditch and jumped clean over them, quite a feat of horsemanship. Once safely to the rear he wheeled the battalion through 90 degrees, so that they were facing the Brussels road, from where they poured volleys into the right flank of Piré's men. At the same time the remaining Brunswickers along the edge of Bossu Wood poured fire into their left flank. This effectively destroyed them as a force. Those few who were left galloped on but all they could now do was spitefully cut down any stragglers and wounded they found to the Allies' rear.

The two French lancer regiments, advancing behind the *chasseurs*, were more fortunate. They branched off east of the road once they had passed Gémioncourt, and came up against Picton's main position in the open fields south of the Namur road, effectively where his battalions had halted in line having driven back the initial French attack. The height of the rye and the fact that the French lancers became intermingled with retreating Brunswick and Netherlands cavalry, who, particularly to the inexperienced, looked much the same, meant that they caught up with the 42nd and 44th before they had time to form squares, and many of their skirmishers, deployed forward specifically to warn of enemy attacks, were skewered on the French lances. James Anton in the 42nd was one of those nearly caught by them. The British infantry feared the lancers most of the French cavalry. 'The lance can be projected with considerable precision, and with deadly effect, without bringing the horse to the point of the bayonet,'[33] Anton complained. His commanding officer, Sir Robert Macara fell, pierced through the brain, quickly followed by Robert Dick, who assumed command, and then Major George Davidson. The flank companies managed to close in so that eventually a ragged square was formed and its volleys drove the lancers off. The 44th had no time, and resorted to firing volleys in line, always a dangerous thing for infantry to do in the face of a cavalry attack, but they just succeeded in causing enough casualties for the French attack to falter, although not before their Colours had been torn by a lance.

Ney's attack was now stalled. Piré's cavalry were beaten and all but destroyed. Bachelu's and Foy's infantry divisions had fallen back in disorder although Jérôme's men were still well ensconced in Bossu Wood. The Allies had, though, suffered severe casualties, Picton's battalions having been under constant artillery fire from the 44 guns which Ney had placed on the high ground around Gémioncourt; the majority of casualties at Quatre Bras were caused either by the French sharpshooters or by artillery fire. It was at this point that Ney received one of those messages from hell that every commander dreads. A note arrived from Soult telling him to clear the Allies from his front and then swing right along the Namur road to attack the Prussians at Ligny in their right flank; in other words, supporting the left of Napoleon's force that was attacking them. Soult told him that the Prussian army 'was doomed if you act with vigour' and ended with the helpful advice that the 'fate of France is in your hands'.[34] Minutes later Ney received a second note, from d'Erlon's chief of staff, informing him that d'Erlon's corps had been turned around and was no longer available to clear Quatre Bras because Napoleon wanted it at Ligny. One must feel some sympathy for Ney, who now faced an Allied force of around 25,000 and growing by the hour. His quick advance to Brussels was beginning to look rather doubtful.

It was at this point that he resorted to a tactic that he would use again and again over the coming two days. He called up Kellerman and told him to use his reserve cavalry corps to clear away Wellington's force. Kellerman not unnaturally objected, pointing out that he would be using up his valuable men riding at infantry squares in difficult country where they would find it hard to see what they were doing. He also reminded Ney that he only had 800 cuirassiers immediately available as the rest of his brigades were still two miles to the rear. He may also have pointed out that one of his regiments, the 11th, had no cuirasses, there having been insufficient to go round. His arguments were to no avail and Ney, by this time decidedly agitated, told him to get on with it. Kellerman duly obeyed orders.

'Kellerman thereupon went to the head of Guiton's brigade and led them at a smart trot down the road; while the French batteries redoubled their fire on the British infantry. Arrived at the summit of the plateau north of the Gémioncourt rivulet, he increased his front to a column of squadrons at twice deploying distance, and advanced at a gallop, hurrying his men into action before they could perceive their danger',[35] wrote Fortescue, and the first wave duly hit what was left of the 42nd and 44th battalions, formed into now rather small squares to the east of the road, having been warned of the imminent threat by their skirmishers, who had learned their lesson and just managed to race back in time. Predictably Kellerman's men found it hard to work out exactly where the squares were in the rye and when they did find them their horses were pretty well blown having galloped for the best part of a mile. But they could do little except demonstrate rather ineffectually, as even a well-armoured cuirassier could not penetrate those walls of bayonets, and whilst they galloped around them they were picked off by volleys and individual shots. 'Our last file had got into square, and into its proper place, so far as unequalised companies could form a square, when the cuirassiers dashed full on two of its faces; their heavy horses and steel armour seemed sufficient to bury us under them, had they been pushed forward on our bayonets', remembered Anton, but once the square was formed, 'a most destructive fire was opened; riders cased in heavy armour, fell tumbling from their horses; their horses reared, plunged and fell on the dismounted riders; steel helmets and cuirasses rang against unsheathed sabres as they fell to the ground.' Some of Kellerman's men went straight on down the Brussels road, but were stopped by the 92nd, in their original position just east of the crossroads, where Wellington was still stationed.

For the soldiers in the Allied squares it seemed as if an endless stream of cuirassiers was being launched at them. In fact there were probably four separate waves, each of about 200 horsemen, but as each attack foundered so small groups of French horsemen remained, bravely attempting to penetrate the squares until they were shot down. The Allies badly needed cavalry at this point, who should have been able to sweep Kellerman's now-exhausted troopers aside, but apart from the rather ineffective Netherlands brigade of van Merlen, and what was left of the Brunswickers, the rest of Wellington's horsemen were still forcing their way south down the packed roads to Nivelles. Picton therefore decided to form his two battalions who had so far suffered least, the First Royals and the 28th, they being furthest away from the road and not subject to the intensity of cavalry attack, into a column – a risky manoeuvre with so many enemy cavalry still about – and advance to support the 44th. He then formed them into a large square, a difficult move in itself, whilst he ordered the 32nd and 79th to do likewise. Best's Hanoverians moved forward to occupy the cutting on the Namur road, but pushed one battalion forward of it.

The French cavalry attacks continued, achieving little except mounting casualties for the cuirassiers, until the attacks paused, allowing the French guns around Gémioncourt to open up again and the infantry sharpshooters to creep forward, both of which started causing serious casualties amongst the squares. Lieutenant John Malcolm in the 42nd was wounded at this point. He took a musket ball in the arm, but, although collapsing from loss of blood, the battalion being completely surrounded he could not go to the rear to find a doctor.[36] Picton sent skirmishers forward to ferret out the sharpshooters, but no sooner had he done so than a fresh cavalry attack materialised. Lancers and cuirassiers charged forward together, and although they made little progress against the squares, they did catch some of the unfortunate skirmishers as they desperately rushed back, and also caught Best's forward battalion in line and quickly destroyed it.

Picton's division was now in trouble. They had lost approximately half their men, and many of the remainder were wounded; all were exhausted and running short of ammunition. Although the French had been repulsed on the east side of the Brussels road, they were still in strength in Bossu Wood and slowly pushing the Netherlands infantry back. Many of these now gave up, and Colonel James Stanhope, advancing to

the battle with his division, saw 'Soon after passing Nivelles . . .
a great many wounded men going to the rear with ten times
their number to take care of them'.[37] There was a serious risk
of Wellington being outflanked and of the French infantry
clearing the wood, turning right and taking Picton's battered
men in their flank. It was at this point, to Wellington's and
Picton's relief, that two brigades of the Third Division arrived,
Colin Halkett's brigade, with four British battalions, and
Count Kielmansegge's Hanoverians. They were just in time.

Picton directed the Hanoverians to the extreme left, mindful of the need to keep the Namur road open, whilst Halkett
was told to stop the French advance through Bossu Wood and
to reinforce Kempt's weakened battalions to the east of the
Brussels road. His men duly moved forward. The 73rd led off
in column, moving south along the road and then peeling off
to the west across the open ground between the road and
Bossu Wood. The 33rd followed them, and then the 30th,
who ended up almost on the road itself. The 69th peeled off
east to attempt to reinforce the by now very battered 42nd
and 44th. Had this manoeuvre worked as intended, there
would have been a ragged line of battalions south of the crossroads stretching from Bossu Wood across the Brussels road and
linking to Picton's squares. As Halkett rode forward to reconnoitre, he saw the French massing for a fourth major cavalry
attack, so quickly sent word back to his advancing battalions
to form square.

The 69th duly obeyed but, as they were doing so, they were
stopped by the Prince of Orange, who appears to have been
riding around the battlefield causing chaos for much of the day
despite Wellington being in tactical command. The Prince
told Lieutenant-Colonel Charles Morice that there were no
cavalry about and that he should get on forward. No sooner

had Morice changed his orders than the French cavalry were upon them. His battalion tried a desperate last-minute attempt to form square, and might just have done so had not the grenadier company wheeled around to fire at the enemy rather than closing the remaining face. The French got in, and two companies were destroyed completely. One hundred and fifty men were killed either by being run through with lances or cut down with swords in a few minutes and the King's Colour was lost, 'wrenched from the hands of the officer who bore it'.

Christopher Clarke, a cadet from the recently founded military college, was one of those volunteers who were serving in the ranks, hoping to get recommended for a commission. He was carrying the Regimental Colour and was 'cut and hacked in the most fearful manner', being wounded 22 times trying to save it, killing three cuirassiers before falling, but survived and was duly awarded the commission he craved.[38] Those men that could get away ran to take refuge with the 42nd and 44th. It was a disaster which demonstrated to anyone who doubted it what cavalry would do to infantry caught in the open. The 30th, who were also attacked, stood firm in their square, although the 33rd melted into the wood. Halkett's brigade had, within half an hour of arriving, been rendered ineffective.

Ensign Edward Macready of the 30th, the 17-year-old ensign who had originally signed up as a volunteer in Holland, was now fighting in his first action.[39] As his battalion arrived with Halkett's brigade, what struck him most was the apparent chaos of the battlefield: 'The roaring of great guns and musketry, the bursting of shells, and shouts of the combatants raised an infernal din, while the squares and lines, the galloping of horses mounted and rider less, the mingled crowds of wounded and fugitives, the volumes of smoke and flashing of fire'. The battalion marched to join up with Picton's men, 'passed a spot where the 44th, old chums of ours in Spain, had suffered considerably, the poor wounded fellows raised themselves up and welcomed us with faint shouts, "Push on old three tens – success to you, my darlings." Here we met our old Colonel riding out of the field, shot through the leg; he pointed to it and cried, "They've tickled me again, my boys – now one leg can't laugh at the other."' They formed square and successfully repulsed the French cavalry, unlike the poor 69th. Picton rode up to thank them. With the relief of their brief success they were 'laughing and shaking hands with all about us' in the square, so Picton, true to his reputation for direct speaking, then damned them for making such a noise.

Things were not so happy in the 33rd. Their commanding officer, Colonel Elphinstone, had assembled the officers before they reached Quatre Bras and given them all one of those rather irritating pep talks about what the regiment and country expected of them. Lieutenant John Boyce's reaction was to say that he was certain he would be killed, and when Frederick Pattison duly passed the colonel's words to his company, he reported it had an electric effect. James Gibbons, one of his men who had been a journeyman hairdresser, came and asked to be sent to the rear as he didn't feel well. The doctor was called to examine him but declared him fully fit, unluckily for Gibbons, who was killed later that day. As they followed the 69th and 30th they managed to form square, like the 30th, but found themselves under the direct fire of the Gémioncourt battery. 'Down went the men like before the scythe of the mower. Lieutenant Arthur Gore of the Grenadier Company, who was standing close by me (an exceedingly handsome young man; like Saul, from his shoulders upwards, he was higher than any of his compeers), was hit by a cannon ball, and his brains bespattered the shakos of the officers near him.

'Captain Haigh, perceiving that the front of the square facing the artillery was bending inward, left his place much excited, and, flourishing his sword, called aloud with an oath "Keep up, keep up; I say keep up". The words were vibrating on his lips when a cannon ball hit him in the abdomen, and cut him nearly in twain. He fell on his back; the separation between soul and body was most appalling.' Boyce was also duly killed, as he had predicted, and it was a much shaken battalion that heard the cry that cavalry were approaching. 'We immediately tried to form square to receive the cavalry', Private George Hemingway wrote to his mother, 'but all in vain, [for] the cannon shot from the enemy broke down our square faster than we could form it; killed nine and ten men every shot; the balls falling down amongst us just at the present and shells bursting in a hundred pieces. We could not be accountable for the number of men that we lost there; and had it not been for a wood on our right, about 300 yards, we should have every man been cut in pieces.'[40] It was at this point that they ran into the edge of Bossu Wood to hide, and the battalion was unable to play any further part in the fighting. Wellington and Halkett were later very hard on them, possibly unfairly. Many of their soldiers were young volunteers who had joined up a few weeks before and within hours of Elphinstone's little talk they had lost ten officers and 100 men killed.[41]

The 73rd Highlanders also ran for the cover of Bossu Wood, where they managed to recover, and once the cuirassiers had retired they reformed, two companies being sent forward to skirmish, one of which was Thomas Morris's.

His company commander was still Captain Robinson, the 60-year-old who had no active service, and 'knew nothing of field movements'. As they moved forward, through the rye on the eastern side of Bossu Wood, they saw the cuirassiers forming up for another charge. Robinson froze, not knowing what to do, so that the company were in imminent anger of being cut down. Luckily for them the battalion's adjutant saw what was going on and quickly intervened, the company racing back to the safety of the square and making it just in time.

It was now evening, but the Allied position remained precarious. Although the French cavalry attacks had stopped, Kellerman's troopers having suffered over 300 casualties and now virtually ineffective, there was still the danger of Wellington being outflanked through Bossu Wood, where Halkett's battalions had failed to stop the French infantry. It was at this point, about an hour after Halkett's arrival, that the Guards Division arrived after a forced march of 15 hours without food or drink. There was something about the reputation of the Guards that always frightened the French and encouraged the British, rather as Napoleon's Imperial Guard did for the French army. 'As a soldier I love the Guards and have always done so for the noble way in which they do their duty', wrote Pattison,[42] then trying to reorganise his shattered company at the southern edge of the wood.

In fact the Guards Division had a very high proportion of raw recruits, 'the largest part of whom were young soldiers and volunteers from the militia who had never been exposed to fire of an enemy',[43] but there were 4,000 of them, they were comparatively fresh and they were the Guards. As they approached they 'constantly met wagons full of men, of all the various nations under the Duke's command, wounded in the most dreadful manner. The sides of the road had a heap of dying and dead.'[44] The Prince of Orange rushed out to meet Lord Saltoun, who commanded their lead battalion – in fact, the light companies grouped together – as they marched in from Nivelles, and ordered him to advance immediately into the western side of Bossu Wood. The experienced and direct Saltoun remarked that he could not see any French, to which the Prince of Orange replied that if he did not 'like to undertake it' he would 'find someone who will'.[45]

Saltoun was not to be easily fazed and sent men forward to find out where the French were. 'We now loaded our muskets and very hastily advanced up the rising ground in the open field; (the shot from the enemy now whizzing amongst us,) we quickly attained the summit and bringing our left shoulders forward, the enemy retiring before us', recalled Private Mathew Clay, the Nottinghamshire weaver who fought under Saltoun's command.[46] 'As we entered the wood', continued Robert Batty, 'a few noble fellows, who sunk down overpowered with fatigue, lent their voice to cheer their comrades. The trees were so thick, that it was beyond anything difficult to effect a passage. As we approached, we saw the enemy behind them, taking aim at us; they contested every bush, and at a small rivulet they attempted a stand, but could not resist us.' But the Guards also took severe casualties. 'Our loss was tremendous, and nothing could exceed the desperate work of the evening', Batty continued. Clay was struck by the 'numerous bodies of the slain; I particularly noticed a young officer of the 33rd Regiment lying amongst the slain, his bright scarlet coat and silver lace attracted my attention when marching over his headless body', which could have been the handsome Arthur Gore, who had fallen in the square of the 33rd.

Emerging from the wood, the Guards arrived in the fields

between its eastern edge and the Brussels road, where they formed square as they saw French cavalry, what remained of Kellerman's men, preparing to attack from beyond Gémioncourt. They were also in range of the French battery, which predictably started to shell them. 'I being one of the outward rank of the square, can testify as to the correct aim of the enemy,' Clay noted, 'whose shells having fallen to the ground and exploded within a few paces of the rank in which I was kneeling, a portion of their destructive fragments in their ascent passing between my head and that of my comrade next in rank; its force and tremulous sound causing an unconscious movement of the head not to be forgotten in haste.'[47] The volleys from the Guards' squares, together with the fire from the Brunswick battalions along the edge of Bossu Wood, drove off the cuirassiers for what would prove to be the final time that day. Just before dark Ensign Sam Barrington, who had been so bored that he had sent for his shotguns, fell dead. He had his hat off and was cheering his men forward when he fell, shot through the head by a sharpshooter.[48]

It was now nearly dark. The Guards' advance had finally succeeded in clearing Bossu Wood, and, with Picton's battered battalions still holding the ground just east of the Brussels road, the Allied line was roughly back to that which the Netherlanders had occupied the night before. The Hanoverians and 95th held on to the far left around Thyle. Picton occupied the area between Piraumont and Gémioncourt, with the Guards and Halkett's brigade, together with some Brunswickers, occupying Bossu Wood and across to Pierrepont Farm. The French attacks ceased as it grew dark, and both armies settled down to reorganising themselves and doing what they could for their wounded. It was an uncomfortable and dangerous night, very close to the French lines, and they fully expected to be attacked in strength the next morning.

Whilst the action was raging at Quatre Bras, Napoleon had been proceeding with his plan to destroy the Prussian army a few miles to the east, between the villages of Fleurus and Ligny, just to the south of the Namur road. Blücher and Gneisenau had taken up positions in front of the small village of Ligny, on a forward slope, incurring raised eyebrows from Wellington, who thought such deployments played into the hands of the formidable French artillery. Napoleon had attacked them at roughly the same time Ney had attacked at Quatre Bras, and had quickly realised that he was facing 80,000 troops rather than the 40,000 on which he had planned. The slow progress of his attack was what had made him send the message to Ney to release d'Erlon, who had obediently left Frasnes to attack the Prussian right, only to be recalled by Ney, so that his corps of 20,000 men, who would have made a decisive difference to either battle, instead spent the day marching pointlessly to and fro. D'Erlon was to be much blamed for his indecision that day, Fortescue describing him as 'a man not to commit himself upon any side so long as he could find a safe way in the middle' after his command in Spain, but it hardly seems fair that he should shoulder all the blame when the orders ultimately came from Napoleon and Ney.

By nightfall on 16 June Napoleon thought he had defeated the Prussians regardless of d'Erlon's non-appearance, and he based his plans for the next day on the belief that they were not in a fit state to fight again. Although Ligny was, narrowly, a French victory, Blücher's army had lost only 6,000 men and 20 guns, and instead of streaming back in disorder on its line of communications via Namur and Liège, as Napoleon firmly believed that it would, Blücher instead withdrew in a relatively well conducted move to Wavre, between Ligny and Brussels, much further west than the French anticipated. Blücher fully intended to join forces with Wellington, as they had originally planned, although some rather muddled staff work at Gneisenau's headquarters meant that Wellington did not find out about his plans until nine a.m. on the morning of Saturday 17 June, much to the embarrassment of von Müffling, Blücher's liaison officer on Wellington's staff. It was now clear to Wellington that he would also have to withdraw from Quatre Bras to take up a position further north, where he could conform to the Prussians and from where they could support one another in the face of what would inevitably be a subsequent French attack.

Napoleon meanwhile detached 30,000 men under Grouchy, ordering them to pursue the supposedly fleeing Prussians, taking a route much further east based on what he assumed that Blücher would do rather than based on any intelligence. The Emperor himself spent the morning of 17 June visiting the wounded from Ligny and ordering his army to sort itself out and resupply. The rushed way in which it had been assembled meant that serious logistical shortcomings were now becoming apparent, as was a lack of discipline amongst many of the newly recruited soldiers. The French Provost Marshal, responsible for arresting deserters, resigned on 17 June in despair at his inability to do anything about the growing numbers.[49] Certainly very little in the way of rations reached Ney's exhausted troops behind Quatre Bras that night, and Foy's divisional staff had to make do with curdled milk from Frasnes whilst, to their considerable annoyance, Jérôme Bonaparte dined in splendour with his own cook.[50]

Consequently it wasn't until one p.m. on 17 June that Napoleon ordered Ney to move forward again, now attaching himself and the Imperial Guard to Ney's wing of the army and directing that the advance should be by way of Genappe and Mont St Jean to Brussels.

Both the French and the Allies lost about the same number of men at Quatre Bras, the French about 4,200 as far as it's possible to tell, and the Allies about 4,800, of which 2,300 were British. Picton's Fifth Division was down to half strength, and the First Guards Division had lost over 500 men in the last desperate fighting in Bossu Wood. Halkett's brigade had not suffered that badly, although both the 33rd and the 69th had taken significant casualties. The Brunswick and Hanoverian contingents, both of whom had fought very bravely, had suffered severely as well, and the Black Brunswickers had lost their charismatic duke. The general feeling was that the Netherlands infantry had not been very distinguished, although van Merlen's cavalry had performed well. By nightfall Wellington had 45,000 men forward, with the remainder of his army in reserve on the Mont St Jean ridge. His trick now was to break contact from his positions directly in front of Ney and to withdraw to conform to the Prussians' new position at Wavre. Withdrawals in contact are amongst the most difficult tactical moves to execute, and the morning of 17 June was not without its anxiety.

The exhausted Allied troops had spent the night after Quatre Bras holding the positions in which they had finished fighting. Their first priority, parched after their approach march and the hours of tearing off black-powder cartridges with their teeth, was to get hold of water. Taking a camp kettle off a dead man, Mathew Clay followed a ditch he had noticed earlier back into the wood to its source in a pond.

Filling the kettle and drinking freely, as did the wounded around him, he only realised in the light of early morning that they had been drinking mostly blood from the dead who had been floating in the water. The next priority was food. There was no possibility of any resupply from the commissariat, still way behind the Army in Brussels, so they had to rely on what they had managed to pack in their kit as they had left their billets in such a rush that morning. Some of the cavalry did manage to find some cattle, which were duly slaughtered and the meat cooked using a French front cuirass from one of Guiton's dead troopers as a frying pan.

Then there were the wounded. Those that could walked or else got themselves carried to the rear, which effectively meant further north up the Brussels road into the large village of Genappe. John Malcolm of the 42nd, wounded in the arm by a sharpshooter's musket ball in the square, managed to find their regimental surgeon, John Stewart, beside the road. He cut out the musket ball on the spot, sending Malcolm back to the field hospital. Here he spent a horrible night 'between the pain of my arm and cramp in my legs and arms from loss of blood and fatigue'. The next morning he tried to find a sprung cart to take him back to Brussels, but all that was available to him and two officers from the 92nd was a very un-sprung small wagon that belonged to an old couple who had been selling gin to the Army. The old couple then left them with an obstinate horse that 'could not speak anything but Flemish' and eventually refused to move. They got rid of it, finding a spare horse that had been taken off the French lancers the day before, but had no more success – presumably this horse spoke only French – and it took a good beating to get it to pull the cart to Brussels, where they eventually arrived at five p.m. From there the system improved. Malcolm was processed by a hospital orderly, who dressed his wound and evacuated him on a barge to Antwerp.[51] It is strange, given all the administrative reforms that had taken place in the British Army in the preceding decade, that no one had thought to create an ambulance corps or to make arrangements for collecting and evacuating the wounded. It was about to become a problem on a much larger scale.

Malcolm was, though, comparatively lucky.[52] The woods and cornfields were full of groaning, dying men, all desperate for water and assistance but, 'with a very formidable and watchful enemy before us',[53] it was difficult to reach them. The 95th had many wounded who were lying in no man's land, too near the French lines to be recovered. Once they had 'halted and laid on the ground and talked over our exploits', Sir Andrew Barnard (the commanding officer who had Corporal Pitt flogged for smuggling his wife on board their transport) pointed to a poor rifleman laid a little in front of the French advanced sentries, observing both his legs were sadly shattered. 'Gentlemen, if one of you would remain here with two or three men and when it is dark try to bring him off, it would be a glorious act indeed.' George Simmons immediately volunteered, which was indeed brave, but when relating the story he cannot resist telling us that Barnard replied, 'George Simmons, you are a good fellow, it is just what I expected from you.' Simmons duly marked the man's position with sticks. The night was very dark and he was able to crawl forward and recover the poor man, who he tells us greeted him with the words 'God bless you Mr Simmons, I am in a sad forlorn state indeed'. His 'smashed legs only hung together by lacerated muscles and tendons', so it is possibly unlikely that he was so articulate, but Simmons did get him back despite having to get past German-speaking sentries

after the Hanoverians had replaced the 95th in that part of
the line. When they challenged him he replied loudly
'Englishmen! Englishmen! What the devil more do you
want?', which eventually seemed to satisfy them.[54]

Some of the wives and families who were with the Army
had accompanied their husbands on the march to Quatre Bras
and, much as they might have prized their being in Belgium,
they now faced the harsh reality of being near the front line.
The First Guards Division had halted to allow the married
men a few minutes to say goodbye as they came up to the battlefield. Other men joined them, trusting their valuables to
their friends' wives and asking them to pass on messages to
their own families. It was a poignant moment, 'sincere and
affectionate and expressed with deep emotions of grief as
though a state of widowhood had suddenly come upon them,
with the loud thunder of the destructive cannon sounding in
their ears'.[55] It is difficult not to sympathise with Wellington
at this stage, as a group of emotional wives and children is not
exactly what you need just to the rear of your army when you
have a complicated battle on your hands.

Ensign Thomas Deacon of the 73rd Highlanders had been
wounded in the arm whilst fighting in one of the squares. He
got his wound dressed and then went back in search of his
wife, who was following him together with their three children. He looked for her in vain the whole night, and was so
exhausted that he collapsed and was taken into Brussels by a
baggage wagon. 'The poor wife, in the meantime, who had
heard from some of the men that her husband was wounded,
passed the whole night in searching for him' as well. She was,
to make matters worse, 'in the last state of pregnancy', and
'wearing only a black silk dress and light shawl'. As the Army
withdrew on 17 June she had no option but to walk back to

Brussels 'exposed to the violence of the terrific storm' which would break that afternoon.[56]

The scene that greeted the British Army the next morning, Saturday 17 June, was a sombre one. As they woke, to a colder morning, they saw the trampled cornfields and everywhere great piles of the dead. In front of Quatre Bras were heaps of metal with orange and blue, mixed with tartan and red, the massed corpses of the cuirassiers and highlanders. Mounds of red and blue marked where the squares had been. In front of Mathew Clay, on the edge of Bossu Wood, was a pile of dead Foot Guards 'laying very thick on the ground' and lying with the wounded who had been gathered for evacuation.[57] The light cavalry were now tasked with gathering what wounded they could, carrying them across the fronts of their saddles. Skirmishing continued with the French, but in a fairly desultory fashion. Simmons found a dead cuirassier officer and tried on his front cuirass, which he then paraded in front of his men. 'It was not wide enough for my brawny shoulders,' he confided, but his antics infuriated the watching French infantry, who took pot shots at him. One hit Sergeant Fairfoot, a valued Peninsular veteran who had been badly injured in the storming of Badajoz. Off came the cuirass, put to better use as a frying pan when the local farmer had produced eggs and bacon and 'some fowls'.[58]

The British and Allied commanders had an anxious morning, awaiting the anticipated French renewal of their attack; but it never materialised. Ney was, as we now know, awaiting Napoleon's orders and for the Emperor to join him. At nine a.m. a staff officer arrived with Wellington from Blücher confirming that the Prussian army was concentrating at Wavre, and Wellington confirmed in return that he would withdraw to the ridge line of Mont St Jean, just south of the Forest of Soignes and ten miles due west of Wavre. Orders were issued immediately for the infantry battalions to leave their skirmishers out but for their main bodies to concentrate from left and right and march north up the Brussels road through Genappe to their new positions. It was a very delicate time. Had the French attacked whilst the battalions were moving back it would have been difficult for them to reform from their columns.

In the 73rd a new officer, Lieutenant Strahan, had arrived in Thomas Morris's company overnight, one of the many still coming in from Ostend. He had been desperate to join his battalion in action, but had arrived too late. Morris had heard him talking during the night, hoping that there would still be plenty to do the next day. As the battalion moved off they were ordered to carry their muskets at the trail; that is, 'the middle of the firelock is grasped by the right hand, and carried horizontally, the muzzle in front'. As Lieutenant Strahan ordered his new command into file, the musket of the man immediately behind him went off accidentally, the ball smashing through his back and straight into his heart. 'The loose earth was removed with swords, a rude grave was formed, the body placed in it, covered over and the line, which had halted when the accident took place, now resumed its march.' The accident was caused by a stalk of rye getting round the flint, cocking it fully, and then around the trigger, and 'he, who had travelled with such extraordinary haste in pursuit of honour and glory' was no more.[59]

Wellington's luck held and by eleven a.m. the last of the infantry were away, leaving the cavalry and horse artillery under the command of Uxbridge to screen their rear. There does not seem to have been any attempt to brief the men as to what the new plan was; briefing and the passage of information was not really Wellington's style, often only passing the curtest of orders even to his senior commanders. None of them knew what had happened at Ligny, although they all realised from the noise and smoke that the Prussians had fought a major engagement. There was quite a bit of grumbling amongst the battalions as they started to march away, not least because they were leaving many of the wounded whom the light cavalry could not carry. They thought they had won a victory and that they should now be pursuing the French, the lack of activity from whom they thought might mean they were retreating. To Standish O'Grady, whose 7th Hussars were the last regiment and soon engaged in skirmishing, it was 'very unpleasant intelligence', and his men were annoyed that the French gave three loud cheers when they saw them move. O'Grady and his men, anxiously waiting alongside Mercer and his troop of horse artillery, then saw the French light fires. Someone remarked that it would not be long before they attacked as they always dined before they moved.[60] They were right and soon O'Grady was too busy to be annoyed. At one p.m. two things happened. First, Napoleon told Ney to move forward and the French advance began. Secondly, the weather, which had started cold, became overcast and sultry. As the French moved, the heavens unleashed the most violent thunderstorm, which continued all afternoon, some attributing its start to the vibrations from British cannon fire.

Uxbridge had divided his force into three columns. The two heavy brigades, together with O'Grady's 7th Hussars and the 23rd Light Dragoons, were to cover the main Brussels road, whilst the remaining light brigades deployed to the east and west. The heavy brigades moved off first, with the 23rd Light Dragoons and 7th Hussars coming behind them, soon to be closely pursued by the French 1st Lanciers, Ney's leading cavalry. The French advance concentrated on the main road towards Genappe but south of the village the 7th Hussars' delaying action was moderately effective. 'We continued disputing the ground by inches, until near 5 in the evening', O'Grady wrote to his father, and they continued to hold the French back until they came to the outskirts of Genappe itself. This gave them a problem, as they had to slow down and concentrate to pass through the defile where the main road narrowed into the high street and across the bridge over the Dyle. This was dangerous, as it would give the French an ideal opportunity to charge them. O'Grady's squadron was the very last, and they decided the best thing they could do was simply to gallop for it, which they duly did, just getting every man over the bridge and clear to the north of the last houses as 20 squadrons of French cavalry came up.

Uxbridge's plan was now to do the same thing to the French in reverse, and attack them as they emerged from the village, where they in turn would be delayed as they concentrated to file over the bridge. When the head of the column showed itself the 7th charged it. O'Grady's men were to the fore. 'Their front', O'Grady wrote, 'were lancers, their flanks were protected, for they were in the street, and the mass of cavalry in the rear was so great, that I defy them to go about. They therefore stood firm; we killed the officer who was in front, but we could not reach the men, as the lances of the front and rear rank kept the men at bay.' They kept trying and did not 'relinquish our efforts even after every endeavour had become useless, and I shall esteem it the greatest honour I can boast; to have belonged to that squadron who died in their ranks, rather than relinquishing the attack when success was not even possible'. It was certainly brave and honourable conduct, but it

didn't stop the French and it came at a terrible cost. Seven officers and 46 men were lost, although many were taken prisoner
rather than killed and were later to find their way back.[61] It was
one of the few engagements during the Waterloo campaign
when both sides' cavalry used their carbines. The French shot
three officers' horses but otherwise did not do much damage.
Thomas Playford watched them firing but although he reckoned they fired at each other for 20 minutes he did not see a
single man hit. As the 7th Hussars withdrew, the French cavalry continued their advance, now posing a significant threat to
the withdrawing British.

The 1st Life Guards had spent the previous night sleeping
with their horses just south of Bossu Wood. They were very
close to the French, and 50 men were dismounted and sent
forward as a screen. 'It was now most intensely hot, so much
so that we perspired copiously as we lay on the ground',[62]
Haddy James noted. 'We remained there until the afternoon,
watching the retreating army on our left, and an immensely
heavy cloud on our right, both of which augured us no good.
Their horses waited unconcernedly, munching the green
corn. At last the order came to mount, followed by that of
"the line will retire", which we now did, riding through fields
of rye as tall as ourselves on horseback. We had scarce commenced this movement when the thunderstorm which had
threatened us for so long burst over our heads with the most
tremendous peal I have ever heard, and a torrential fall of rain
soaked us to the skin almost instantly.' They rode through
Genappe, halting in column a few hundred yards further
north, watching the 7th Hussars' ineffectual charge. Edward
Kelly's squadron was at the rear of their column, and he and
Haddy James sat on their horses swigging what gin remained
in James's flask. Kelly commented, 'I should not be surprised

if we have a bit of a fight here. I believe the Duke is surprised that we have not been more pressed by the French before this.'[63]

He was right. No sooner had he spoken than Uxbridge rode up and said 'the Life Guards shall have this honour' and invited Kelly to charge, which he duly did most efficiently. His troop wheeled from column into line, they moved off at the trot, lined themselves up with the leading French lancers and as they came down to the village his trumpeter blew the charge. It was a textbook cavalry charge, over a short distance in open ground so that the troop did not lose formation. The French were taken by surprise, and the impact of the sheer size and mass of a heavy-cavalry squadron shattered them. Although the Life Guards lost 18 men, skewered on French lance points, they had temporarily stopped the French pursuit. The lancers turned tail and fled back through Genappe. Uxbridge was delighted: 'Well done, the Life Guards, you have saved the honour of the British cavalry', words which Kelly never seemed to tire of repeating for the rest of his life.[64]

Colonel Sir John Elley had been with Uxbridge, as his senior staff officer, and he could not resist the temptation to join Kelly's men, claiming that he had cut down two French lancers with a 'right and left' sword stroke. They brought back some prisoners from the French lancers; they were all very young and mounted on small horses and the Life Guards thought some of them were drunk. Their commanding officer, Colonel Sourd, who had not been captured, had, though, led them bravely. His right arm was hacked by six sabre strokes and was amputated in the field by Larrey, Napoleon's personal surgeon, who was travelling with the Emperor a little way behind. Sourd dictated a letter to Napoleon as he was under the knife, assaying that the greatest favour that the Emperor could grant him was to allow him to remain in command of his lancers. Captain John Kincaid of the 95th watched the charge as well. He wrote that the Life Guards were straight-forward fighters and 'the only young thing they showed was in everyone who got a roll in the mud (and owing to the slipperiness of the ground there were many) going off to the rear, according to Hyde Park custom, as being no longer fit to remain on parade',[65] which amused him, however untrue.

The cavalry brigades were supported throughout the withdrawal by both Mercer's and Gardiner's troops of horse artillery, and their guns, fired from a series of positions, were as effective in delaying the French as the cavalry. Liaison between the gunners and the cavalry they supported was good, but not perfect. Mercer had remained far behind, worried that Uxbridge and his staff were still not visible, and with dark masses of the French appearing on the hill opposite him. He had just unlimbered his guns and prepared them for firing when an infuriated cavalry commanding officer rode up, exclaiming, 'What are you doing here sir? You encumber my front, and we shall not be able to charge. Take your guns away sir; instantly, I say – take them away!' Luckily at that moment Uxbridge came back and told Mercer to fire as the French appeared in front of him and then get back as quickly as he could. Mercer was about to do so when he thought he saw Napoleon, 'that mighty man of war – that astonishing genius . . . Now I saw him'. It had long been his ambition to set eyes on the great man and he hesitated, much to Uxbridge's fury, who was yelling 'Fire! Fire!' at him. Mercer's first gun 'seemed to burst the clouds overhead, for its report was instantly followed by an awful clap of thunder, and lightning that almost blinded us, whilst the rain came down as if a waterspout had broken over us'. Mercer was irritated to see that, somehow, Whinyates had managed to get his rocket troop between him and the enemy. He had disobeyed the order to retreat and 'remained somewhere in the neighbourhood until this moment, hoping to share whatever might be going on'.[66]

'We', Mercer continued, 'then galloped for our lives through the storm, striving to gain the houses of the hamlets', by which he meant Genappe. Uxbridge rode with them, telling Mercer to follow him as they reached the apparent safety of the village. Taking the poor gunners down a twisting street, Uxbridge finally emerged on the southern edge only to find himself within 50 yards of a large group of French *chasseurs*. 'By God! We are all prisoners,' exclaimed Uxbridge, and, putting his horse at a garden bank, he cleared it leaving poor Mercer to extricate his guns as best he could.[67] 'Reverse by unlimbering!' Mercer shouted. This was a complicated manoeuvre at the best of times, but in the face of the enemy and in a very restricted space it was almost impossible, but his men managed to do it, unlimbering the guns, turned round with one wheel up on the bank, the limber passed to the other side and then hitched up again. Mercer later admitted he never really expected them to achieve this, and the French cavalry stood watching them in stupid inactivity.

Once turned round, the gunners galloped back through the village, hardly able to see for the mud and sheet rain, just getting clear of the bridge before the French cavalry came up. They established a new position outside Genappe, alongside the waiting heavy cavalry. Here they found Whinyates's men once again; they had set up a little iron triangle in the road with a rocket lying against it. It fired and, to Mercer's amazement, actually hit a French horse-artillery battery; its gunners fled. The second and third rockets did not perform so well. None of them followed the first, most 'arriving about the middle of the ascent, took a vertical direction, whilst some actually turned back on ourselves – and one of these, following me like a squib until its shell exploded, actually put me in more danger than all the fire of the enemy throughout the day'. The French gunners saw what was happening, returned to their guns, and started firing case-shot. It was time for Whinyates to withdraw.

There were other skirmishes and clashes during the afternoon, but the action at Genappe was the last serious French threat to disrupt the British withdrawal. By the early evening the Army was beginning to occupy its new positions, with the French now some 1,000 yards behind. The joint cavalry and horse-artillery action had covered the withdrawal admirably. Uxbridge called it 'the prettiest field-day of cavalry and horse-artillery [he] ever witnessed', which, although self-congratulatory, was probably true.

4

18 JUNE 1815

Morning and Afternoon

'What a sight, even to we old campaigners, but more particularly to the young soldiers', thought Thomas Wheeler of the 51st Foot, as he witnessed the withdrawing Army near the ridge at Mont St Jean. 'The cavalry retiring in sullen silence as often as opportunity served would wheel round to check the enemy. The rain beating with violence, guns roaring, repeated bright flashes of lightning attended with tremendous volleys of Thunder that shook the very earth and seemed to mock us with contempt.'[1] Surgeon John Haddy James had ridden on back after treating Captain White, who had been severely wounded by a lance which had gone through his back into his rib cage. As James reached the top of the ridge he looked back over the cavalry coming in. 'The view was of the most tremendous description, commanding the field of Waterloo and an immense tract of country, dark with woods and coloured with columns of troops, both French and English. The storm was breaking up, leaving patches of light and grey isolated showers in different parts of the landscape. At intervals wraiths of vapour were gathering.'[2] He soon saw his own 1st Life Guards coming in,

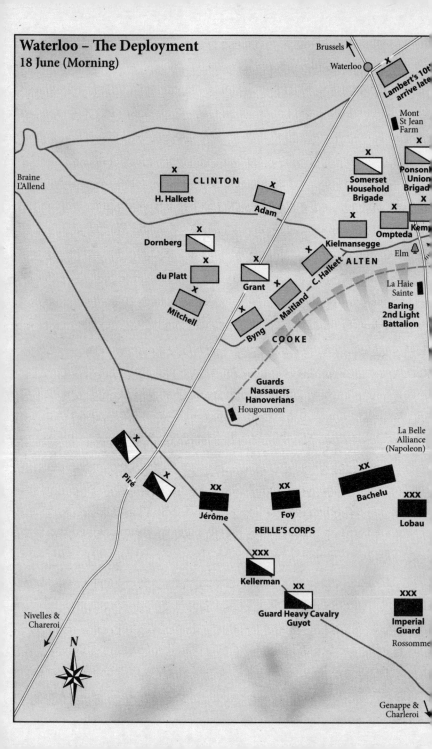

Waterloo – The Deployment
18 June (Morning)

Brussels

Waterloo

Lambert's 10th arrive late

Mont St Jean Farm

Braine L'Allend

CLINTON

x
H. Halkett

x
Adam

x
Somerset Household Brigade

x
Ponsonby Union Brigade

x
Dornberg

x
Kielmansegge

x
Ompteda

x
Kem

x
du Platt

x
Grant

x
C. Halkett

ALTEN

Elm

x
Mitchell

x
Maitland

La Haie Sainte

x
Byng

COOKE

Baring 2nd Light Battalion

Guards Nassauers Hanoverians

Hougoumont

La Belle Alliance (Napoleon)

x
Piré

x

xx
Jérôme

xx
Foy

xx
Bachelu

xxx
Lobau

REILLE'S CORPS

xxx
Kellerman

xx
Guard Heavy Cavalry Guyot

xxx
Imperial Guard

Rossomme

Nivelles & Charleroi

N

Genappe & Charleroi

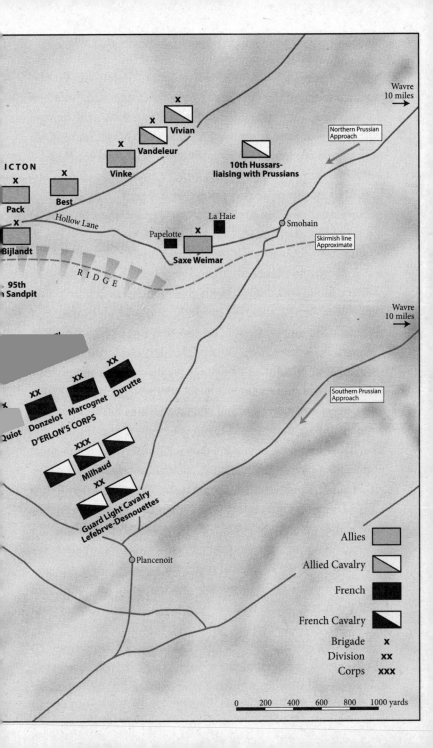

ICTON

x
Pack

x
Best

x
Bijlandt

Hollow Lane

95th
in Sandpit

R I D G E

x
Vinke

x
Vandeleur

x
Vivian

10th Hussars-
liaising with Prussians

Papelotte

La Haie

○ Smohain

x
Saxe Weimar

Northern Prussian
Approach

Skirmish line
Approximate

Wavre
10 miles →

Wavre
10 miles →

xx
Quiot

xx
Donzelot

xx
Marcognet

xx
Durutte

D'ERLON'S CORPS

xxx
Milhaud

xx
Guard Light Cavalry
Lefebrve-Desnouettes

Southern Prussian
Approach

○ Plancenoit

Allies	

Allied Cavalry	

French	

French Cavalry	

Brigade   **x**

Division   **xx**

Corps   **xxx**

0   200   400   600   800   1000 yards

'so covered with black mud that their faces were hardly distinguishable, and the colour of their scarlet uniforms invisible. The ground was a quagmire and if any man took a fall he rose with a coat of mud from head to foot. The horses were in no better case.' Actually Colonel Ferrior, who was leading 1st Life Guards, got lost, and the regiment ended up behind their intended position in the Forest of Soignes. Amidst much grumbling they retraced their steps and found their bivouac in a dip behind the ridge.

The Army was in position by the time it got dark, which was a significant achievement and owed much to De Lancey's staff work. A withdrawal, with the French cavalry harassing them, and across soaking ground, was a complicated and dangerous manoeuvre, but the gap that the cavalry action at Genappe had opened up allowed them to complete the move into their new positions without further significant disruption and, Wellington hoped, unobserved. His intention was to conceal his army behind the ridge, out of view of the French so that they would not know his exact positions nor in what strength he occupied them. At dusk the French were approximately 1,400 yards away, along the ridge to the south of Mont St Jean, straddling a crossroads with a small inn called La Belle Alliance, but lower than the Mont St Jean feature and unable to see over it. As Napoleon himself drew up, he told his accompanying horse artillery to fire speculative shots at the Allied positions, trying to gauge whether he was facing the main force or just a temporary blocking position; Napoleon was still fixated on his idea that Wellington would withdraw west towards the Channel, just as he had convinced himself that Blücher was falling back on Liège. To Wellington's understandable fury, two British batteries, Cleeves's and Lloyd's, returned fire, confirming to Napoleon that he did indeed face the main Allied army and that he would most likely have to fight a pitched battle the next day.[3]

That Allied army was very wet and very muddy and now settled down to the most miserable night many of them could remember. They had no greatcoats, which had been thought unnecessary in the summer and which had been collected and sent back to Ostend, although they did have their smart new blankets. The rain, which had looked as if might have let up in the early evening, now 'poured down in torrents all night, and that so powerfully as to preclude all possibility of kindling a fire'.[4] The ground was already soaked when the army arrived and it now became even wetter. 'There was no choice; we had to settle down in the mud and filth as best we could. I looked for a drier place, but it was all mud,' complained William Gibney, Assistant Surgeon to the 15th Hussars. 'We got some straw and boughs of trees, and with these tried to lessen the mud and to make a rough shelter against the torrents of rain that fell all night; wrapping around us our cloaks, and huddling close together, we lay in the mud and wooed the drowsy God.'[5]

In Mathew Clay's company of the 3rd Foot Guards two men out of every four were detailed to unpack their blankets. These had been previously prepared to act as makeshift tents, with button holes stitched into the corners and along each side of the centre and fitted with small cords. They now used two of their muskets as tent poles, pegged out the long sides of the blankets, and then all four men crawled underneath with their kit in some effort to keep dry. It was fairly pointless, and they were all soon even wetter, leaving Clay with the added problem of trying to pack away soaking blankets with numb fingers when they had to crash out after the French artillery opened up; Clay was not the sort of soldier to leave his blanket behind, even under artillery fire.[6]

There were a few farm huts around and Haddy James's men found him a space in one. He decided that as he was already soaking he might as well undress and put on what dry clothes he had with him. 'It seemed', he wrote later, 'a cruel thing to strip naked under a pouring rain, but it was the best thing I could do.'[7] Finding the corner of a chair, he huddled in front of a meagre fire all night without sleep, being too wet to leave it and lie down. He spent much of it regretting that he had allowed Kelly to drain his gin flask. Even Charles Foster of the Royals, who had greatly amused the Secretary by equipping himself 'with a double oilskin and had taken every precaution was alike wet to the skin with everyone else in two minutes'. Foster would never be dry again in his life.[8] William Hay decided the best tactic was to lay his cloak on the highest ridge of mud he could find. He 'never slept sounder' but when he woke he found he had sunk six inches overnight and was now encased in water and clay.[9]

What made matters worse was that there was still no food other than what the men carried with them, supplies which had already had to last 36 hours. The cavalry had dumped their hay nets in preparation for action at Quatre Bras, so neither was there anything for the horses except wet grass. Wellington had relaxed the usually harsh rules about 'living off the country' as looting was termed, but even when Thomas Jeremiah, who felt that 'hunger bites harder than a wet shirt',[10] went into the village of Waterloo he couldn't find anything and only came back with gin, which, on an empty stomach, made several of the less hardened men fall down drunk. The gunners of Mercer's troop had managed to trap an unlucky stray chicken but none of them knew how to 'pluck and truss it until the troop tailor undertook the important affair'.[11]

William Wheeler had found a man selling brandy and hollands gin as they marched through the village of Waterloo, the 51st not having been at Quatre Bras, and he and his company had filled their flasks. As night came on they were wet to the skin but, having plenty of liquor they were 'wet and comfortable. It would be impossible for any one to form an opinion of what we endured this night. We sat on our knapsacks until daylight without fires; the water ran in streams from the cuffs of our jackets, in short we were as wet as if we had been plunged overhead in a river. We had', he added, 'one consolation, we knew the enemy were in the same plight.'[12]

Arguably the enemy was worse off. The Allied army had at least got into position in daylight, whereas most of Napoleon's troops came up in the dark, exhausted after a long march through the mud. There was no food for them either, and many regiments broke their march to pillage. The infantry of the Imperial Guard got completely lost, not something they were expected to do, ending up several miles from their intended position between La Belle Alliance and the hamlet of Rossomme, where the Braine-l'Alleud road branches off the main road north of Genappe. The cavalry mostly slept on their horses, which was not a very good way of keeping dry nor of resting their horses, who, already unfit, had now been marching for three days, mostly without any fodder. This would tell the next day. The French move continued to indicate faulty staff work, and a lack of clear and timely orders. Soult's system was evidently under strain. Napoleon himself slept at the farm of Le Caillou, about a mile and a half south of La Belle Alliance, and half a mile behind Rossomme, again on the main road.

The rain stopped early on the morning of Sunday 18 June, leaving, as so often after a violent storm, a bright clear day. 'The sun began to warm us about 7 o'clock' and the Army's first thought remained food.[13] The skirmishers, who had been deployed in front of the ridgeline all night so they could warn of any French moves, were called in, much to their relief, and foraging parties were sent back by their regiments to see what they could find. Some were quite lucky. Major-General Frederick Adam, who commanded the 3rd Brigade, all of whom were light infantry, gave his men leave to plunder three farmhouses in the nearby hamlet of Merbe Braine, which revealed a rich haul of 'beef, pork, veal, duck, chicken, potatoes and other delicacies' which the 95th made into 'as delicious a breakfast as I ever made an attack upon'.[14]

Thomas Playford went with Corporal Shaw to see what they could find for their squadron of 2nd Life Guards. They had suffered a particularly miserable night standing with their horses 'on soaked ploughed ground, shivering, wet, and hungry. Some soldiers complained of the hardship, some jested at their sufferings, and others tried to guess at what would take place on the morrow; and some hinted at the probability that not many of us would see the 19th of June.' Sadly they were correct as 2nd Life Guards would suffer the worst casualties of any regiment, but for the time being 'no one believed in gloomy prognostications. We pulled down a fence and made a fire, but we gained little good by standing round it, for while one side was warming the other was cold and wet.' As the Reserve Champion of All England and the reclusive farmer's son from Yorkshire searched for food they had the good luck to find an abandoned bread wagon. They took a sack full of loaves each and then found a farmhouse with 'cheese, butter, or bacon, to be eaten with the bread'.[15]

As well as foraging, the Army also looked to its weapons. 'For the first time ever known in our army, the cavalry were ordered to grind the backs of their swords, so as our Captain Clark said, we should have to use both sides. It was thought by the men that this order had been given because we had to contend with a large number of French cuirassiers, who had steel armour, and through this we should have to cut', wrote Private Smithies of the Royals. Corporal Shaw, whose word seems to have been law in 2nd Life Guards, told them that this would make it easier to swing at the back of the cuirassiers' necks; this was where they were most vulnerable, their fronts being so encased in steel. It is an easier sword stroke on a galloping horse to swing a sword straight back rather than trying to turn to use the front edge. Actually this was an old Peninsular trick, but that several cavalrymen mention it shows how worried they were about the cuirassiers and their fearsome reputation.

The infantry cleaned and reloaded their muskets. It says something for the lined cartouche boxes that their cartridges seem to have remained relatively dry. It was an established drill to reload muskets prior to an action. The more carefully the process was carried out, and the more deliberate the wadding and ramming, the tighter would be the resulting seal and the more accurate the subsequent shot. 'The powder was', in fact, 'moistened in the piece and completely washed out of the pan', so the 'shots [the balls] were drawn, muskets sponged out, locks oiled and everything put to rights'. The easiest way to get rid of the old 'moistened' powder in the barrels was to fire it off without the ball, so there was a general sound of irregular firing along the lines, which the more nervous thought was French skirmishers advancing. They also fitted new flints.[16]

The artillery's cartridges had also been kept fairly dry in their covered caissons, under which many of their crews had also slept. It hadn't done them much good, and even though Mercer's troop had a small tent, it was soon soaked as well. The crews wrapped themselves in their wet blankets and huddled together for warmth, none of them really sleeping but lying in silence and thinking of their lucky escape from Genappe that afternoon and of what might be about to happen. The 'old Peninsular hands disdaining to complain before their Johnny Newcome comrades, and these fearing to do so lest they should provoke some such remarks as "Lord have mercy on your poor tender carcass! What would such as you have done in the Pyrenees?" or "Oho my boy this is but child's play to what we saw in Spain"'. Mercer had given up trying to sleep and instead smoked a cigar sitting under an umbrella that one of his officers had with him, which was brave given that Wellington had very firm views that umbrellas had no place on the battlefield. As it got light Mercer sent back ammunition wagons under a bombardier to collect fresh cartridges from a dump that had been established on the Brussels road. The bombardier, the name given to corporals in the artillery, returned quickly not only with the ammunition but also a cask of rum and beef, biscuit and oatmeal, which they 'eagerly started to cook'[17] and which must have been welcome after that one chicken.

Several regiments were not quite where they should have been, having moved in when it was almost dark, and there was now also a general adjustment of the line. This, together with the cleaning, cooking and general sorting-out meant that there was a continual rumble of noise, 'the buzzing [of voices] resembled the distant roar of the sea against a rocky coast'[18]. About eight a.m. most regiments also issued rum, which had come up from Brussels, and which was 'the most welcome thing' Thomas Howell 'ever received', he being 'so stiff and sore from the rain'.[19] Even from their new positions, they were still under the top of the ridge and few of them could see much more than the ground and troops immediately around them; very few could see the French on the opposite slope, which was probably just as well. Thomas Morris did get to see them, though, as, after managing to shave and even put on a fresh shirt so that he felt 'tolerably comfortable', he went down the ridge to La Haie Sainte farmhouse to find water; from there he could see most of the battlefield.[20]

The ridge behind which the Allies were sheltering ran for about a mile and three-quarters from a cluster of hamlets around Papelotte in the east, or the left of the Allied line, to Braine-l'Alleud in the west, which was their right flank. It was broken, almost in the middle, by the Charleroi–Brussels road, which cut the ridgeline at a right angle. Around Papelotte the ground was, and still is, close, wooded and broken, with poor visibility. Wavre, where Blücher was concentrating, was ten miles to the east of Papelotte, via small and overgrown lanes along which movement was slow. There were two usable routes. The more southerly ran via the villages of Chapelle St Robert and Chapelle St Lambert to Lasne where there was a single narrow bridge over the River Lasne. It then crossed the small Bois de Paris before arriving uphill into Plancenoit, which sizeable village formed the right of the French position. The more northerly ran via Rixensart, crossed the Lasne short of Genval, and then passed the hamlet of Ohain, where, passing north of Papelotte, it ran along the ridgeline. It is easier to understand the significance of these routes on the map on pages 174–5.

From Papelotte west the ground opened up into wide fields. Along the ridgeline itself these were mostly rough grass and scrub, but the valley was intermittently sown with rye which, nearing harvest, was as tall as it had been at Quatre Bras. Up the centre of the Allied position ran the main Charleroi and Genappe to Brussels road, the route the Army had taken on its withdrawal the previous day and the axis along which Napoleon was advancing. Just before it crossed the ridge it passed a substantial farm complex called La Haie Sainte, which roughly translates as the Holy Hedge. Behind the farm, and as the road disappeared over the ridge, was a small crossroads where it met the lane from Papelotte to Braine-l'Alleud, a continuation of the Ohain road from Wavre. This lane was 'hollow' – in other words, sunk down – and lined with beech hedges, and was a serious obstacle, more so on the east end of the ridge and particularly so just above La Haie Sainte, which took its name from them. Just north of the crossroads, and again on the main road, were the farm buildings of Mont St Jean, from which the ridge took its name.

Beyond the Brussels road, the open ground continued westwards to a cluster of woods and buildings around the small château at Hougoumont, a comfortable country house with a walled farmyard, formal gardens, also walled, and a large orchard extending east. In front of the château, to the south, was a substantial wood, which has all but disappeared today. From La Haie Sainte to Hougoumont was about 1,000 yards. West of Hougoumont the ridge falls away sharply and merges into downland, although today it is dissected by a motorway. Behind the ridge, to the north, lay the sizeable Forest of Soignes, where movement off the road was difficult. Once it crossed the ridge, the Brussels road passed the farm complex of Mont St Jean, and then ran through the village of Waterloo, before disappearing into the forest to re-emerge in the outskirts of Brussels itself. Today it is a dual carriageway.

The ridgeline had been selected by De Lancey, who had been told by Wellington to find a defensive position which blocked the Charleroi–Brussels road south of Waterloo, or in other words before it entered the Forest of Soignes. Wellington was not specific about exactly where, but De Lancey was schooled in the defensive tactics of the Peninsula and knew what was required. The idea of a ridge was twofold: first, it offered protection from French artillery, always the part of the Napoleon's army that the British feared most; and secondly it meant the enemy had to attack uphill, which favoured the British line formation. De Lancey could have chosen the lesser ridge to the south, which would have given more space between the Army and the forest if things had gone wrong, but the Mont St Jean position was higher and had the added advantage of covering both the Charleroi and Nivelles roads to Brussels should the French swing to the west, their left, and try to take the Allies in the flank. Wellington remained concerned that this might be Napoleon's plan right up until the main attack started. It was the French who now occupied the more southerly ridgeline. With their right wing, in the east, in front of the village of Plancenoit, almost opposite and about a mile and a half from Papelotte, the French positions stretched across the open ground, over the Brussels road at the inn at La Belle Alliance, from where Napoleon had observed the Allies the previous evening, continuing in open ground to their left, which was in front of Hougoumont Wood, and finishing on the Nivelles road. Whereas the Allied positions were hidden, every move the French made was clearly visible to Wellington and his staff.

The second disadvantage of the French position, as De Lancey had calculated, was that they would be attacking uphill and across saturated ground. The Allied ridgeline was sharper in 1815 than it is today, much of the earth having been excavated to build the enormous Belgian Lion Mound memorial (for a modern guide to the battlefield see page 413), and it represented a significant climb even when dry. The storms of the preceding 24 hours had made land already soaking from a particularly wet spring even heavier and very slippery, which made it difficult for the French to manoeuvre their larger guns and imposed additional strain on their already unfit and tired horses. The soil in the valley between the opposing armies is also different to that on the ridgelines. Napoleon thought if he delayed his attack the ground would dry out; it may have done where he was standing, but the clay in the valley would hold water for several days.[21]

The adjustments Wellington made to his positions at first light saw the Allies occupying the ridge from Papelotte to Hougoumont, and are shown on the plan on pages 174–5. On his far left, from where he expected the Prussians to appear, he placed two brigades of light cavalry. Vivian's brigade, with Henry Murray's 18th Hussars and the 1st Hussars of the King's German Legion, were the furthest east, with the 10th Hussars given the task of liaising with Blücher's forces. Next came Vandeleur's brigade, the 11th Light Dragoons with George Farmer, William Hay and the 12th Light Dragoons, and Tomkinson's 16th Light Dragoons. Both light-cavalry brigades were drawn back from the lane, along a farm track which still runs a few hundred yards north, and which offered more cover where the ridgeline began to flatten out. In front of them, in the broken ground around Papelotte Farm, and the farms of La Haie (a different one – not La Haie Sainte) and Frichermont, and in the hamlet of Smohain, was Prince Bernhard of Saxe-Weimar's Nassau brigade, who had suffered so much in Bossu Wood. To the right of the light cavalry came Vincke's Hanoverian brigade, then Best's Hanoverians, the same men who had lined the Namur road at Quatre Bras and who had already lost one battalion to the cuirassiers.

To their right were the two British infantry brigades of Picton's Fifth Division. First, Pack's brigade, with the 1st, the 42nd Highlanders with James Anton, the 44th and the 92nd Highlanders, all substantially reduced from the fighting two days before. The 42nd had formed a hollow square as they arrived, to witness one of their privates flogged for an undetermined transgression at Quatre Bras. His offence is not recorded but it is likely that he did something that endangered the square. Anton felt the punishment was justified as 'it is better that this should be awarded and inflicted, than to see hundreds fall victim to the rapacity that might ensue from not timely visiting the aggressor with punishment'.[22] Then, to their right, hard up against the Brussels road at the crossroads were Kempt's brigade, with the 28th, 32nd, 79th and the 95th with Andrew Barnard and George Simmonds. They occupied an old sandpit which stood just at the south-east corner of the junction, and which they fortified after a fashion with a latticework of trees and branches. Behind the crossroads was a tree, by which Wellington would spend much of the day and which afforded a good view south over the valley to the French lines. In front of Kempt's men were the rest of Perponcher's men, Bijlandt's 1st Netherlands infantry brigade, just forward of the sunken lane; his second brigade was Prince Bernhard's, already deployed around Papelotte. This was where the Allies were weakest, with understrength battalions and a preponderance of Netherlands troops.

Across the road, where Wellington felt the main attack would develop, he placed Alten's Third Division. The first of their brigades was Ompteda's brigade of the King's German Legion, with Edmund Wheatley in the 5th line battalion; then came Kielmansegge's Hanoverians and Halkett's British, with the shaken battalions who had suffered so much in Bossu Wood – the 30th, with Edward Macready, the 33rd, hoping for a better day than that they had endured at Quatre Bras, the 69th, minus their Colour, and the 73rd Highlanders, with Thomas Morris. One battalion of Ompteda's King's German Legion, the riflemen of Major George Baring's 2nd Light, with Frederick Lindau, was detached forward, and told to hold the farm buildings at La Haie Sainte, about 300 yards in front of the crossroads. Behind the crossroads were the two brigades of heavy cavalry, those lines of brick-red menace. On the east, behind Kempt's men, was Ponsonby's Union Brigade; here were Ben the Ruler and the Secretary with the Royals and the Inniskilling Dragoons in the first line, and the Scots Greys with Francis Kinchant and Charles Ewart in the second.

Across the road, drawn up in the dead ground behind Ompteda's men, who found them a reassuring sight, was Edward Somerset's Household Brigade, formed in two lines. On the right, in the front line, were 1st Life Guards with Edward Kelly, fresh from his much self-advertised glory at Genappe, and their surgeon, Haddy James. Forward dressing stations had been set up in La Haie Sainte and Hougoumont, but the main collection point for the wounded was behind the crossroads at Mont St Jean Farm. Beside them were the King's Dragoon Guards, with Private Thomas Hasker. The 2nd Life Guards were on the left, with Corporal Shaw and Thomas Playford, although at this stage both were still away foraging;

behind them, in the second line, were the Blues, with John Bingley. On the right was their commanding officer, Robert Hill, with his trumpeter, Tom Evans, whom he had initially refused to bring with him, saying he was too fat.

Beyond Alten's Third Division came the First Guards Division, Maitland's and Byng's brigades, with their four light companies detached to garrison the château and buildings at Hougoumont, where Mathew Clay had spent the night. They were joined by 200 of Kielmansegge's Hanoverians and one of Prince Bernhard's Nassau battalions. On their right, and astride the Nivelles–Brussels road, was Mitchell's 4th Brigade, Frank Tidy with his very young battalion of the 14th, the 23rd, and the 51st with William Wheeler. Behind the Guards were the two remaining light-cavalry brigades, Dörnberg's, with the 23rd Light Dragoons, and the two King's German Legion light-cavalry regiments, and then Grant's brigade, with Standish O'Grady and the 7th Hussars, the 13th Light Dragoons and the 15th Hussars. Behind them again was Clinton's Second Division, in reserve, and able to deploy forward to block either the main Charleroi–Brussels or the Nivelles–Brussels road. Clinton had a King's German Legion brigade under du Platt, a Hanoverian brigade under Halkett and then the 3rd British Brigade under Adam.

His troops thought the world of Adam. He was 34 at Waterloo, having been in the Army since he was 14, and one of his private soldiers described him as as 'brave a soldier as can be'.[23] He had two light-infantry battalions, the 52nd Light Infantry, under Sir John Colbourne, with Thomas Howell in their ranks, and the 71st Highland Light Infantry under Thomas Reynell, as well as the 2nd Battalion of the 95th Rifles, and two companies of the 3rd Battalion (the first being under Andrew Barnard under Kempt). Behind them again were the mauled Brunswickers, raw about the loss of their duke; and to their right were two of the less reliable Netherlands brigades, from Chassé's Third Netherlands Infantry Division, in Braine-l'Alleud, which Wellington probably hoped was a safer place for them. Finally there was Lambert's brigade, literally just off the ships from America. They came up to join the Army after marching 50 miles from Ghent, arriving behind the Mont St Jean crossroads at 10.30 a.m. It had three British battalions – the 4th, who had suffered badly at the siege of New Orleans and who were short of captains as a result, the 27th, an Irish battalion confusingly also called the Inniskillings like the 6th Dragoons, and of whom we will be hearing much more, and the 40th, with Sergeant William Lawrence, commanded by Major Arthur Rowley Heyland. (Lambert's fourth battalion, the 81st, had been left in Brussels.)

Heyland was one of the very few men to write home on the eve of Waterloo, something he must have done during a brief halt on their forced march from Ghent. Telling his poor wife Mary, pregnant with their seventh child, that 'I cannot help thinking it is almost impossible I should escape either wounds or death', he left detailed and poignant instructions as to what she do, that their sons should be educated at the Military College, and that they should all follow him into the Army, except Arthur, who wasn't strong enough, advice the poor woman may have felt was not, in the circumstances, exactly what she wanted to hear. She should sell their Irish property, the Heylands being an Ulster family, and buy a house in Wales, 'or elsewhere if you prefer it, but I would advise you, my love, to choose a permanent residence'. The letter then becomes very touching: 'My Mary, let the recollection console you that the happiest days of my life have been from your love and affection, and that I die loving only you, and with a fervent hope that our souls may be reunited hereafter and part no more. The only regret I shall have in quitting this world will arise from the sorrow it will cause you and your children'.[24]

Wellington spaced his artillery batteries out along his line. The horse-artillery batteries were with the light-cavalry brigades; three batteries were in reserve, held centrally behind the crossroads. One battery, Ross's, was behind La Haie Sainte, with its guns initially pointing down the road, two batteries were in front of the Third Division, two in front of the First Guards, and two more were back with Clinton's division in reserve. The Brunswick batteries were with their own battalions. Mercer was on the right, on the ridge behind Hougoumont, with Grant's 5th Cavalry Brigade.

About 200 yards in front of the ridge, thus clearly visible to the French, the skirmish line was re-established. This was made up mostly from the light companies of the infantry battalions, the Foot Guards' light companies being in Hougoumont itself. From there the line stretched from the edge of the Hougoumont orchard to La Haie Sainte, and then eastwards, gradually creeping further south as the ground dictated, so that its eastern end linked up with the Nassauers in Papelotte. Traditionally the 95th Rifles would have been in the skirmish line as well, but they were kept back around the sandpit at Mont St Jean crossroads, or with Adam's brigade.

Wellington's deployment had to take into account that, although he was now reasonably confident that Napoleon would attack, he did not know exactly where. It was only later on the 18th that it became clear that the French would make the Charleroi–Brussels road their main axis. Wellington still thought it possible that Napoleon might try to outflank him to the west, cutting him off from his links to the Channel ports and attempting to take Brussels via Mons. He had in his initial deployment from Brussels therefore sent Lord 'Daddy' Hill with 17,500 of his corps to the area of Hal, about ten miles west of Waterloo. Most of Hill's troops were Netherlanders, including the Dutch Indian Brigade, but he also had one British and one Hanoverian brigade. By the time Napoleon's intentions were clear, it was too late to recall them, although Hill himself did ride back to command the right wing.

Only 1,200 yards away from them, across the valley, Napoleon's legions were finally sorting themselves out. This was taking some time after their late arrival the previous evening, and the state of the ground made movement slow. Effectively Napoleon put his two strongest corps in line: d'Erlon's, tired from their rather pointless marching of two days before but which had still not been engaged, on the right of the Charleroi–Brussels road; and Reille's, which had been so heavily involved at Quatre Bras, on the left of La Belle Alliance between the Charleroi and Nivelles roads. In the middle, straddling the Charleroi road and forming a second echelon, was Lobau's smaller corps, kept in column formation; and behind them, central and in reserve as was its custom, was the Imperial Guard – the Young Guard in front, then the Middle Guard, and finally the Grenadiers and *chasseurs* of the Old Guard. Behind d'Erlon's corps was Milhaud's cavalry corps, and behind Reille was Kellerman's, almost exactly as it had been at Quatre Bras. Much as Wellington had despatched Hill on a separate mission, so Napoleon was without Grouchy, who was still pursuing the supposedly defeated Prussians with 30,000 men some way well to the east of where Blücher was actually gathering his army.

Ney remained nominally in tactical command of the troops at Waterloo, although Napoleon would in fact direct the course of the battle from his command post which he set up near La Belle Alliance. What Napoleon did very differently was to mass his artillery, a common tactic of his, detaching guns from his various corps and assembling 60 cannon, including 18 twelve-pounders, and 20 howitzers in a Grand Battery. He placed this about 350 yards forward of his main line, on the forward slope where a half ridge of high ground that ran for about 900 yards in front of d'Erlon's corps made a natural gun position. Deploying the guns forward meant that the range to the Allied lines was reduced, to on average about 600 yards, greatly increasing the effectiveness of the six-pounders in particular. It did not worry Napoleon that his guns were so far exposed from the cover of his infantry as his intention was to attack, which was why he needed the artillery as far forward as possible.

No one knows exactly how many troops were to fight this day. On paper Wellington had about 73,000 men at Waterloo, allowing for those detached at Hal and for a rough estimate of losses at Quatre Bras; 14,000 of these were cavalry and 5,000 were gunners. However, no one had taken an accurate count of exactly who had been lost over the previous two days, except the sergeant-majors responsible for manning in each squadron and company, and their returns had not been col-lated. Napoleon, allowing for those detached with Grouchy, had marginally more at about 77,000, but he had significantly more artillery with 246 guns, including 36 of his powerful twelve-pounders, those wonderful brass affairs known as 'the Emperor's Beautiful Daughters', against the Allies' 157, although Wellington did, of course, also have Whinyates's rockets.[25]

It is hard for modern readers to imagine just how close the distances involved at Waterloo are and how very localised were the various actions during the day. The armies started only 1,200 yards apart and the nature of the fighting meant that much of it was hand to hand. The skirmishers on both sides were close enough to talk to one another across no man's land.[26] The action took place in a box which was roughly two miles long and about one mile deep. You can walk from Papelotte to Hougoumont in about half an hour, and gallop it on a horse in under five minutes. Into this confined space, roughly 200,000 men, once Blücher arrived, and 60,000 horses would fire, hack, smash and gorge at each other. The size of battlefields is governed by the range of and ability to target weapons, by the troops' ability to move and by their commander's ability to control them. At Waterloo the weapon with the longest range, Napoleon's twelve-pounders, could fire effectively only 900 yards, and the most common weapon, the musket, was, as we have seen, only useful under 200 yards and ideally at 100. All the other weapons were swords or bayonets, which necessitated hand-to-hand fighting, so we should not be surprised that the battlefield was so small, or that the carnage was so concentrated. By way of contrast, a modern battle tank can fire a direct shot over two miles, the whole length of the Waterloo battlefield. Modern field artillery would have engaged the French as they were leaving Genappe, five miles away, and could have done so much further out. A machine gun sited on Mont St Jean ridge would have destroyed the Imperial Guard back behind La Belle Alliance. Such is the progress, or otherwise, of military technology.

Napoleon's plan was simple. Assuming that the Prussians were a spent force, and that Grouchy would deal with any remaining threat on his right or eastern flank, he intended now to smash his way through the Allies by concentrating overwhelming force to break what he thought was a weakly held line. He would do this by a preliminary bombardment, hence his assembling the Grand Battery, then a massed infantry attack which would be followed up by his cavalry. The Imperial Guard would administer the *coup de grâce* should it be needed. His aim was to be in Brussels by nightfall with a defeated British Army fleeing back towards Ostend. He had even ordered his dinner – lamb, well done. Napoleon had never faced British infantry before, and he was warned by his generals who had fought in Spain that, when well positioned and commanded, they could be a formidable adversary. Both Soult and Reille warned of the dangers of a frontal attack, Reille even daring to say that that 'When well posted, as Wellington knows how to post them, I consider them invincible by a frontal attack'. He advised the Emperor to consider a flanking move, as Wellington had feared, continuing 'but [the British Army] is less flexible than ours. If one cannot beat them by direct attack, one can do so by manoeuvring'.

A flanking attack, from the area of Braine-l'Alleud, where the ground was open, would have nullified some of the advantages the ridge gave the Allies, and given Wellington a problem as he would have had to manoeuvre his very inexperienced army through 90 degrees. But Napoleon was not to be moved. He told Reille that 'You think Wellington is a great general because he beat you. I tell you that he is a bad general and that English troops are bad troops, and that we will shortly make short work of them.' Neither was he prepared to listen when Jérôme reported that a sympathetic waiter in the inn at Genappe had heard some of Wellington's staff talking about joining up with the Prussians at the 'entrance to the forest of Soignes'. He snorted that such a juncture was impossible after Ligny, that the Prussians could not hope to be effective again for two days and that anyway Grouchy was 'at their heels'.[27]

Who knows what was really going through Napoleon's mind? Events in France were certainly pressing, and he knew that he needed a swift and decisive victory to silence his many critics in Paris. He probably saw the urgency of taking Brussels more than his generals, and he felt that he could sweep Wellington's mongrel army aside. His tactics had worked so very well so many times in the past. The artillery, the massed and menacing columns, the threatening drums, the fear of the Imperial Guard, the élite cuirassiers: all relied to a degree on destroying the enemy's morale so that they were half beaten before the actual attack began. Napoleon was confident that would happen again.

Wellington's plan in response was equally simple. He would defend the ridge until the Prussians came to join him when, he reasoned, together they would be strong enough to stop Napoleon's advance. For much of the day his telescope would be trained on the eastern end of his line, towards Wavre, whence he hoped to see the grey and black columns of Blücher's leading corps appearing at any minute. It was to be a long wait. In the meantime he had but few orders to give. 'Form as usual' was his instruction to his generals and when Uxbridge, as his designated second-in-command, sought him out to ask what his orders were, Wellington replied, accurately if unhelpfully, 'Bonaparte has not given me any idea of his projects: and as my plans will depend upon his, how can you expect me to tell you what mine are?' The Duke then rose, put his hand on Uxbridge's shoulder, and said, 'There is one thing certain, Uxbridge, that is, that whatever happens, you and I will do our duty.' Splendid words, but poor Uxbridge went away none the wiser and probably rather cross.[28]

The sun was up by the time the line had been adjusted. The Allies had been expecting an early attack, as they had at Quatre Bras, and were rather surprised that nothing happened. Hidden behind the ridge, they could not see the French and could only guess from the various noises they could hear what was going on just 1,000 yards away. Their sodden clothes slowly began to dry out, steaming in the summer warmth. Their weapons were ready, they were in the positions from which they knew they would now fight, they had mostly had a tot or more of drink if not much to eat, and now they had to wait, and the waiting is the worst part of a battle. Rees Gronow was waiting not with Picton's staff but with his own Coldstream Guards, with Byng's brigade above Hougoumont. He thought the day had been 'chosed by some providental accident for which human wisdom is unable to account. The sun shone most gloriously, and so clear was the atmosphere.'[29] Others thought the rain during the night showed that God was very much on their side, it often having rained in the Peninsula before their victories, and it was taken as a good if uncomfortable omen.

Many turned to prayer now. William Hay, waiting with the 12th Light Dragoons on the far left above Papelotte, asked 'the Almighty Dispenser of all good to bestow on me the power to do my duty' and this for a man whose friends would, he thought, have laughed at him as he 'made as little outward show of religion as any man living'; but the circumstances today were rather different.[30] As there were no chaplains there were no regimental services, which the older soldiers regretted. Once he had said his prayers Hay felt 'moved to capability of any performance that might be required of either mind or body' and it was the fear of not playing his part, or of getting it wrong and letting down his comrades, or even worse of his nerves failing, that motivated him as it did so many others.

But some of those waiting were nervous, and very nervous indeed. Edmund Wheatley, an experienced Peninsular veteran, stood next to a 'swelled-faced, ignorant booby, raw from England, staring with haggard and pallid cheeks. One could perceive the torture of his feelings by the hectic quivering of his muscles, as if fear and cold were contending for the natural colour of the cheek. And this man is one of the mighty warriors shortly to deal out thunder and confusion to the opposers of the British constitution',[31] which is an unkind but truthful description of so many of those young men who only three months before had been peacefully going about their business in England. Wheatley himself steadied his nerves by thinking of 'the occupation of all at home'. He thought of his 'dearest Eliza, you, whom I always regretted, I was certain was asleep innocent and placid. The pillow that supported you was unconscious of its lovely burden. But the breast, then cold and chilled with the prospect of approaching dissolution, felt that morning one or two warm sensations. It is an awful situation to be in, to stand with a sharp edged instrument at one's side, waiting for the signal to drag it out of its peaceful innocent house to snap the thread of existence of those we never saw, never spoke to, never offended.' Wheatley took the opportunity to look around. 'It was singular to perceive the shoals of cavalry and artillery suddenly in our rere [sic] all arranged in excellent order as if by a magic wand. The whole of the Horse Guards stood behind us. For my part I thought they were at Knightsbridge barracks or prancing on St James's Street.'[32]

Ensign George Keppel, with Frank Tidy's 14th Foot, had carried out a rigid inspection of every one of his soldiers' muskets and ammunition pouches. They had then 'piled arms', which means propping them barrel-up in a tripod, and the men fell out. As he waited he tried to calm his nerves by thinking of home but his mind constantly went back to an account his father had given of a 'conversation with Henry Pearce, otherwise known as The Game Chicken, before his fight with Daniel Mendoza for the All England championship. "Well, Pearce", asked my father, "how do you feel?" "Why, my lord", was the answer, "I wish it was fit (fought)". Without presuming to imply any resemblance to the Game Chicken, I had much in common with that great man – I wished the fight was *fit*.'[33]

Private Jack Parsons was 'one of the best-hearted, good humoured, generous fellows' in the 73rd and a good friend of Thomas Morris. He was also a habitual drunk, which meant he was often in trouble. He always carried a piece of bacon in his haversack, which he would never eat, not even now when he was starving, as it had been 'the last gift of his poor old mother' before she died and he treated it as if it had been the most valuable relic. He was known in the regiment to be too fond of the bottle to bother much with girlfriends, but, totally out of character, when they had been billeted near Antwerp, he had fallen madly in love with a local girl called Thérèse. She had also had a marked impact on his drinking, and consequently his behaviour, so that when he asked his company commander whether she could accompany the battalion when they marched, he had quickly agreed. As they waited, nervously making their preparations, Jack suddenly produced a will out of his knapsack and asked his company commander to witness it. The officer asked why he had decided to have one prepared, which may sound rather an unnecessary question in the circumstances but it was unusual for soldiers to bother with such formalities, relying instead on their friends to ensure that anything they had reached their families. Jack replied his mother had appeared to him in a dream during the night and 'solemnly assured him that this day would be his last'. Now he felt responsible for dear Thérèse, he wanted her to have his arrears of pay, which was all he possessed in the world. The company commander duly signed and Jack stuffed the completed document back in his pocket.

The cavalry waited, mostly at their horses' heads or resaddling, checking equipment, rerolling their cloaks, endlessly drawing and redrawing their swords from their scabbards. At La Haie Sainte, Frederick Lindau had spent a moderately comfortable night. They had found animals to kill and roast and half a barrel of wine in the cellar, which predictably soon disappeared. When he woke his neighbour, Private Harz asked for some, saying that he knew the day was going to be a tough one as he had just dreamt that he was going to die from a bullet through the body. Lindau obliged, told him dreams were just that, and together they went to work trying to fortify the buildings as best they could. This was not easy as the main doors of the farmyard facing the French had been burned as firewood, but they did what they could using ladders and farm implements.[34]

One of the most difficult things for the ordinary soldier was not knowing what was going to happen. There had been little attempt to brief them as to any plans. Wellington's negotiations with Blücher remained between him and his staff, and the instruction 'Form as usual' did not satisfy many.

Henry Murray, who did not like Wellington, noted that at this stage in the morning 'There were rumours of an intended general action – rumours also that the French were about to attack & that the Duke of Wellington was absent having gone to the Prussian army. The same ignorance which had disfigured the movement of the previous evening – was abroad with idle fears its offspring.'[35] Certainly British officers did not favour stirring eve-of-battle speeches, even Colonel Elphinstone of the 33rd keeping quiet; rather there was the odd word of comfort to the most terrified, and a general reassurance that they would be all right, coupled with quite a bit of cynical humour as to who would be killed or maimed. Although they had a general idea that the plan was for the Prussians to come up, no one knew for sure. 'We (I mean the multitude) were not aware that Blücher could afford us any assistance', Ensign Macready wrote afterwards, 'as we heard that he was completely beaten and hotly pursued – but no British soldier could dread the result when Wellington commanded.'[36] Despite the fascination Napoleon exercised on the whole British Army, and the fact that they had seen the French fight bravely at Quatre Bras, there were few if any who doubted that they were the better army and that they would win. That well placed faith would be sorely tested before the end of the day.

At about eleven a.m., the Allies, hidden behind their ridge, heard wild cheering from the French lines. Napoleon had come forward from Rossomme and was riding down the front of d'Erlon's, Lobau's and Reille's corps. He was greeted with huge enthusiasm, the French cheers of 'Vive l'Empereur' sounding ominously across the valley. Eyewitnesses on the French side said it was a magnificent spectacle. 'The bayonets, the helmets, the cuirasses gleamed; the colours of the flags,

Guidons and pennants of the lancers waved in the breeze; the drums beat, the bugles sounded, all the regiments' bands struck up the tune *Veillons au salut de l'empire*. Never have I heard the cry "Vive l'Empereur" cried with more enthusiasm, never had more absolute devotion been engraved in the features, in the gestures and in the voices of his soldiers', thought Lieutenant Martin, a Swiss serving with the 45th Regiment of the Line in d'Erlon's corps, which was about to have a sobering experience at the hands of the Scots Greys. Corporal Canler, of the 28th line regiment, said it reminded him of the review before the Grand Army crossed the Niemen on their way to Moscow, although it is not entirely clear whether he meant this positively or as an omen.[37]

Wellington did nothing so ostentatious but, having spent the night in Waterloo village, he was back early in the morning, quietly inspecting the lines, ordering more troops down to Hougoumont, and visiting most brigades, although he does not seem to have made it to the far left, where Henry Murray was complaining. He seemed very relaxed to Haddy James: 'At half past ten we saw the materials for erecting a telegraph [semaphore machine] carried along our front, and a little later there was a stir and bustle as the Duke of Wellington passed us on his chestnut, with his staff looking entirely unconcerned and as smart as if they were riding for pleasure. All now became silent and the order was given to mount.'[38] Unconcerned as he may have appeared, Wellington was in fact anxiously waiting for news of the Prussians, and for some idea as to when he might expect them on the battlefield. Prussian patrols had been spotted as early as ten a.m. but it wasn't until eleven a.m. that word came from the 10th Hussars that they had linked up with their leading elements and not until one p.m. that Wellington had confirmation from

Blücher that von Bulow's IV Corps had crossed the River Lasne. Every hour that passed without the French attacking played into his hands; every hour Napoleon delayed brought the Prussians that much nearer.

Napoleon had intended to start his attack at nine a.m., and had issued orders to Ney to that effect, but the delay in moving his troops into position, partly because of the boggy state of the ground and partly due to many units still moving up, meant that he had to wait. Many of his soldiers had also taken themselves off foraging, and had not rejoined their units, several of whom were still in some state of disorder. The Middle Guard and Old Guard were still moving into Rossomme when the attack started. The orders to assemble the Grand Battery were not given until eleven a.m., and moving that number of guns with their ammunition wagons and caissons also took time. They were only finally getting into position at one p.m. In his memoirs Napoleon is at pains to point out that his columns 'deployed with such precision that there was no confusion; each man took up exactly the place which had been planned for him in the very mind of his leader. Never had such masses moved about with such ease', which, given his propagandist tendencies, would seem to reinforce the view that his army was far from ready.[39] He had not, in fact, decided on his detailed plan until eleven a.m. The attack would now begin on the left, with Reille's corps attacking Hougoumont. This was intended to compel Wellington to reinforce the château complex, thus weakening his centre. The Grand Battery would then blast a hole in this weakened centre, after which d'Erlon's corps would attack en masse, followed by the cavalry and the Imperial Guard.

*

At 11.20 a.m. Bauduin's 1st Brigade from Jérôme's 6th Division in Reille's corps attacked the wood in front of Hougoumont. The battle had begun. It is not clear why Reille trusted this move to Jérôme, never the most astute field commander, and it may be because he considered it, as a diversionary attack, to be less important than the work his divisions would have to do later against the Allied centre. Neither Napoleon nor Ney seemed to regard Hougoumont as part of their main effort, although Wellington most certainly did, realising that if the château complex fell it could lead to the collapse of his right wing. The struggle for Hougoumont began, however, to absorb more and more French troops, and as the day wore on, it became a battle within the battle, and the scene of some of the most heroic and bloody fighting. The Allies had originally deployed the light companies of the four Foot Guard battalions there on the evening of 17 June, including Mathew Clay, under the command of the vinegary Lord Saltoun, who had seen off the Prince of Orange at Quatre Bras, and also a Hanoverian battalion from Kielmansegge's brigade. They had 'stood to' a couple of times during the night as French patrols had approached, which had caused Clay to have to pack up his soaking blanket tent in a hurry. Some French *tirailleurs*, advance pickets of Jérôme's division, actually spent the night in the forward edge of the wood, and one is alleged to have crept forward into the corn and to within ten yards of the lane down to Hougoumont along which Wellington would ride in the morning, although there is no record of his having had a shot at the great man. As morning came the Guards set about defending the complex, barricading windows and gates and knocking loopholes in the walls.

Hougoumont (see plan opposite) consisted of a small château, with a chapel, and substantial farm buildings in a

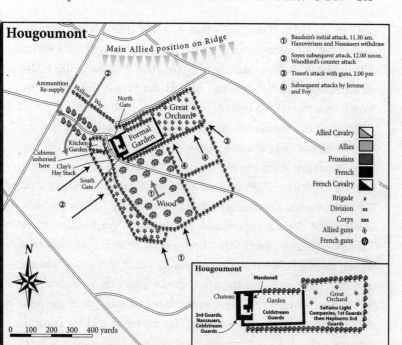

Hougoumont

Main Allied position on Ridge

Ammunition Re-supply

Hollow Way

North Gate

Great Orchard

Formal Garden

Kitchen Garden

Cubieres unhorsed here

Clay's Hay Stack

South Gate

Wood

N

0   100   200   300   400 yards

① Bauduin's initial attack, 11.30 am. Hanoverians and Nassauers withdraw

② Soyes subsequent attack, 12.00 noon. Woodford's counter attack

③ Tissot's attack with guns, 2.00 pm

④ Subsequent attacks by Jerome and Foy

Allied Cavalry
Allies
Prussians
French
French Cavalry
Brigade   x
Division   xx
Corps   xxx
Allied guns
French guns

Hougoumont

Macdonell

Chateau

Garden

Coldstream Guards

3rd Guards, Nassauers, Coldstream Guards

Great Orchard

Saltains Light Companies, 1st Guards then Hepburns 3rd Guards

walled courtyard with two gates. The main gate, to the north, faced back towards the Allies' main positions about 500 yards away, which were occupied by the First Guards Division. There was also a southern gate, that opened onto an area 30 yards wide, which ran in front of a formal wood, about 300 yards square, with single upright trees and little undergrowth. To the east of the château buildings was a large ornamental garden, surrounded on two sides by a substantial wall six foot high. This ran along the south side, thus opposite the wood, and on the east side, thus towards La Haie Sainte. There was a thick hedge on the north, which covered a hollow lane back to the north gate. To the east again of the walled garden was a large orchard, about 200 yards square, which opened onto the fields towards La Haie Sainte. The buildings, the garden and the wood all offered good defensive positions, and it was, in effect, a forward detachment of the First Guards Division's positions anchoring the Allied right wing. The main Allied skirmish line ran back to La Haie Sainte from the north-east corner of the orchard.

During the course of the day it would be defended by various different Guards units, for whom the hollow lane offered some cover as they moved up and down from the ridgeline. Early on 18 June, Wellington had inspected the defences. As he rode down, he had met Saltoun, who had been ordered back to the main position with his two light companies of the 1st Foot Guards' battalions. Wellington countermanded that order, telling Saltoun to stay where he was for the time being, and ordered up the 1st Battalion of the 2nd Nassau Regiment as reinforcements. As Bauduin's attack started, the western edge of the wood was defended by the Hanoverians and the eastern side by four companies of the 1st Nassauers. Behind them, around the buildings, the light company of the 3rd Foot Guards was positioned in the kitchen garden to the south-west of the farmyard, to prevent any move around to the west or north; the light company of the Coldstream Guards and the remaining four companies of the 1st Nassauers held the buildings themselves and the walled garden, whilst the Nassauers held the orchard. Wellington had put Lieutenant-Colonel James Macdonnell, a trusted Maida and Peninsular veteran, in overall command.

At around 11.30 a.m. the skirmishers of 1st Légère Battalion of Bauduin's brigade closed to the wood under their charismatic commanding officer, the 29-year-old Marquis de Cubières, riding with his arm in a sling from a wound at Quatre Bras. They started slowly to force back the Hanoverians and Nassauers. The Hanoverians were the Jaeger, or light, companies of the Lüneburg and Grubenhagen battalions and fought bravely. The Guards were less complimentary about the behaviour of the Nassauers. The 16-year-old ensign Charles Short noted that 'when one man was wounded at least a dozen would carry him out, so that the chief of the work was left to our men'.[40] At the same time Piré's light cavalry began to work their way round to the west. Piré's men do not seem to have contributed much over the coming hours, in the words of one of their officers 'we only skirmished', which may be because they could do very little against the well-defended buildings and, possibly, because they were still reeling from their horrific casualties at Quatre Bras.[41]

There was little cover in the wood, but the German troops fought skilfully, fighting back from tree to tree. Bauduin committed the rest of his brigade, before being killed himself as he was directing the attack from his horse. Cubières took over command, and slowly the German troops were forced back against the hedge which ran along the northern edge of the wood, and then back to the buildings themselves. Wellington now ordered two artillery batteries, Sandham's and Cleeves's, to fire in support from the ridge behind the château, and then added Bull's battery of howitzers, who dropped shells into the wood itself with devastating effect; the first salvo killed 17 of Cubières' men. Reille had positioned his own corps artillery to fire in support of the attack, and two batteries of horse artillery from Kellerman's corps were now sent to reinforce them. Because their view was blocked by the wood, and because they were unable to depress their barrels enough, they could only fire onto the ridge behind rather than into the buildings themselves; thus, despite the French ending up with 42 guns firing in support, the defenders reported few casualties from artillery fire until later in the day.

What stopped Cubières' attack was that, as his men fought through to the hedge, they emerged in the open ground that ran along the north edge of the wood, where they were met by volleys from the Guards, firing from the protection of the farm buildings and the garden wall. This seems to have taken them by surprise, rather as if they had not realised that the buildings would be there or would be so fiercely defended. With their artillery well behind them, and unable to depress enough to blast the buildings, Cubières' men began to take significant casualties. There is little a man armed only with a musket can do against well-positioned defenders protected by a wall, other than try to pick them off individually through their loopholes, but muskets were too inaccurate to do that effectively. On the right they had some initial success, forcing the Nassauers, who had no wall to protect them, back through the orchard, but they were driven out by Saltoun's two companies counter-attacking.

At this point Jérôme, stung by his failure, decided to launch his second brigade, Soye's, who would attack from the south-west. Jérôme seems to have done this against his corps commander's wishes. Reille is reported as feeling that they had already done enough to create a diversion, and he was worried about the high casualties. Soye's six battalions moved through the now-cleared wood but came up against the same withering fire as they neared the buildings. They made little progress, except on their left, where they skirted the wood through a cornfield until they made contact with the Light Company of 3rd Foot Guards, who were in the kitchen garden and the scrub at the western end. Mathew Clay was with them. They were in 'a long and narrow kitchen garden, which was extended under cover of a close hedge, next to a corn field, through which the skirmishers of the enemy were advancing to attack. We remained in a kneeling position under this cover, but annoyed by a most galling fire ... indeed that the spreading of their small shots rarely escaped contact with our knapsacks and accoutrements, even the heels of our shoes were struck by them. We remained in this position for a considerable time, and the enemy now advancing in greater force to attack the chateau. Our commanding officer on his charger remained on the road between the fence of the garden and the exterior wall of the farm to our rear, it being a higher position whence he could more perfectly watch the movements of the enemy.' Weight of numbers slowly forced the 3rd Foot Guards back, and they began to withdraw in contact to the north gate, which was kept half open to let them in. Clay was in the last group to leave the kitchen garden, and as he emerged onto the track, they were led by Lieutenant Standon in a counter-attack to hold off the French skirmishers whilst the remainder made good their escape. Clay and Private Gann, a 41-year-old veteran, took up firing positions behind a haystack, where they became involved in a firefight with Soye's leading men and didn't notice what was going on behind them.

Soye's attack had in fact come at a critical time for the defenders. As he was readying his six battalions, Cubières had gathered his surviving troops and they had slowly worked their way around the western end of the buildings. They were more sheltered from fire here, as there were no openings in the western wall for the Allies to fire through, although they were also engaged by Clay and his comrades in the Light Company of 3rd Foot Guards. Cubières now sorted out a group from his remaining men which he put under a giant *sous-lieutenant* called Bonnet, nicknamed Le Gros, who had been commissioned in Spain by Marshal Suchet for being the first into the breach at Tarragona. Le Gros took about a hundred men, and they worked their way round, under cover of Soye's attack, to beside the still half-open north gate. As Cubières was moving round, still riding his horse with one hand, he was attacked by Sergeant Ralph Fraser, a Peninsular veteran of the 3rd Foot Guards, who used his halberd, which some sergeants still carried (although most discarded them for muskets), to wrestle him to the ground. Cubières fell, and Fraser swung himself into the saddle, galloping the horse through the still-open north gate, joining what were now most of the Light Company inside the farmyard walls, but leaving Clay and Gann still by their haystack.

The north gate was still just open, and Le Gros's group now rushed it. Le Gros seized an axe, carried by the French pioneers, and smashed his way through the gate panels. About a hundred men followed him as they rushed into the main yard. Desperate hand-to-hand fighting ensued as the Coldstream Guards and Hanoverians rallied to stop the French, wielding their muskets by the barrel as clubs and using swords and axes as they tried to prevent Le Gros's party fighting their way towards the château. The French caught a Hanoverian officer, Lieutenant Wilder, as he was trying to open the door into one of the outhouses, and cut off his hand with an axe as he was turning the handle. Slowly, with musket fire from the château, and the fighting in the yard, the French were killed one by one. Le Gros himself was killed near the château. Had not the 3rd Foot Guards held up Soye's leading battalion by their delaying action, and had Cubières still been in action to bring forward more troops, Hougoumont could have fallen at that point, and Wellington's flank would have been turned.

Clay and Gann, meanwhile, realising rather late that they

had been left behind, had to get back from their haystack, along the west wall of the farmyard, and try to reach the north gate. They had been getting the worst of their firefight with Soye's skirmishers, musket shots hitting the farmyard wall behind Clay's back, and Clay's musket had packed up, which was not unusual in a sustained action. Grabbing another, warm from recent use, they quickly saw their predicament and were 'for a moment or two quite at a loss how to act'. But turning round they saw that the north gate had been forced open by Le Gros, and made a run for it. As they panted in they saw 'many dead bodies of the enemy; one I particularly noticed which appeared to be a French officer, but they were scarcely distinguishable, being to all appearance as though they had been very much trodden upon, and covered with mud'. They had just made it in time, as the next thing they saw was Lieutenant-Colonel Macdonnell carrying a large piece of wood or tree trunk in his arms (one of his cheeks marked with blood, his charger lay bleeding within a short distance) with which he was hastening to secure the gates against a rush by Soye's leading companies, who were now following Le Gros.[42] Shouting to three Coldstream officers near by, Lieutenant-Colonel Henry Wyndham and ensigns James Hervey and Henry Gooch, Macdonnell flung himself at the gates. Two more Coldstream Guards corporals, James and Joseph Graham, joined them, together with four men who had just rushed in with 3rd Foot Guards – Sergeant Ralph Fraser, who had de-horsed Cubières, Sergeant Bruce McGregor, Sergeant Joseph Aston and Private Joseph Lester. These ten men jammed themselves against the gates, slowly trying to force them shut against the increasing mass of French. Inch by inch the great gates moved, until finally they could drop the locking bar in place and barricade them. Some

French had managed to climb the walls, and a grenadier, standing on a comrade's shoulders, was about to fire at Wyndham when Corporal Graham shot him through the head.

Soye's men may have failed to force the gates, but they were still all around the perimeter and keeping up a steady fire on the defenders, who had been in constant action for over an hour. Major-General Byng, who commanded the 2nd Guards Brigade back on the ridge, had seen what was happening, and now sent the remainder of 2nd Battalion Coldstream Guards down the hill in a counter-attack to drive Soye off. Led by Lieutenant-Colonel Alexander Woodford, with two companies leading and two in reserve, they raced down the hill, forming line as they came up to the north gate, spreading out along the château drive, and clearing Soye's men back into the wood. They then joined their exhausted light company in the farmyard, a welcome relief. Soye's attack had failed just as Bauduin's had, and Jérôme had used up the fighting power of his brigades.

French plans now become confused. Apologists tell us that the continued effort against Hougoumont was partly because of Jérôme Bonaparte's hubris, but at this point Reille despatched Gauthier's brigade from Foy's division to attack the château as well, suggesting Reille was beginning to see the real significance of the position. In fact Gauthier had fallen at Quatre Bras, and Colonel Tissot was in command. Within 15 minutes of Soye's men falling back into the wood, Tissot's lead battalions attacked the orchard from the south-east; this could have been much more dangerous as there was no wall or buildings there to help the defenders as the unfortunate Nassauers had discovered an hour earlier. Saltoun's two light companies were still in possession of the orchard, after their earlier successful counter-attack against Bauduin, but they were now potentially massively outnumbered. Seeing Saltoun's predicament, Byng sent down two more companies of 3rd Foot Guards under Lieutenant-Colonel Francis Home. They succeeded in driving the French back part of the way, and, helped by flanking fire from the Coldstream Guards behind the east wall of the garden, they broke the impetus of Tissot's attack. But Tissot remained in possession of the south-eastern part of the orchard, to which he now brought up howitzers, something which arguably should have happened at the outset, and he began to fire incendiary shells into the thatched buildings in the farmyard complex. The main battle for Hougoumont was about to begin.

Whilst the battle for Hougoumont had been raging, the rest of the Allied line had continued to wait. Rees Gronow was on the ridge with the Guards, who were watching but not yet involved in the fighting. 'We heard incessantly the measured boom of artillery, accompanied by the incessant rattling echoes of musketry. The whole of the British infantry not actually engaged were at that time formed into squares; and as you looked along our lines, it seemed as if we were a contin-uous wall of human beings. I remember distinctly being able to see Bonaparte and his staff; and some of my brother officers using the glass exclaimed "There he is on his white horse".'[43] Napoleon exerted a fascination on almost every soldier in the Allied army. Many, like Blücher and his Prussians, and Frederick Lindau and the King's German Legion, hated him and the French with a violent loathing, never able to forgive what the occupation of their homeland had meant for them and their families. Most of the British, however, not neces-sarily having suffered directly from French atrocities, regarded him with a mixture of fascination, awe and superstition. Gronow must have moved forward to see Napoleon at this point, as the main body of the Guards was still back behind the ridge.

But this voyeuristic calm was about to be shattered. At one p.m., after all the work on the part of Napoleon's gunners to drag and manhandle their 80 guns into place, the Grand Battery opened fire. 'A ball whizzed up in the air. Up we started simultaneously. I looked at my watch. It was eleven o'clock, Sunday (Eliza just in Church at Wallingford or at Abingdon) morning. In five minutes a stunning noise took place and a shocking havoc commenced',[44] wrote Edmund Wheatley, whose watch or memory was somewhat out. 'One could almost feel the undulation of the air from the multitude of cannon shot. The first man who fell was five files on my left. With the utmost distortion of feature he lay on his side and shrivelling up every muscle of the body he twirled his elbow round and round in acute agony, then dropped lifeless, dying as it's called a death of glory.'

The Grand Battery fired continuously for half an hour. The bombardment was a precursor to the main attack on Wellington's centre, and so the French gunners were aiming for the area along the ridge either side of the Mont St Jean crossroads, which was where Napoleon intended d'Erlon's corps to strike. They probably fired about 3,350 shots, of which three-quarters would have been round shot and the remaining quarter shells from their howitzers. About half the round shot hit the forward slope. It did some damage to the gunners and the skirmish line here, which was all they could see, but much of the shot ploughed harmlessly into the wet ground; Bijlandt's Dutch infantry, who had been standing forward of the sunken lane, had already been pulled back.

Round shot was at its most dangerous when it bounced, so the weather was an added advantage for the Allies. The other half either landed over the ridge or did bounce over the top, and landed amongst the infantry battalions massed behind. They had been told to lie down once the barrage started, and the true advantage of Wellington's choice of position now became apparent. Most of the French shot flew too high to cause many casualties. The howitzer shells did more damage when they burst, but again many passed over the infantry's heads or buried themselves in the wet ground. The whole barrage therefore probably only accounted for an estimated 500 casualties,[45] but its psychological effect was rather worse. There is something about the indiscriminate nature of artillery fire that makes it particularly difficult for soldiers to endure, added to the fact that in this case they just had to lie still and were unable to retaliate. Later in the day many regiments would suffer much worse artillery casualties, but for some this initial bombardment was the first time they had been under fire. It is not a particularly pleasant experience to have to lie unprotected on the ground with someone else trying to kill you, especially if you cannot see them or from where they are firing at you. 'All I could do would not hinder me from bobbing though the balls went 100 yards over my head', the 17-year-old Lieutenant John Hart of the 52nd wrote to his father, 'but that was only for a little while as I soon got accustomed to them'.[46]

Thomas Howell of the 71st recalled 'a young lad who had joined but a short time before', one of those militiamen who had made up their numbers in that rush during March. He said to Howell, 'Tom, you are an old soldier, and have escaped often, and have every chance to escape this time also. I am sure I am to fall.' 'Nonsense, be not gloomy,' Howell replied, but the lad was certain and asked Howell that he 'would tell his parents when you get home that I ask God's pardon for the evil I have done and the grief I have given them. Be sure to tell I died praying for their blessing and pardon.' At about twelve noon, Howell wrote, but probably later, the battalion marched up to a bank and lay down covering 'a brigade of guns'. They were so tired after marching for two days that many soon fell asleep. Howell 'was suddenly awakened. A ball struck the ground a little below me, turned me heels-over-head, broke my musket in pieces and killed a lad at my side. We lay thus about an hour and a half, under a dreadful fire which cost us 60 men, while we had never fired a shot. The balls were falling thick amongst us. The young man I lately spoke of lost both his legs by a shot at this time. They were cut very close; he soon bled to death. "Tom", he said, "remember your charge: my mother sore wept when my brother died; if she saw me thus it would break her heart. Farewell! God bless my parents!" He said no more, his lips quivered and he ceased to breathe.'[47]

William Lawrence was marching towards the crossroads with the 40th, still coming up to join the Army at Mont St Jean. 'An enemy shell cut our deputy sergeant-major in two', he recalled, 'then went on to take the head off William Hooper, one of my grenadiers. It exploded in the rear no more than a yard from me, the impact hurling me six feet into the air. The tail of my sash was completely burned off and the handle of my sword was singed black, but fortunately the only injury it did me was to take a small piece of skin off the side of my face. This event frightened young Bertram, one of the new recruits in my company. He had never been in action before and did not like the curious evolutions of the shell. He called out, saying he suddenly felt very ill, and had to fall out of rank. I pushed him back. "Why, Bertram," I said, "it's only the smell of a little bit of powder that's making you sick." But my diagnosis did no good – he fell down and would not go another inch. I was very put out. He ought to have been shot, but I left him.'[48]

The cavalry could not lie down but they did move around. 'Some shot passed over our heads and through the ranks, others struck the ground a few yards in front of us, at last one struck a man and horse and killed them both, which obliged us to move as they had got their distance', noted Private Joseph Lord, standing with his squadron of 2nd Life Guards in the dip behind the crossroads.[49] If the French gunners had 'got their distance', then it was more by luck than judgement as they could not see where the shots fell. On the right of the line Private John Smith, from Dumbarton, with the 71st, saw 'cannon shot and shell, big gun shot of all descriptions as thick as it could fall, I could not mention what it had the appearance of. Limbs, arms, heads was flying in all directions, nothing ever touched me in the smallest [way]. There was a great many of us killed, there a great deal of them fell asleep with the fatigue for all their neighbours being knocked to pieces beside them.'[50] There are many records of men falling asleep during the day, even when under heavy fire, which, although it may seem extraordinary, shows the effect of the exhaustion of three days' marching and fighting with very little food. Thomas Morris wrote that 'as the enemy's artillery was taking off a great many of our men, we were ordered to lie down to avoid the shots as much as possible; and I took advantage of this circumstance to obtain an hour's sleep as comfortably as I ever did in my life'.[51]

Mercer, whose troop were in position on the ridge behind Hougoumont, just in front of Frank Tidy's 14th Foot, was too far away to be hit by shots from the Grand Battery, but he was being engaged by Kellerman's lighter guns firing in support of Jérôme's repeated assaults on Hougoumont itself. Wellington's orders to his artillery were very clear; they were to reserve their ammunition for infantry and cavalry and not waste it on firing at the French artillery, or what gunners like to call 'counter-battery fire'. But Mercer, in typical Mercer style, thought that, with his nine-pounders, he could quickly silence the French battery and he started a 'slow deliberate fire'. To his great surprise, the French replied with larger guns, 'half-a-dozen gentlemen of very superior calibre', so much so that he quickly stopped firing, but not before the first man of his troop was hit. 'I shall never forget the scream the poor lad gave when struck. It was one of the last [shots] they fired, and shattered his left arm to pieces as he stood between the wagons. That scream went to my very soul, for I accused myself of having caused his misfortune.'[52] His guilt at poor Gunner Hunt's wound was interrupted by three officers who 'lounged up to our guns to see the effect. One was a medico, and he (a shower having just come on) carried an umbrella.' No sooner had the French incoming fire started than they 'scampered off in double quick, doctor and all, he still carrying his umbrella aloft'. A shot landed rather too close to the good doctor, who dropped to his hands and knees, and scrambled away 'like a great baboon', one hand still holding the umbrella, 'his head turning fearfully over his shoulder, as if watching for the coming shot, whilst our fellows made the field resound with their shouts and laughter'. Sadly it does not seem as if he came back to treat poor Hunt.[53]

That stray doctors were still wandering around the battlefield at one p.m. shows that, unless you were at Hougoumont, or under the 'grand barrage' at Mont St Jean, the battlefield remained relatively quiet. Mercer had been surprised earlier to see the Duke of Richmond galloping across his front with his two sons, although they were the last civilians he saw. Richmond was, as a serving general, annoyed at having no active command and had come up with his boys to attach himself to Wellington's staff. They were not the only civilians to do so. There is an unsubstantiated story that an English travelling salesman, a bagman as they were called, had been showing samples from his Birmingham factory to clients in Brussels, and was on his way home when he heard what was going on. Determined not to miss out on what he saw as the 'fun', he rode up behind Lambert's 10th Brigade, and headed for the highest point, which was just behind Mont St Jean crossroads. There he came upon Wellington and his staff. Wellington was, at that point, allegedly short of ADCs, and, seeing the bagman, assumed he was there to help, so he asked him to take a message to one of his brigades. The bagman, very pleased to be of service, and no doubt mindful of how he would tell the story when he was safely back in Birmingham, galloped off on his errand but soon shells and bullets were landing all around him. He duly delivered his message but was never seen again. Years later he approached Wellington rather sheepishly at a public gathering in England. The Duke recognised him and asked what had happened, saying he wished to thank him for his services. The bagman confessed that one ride through the bullets was enough, and that his curiosity had been well satisfied.[54] Otherwise there was 'not a living soul in sight', apart from the two armies and, still, the odd redoubtable wife. Madeleine De Lancey may now have been safely in Antwerp, but Mrs Ross, wife of Alexander Ross, who was quartermaster of Frank Tidy's 14th Foot, refused to leave her battalion. She stayed with them 'for some time after the firing had began' and only with difficulty and, possibly, some of the remaining gin ration, was she persuaded to retire to the relative safety of Waterloo church.[55]

Several foraging parties were still out when the artillery barrage started. Thomas Playford and Corporal John Shaw heard the first guns as they were filling their sacks in the farmhouse in Waterloo. 'The work is beginning,' Shaw shouted. 'Come lads, let us hasten back to our regiment; we have each our share of duty to perform today.' They hastened back to 2nd Life Guards − 'the firing had become very brisk before we joined the ranks' − but by the time they got back the barrage was coming to an end as Napoleon was now ready to launch his main attack. Shaw had told Playford that he had had a premonition of being killed. He had been catnapping in the corn on the morning of the withdrawal from Quatre Bras and had suddenly leaped up shouting, 'I have just dreamed that a Frenchman shot me.' Playford did not pay much attention, Shaw being 'as little addicted to superstitious fears as any man on earth, and instantly shaking off the unpleasant feeling his dream had produced, he joked about the alarming apparition he had seen in his sleep'.[56]

The sound of the 'grand barrage' had carried the twelve-odd miles to Brussels very clearly on that still June morning and the centre of the city had dissolved into chaos. Edward Heeley heard the noise of cannon 'about as loud as if you had taken a number of cannon balls and rolled them down a wooden staircase and then heard them at about 20 yards off. People were in a dreadful state of anxiety, every now and then the noise would appear a little louder and the people would exclaim "Oh they are coming, the English are beaten".'

Around the time the grand barrage was ending, his father despatched him on his mule to collect hay and corn from the forage store about a mile and a half away through the centre of the town. Whilst his father met an 18th Hussar he had known in Canterbury, and disappeared into a wine shop with him, young Heeley was sent on alone. The mule was never the easiest of animals, and was now to have its temper sorely tested. He had not gone far when he met 'about 50 Brunswickers coming at full gallop, crying out "Franceuse, Franceuse, the French, the French". My mule, being a very headstrong animal, immediately turned round and mixed with this flying mass. I must say now that I was most desperately frightened. Such a scene of confusion had now began as baffles all description. Carriages and horsemen, in trying to pass each other, were all thrown down together. My mule was at full gallop, and nothing could stop her.' Luckily the mule bolted back to her stable. Heeley wanted to join the throng crowding out along the Antwerp road, but his father and Scovell's other staff, Peninsular veterans, had seen it all before and they stayed put.[57]

It was now 1.30 p.m., and the Grand Battery began to fall silent. There was a momentary calm, interrupted by the sound of the battle still being fought at Hougoumont, and the screaming of the wounded behind the ridgeline. The Army waited, the infantry still lying down in their ranks, the cavalry standing by their horses, the gunners ready by their loaded guns. The gun batteries that had been behind the crossroads were now brought forward to line the sunken lane. Then they heard the beating of massed drums, the shouted words of command, and the bugle calls, as the 20,000 men of d'Erlon's corps made their way slowly down the valley. Napoleon's mass attack to shatter the Allied line had begun. D'Erlon's four divisions moved slowly at first, threading their way through the wagons and caissons, the guns and the piles of ammunition of the Grand Battery, the thick smoke clearing only slowly. As they passed through the gun line, the guns opened up again, briefly, firing over the heads of the packed columns as they took up their attack formation. D'Erlon moved to their head 'and with a strong and clear voice pronounced these few words "Today it is necessary to vanquish or die".'[58] Corporal Canler in Bourgeois's brigade remembered his NCO, Hubant, a veteran of all Napoleon's campaigns, looking preoccupied and very pale as he directed his men into position.

The *voltigeur* company of each battalion, the French skirmishers, over 2,000 of them, moved off in front, their job being to mask the mass behind them and to drive in the Allied skirmish line. Then came the dense battalion columns of infantry, marching with their arms at the shoulder, moving down the slope and then slowly up the far side, plodding rather than marching over the soaking ground, struggling to keep pace through the sodden corn: 'the soldier, who still had a long march before encountering the enemy, was soon tired out by the difficulty of crossing the greasy and water-logged ground, in which he broke the straps of his gaiters and even lost his shoes, weighed down by the amount of dirt that attached itself to them and stuck to the soles and to the ground, and because the commands could not be heard, lost in the thousands of repeated cries and drumming'.[59]

They moved in echelon, one division slightly behind the other, Quiot's division on the left stepping off first, then Donzelot's, then Marcognet's and finally Durutte's on the right. On the very far left, guarding d'Erlon's flank, were two

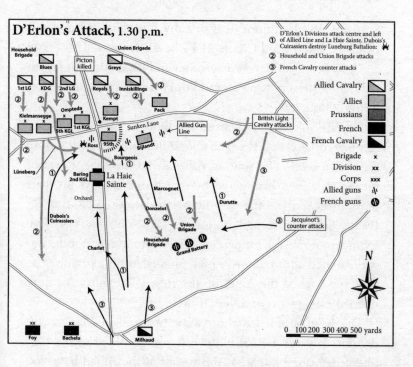

D'Erlon's Attack, 1.30 p.m.

① D'Erlon's Divisions attack centre and left of Allied Line and La Haie Sainte. Dubois's Cuirassiers destroy Luneburg Battalion:

② Household and Union Brigade attacks

③ French Cavalry counter attacks

Allied Cavalry
Allies
Prussians
French
French Cavalry

Brigade x
Division xx
Corps xxx
Allied guns
French guns

regiments of heavy cavalry, 780 cuirassiers commanded by Dubois. They moved up at the walk, just to the left of the Brussels road, working their way through the corn, and in line with the infantry of Quiot's division on their immediate right. Quiot had two brigades; Charlet's came straight up the road, his 54th and 55th Ligne making for La Haie Sainte, whilst Bourgeois's was just to their right, led by 105th Ligne, and they had the crossroads as their objective. These brigades moved separately, but Donzelot's and Marcognet's to their right moved in dense battalion columns. Each battalion deployed in a line three ranks deep, with roughly 200 men in each rank, one battalion behind the other. The columns were therefore wider than they were deep, but with eight battalions in each division, they were still a massed formation. Beyond

Durutte was Jacquinot's cavalry division, the 3rd and 4th Lanciers, and the 3rd Chasseurs à Cheval, acting as flank guard and advancing close to Frichermont and Papelotte. His fourth regiment, the very experienced 7th Hussars, had been sent off to find Grouchy.

As d'Erlon's infantry started to climb so the French guns stopped for a second time, unable to fire now without hitting their own men. The waiting Allies heard the urgent beat of the *pas de charge*, hammered by the drummer boys on their brass drums, the officers and NCOs shouted 'Serrez les Rangs! Serrez les Rangs!' (Close up! Close up!) The cry 'Vive L'Empereur! Vive L'Empereur! came from every mouth, and we marched ahead, closed ranks, aligned as on a parade',[60] as they approached the Allies up the ridge. The guns that now opened carried a very different message.

The most junior battalion went first and in Marcognet's division this was the 45th Ligne. A young soldier in this regiment described just what this meant as the Allied batteries, hidden in the hedge line of the sunken lane, raked them with canister fire as they started to climb. Canister, effectively a giant shotgun cartridge, was devastating at 300 yards. 'We were met by a hail of balls from above the road at the left. Two batteries now swept our ranks, and the shot from the hedges a hundred feet distant pierced us through and through.'[61] 'Death crept up on us from every side; entire ranks disappeared under the case shot', wrote Corporal Canler.[62] 'Hardly had we gone a hundred paces when the commander of our second battalion, M. Marins, was mortally wounded; the captain of my company, M. Duzer, was struck by two balls; adjutant Hubant [who had looked so pale forming them up just a few minutes earlier] and the man carrying the colour, Post Drapeau Crosse, were killed. At the second discharge of the English battery, the drummer of grenadiers Lecointre had his right arm taken off by case shot, but this courageous man continued to march at our head beating the charge with his left, until he lost consciousness through loss of blood. The third discharge from the English battery reduced the frontage of the battalion to that of a company and the terrible cry of "Serrez les Rangs!" was heard again.' The climb was only 300 yards, 'and an average person on foot would have taken no more than five or six minutes to cover the ground; but the soft and rain-sodden earth and the tall rye slowed up our progress appreciably. As a result the English gunners had plenty of time in which to work their destruction upon us.'[63]

But the pressure of numbers and the bravery of the French infantry meant that the advance didn't falter. 'Nothing was able to stop our march; it continued with the same order as before, with the same precision. The dead were immediately replaced by those who followed; the ranks, although becoming fewer, remained in good order'.[64] The Allied skirmishers fell back, partly so that the guns could have a clear field of fire. The French *voltigeurs* and *tirailleurs*, their skirmish line, who had started off only 15 minutes earlier with two men per yard across the whole corps front, now closed towards the sunken lane, although with huge holes blown in their ranks. They were about 50 yards in front of the main columns, and as they closed to the hedge they were met by rather disjointed volleys from Bijlandt's Netherlands Brigade, their blue uniforms temporarily surprising Donzelot's men. 'Our battalion opened fire as soon as the skirmishers had come in. We were so close that Captain Henry l'Olivier, commanding our grenadier company, was struck on the arm by a ball, of which the wad, or cartridge paper, remained smoking in the cloth of his tunic', remembered Lieutenant Scheltens of Bijlandt's 7th

Infantry Battalion.[65] But the head of Bourgeois's and Donzelot's columns were now approaching the hedge as well, and their front ranks were firing effective volleys of their own. Together with their mass of numbers, and all the Napoleonic paraphernalia of terror, the drumming, the trumpets, the shouting, the Netherlanders began to falter. 'The Belgians, assailed with terrible fury, returned the fire of the enemy for some time with great spirit', wrote Lieutenant Hope of the 92nd, who were watching from their positions 50 yards to the rear, but then they broke. Their officers succeeded in rallying them for a time, but not for long and, with the exception of Scheltens' 7th battalion, they poured back in disorder.[66] Some were rallied behind the Allied lines, but they were ineffective as a fighting force for the rest of the day, apart from being used to escort prisoners.

The 95th Rifles, in their sandpit at the crossroads, were still pouring fire into the left-hand flank of Bourgeois's column, which caused them to veer to the right, but from the French perspective it now seemed as if they had gained the ridge. They could not see any other Allied troops immediately ahead of them and they saw the Allied gunners abandoning their guns as they came up. This was a deliberate tactic, the gun crews running back so they were not slaughtered but bargaining on the French not being able or inclined to drag their guns away, and then returning to them later. One crew did panic at this stage in the battle, and 'spiked' theirs – this meant hammering a nail down the vent hole, which put it out of use – but they were the only ones. Bourgeois's men, still in the lead, but with Donzelot's and Marcognet's closing fast in echelon behind them, had not, however, realised quite what an obstacle the sunken lane was; several French officers referred to it as a 'ravine with banks so steep it could not be crossed'.[67] Trying to manoeuvre the dense columns through the first hedge, across the lane and up the other side temporarily broke their momentum, which pause meant that they could not immediately exploit Bijlandt's flight. It was also getting increasingly hard to see what was going on as by now the repeated volleys and artillery fire meant that the area east of the crossroads was covered in dense white smoke. The disadvantages of the French massed-column formation now became clear. Unable to see, and with the din and chaos making it almost impossible to hear orders, some battalions went left and some right, milling along the front of the hedge, and quickly losing their formation, which until now they had managed to preserve.

General Picton had been watching the débâcle of Bijlandt's brigade, and appreciated that there was a real danger of the French breaking through. This was, of course, the weakest part of Wellington's line, and Picton only had his two below-strength British brigades, which had been so badly mauled at Quatre Bras. Pack's brigade numbered only about 1,400 men and there were now 8,000 of Marcognet's men about to breast the ridge in front of them. Kempt, on Pack's right and between him and the crossroads, had rather more, but faced Bourgeois's brigade. Picton, who was dressed in civilian clothes and wearing a top hat as his uniform was still en route from Ostend, now ordered both brigades forward. Leaving the 44th in reserve, Pack formed the 1st, 42nd and 92nd Highlanders into line and marched them forward. They didn't have that far to move, only about 50 yards, until they were within 20 yards of the French columns. They then halted and delivered three volleys into the head and flanks of Marcognet's struggling battalions as they tried to cross the road. Kempt made the same manoeuvre on the right, urged on by Picton, who was at this point shot through the head by a French sharpshooter and fell dead from his horse. The battalions were only too keen to move. Anything was better than lying there under the fire of the Grand Battery; to hear the noise of the French advance but not be able to react to it had stretched their endurance.

Their move up was not quite the textbook advance in line that may be supposed. The men were tired after Quatre Bras. Few had eaten, they had had little sleep the previous night, and the going through the corn and over the wet ground was as difficult for them as it was for the French. Edward Stephens of 32nd described it more as 'wading up to our middle in corn' and 'not being able to get up to them' but that 'we peppered them pretty well as they were getting through the gaps in the hedges'. On the right, the 95th were relieved when Kempt's men came up. 'They had arrived at the very hedge behind which we were – their muskets almost muzzle to muzzle, and a French mounted officer attempted to seize the Colours of the 32nd Regiment', wrote an officer in the sandpit. The Frenchman was instantly run through by Sergeant Switzer with his pike, and then finished off by Ensign John Birtwhistle with his sword. When they saw Kempt's men rushing through the hedge they turned, but 'walked off in close columns with the greatest steadiness', although rather surprised by the sudden appearance of British infantry who had been hidden by the ground and smoke until they were suddenly upon them with 'our tremendous huzza'.[68]

Captain Duthilt, in the front French ranks with his 45th Regiment, was rushing at the batteries, the line of now-deserted Allied guns along the hedge line, when 'suddenly our path was blocked: English battalions concealed in the hollow road, stood up and fired at us at close range'.[69] Picton's move served temporarily to halt d'Erlon's advance but his weak brigade could not hope to defeat it. Looking along the line to the east of the crossroads, Bourgeois's men had been pushed into Donzelot's columns by the fire of the 95th in the sandpit, but both formations were still occupying the sunken lane. Beyond them Marcognet's men, with the 45th Ligne in the lead, were also on the lane; and beyond them Durutte's division, the last to move and furthest on the French right (Allied left), was now only a hundred yards from the ridge. There was a large gap in the Allied line opposite them where Bijlandt's men should have been, a space temporarily now filled by a very thin line of red coats. From Napoleon's command post 900 yards away down the hill at La Belle Alliance, it looked as if he had taken the ridge. The Allies' position was critical. A renewed push by d'Erlon must break through and penetrate Wellington's position, outflanking his main force to the west of the road and opening the way to Brussels.

The Allied position immediately to the west of the road at La Haie Sainte seemed little better. Of Quiot's two brigades, Charlet's infantry, supported by Dubois's cuirassiers, had made the farmhouse their immediate target. As Bourgeois had advanced just to the east of the road, Charlet's men had marched in column up to the hedge which marked the southern edge of the orchard, whilst the cuirassiers had branched off into the open fields on the west. La Haie Sainte was a large farmhouse, not a château like Hougoumont, but, like all prosperous Brabant farms, it had a large yard with barns. It was tactically important as, if Napoleon seized it, the French would have an advanced protected position from which they could use their guns. The struggle for La Haie Sainte became, rather like Hougoumont, a battle within the battle, with the defenders fighting on doggedly against numerous assaults sometimes in isolation from what was happening elsewhere.

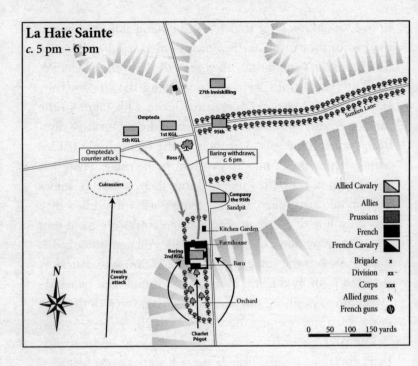

La Haie Sainte
c. 5 pm – 6 pm

27th Inniskilling

Sunken Lane

Ompteda

5th KGL   1st KGL

95th

Ompteda's counter attack

Ross

Baring withdraws, c. 6 pm

Cuirassiers

Company the 95th

Sandpit

Kitchen Garden

Farmhouse

Baring 2nd KGL

Barn

French Cavalry attack

N

Orchard

Charlet Pégot

Allied Cavalry	
Allies	
Prussians	
French	
French Cavalry	
Brigade	x
Division	xx
Corps	xxx
Allied guns	⁝
French guns	◖

0   50   100   150 yards

The farmhouse itself formed part of the north side of the square of buildings that made up the complex, thus closest to the Allied lines, and only 200 yards from the crossroads. North again was the kitchen garden, which was directly across the road from the sandpit held by the 95th Rifles. Beside the farmhouse was a large cowshed, then a range of stables on the western side. On the south side was a large barn, the one whose door had been stolen for firewood and which was giving Frederick Lindau such a problem to barricade. A wall ran from the barn to the road, then north along the road, via the main gate, until it joined the farmhouse again. Just beyond the gate was a small piggery. South of the barn was a long formal orchard, bounded by a hedge, and it was against the southern side of that hedge that the 2,200 men of Charlet's brigade were now forming up for their assault. The farm was held by the six companies of Major George Baring's 2nd Light Battalion of the King's German Legion, about 400 men, including, of course, Frederick Lindau and his brother. They were a forward outpost of their parent brigade, Ompteda's, deployed behind the ridgeline immediately to the north, in much the same way that the Guards occupied Hougoumont as a forward detachment for the two Guards brigades. Baring had not had the time or resources to fortify the buildings properly. His pioneers, those soldiers trained in making defences, had been detached and sent to Hougoumont (where they had not been able to do much either) and his men resorted to knocking loopholes in the walls. The barn door was never fully blocked, and was held during the day by the bravery of the soldiers defending it.

As Charlet's men formed up, Baring had three companies in the orchard, two in the farm buildings and one in the kitchen garden behind, linked in with the Rifles across the road in their sandpit. Lindau's company, commanded by Captain Graeme, were, from midday, standing behind the hedge at the southern end of the orchard waiting for the enemy. It was not long before 'a swarm of enemy skirmishers came', Lindau wrote, 'a thousand rifles exploded and a jubilant cry of "en avant!" resounded; behind them were two columns of enemy troops of the line who marched forward so quickly that we said to one another "The French are in such a hurry, it's as if they wanted to eat in Brussels". At first, the enemy were packed in front of our hedge we opened such a murderous fire on the dense crowd that the ground was immediately covered with a mass of wounded and dead. For the moment the French halted, then they fired, causing major destruction on us. My friend Harz collapsed at my side with a bullet through his body, Captain

Schaumann from the 2nd battalion fell too, my brother took him on his back and carried him into the farm, where he laid him down but he was already dead.' Poor Harz's gloomy prediction from his dream had come true in the first few minutes of fighting. Many more would soon follow him. There was a particular bitterness to the fighting in La Haie Sainte, as if all the pent-up fury and hatred the Germans felt for the French after their appalling behaviour as occupiers was now being unleashed. Charlet's men would pay dearly for what their compatriots had done.

The weight of their numbers forced Lindau and his comrades slowly back through the orchard and into the farm buildings. They went slowly, fighting from tree to tree, covering each other as they reloaded, the French so closely packed that several times three of four fell to one bullet, but relentlessly pushing the German riflemen back into the farmyard. Baring, still on his horse, had his bridle broken by a bullet and Major Bosewiel, his second-in-command, was killed, along with three other officers and six were wounded. This was about the time when Picton brought his battalions forward. Alten, the divisional commander, who had been observing the action from behind the crossroads, and, realising the importance of holding the buildings, told Kielmannsegge to detach a battalion from his Hanoverian Brigade and double it forward the 200 yards from the ridge to reinforce Baring's men. Kielmannsegge sent Lieutenant-Colonel Klencke's Lüneburg Battalion, who set off in column across the open ground. Baring sent men out to guide them in, and they were just on the point of meeting up north of the farmyard when they were seen by Dubois.

The ground immediately west of La Haie Sainte is undulating, and Dubois's cuirassiers, all 780 of them, appear to have approached more or less unseen, also masked by the smoke rolling across the battlefield. Actually Colonel Ordener, who commanded the 1st Cuirassiers, claimed to have been told by Ney to attack Ross's gun battery, which was positioned just forward of the crossroads and which was causing huge casualties to Quiot's men. He was advancing behind La Haie Sainte to take Ross in the flank when he unexpectedly saw poor Klencke's Lüneburgers, moving in a column from left to right across his front. Attacking infantry in column in the open was the cuirassiers' dream. Ordener ordered his trumpeter to blow the charge. It was not a very fast charge; the ground was too wet and the horses too blown to manage more than a trot, but each of his squadrons in turn rode over the now-condemned battalion. There was no time for the German infantrymen to form square; they were too strung out even if their training had been of a sufficient standard. Ordener himself claimed to have killed three officers, the Colour was taken, and within minutes the Lüneburg Battalion had ceased to exist. Half the battalion were killed or wounded, including Klencke, and 180 later listed as missing, meaning either that they were taken prisoner and had not found their way back, or their nerves had got the better of them and they had run. The wounds were bad. The height of a cuirassier on his horse, and the length of his sword, meant that he hardly needed even to rise in his stirrups to bring his stroke down on an infantryman's head. The most common stroke was directly onto the crown, usually splitting the head in two; alternatively, a diagonal stroke would cut through the shoulder and neck. Almost as an afterthought the cuirassiers made for the guns. Ross's men saw what was happening and ran back, taking their horses but leaving the guns themselves, two of which the French disabled.

Ordener now moved onto the ridge itself, where the remainder of Ompteda's and Kielmannsegge's brigades quickly formed squares, joined by those Lüneburgers who were still alive, more of whom were cut down as they ran back. The cuirassiers milled around the squares, who held their fire, finally giving them several volleys that proved fairly ineffective. Ordener would later say that this was Napoleon's great opportunity. He had encircled La Haie Sainte, disabled Ross's battery, and was occupying the ridge together with Crabbe's regiment. He would also claim that he had taken 24 guns, which was a gross exaggeration. Foy's and Bachelu's divisions from Reille's corps, not yet involved at Hougoumont, stood waiting only 800 yards to the south. East of the road Bourgeois, Donzelot and Marcognet held the sunken lane. The Allied position suddenly looked very, very precarious.

Another man who had been watching the situation deteriorate, and who had greater tactical sense than Wellington would credit him with, was Uxbridge. He was positioned behind the crossroads, and could see what was happening on both sides of the road. Behind him, still motionless, hidden from sight and, masked by the thick smoke and rising ground, unable themselves to see what was happening the far side of the sunken lane, were his two heavy-cavalry brigades. Somerset, with his Household regiments, was on the right behind Kielmannsegge and Ompteda, whilst Ponsonby with his Union Brigade, was on the east side of the road, his regiments forming a line behind Kempt's and Pack's men. They were still dismounted, standing in columns, having been moving around behind the ridge to avoid the fire from the Grand Battery. Captain William Elton of the King's Dragoon Guards noted that they were safer when they moved further forward, nearer the ridge, 'the shot passing over us and killing the Belgian cavalry who took our ground during the time they stayed in the field, and previous to their running away and plundering our baggage',[70] which was a bit unfair as it was in fact the Hanoverian cavalry who would flee. It was, though, a frustrating time for them. They heard 'the thunder of cannon, the fire of musketry, and the shouts near us; and we saw many wounded men passing towards the rear: some were carried in blankets, others walked slowly along, and several fell and died'.[71] They knew it could not be long until it was their turn.

Uxbridge saw that the weight of both brigades could throw back d'Erlon's infantry from the east of the crossroads and Dubois's cuirassiers from the west, and rode over himself to both Somerset and Ponsonby, telling them to close up to the lane. 'A slight murmur of gladness passed along the ranks'.[72] The word 'Mount' was given, then the order 'Draaaaaw Swords!' rang out from each squadron. On the command 'Swords', 2,500 gauntleted right hands reached across to find their sword hilts hanging on their left side. Pulled first so that the hand was level with their face, and the tip just in the scabbard, on a nod from their officers they brought the hilts down on their right knees at the 'Carry'. The next order in the Household Brigade was 'Form line on the leading squadron' then the trumpet sounded 'Walk March', and both brigades started slowly forward. In the first line of the Household Brigade rode the 1st Life Guards on the right, then the King's Dragoon Guards in the middle and the 2nd Life Guards on the left. Behind them came the Blues. In the Union Brigade all three regiments moved as one line. The Royals were on the right, Ben the Ruler chivvying and fussing his trumpeter, then the Inniskillings and, slightly behind, the Scots Greys.

They picked their way forward but still 'saw no enemy; yet there was a strange medley of sounds, musket shots, and the roar of cannon, beyond the rising ground in front of us'.[73] The way the brigades had been formed up meant that the Blues and the Greys should have formed a second line, a reserve to be deployed to support the first line, but that was not how things were to work out. The trumpets sounded 'Trot'. The odd cannon shot was coming into their ranks. Private Youeson nudged Playford as they rode tightly packed together, saying 'Shaw is hit!' Looking to his left Playford saw Shaw's head had fallen, his right hand was in the air and his sword dangled by its knot from his wrist. Moments later they saw Shaw's horse, generally reckoned to be the best in the regiment, gallop off riderless in front of them, but Playford thought Shaw had only been winded by a spent round.

Just short of the lane, Ponsonby's ADC, de Lacy Evans, simply raised his hat, which was enough for the Union Brigade commanding officers to know what they had to do, rather disconcerting Colonel Joseph Muter of the Inniskilling Dragoons, who had dismounted to adjust his cloak, which had slipped behind his saddle. It was now that the trumpeters blew the urgent call 'Charge', two sets of sharply ascending notes, and it is a testament to their training that they could do so through lips dry with fear. Uxbridge gave the same signal to Somerset, and the 16-year-old John Edwards of the Blues, just over five foot tall, who had joined the regiment as a boy aged eleven, and who was the duty trumpeter for the day, took up the call. The Household Brigade charged. Where they were, on the right, the hedges along the sunken lane were not so much of an obstacle, and the front rank were mostly through them when the 'Charge' was blown. There was a great cheer 'and at that moment a line of French horsemen in bright armour appeared in front of us; they were shouting, waving their swords and sabring English infantry and artillerymen who had not got out of our way. Our shouts arrested their attention, and looking up they saw fearful ranks of red horsemen come galloping forward, shouting and brandishing their swords.' These were Dubois's cuirassiers, some on the ridge itself, others milling around in the open around La Haie Sainte, still butchering the odd Lüneburger, their horses blown, and not expecting British cavalry. 'The charge of the Life Guards was tremendous! They rushed with overwhelming fury on the ranks of the enemy and hurled them back in confusion.' In fact the next ten minutes were a bloody mêlée of heavy cavalry on heavy cavalry. The better armed and protected cuirassiers, with their long swords, gave as good as they got but they rode tired horses, and the Household Brigade had the advantage of being fresh, having the slope behind them, and generally being better trained.

As the Life Guards and the cuirassiers met it was 'like the ringing of ten thousand blacksmiths' anvils'.[74] The short distance they charged meant that the Household Brigade hit the French still in relatively tight formation, although those who had crossed the lane where the hedges were more impenetrable lost their order. However, once engaged, this violent mêlée became a series of individual duels and fights between small groups. It reminded Corporal Richard Coulter 'of Mr Greenwood's Braziers Shop, such a rattling of swords about their backs and helmets' it was 'almost laughable'. He received a cut on his bridle hand, his left hand in which he held his reins. A cuirassier's sword ran through his shoulder but did not reach his skin. His horse had his eye almost cut out.[75] Shaw appears to have found another horse, as Corporal Webster then saw him attack a cuirassier who thrust at him.

Shaw parried the thrust, and before the man had a chance to recover he had cut him right through his brass helmet to the chin so that 'his face fell off like an apple'. Private Dakin, who was with Shaw, knocked two cuirassiers off their horses before being dismounted himself. Fighting on his feet, he 'divided both their heads with cuts five and six'.

Private Hodgson, another fighter and artists' model, 'a perfect Achilles', attacked a cuirassier who was an Irishman in French service. He dashed at Hodgson shouting 'Damn you, I'll stop your crowing'. It was the first time Hodgson had fought with swords other than at drill, and he shuddered. His first blow landed squarely on the Irishman's cuirass with such force that it nearly broke his arm. Watching the Irishman, he realised he could move his own horse quicker. 'So, dropping the reins, and guiding his horse with his knees, as the cuirassier at last gave point, Hodgson cut his sword hand off, and then dashing the point of his sword into the man's throat, turned it round and round.'[76] Poor Thomas Playford found it all rather more difficult because he couldn't find any cuirassiers to fight. The first who 'looked me in the face rode off before we crossed swords, not I suppose from fear of personal conflict, but from noticing that it was impossible for them to maintain their ground against our numbers'. He got held up trying to get through the hedge, but once the other side saw 'fearful carnage' on the Brussels road; however, by the time he got there all he 'could do was to ride after some cuirassiers who contrived to escape. But in whatever direction I turned every Frenchman got out of my way, excepting one cuirassier who fell completely into my power. He was unhorsed, his helmet was knocked off, and I raised my hand to cleave his skull; but at that moment compassion sprung up within me, I checked the blow and let the conquered cuirassier escape with a wound on the side of his head.'[77]

Elton's squadron of the King's Dragoon Guards, the left-hand squadron, thus nearest to the 2nd Life Guards, had found themselves amongst the cuirassiers as soon as they got into the lane, and the first part of their fight was spent clearing it. They lost several men killed as they fell trying to get over the first hedge, and then cornered a large group of cuirassiers, blocking them in between the high banks. They slowly killed them all, but found that 'their cuirasses secured them to such a degree, that not one blow told out of five'. Ironically the time this took was to save many of them. Their right-hand squadron, who had an easier time at the beginning, galloped straight through, and their momentum took them well on down the slope to their front.

The Blues, who should have been kept back to act as a reserve, had become entangled with the first rank as they were crossing the sunken lane and became enmeshed in the same fight. Uxbridge would later never stop criticising himself for not insisting that they and the Scots Greys behind the Union Brigade stay back, but for now the Blues were fighting for their lives as well. Robert Hill, their commanding officer, was soon shot in the arm by one of the voltigeurs, the skirmishers who had led the French advance, and who were now hiding in the hedges along the Brussels road, from where they were taking pot shots. Surrounded by five cuirassiers, he thought his hour had come, until the fat Tom Evans, his trumpeter, came to his rescue. He killed three before his sword broke as he was despatching the fourth; undeterred, he used the hilt as a knuckle duster and duly despatched the fifth. Elley, who should have stayed with Uxbridge to exercise some control, had got carried away and charged with his old regiment. He was wounded by a French officer, but managed to kill him, taking his cuirass as a trophy which he would later wear on parades, to the slight irritation of his brother officers. Cornet George Storey was about to kill another French officer when his victim shouted, 'Don't kill me! Don't you remember me?' Storey, who was a long-serving officer, had been taken prisoner in 1794 and for seven years kept in gaol in Verdun, where this man had been his compassionate gaoler. He duly spared his life.

Slowly – and the whole action only lasted about 15 minutes – the strength and weight of the Household Brigade began to tell and, where they could, the cuirassiers started to break off and ride back. Although there was little that could be done for the Lüneburgers, lying bleeding and screaming around La Haie Sainte, the guns were safe and the threat to the ridge was over, at least for the time being. Across the road, the Union Brigade had charged at the same time. The first regiment to engage were the Royals. Phil Dorville's and Alexander Kennedy Clark's squadrons on the right smashed into those of Dubois's cuirassiers who had worked their way onto the Brussels road and also into the left-hand columns of Bourgeois's brigade, hitting Colonel Gentry's 105th Ligne while it was struggling across the sunken lane. Charles Radcliffe's squadron hit the left flank of Donzelot's men. It wasn't really a cavalry charge, as no sooner had Ponsonby given the signal and the trumpeters blown but the Union Brigade regiments were on the enemy and became tangled up with them in the hedges and along the lane. Kennedy Clark reckoned his squadron were only 80 yards away when they 'charged' and, although a few may have broken into a gallop, most were trotting uphill. His squadron also had to get past Kempt's battalions, who were still firing from the corn in front of them. As the French saw the Royals approach they became 'seized with panic, gave us fire which brought down about twenty men, went instantly about and endeavoured to regain the opposite side of the hedges'.[78] Captain Edward Windsor, Peninsular veteran and the Secretary's (Sigismund Trafford) close friend, was one of those killed. This left his poor widowed mother Dorothy penniless as she had used up what money she had purchasing his commission.[79]

Clark now saw the Eagle of the 105th Ligne. 'The officer who carried it, and his companions, were moving with their backs towards me, and endeavouring to force their way through the crowd. I gave the order to my squadron "Right shoulders forward! Attack the colour!" On reaching it I ran my sword into the officer's right side, a little above the hip-joint. I called out twice "Secure the Colour! Secure the Colour! It belongs to me". On taking up the Eagle I endeavoured to break the Eagle off the pole, with the intention of putting it in the breast of my coat, but I could not break it. Corporal Styles said "Pray Sir! Don't break it!", on which I replied "Very well. Carry it to the rear as fast as you can. It belongs to me."'[80] This incident, which was to be relived so many times in the coming years, was to become one of the bitterest controversies of the battle.

Private Smithies rode in Dorville's squadron and hit the cuirassiers. 'It was desperate work indeed, cutting through their steel armour', he wrote. 'On we rushed at each other, and when we met the shock was terrific. We wedged ourselves between them as much as possible, to prevent them from cutting, and the noise of the horses, the clashing of swords against their steel armour, can be imagined only by those who have heard it. There were some riders who caught hold of each other's bodies – wrestling fashion – and fighting for life, but the superior physical strength of our regiment soon showed itself.'[81] Smithies' description gives an indication of just how many men were packed into a very small space.

Next to the Royals, the Inniskillings attacked the right of Donzelot's column whilst the Scots Greys smashed their way into the 45th Ligne, the leading battalion of Marcognet's division. They were reorganising themselves on the Allied side of the hedge and their officers were confident that they had gained their objective. The Greys should have been kept back by Ponsonby, but in the excitement and confusion they had come up level with his two right-hand regiments, and when they saw the French their colonel, Inglis Hamilton, shouted, 'Now then, Scots Greys, charge!' This they duly did. Hamilton rode straight at the hedges in front, 'which he took in grand style' exactly as if he was hunting, and landed in the middle of the startled and quickly terrified French infantry with his squadrons piling in behind him.[82] A great cheer rose from the Greys' ranks as they surged forward. John Dickson dug his spurs into brave old Rattler, his beloved charger, and 'we were off like the wind'. As he surged forward he saw his squadron leader, Major Hankin, fall but he felt 'a strange thrill run through me, and I am sure my noble beast felt the same, for, after rearing for a moment, she sprang forward, uttering loud neighings and snortings, and lept [sic] over the holly-hedge at a terrific speed'. The lane here was sunk deep, and the hedges high; rather than clear them they must have scrambled down one bank and then up the other side. Amazingly only a few of the Greys in their tall bearskin helmets fell. Although the right-hand squadrons hit the French on the lane itself, those on the left, having cleared the hedges, charged on downhill and hit the French in the side. As they went they had passed through the 92nd Highlanders, who had been firing volleys into Marcognet's forward battalion as part of Picton's advance, and some of them now charged forward with the Greys, grabbing hold of their stirrups, which must have been as annoying and dangerous for the poor horsemen as it was convenient for the war artists. Dickson afterwards claimed that he saw his old friend Pipe Major Cameron of the 92nd playing 'Johnny Cope' as they passed, but his memory may have matured with age as the din was tremendous. Beside Dickson rode 'young Armour, our rough-rider from Mauchline' – a rough rider was one of the staff in a cavalry regiment who broke and made the young horses. Dickson was very impressed that Armour was a relation of Robbie Burns's wife. Sergeant Ewart rode on the right of their line beside their troop officer, the whoring young Francis Kinchant.

The first Frenchman Dickson encountered was a young officer who slashed at him with his sword, but Dickson parried the blow and broke his arm with his sabre. 'The French were fighting like tigers. Some of the wounded were firing at us as we passed; and poor Kinchant, who had spared one of these rascals, was himself shot by the officer he had spared.' There would be no more visits to brothels, no more amusing letters to John Hall, nor begging ones to the 'Old Goat', and no one to dream of keeping the divine Letitia warm at night. Ewart saw what had happened. A French officer begged Kinchant for mercy. Kinchant refrained from killing him and asked for his sword. Ewart told the inexperienced Kinchant it was no time for mercy but Kinchant's better instincts had prevailed and he had taken the Frenchman prisoner instead. As soon as Kinchant's back was turned the French officer drew out a pistol and shot him so that Kinchant fell backwards off his horse. Ewart wheeled round, 'and was again entreated by this villain for mercy in the same supplicating terms as before, the only answer to which he [Ewart] returned was "ask mercy of God for the devil a bit will ye get at my hands" and with one stroke of his sabre severed his head from his body'.[83]

They came to an open space where Dickson saw Ewart attacking five or six men who were attempting to run with the Eagle of the 45th. Armour and Dickson forced their way over to him, just as Ewart killed the last of them and took the Eagle. 'He and I had a hard contest for it', Ewart recalled, 'he thrust for my groin – I parried it off, and I cut him through the head; after which I was attacked by one of their lancers, who threw his lance at me, but missed the mark by my throwing it off with my sword by my right side; then I cut him from the chin upwards, which cut went through his teeth. Next I was attacked by a foot soldier who, after firing at me, charged me with his bayonet; but he very soon lost the combat, for I parried it, and cut him down through the head; so', he added in a matter-of-fact way, 'that finished the contest for the Eagle.'[84]

James Anton was one of the Highlanders swept along by the Greys. He wrote a very vivid description of it. 'Horses' hoofs sinking in men's breasts, breaking bones and pressing out their bowels', he recorded, which again shows just how crowded the battle space was. 'Riders' swords streaming in blood, waving over their heads and descending in deadly vengeance', he continued. 'Stroke follows stroke, like the turning of a flail in the hand of a dextrous thresher; the living stream gushes red from the ghastly wound, spouts in the victor's face and stains him with brains and blood. There the piercing shrieks and dying groans; here the loud cheering of an exulting army, animating the slayers to deeds of signal vengeance! It is a scene of vehement destruction, yells and shrieks, wounds and death; and the bodies of the dead served as pillows for the dying.'[85]

For the French infantry, these cavalry attacks were completely unexpected. Captain Duthilt of the 45th had been trying to re-establish some sort of order in the bloody confusion and to 'reform the platoons, since a disordered group can achieve nothing. Just as I was pushing one of our men back into the ranks I saw him fall at my feet from a sabre slash. I turned round instantly – to see English cavalry forcing their way into our midst and hacking us to pieces. Just as it is difficult, if not impossible, for the best cavalry to break into infantry who are formed up in squares, so it is true that once the ranks have been broken and penetrated, then resistance is useless and nothing remains for the cavalry to do but slaughter at almost no risk to themselves. This is what happened. In vain our poor fellows stood up to bayonet those cavalrymen mounted on powerful horses, and the few shots fired in this chaotic mêlée were just as fatal to our own men as to the English.'[86]

The French infantry now began to throw down their weapons and belts and run back down the hill. Whereas just ten minutes earlier they thought they had carried the main Allied position, as had their emperor watching from La Belle Alliance, they were now streaming in disorder through the trampled corn through which they had so laboriously just attacked. They had lost two Eagles, regarded as just as sacred by French regiments as their English counterparts valued their Colours. Most Eagles had understandably been removed by the Bourbons whilst Napoleon was on Elba, but he had re-presented them at a very grand ceremony on Champ de Mars on 1 June just before his army marched. Dressed in his imperial robes, rather than uniform, his soldiers were told to swear to defend them with the sacrifice of their blood, to which they roared 'We swear it! We swear it!' in reply. The Eagle of the 45th carried the great Napoleonic battle honours on coloured streamers under the silver eagle itself – Austerlitz, Jena, Friedland, Essling and Wagram – all battles at which the 45th had fought with distinction. Waterloo would not be amongst them, and an awful lot of blood had now been shed in its vain defence.

On the French right, Durutte's men had attacked Papelotte and driven out the Nassauers but were now attacked in turn by the 12th Light Dragoons. William Hay was commanding the leading squadron, and was ordered by his commanding officer, Frederick Ponsonby, to move them forward through the hedges in front of their position to the field beyond so that they could form line. Hay was about to move off when there was a great barking and he saw his dog Dash, who should have been secured way back with the baggage. Dash adored his horse, and 'up he came in delight, jumping at the horse's head and my knee in turns, having satisfied himself at finding us out he was in raptures. With the shooting going on I dare say he fancied himself transported to a field-day on the Lammermuir Hills.'[87] Forming up at the top of the ridge, which was much less marked on the left of the Allied line, and with Dash still barking at his horse's heels, Hay saw Durutte's skirmish line firing at the 71st Foot across the lane, and French infantry forming squares just 80 yards away, which they had time to do on that flank. Ponsonby placed himself in the centre and shouted 'Forward', and they charged, one of the few times during the Waterloo campaign when British cavalry engaged at a gallop.

Hay assumed the squares were their target but they suddenly saw several squadrons of Jacquinot's cavalry, deployed by d'Erlon as his flank guard; these had been hidden from view, and were now just in front of them. 'On we went at a gallop, sweeping past, and close to the muskets of the French, and over the skirmishers, who were running in all directions seeking shelter' until they were engaged hand to hand with the *chasseurs à cheval*. As Hay passed, one skirmisher fired at him from point-blank range but missed. Hay took a cut at his head but also missed and was going too fast to turn. This was a more unequal contest. The *chasseurs* were bigger men on heavier horses and there were three times more of them than the two squadrons of the 12th, their third squadron having not, for some reason, joined them. Ponsonby went back to see what had happened to it, telling Hay to extricate the rest of the regiment as best he could and take them back behind the sunken lane. As Hay was doing so a shell burst under his horse, which 'sat down as a dog would do'. Hay did not realise what had happened, and kept kicking the poor animal, until he had to slide off backwards over its tail. Two French lancers charged him. He jumped down into the lane, and they were brought down by musket fire from the 71st, 'leaving their carcasses where they intended mine should be laid'. Hay recovered, and witnessed the Union Brigade charge 'like a torrent, shaking the very earth, and sweeping everything before them'. Sadly Dash had not returned. One of Hay's dragoons had seen him shot by the French. He was much regretted.[88] He was not the only loss. Of 155 men who had charged ten minutes earlier, only 47 had made it back. A light regiment like the 12th were no match for heavy cavalry like the *chasseurs*, but their action, combined with the collapse of the divisions on his left, had succeeded in making Durutte pull back.

Colonel Frederick Ponsonby was also missing. He had been

wounded in both arms in the mêlée. A few of his men tried
to reach him but were cut down. Unable to control his horse,
Ponsonby was carried on towards the French lines. He was hit
on the head by a sabre and fell senseless to the ground.
Coming to, and looking round to see if he could make his
escape, a passing *lancier* saw him and, muttering 'Tu n'es pas
mort, coquin', stuck his lance through his back. 'My head
dropped, the blood gushed into my mouth, a difficulty of
breathing came on and I thought it was all over.' Not long
afterwards he came to again, only to find a *tirailleur* rifling his
pockets. He told him which pocket he had three dollars in
and the man ripped open his clothes, took it and left. A
second *tirailleur* came along also intent on robbing him, but so
did their officer, who said he 'feared I was badly wounded. I
replied I was and that I wished to be removed to the rear.' The
Frenchman said it was against orders to move any of the
wounded until after the battle, but that it would soon be over
as he had heard that Wellington had been killed and six British
battalions had surrendered. He gave Ponsonby some brandy
and made him as comfortable as he could. Later another
tirailleur came up and used his body as cover, firing over him
and, when he finally left, saying cheerily, 'You will be glad to
know that we are now withdrawing! Goodbye, my friend!'[89]

It was now about 2.30 p.m. Uxbridge's initiative had, at this
stage, been successful. The Allied position was safe, the main
French attack had been repulsed and d'Erlon's corps were
streaming in a disorganised rabble back to whence they had
started. It had, so far, been an almost textbook cavalry attack,
launched at exactly the right time, and under fairly tight control. What was about to happen would be very different. By
the time both the Household and the Union brigades had
hacked their way through the enemy immediately in front of

them, they found themselves at the bottom of the valley in front of the Allied position. This was not actually very far, only about 400 yards from where they had started but their blood was up, their horses still relatively fresh, the ground apparently in their favour and they now saw in front of them the tempting target of 10,000 fleeing Frenchmen. They also saw, on a slight rise just 200 yards away, Napoleon's Grand Battery that they had just witnessed killing so many of their comrades. John Dickson was more circumspect than most. He saw that the ground at the bottom of the slope, already slippery, had been churned into deep mud by the French advance. He also thought there was a ploughed field in front of the Grand Battery. This was unlikely and it was more probably the trampled field of corn, but whatever it was poor old Rattler sank to her knees as he struggled on. Fresh as she may have been, she was now tiring quickly.

At this moment, however, Colonel Inglis Hamilton, still possibly enjoying the charge rather like a hunt, rode up shouting 'Charge! Charge the guns!' and went off like the wind up the hill 'towards the terrible battery that had made such deadly work among the Highlanders. It was the last we saw of our colonel, poor fellow! His body was found with both arms cut off.' But they followed of course and then got amongst the guns 'and we had our revenge. Such slaughtering! We sabred the gunners, lamed the horses, and cut their traces and harness. I can hear the Frenchmen crying "Diable!" when I struck at them, and the long drawn out hiss through their teeth as my sword went home. The artillery drivers sat on their horses weeping aloud as we went among them; they were mere boys.' Even 'Rattler lost her temper and bit and tore at everything that came her way. She seemed to have got new strength.'[90] Fifteen guns were put out of action but that was only a fraction of the Grand Battery. The gunners could be replaced, and it was an action that would now start to come at a terrible cost. The French 85th Ligne regiment had been rushed forward to help protect the guns, and as the Greys approached they formed square and poured fire into them. Soon the 'ground was strewn with red jackets and grey horses, and our cries of "Vive L'Empereur" proved to them that it would not be easy to beat us'.[91]

Robert Hill, and the Blues, who had been slightly behind the Household Brigade, realised what was happening and managed to rally at least their right-hand squadrons, who had come under fire from Reille's divisions drawn up in the open ground behind La Haie Sainte. Fat Tom Evans blew the 'Rally' as hard as he could, but it had little effect. Uxbridge, having charged with 2nd Life Guards, had checked his horse and was now back on the ridge, His visibility was limited by the smoke, but what was about to happen gradually became horribly apparent to him. Jacquinot's cavalry division, which had been guarding d'Erlon's right flank, and which had been attacked by William Hay and the 12th Light Dragoons, had not been seriously damaged and was regrouping. The 3rd and 4th Lanciers and the 3rd Chasseurs,* who had killed so many of the dragoons and Dash the dog, were hovering in the open, to the right, in other words the east, of the Grand Battery and neither Ponsonby nor Somerset had seen them. Behind the Grand Battery were a further 1,500 uncommitted cuirassiers of Milhaud's cavalry corps, initially deployed in support of Lobau; 450 from Watier's 13th Cavalry Division, and nearly 1,000 from Delort's 14th Division. De Lacy Evans, on Uxbridge's staff, recalled later that 'our men

---

* The 7th Hussars had been detached from Jacquinot by Napoleon and sent to find Grouchy.

were out of hand. The General, his staff and every officer within hearing exerted themselves to the utmost to reform the men; but the helplessness of the enemy offered no greater temptation to the dragoons and our efforts were abortive.'[92] Napoleon now loosed these cavalrymen on the rapidly tiring British regiments.

There were, in effect, two attacks. Milhaud's cuirassiers rode straight up the Brussels road and hit the Household Brigade in the side, whilst Jacquinot's men attacked from the east, sweeping into the Union Brigade as they struggled back up to the ridge from the Grand Battery. Some gave as good as they got. A cuirassier officer attacked Private Hodgson, fresh from despatching the Irishman. Hodgson turned, cut his horse at the 'nape' and, as it fell, the man's helmet rolled off. Hodgson saw he was a 'bald man with grey hairs'; the officer begged for mercy, but at that instant a troop of lancers were coming down full gallop, so Hodgson clove his head in two at a blow and escaped. Before he got back to the ridge the lancers caught up with him. As one of them thrust at Hodgson's back, he turned and cut the man's head off at the neck with one blow. The head bobbed onto his haversack, and he rode back with this grisly trophy into his own lines. Another cuirassier rode at one of the 2nd Life Guards trumpeters, and was about to decapitate him when he saw he was only a boy; he raised his sword and galloped past, only to be instantly cut in two by another Life Guard who hadn't seen his act of mercy. Cavalry trumpeters were at distinct disadvantage on the battlefield. They carried swords, but couldn't draw them as they had to hold onto their trumpets with their right hand and hold the reins in their left. In the Household Cavalry they also rode grey horses, as opposed to the blacks of the rest of the regiment, which made them very distinctive.

Private Thomas Hasker, who had charged with his squadron of the King's Dragoon Guards, was less fortunate. He engaged a cuirassier; they made several ineffectual passes at each other and then the man rode off. Hasker followed his regiment but his horse fell, and whilst he was getting up he found a second cuirassier cutting and slashing at his head. He fell again, and whilst he was lying on the ground a lancer stabbed him. He staggered around, only to be stabbed by a third with a sword. 'Very soon after, another man came up with a firelock and bayonet, and raising both his arms, thrust his bayonet (as he thought) into my side near my heart. The coat I had on was not buttoned, but fastened with brass hooks and eyes. Into one of these eyes the point of the bayonet entered, and was thus prevented penetrating my body. One of my fingers was cut off before I fell; and there I lay bleeding from at least a dozen places, and was soon covered with blood. I was also at that time plundered by the French soldiers of my watch, money, canteen, haversack and trousers.'[93]

Hasker was not alone. No one ever really knew what happened to the right-hand squadron of the King's Dragoon Guards, the one that had not been held up as Elton's had on the sunken lane, and which had charged on with Colonel Fuller, other than that he and the men around him were surrounded and cut to pieces. Lieutenant John Hibbert wrote afterwards that they 'never having been on service before, hardly knew how to act. They knew they were to charge, but never thought about stopping at the proper time, so that after entirely cutting to pieces a large body of cuirassiers, double their number, they still continued to gallop on instead of forming up and getting into line; the consequence was that they got amongst the French infantry and artillery and were miserably cut up.' Fuller tried to recover. He extricated about half his men from the mêlée and started back but the lancers overtook them. 'Our men were rendered desperate by the situation', Hibbert continued, and 'resolved to get out of the scrape or die rather than be taken prisoners'. And die many of them did, including Fuller, who was knocked off his horse and then skewered by a lance.[94]

Many of the Household Brigade did not seem to appreciate how dangerous their situation now was. Thomas Playford saw some of his friends lose their lives from 'rash bravado'. Still thinking that the French were on the run, they would ride 'singly out of their way to attack two or three enemies, and when a greater number came against them, their horses were blown and they could not escape. They could only sell their lives as dearly as possible'.[95] Playford himself still could not find anyone to attack, 'every enemy avoiding' him. He saw Private Joseph Hindley, whose horse had been killed, running to catch a loose French horse, pursued by a party of cuirassiers. Playford rode between them, and although the cuirassiers fired pistols at them, never easy off a fast-moving horse, they missed and he and Hindley made their escape. As they passed La Haie Sainte they had to fight through Charlet's infantry, who were still formed in squares. They were firing at every retreating British cavalryman, but only ever hit one horse, which, as they were only between 100 and 200 yards away, confirmed the Life Guards' view that the French infantry were bad shots.

Whilst Milhaud's cuirassiers were causing serious attrition to the Household Brigade, Jacquinot's lancers were taking an equally severe toll on the Union Brigade. As unfortunate as any was the Union Brigade commander, Major-General William Ponsonby, both liked and respected by his men. His groom had got lost with his main horse so he was still riding his hack as the Union Brigade advanced. He went with them, swept along in the rush, wearing, as John Dickson noted, his long fur-lined cloak and great cocked hat. He must have looked rather different to the French *lanciers*, and as he tried to ride back from the Battery, his hack not really able to struggle through the mud, he was quickly overtaken. Realising that he could not escape, he handed the locket he wore round his neck to his brigade major, Captain Thomas Reignolds, asking him to give it to his pregnant wife. Seconds later Sergeant Orban of the 4th Lanciers struck him down. Riding on, Orban and Colonel Bro sabred both Reignolds and two other men riding with him. A party of Greys making their way back across the valley stopped when they saw Reignolds, the locket in his outstretched hand, and quickly recovered it before riding on. It was not a good day to be called Ponsonby. The 4th Lanciers had suffered perhaps worst of all Napoleon's cavalry regiments in Russia, crossing the Niemen with 600 men but returning with 18, so perhaps their desire for some sort of revenge is understandable.

Vandeleur's 4th Cavalry Brigade had seen what was happening to the heavy-cavalry brigades but did not dare to move without orders, despite Müffling, Blücher's liaison officer to Wellington, and who was positioned near them, urging him to do so. Vandeleur was a distinguished Peninsular veteran who had seen the fury vented by Wellington on commanders who moved without him telling them to, and he waited too long. When he did finally decide to commit, he found Durutte's infantry still in front of him, and he moved his brigade first about a quarter of a mile to the west, crossing the ridgeline through Best's Hanoverians; sensibly, he ordered his commanding officers not to go further than the bottom of the slope. He only had about 1,000 men with him, the battered

12th Light Dragoons, minus Ponsonby, together with the 11th and 16th Light Dragoons. Placing himself at the head of the 16th, and having picked their way through the German infantry, Vandeleur charged over the ridge and hit Jacquinot's *lanciers* obliquely in the side, but by that stage it was really too late. Although they drove the *lanciers* back, the damage had been done. The casualties had been caused by a combination of artillery and infantry fire, but mostly from the French cavalry, the most feared of which were those *lanciers*. The British light cavalry were alone in Europe in eschewing the lance, thinking it outdated as a weapon, but then in Spain the light cavalry had been used much more for scouting and escorting tasks than in setpiece attacks. Now they had learned a savage lesson in how effective it could be when wielded by well-trained regiments like Jacquinot's. In Brussels some days later the Scots Greys counted several men with 10 or 12 lance wounds in them, and Private Lock had 18.[96]

When the regiments finally struggled back to their positions behind the ridgeline, they were drastically reduced. Of the 2,500 men who had charged under an hour before, over 800 were killed, wounded or missing, as were over 1,000 horses. 'The two finest brigades of the British cavalry' had virtually ceased to exist, and during the long afternoon and evening, Uxbridge would continually bemoan his and their lack of restraint. Those who remained would be used again and again in the hours ahead, but never with the same impact as in those first charges. In the 1st Life Guards only three officers remained unwounded and three never came back at all; Colonel Samuel Ferrior, who had so admired the Brabant farming, had his head cut open with a sabre and a lance wound through his body. Less than half the King's Dragoon Guards returned, and barely a quarter of the 2nd Life Guards.

When Thomas Playford and Joseph Hindley looked round they saw Hodgson but there was no sign of Corporal John Shaw and no one seemed to know what had happened to him. Across the road in the Union Brigade, Ben the Ruler had made it back, as had the Secretary but there was no sign of Edward Windsor nor of Charles Foster, whose oilskin had provoked such mirth only a few hours before. Colonel Muter of the Inniskillings had returned, presumably with his cloak, but the body of Colonel Inglis Hamilton of the Greys lay mutilated in the Grand Battery.

But d'Erlon's Corps had suffered equally crippling losses. There is no accurate estimate of their casualties, but around 3,000 had likely been killed. At one point in front of the sunken lane French muskets and packs lay in neat rows as if 'grounded by word of command'.[97] A further 3,000 had been taken prisoner. Some of these were able to escape in the confusion, as Corporal Canler did. He slipped away during the French cavalry counter-attack, and made a detour. He passed the body of an English dragoon officer. 'A sabre blow had split open his head and the brain had burst out of the skull. His fob pocket held a superb gold chain; despite the speed of my flight, I stopped a moment to grab this chain and a beautiful watch that was also gold. The English having stripped off my pack and arms, I applied the law of an eye for an eye.' Canler was not particular whom he looted from. A few paces further on he found the body of Lieutenant Labigne of 55th Line and took his writing case and linen. Then he legged it as fast as he could, joining the mass of fugitives to which d'Erlon's divisions had been reduced.[98] Although individual brigades would be reformed for limited operations later that day – such as Quiot's, which would soon re-attack La Haie Sainte – the corps had ceased to exist as a formation.

Those prisoners whom the Allies kept hold of were escorted back to the rear. Bijlandt's disgraced brigade made itself more useful by acting as escorts, much to Scheltens' disgust. He was equally irritated at a French battalion commander complaining that he had received a sabre cut on his nose, which was hanging down over his mouth. 'The good fellow might have fared much worse', he wrote. An active freemason, he was slightly mollified when two other French prisoners gave him the Masonic sign. He took them personally to the rear and ensured that they were not robbed, as most prisoners were on both sides. 'It was a great advantage to belong to a Masonic lodge', he noted, somewhat smugly, 'as this enabled one to enjoy very pleasant relations with the leading inhabitants of any town in which one happened to be garrisoned and it ensured protection in time of war.'[99]

5

18 JUNE 1815

Afternoon and Evening

It was now three p.m. It was hot, stiflingly hot, the unwashed soldiers slowly steaming in the sun, the still-sodden ground, the trampled corn, the gunpowder and the wounded giving off a particular stench. Napoleon's main attack had failed, and as he had been committing d'Erlon's corps he had received the unwelcome news that the Prussians had been sighted. Looking to his right, the Emperor had seen troops himself, in the far distance around Chapelle St Robert. At first he may have thought it was Grouchy, to whom Soult had been sending increasingly urgent messages to march to join their right wing, but at 1.15 p.m. a Prussian prisoner was brought in who confirmed that the dark figures emerging from the woods were the advance elements of Bülow's IV Corps, which was leading Blücher's march. Lobau's cavalry were consequently despatched east by the Emperor, to be followed by the rest of Lobau's corps. By now Prussian cavalry patrols from Schwerin's 1st Cavalry Brigade were well across the River Lasne and were beginning to encounter Lobau's cavalry in the Bois de Paris. Schwerin himself was killed in one of the first engagements.

The appearance of the Prussians gave Napoleon two

problems. First, he had to despatch much of his uncommitted infantry, namely Lobau's corps, to block them, which meant these troops were no longer available to Ney for the main assault. Secondly, he realised that he had to force Wellington's position before Blücher joined up with him. He still had several hours, as it would take at least that long for the Prussian main body to come up, but it imparted an urgency to French attacks that had previously followed a more leisurely timetable. Napoleon must also have realised that Grouchy was in danger of failing him, and that he could no longer rely on his 30,000 men, although in his memoirs he is at pains to point out that Lobau's orders were to hold the Prussians until he heard Grouchy come up behind them.

Although there was a lull whilst d'Erlon's shattered divisions tried to regroup themselves, the intensity of the fighting at Hougoumont increased.* At about two p.m. Tissot's men had brought up a howitzer, and started shelling the château and the farmyard buildings, setting them on fire. Mathew Clay, having just got back inside the farmyard before the north gate was closed by Lieutenant-Colonel Macdonnell, had been sent to man one of the upstairs rooms in the château; from here they were able to take well aimed shots at the French infantry still milling around between the wood and the walls. Soon French shells were landing against the building, and the room from which he was firing was set on fire. 'Our officer placed himself at the entrance of the room and would not allow anyone to leave his post until our positions became hopeless and too perilous to remain. We fully expected the floor to sink with us every moment and in our escape several of us were more or less injured', Clay recalled.[1] Ensign George Standen was an officer

---

* You may find it helpful to refer to the map on p.205.

in Clay's company. He saw the haystack, behind which Clay had been hiding earlier, go up in flames. The whole of the barn and cart house now caught fire as well. 'During the confusion three or four officers' horses rushed into the yard from the barn, and in a minute or two rushed back into the flames and were burnt', which surprised him as it was always supposed that horses will not face naked flame. 'Perhaps', he thought, 'some beam or large piece of wood fell and astonished them.'[2]

The burning château became very visible across the battle-field, prompting Wellington to send Macdonnell a curiously interfering message. The experienced veteran must have read it through slightly gritted teeth, particularly as Major Andrew Hamilton, the ADC, had risked his life to gallop down through the Hollow Way (as the British usually described the sunken lane) to deliver it. Hamilton found Colonel Home, who was still outside the buildings on the Hollow Way at that point, and delivered it to him instead. 'I see', wrote the Duke on one of the slips of ass's skin on which he wrote his despatches, 'that the fire has communicated itself from the haystack to the Roof of the Chateau. You must however still keep your Men in those parts to which the fire does not reach. Take care that men are not lost by the falling in of the Roof or floors. After they will have fallen in occupy the Ruined Walls inside of the Garden, particularly if it should be possible for the Enemy to pass through the Embers in the Inside of the House.'[3] Hamilton added insult to injury by then asking Home whether he had fully understood the Duke's orders. 'I do', he replied, 'and you can tell the Duke from me that unless we are attacked more vigorously than we have been hitherto we shall maintain the position without difficulty', which was remarkably sanguine given the circum-stances. Home then forced his way into the château yard and passed on Wellington's dictat but sadly history does not record Macdonnell's or Woodford's reaction.[4]

However, the defenders were now running short of ammunition. Each man would have started with the standard 50 rounds, but they had been in action for three hours and were running low. Captain Horace Seymour was one of Uxbridge's ADCs and happened to be in the vicinity of some of the 3rd Foot Guards officers near the Hollow Way, presumably on some errand to Grant's light-cavalry brigade, which was still positioned just behind the Guards. They asked him what he could do to find a resupply. Riding west along the ridge he came across Private Brewer of the Royal Waggon Train who, in one of those lucky coincidences which seemed to have such an effect on the battle, had a cartload of ball and cartridges. Explaining the desperate situation, he persuaded Brewer to gallop his wagon down the main avenue to the north gate of the château, the one that Legros had forced an hour earlier. Brewer was fired at by the French infantry for almost his entire journey, and his horses were hit, but he made it to the gate and the Guards got their ammunition. It was an act of extraordinary bravery. Brewer was rumoured to have transferred to the Guards after the battle but of this sadly there is no reliable record.[5]

The fire was spreading, and 'the heat and conflagration were very difficult to bear', wrote Colonel Woodford. 'Several men were burnt as neither Colonel Macdonnell or myself could penetrate to the stables where the wounded had been carried.'[6] 'Many of the wounded of both armies were arranged side by side, and we had no means of carrying them to a place of greater safety', Clay continued.[7] Corporal James Graham of the Coldstreams, the man who had recently helped Macdonnell slam shut the north gate, now asked the

Colonel whether he could leave his post in the firing line behind the garden wall. Surprised, Macdonnell asked why. 'I would not,' replied Graham, 'only my brother lies wounded in that building which has just caught fire.' Graham fought his way in through the flames, rescued his brother Joseph, who had also been involved in the savage fighting around the gates, and returned to his post.[8] Joseph Graham was one of the lucky ones, and many of the wounded were now burned to death as the blazing timbers fell in. The chapel, which adjoined the château, also caught fire, the flames reaching the altar at the east end above which was a large wooden crucifix. Bizarrely they only burned the foot of this cross, leaving the body of the crucified Christ untouched, 'which in so superstitious a country made a great sensation',[9] wrote George Standen. The part-burned crucifix still hangs there today.

The French artillery fire, still coming from the south-east corner of the orchard, also now secured a hit near the southern gate and blew it open. Sixty French infantry from the 3rd Regiment de Ligne under Lieutenant Toulouse rushed it and used their rifle butts to smash away the fragments but, as with Legros's effort earlier, there weren't enough of them and they were quickly shot down. 'No one was left inside except a Drummer Boy without his drum whom I lodged in the stable or outhouse', Clay wrote. Their commanding officer, Sarrand, led a second group to try to find another place to break in, but he was hit by a musket ball after only a few yards and fell, his thigh bone shattered.[10] But although the enemy had been forced out, the southern gate was partially destroyed. Clay was posted with Private Philpot under the archway to act as first line of defence against a repeat attack. Soon a second round shot burst what was left of the gates open, and they rushed to gather what pieces of wood they could find in the yard to effect some sort of barrier. Clay was then posted by a breach in the wall in the loft above the gate, to fire down on the French moving up to attack it. The wall was shattered, but they used the dead bodies of their comrades as a barricade, which absorbed much of the incoming musket fire.

Meanwhile Saltoun had been attempting to destroy the French guns which were causing all these problems from their position at the corner of the orchard. He had gathered his exhausted men and they had fought their way forward once more, skirmishing through the trees from their positions lining the Hollow Way. They came up against the 'best part of three French brigades',[11] namely those men left from Bauduin's, Soye's and now Tissot's attacks. Unsurprisingly Saltoun and his men were beaten back. The French howitzers kept firing, and they were forced once again into the Hollow Way. About two p.m. the decision was taken by General Byng, commanding the 2nd Guards Brigade, to relieve him. Colonel Francis Hepburn was sent down to the Hollow Way with the majority of his 3rd Foot Guards battalion. Saltoun withdrew to the ridge with what was left of his light companies, only one-third of the number he had started fighting with three hours before, and this time he was not ordered to return. He had already lost four horses shot from under him. Hepburn, with his fresh companies, knew that he had to regain possession of the orchard, and, as he remarked with extraordinary understatement, 'we advanced upon the enemy, crossed the orchard and occupied the front hedge, which I considered my post'.[12]

These rather matter-of-fact statements disguise the savagery and intensity of the fighting around Hougoumont. By the time Hepburn retook the orchard, the whole of the 2nd

Guards Brigade had been committed to the château, the gardens and the orchard, except for a small party left on the ridge with the Colours of the two battalions involved. At about two p.m. Wellington had moved four Brunswick battalions who had been in reserve around Merbe Braine forward to fill the gap they had left in the line. There was also a brave core of what was left of the Jaeger companies of the Lüneburg and Grubenhagen Hanoverian battalions. Altogether this amounted to 2,600 men, and ranged against them were 12,500 men from Reille's corps. They were fighting in an area not much more than 400 yards long, being the frontage of the farmyard, garden and orchard, by 200 yards – and only 100 yards at the western end. The numbers packed into that small area alone tell why the fighting was at such close quarters and so bloody.

Home complained that despite the pioneers being detached from other brigades to help, there had been hardly any preparatory defensive work carried out: 'not a single loop hole made in the garden wall; at no time was half the advantage taken of it which might have been done. A few picks and irons of the pioneers formed all the tools'.[13] Home thought that the Guards managed to defend the château because it was difficult for the French to bring guns to bear; even when they did get howitzers into the orchard they could only lob shells rather than fire down on the buildings from the ridge. The defenders could also take cover behind the walls whilst they were reloading, only popping up to shoot. Well co-ordinated as they were by their Guards NCOs, it made it very difficult for the French infantry to acquire a target, even for their sharpshooters, who remained all day along the front edge of the wood. It has been estimated that there were 350 French musket shots against the defence every minute of the attack, so about 190,000 shots in total, of which only about 800 hit one of the defenders. French cavalry could do nothing against the walls, and could not get into the orchard. Piré's men were destined to spend their day in some idleness on the left flank.

Napoleon's initial reaction to the repulse of d'Erlon's corps was to make a renewed attempt on both Hougoumont and La Haie Sainte, realising that both positions were more fundamental to Wellington's defence than the French may have at first appreciated. To Hougoumont, which had started as a diversionary attack to make Wellington weaken his centre and had now grown into a key part of the French battle plan, he instructed Reille to commit more troops. It is not entirely clear where they came from, probably two regiments of Foy's division and what remained of Bachelu's division, currently on Reille's right, thus positioned just west of the road from La Belle Alliance.[14] Already severely weakened at Quatre Bras, these battalions had to cross 1,000 yards of open ground where they were in full view of the Allied batteries on the ridgeline. Consequently they were even weaker by the time they closed to the orchard, but they still overwhelmed Hepburn's men, who were driven from their proper 'post' on the hedge line and forced back once more to the Hollow Way. Two King's German Legion battalions were sent down from the ridge to help them, but it was the fire of the Coldstream Guardsmen, directed into their flank from the garden wall, that finally halted the French. The fire 'was so destructive that they were completely staggered', and whilst they were reeling, Hepburn wrote in his economical style, 'we meanwhile advanced and regained our post'.[15] But it came at some cost. 'Poor captain Forbes was shot. I was shot a wee bit above the right temple. Poor Sir David Baird . . . a musket ball struck him immediately above the chin and lodged in his throat. In the space of a few minutes every officer became a casualty and command passed to the senior Sergeant', wrote Ensign Charles Lake of his company.[16]

The Allied batteries which had fired so destructively at the French infantry as they crossed the open ground below the ridge were not having an easy time either. Mercer, whose troop was still facing down the Nivelles road and who were not currently being engaged, remembered watching Captain Bolton's battery, who were positioned away to his left, on the ridge. They were taking considerable incoming fire from Reille's artillery, which Napoleon had recently reinforced with some of the Imperial Guard's twelve-pounders. Mercer saw man after man fall, until Bolton himself was hit. Occasionally, amongst the enveloping smoke, he could see 'still more dense columns of smoke rising straight into the air like a great pillar, the spreading out mushroom-head. These arose from the explosions of ammunition wagons, which were continually taking place, although the noise which filled the atmosphere was too overpowering to allow them to be heard',[17] although when they did score a direct hit the French artillerymen sent up a great cheer. Some shot was landing amongst Mercer's men, one of which struck a horse and 'completely carried away the lower part of the animal's head, immediately below the eyes'. The gunners tried to chase him away, but the wretched animal kept returning, pushing itself up against his companions still harnessed to the ammunition wagons 'eager to identify himself as of their society'. He wouldn't be sent away, and 'still he lived, and seemed fully conscious whilst his full, clear eye seemed to implore us not to chase him from his companions'. Eventually Farrier Price put him out of his misery by running a sabre into his heart. The incident affected Mercer as much as poor Gunner Hunt losing his arm.

A thousand yards to the east, Ney himself was leading the renewed French assault on La Haie Sainte. Gathering what was left of Quiot's infantry, who had suffered the least of d'Erlon's divisions, he pushed them into some sort of order and advanced back up the main Charleroi–Brussels road and into the orchard south of the farmyard. They came on more as a swarm than in the tightly packed columns that had proved so costly in their previous assault and found that Baring's riflemen had withdrawn into the farmyard itself. The fighting in La Haie Sainte was as savage as anywhere that day, driven as much by men like Frederick Lindau's virulent loathing of Napoleonic France as by the tactical situation. Captain Graeme ordered Lindau to bar the gateway, which was difficult with so few materials about. They held off the skirmishers easily enough, with Lindau firing through a loophole. 'We shot at the enemy where they were densest, then quickly stepped back to load and make room for the others. Of course the French also put their muskets in the opening and more of my comrades fell near me; some also falling down from the stand above, from which our people were shooting down over the wall. But that only increased my determination, so I could hardly wait until I fired another round and I loaded my rifle with such eagerness that I shot over a hundred rounds that day.'

The French continued to press their attack, with Ney urging them on in person. Baring recalled that 'every bullet of ours hit, and seldom were the effects limited to one assailant; this did not, however, prevent them from throwing themselves against the walls, and endeavouring to wrest the arms from the hands of my men, through the loop-holes; many lives were sacrificed to the defence of the doors and the gates; the most obstinate contest was carried on where the gate was wanting, and where the enemy seemed determined to enter. On this spot seventeen Frenchmen already lay dead, and their bodies served as protection to those who pressed after them to the same spot.'[18] Captain Graeme – actually a lieutenant but Lindau always referred to him as captain – wrote that 'The ground was literally covered with French killed and wounded, even to the astonishment of my oldest soldiers, who said they had never witnessed such a sight. The French wounded were calling out "Vive L'Empereur", and I saw a poor fellow, lying with both legs shattered, trying to destroy himself with his own sword.'[19]

Lindau had been watching a French officer who had been 'constantly riding round the battlefield in front of us and showing the way to the advancing columns. For some time I had him in my sights – at last, just as he was leading up new troops, he came into my fire. His horse made a bound, reared up and fell with the rider beneath it. Soon afterwards we made a sally. I opened the gateway, the nearest enemy were bayoneted and the others fled.' Lindau now saw the officer he had shot. He rushed over to him and grabbed his gold watch chain. The wounded officer managed to raise his sabre but Lindau bashed in his head with his rifle butt 'so that he fell back and dropped dead'. Lindau noticed a small bag on the saddle, which he took, and was about to cut off the officer's finger to take a gold ring when his comrades yelled that more of the enemy were approaching. They halted this fresh attack on the road, and Lindau was gratified to see enemy dead now lying a yard high around the barricade they had built by the main gate. There were loose Household and Union Brigade horses galloping around. Lindau grabbed hold of one for

Major Baring, whose own horse had just been shot, but Baring was unimpressed, probably realising that he was rather less conspicuous to the French *tirailleurs* on his feet in the very confined space in the farmyard. He told Lindau to get rid of it. Lindau had better luck when he opened the bag he had taken from the French officer's saddle and found it full of gold coins.[20]

Neither the attacks on Hougoumont nor La Haie Sainte achieved the desired effect. Whilst they had been in progress Napoleon had ordered infantry to replace the gunners who had been massacred in the Grand Battery and within an hour of the Household and Union Brigades' charge the majority of the French guns were back in action. Reille, on the French left, had also been reinforced with twelve-pounders from the Imperial Guard, and now had 34 guns which were also firing regularly at the ridgeline. Artillery fire would play an increasingly deadly role over the next four hours. In response to this, and to the slight pause in attacks against his main position, Wellington made some adjustments. He had, as we have seen, brought the Brunswickers forward to replace the 2nd Guards Brigade, now fully committed to Hougoumont. At the same time he moved Chassé's Netherlands Division from Braine-l'Alleud, finally confident that Napoleon was not intent on outflanking him from the west. He moved Lambert's brigade up to reinforce the area just behind the crossroads, where Bijlandt's Netherlands brigade, which had fled earlier, should have been. George Simmons and the Rifles reoccupied the sandpit on the south-eastern corner of the crossroads, which they had vacated during d'Erlon's attack.

The area behind the Allied lines, where the Brussels road passes Mont St Jean and starts to think about entering the

Forest of Soignes, was also full with wounded and prisoners moving to the rear. From the French positions, and in particular where Napoleon and Ney were looking from the slight rise at La Belle Alliance, from where they could see beyond but not under the ridge, this movement may have given the impression that at least part of the Allied army was withdrawing. It was close to four p.m. and word was coming back from Lobau at Plancenoit that Bülow's infantry were entering the Bois de Paris. Napoleon needed to force the Allied lines, and he needed to do so soon, yet he had no infantry available. Reille's corps, already damaged at Quatre Bras, was consumed at Hougoumont. Grouchy was God knows where to the east but certainly not about to engage Blücher; d'Erlon's corps was in pieces after its attack, and what usable formations he had left were hammering at La Haie Sainte, whilst Lobau was en route to block the Prussians.

What Napoleon did have, though, was his cavalry – the independent cavalry corps of Milhaud and Kellerman, which he had anyway always planned on using after d'Erlon's attack against what he may have still thought was an almost defeated enemy. And he had the Imperial Guard, with their own light cavalry, 2,500 men under Lefèbvre-Desnouëttes, and 2,000 heavy cavalry under Guyot. Ney would now lead these horsemen in an attack to drive the Allies, whom Napoleon may have thought were on the point of withdrawing, from their positions and clear the Brussels road before Blücher could bring up his main force.

Their attacks would be preceded by a renewed artillery barrage. The Grand Battery and Reille's corps artillery, already reinforced, now had the cavalry and the Imperial Guard's integral horse artillery attached, meaning at least 80 guns were available, and the fire they unleashed was very, very much more concentrated than what the Grand Battery had managed that morning. As the artillery fire intensified, the cavalry started to move. Ney took personal command, issuing orders directly to regimental commanders to form up in the open ground to the west of La Belle Alliance. It was the only usable space although it would mean that their attack frontage would be reduced to 800 yards, sandwiched between Hougoumont and La Haie Sainte, both of which positions would be able to fire into their flanks. Ney's ADC took his orders straight to General Farine, who commanded one of Milhaud's brigades, rather than to Milhaud himself or Delort, the divisional commander. Farine started to move his two regiments of cuirassiers forward but the experienced Delort halted them, telling the ADC that he had received no orders from Milhaud.

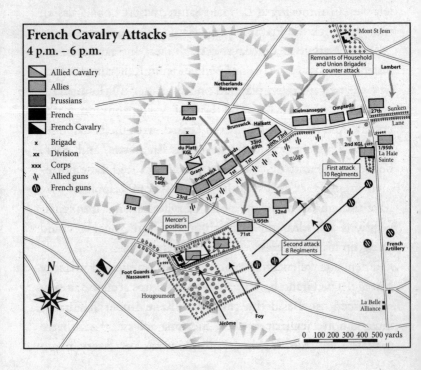

French Cavalry Attacks
4 p.m. – 6 p.m.

Allied Cavalry
Allies
Prussians
French
French Cavalry

x   Brigade
xx   Division
xxx   Corps
\|/   Allied guns
●   French guns

Mont St Jean

Remnants of Household and Union Brigades counter attack

Lambert

Netherlands Reserve

x Adam

Kielmansegge   Ompteda   27th   Sunken Lane

Brunswick   Halkett

x du Platt KGL

33rd 69th   30th 73rd

2nd KGL

1/95th La Haie Sainte

Ridge

Guards   1st

Grant   1st

Brunswick

First attack 10 Regiments

Tidy 14th

23rd

51st

3/95th

52nd

Mercer's position

71st

French Artillery

Second attack 8 Regiments

Pire

Foot Guards & Nassauers

Hougoumont

La Belle Alliance

Jérôme

Foy

0 100 200 300 400 500 yards

Ney himself then galloped up 'bristling with impatience. He insisted not only on the execution of his first order, but demanded in the name of the emperor both [my] divisions. I still hesitated ... I explained that heavy cavalry should not attack unbroken infantry on heights which was well prepared to defend itself. The Marshal replied "En avant! The salvation of France depends on it". I obeyed with regret.'[21] The planning of this attack was necessarily rushed, but it did by now seem as if Ney was acting with almost rash impetuosity. Lefèbvre-Desnouëttes' Light Cavalry of the Imperial Guard followed Delort, so that eight regiments of cuirassiers, one of lancers – the famous Red Lanciers of the Imperial Guard, many of whom were foreigners from the further reaches of the Empire – and one of mounted *chasseurs* followed Ney to form up. Some regiments were better manned than others; Lallemand's Chasseurs à Cheval of the Guard, Napoleon's favourite and whose green uniform he habitually wore and was eventually buried in, numbered 1,200, whilst the 7th Cuirassiers, who were very short of horses, only numbered 180. Altogether they totalled 4,500, and the limited space meant that they had to line up in echelons of squadrons, one behind the other, with all ten regiments in line, and on a frontage of about 1,000 men, closely packed, with little room to manoeuvre.

On the far left were Lefèbvre-Desnouëttes' two light regiments, the *chasseurs à cheval*, with the short green jackets and round fur caps. There were eight regiments of *chasseurs* at Waterloo but Lallemand's men were the Imperial Guard, the élite. They carried the curved French light-cavalry sabre as well as carbines. Beside them were the *lanciers*, five squadrons under Colonel Jerzmanowski. The first squadron, riding hard up against the *chasseurs*, was Major Balinski's Polish squadron, who wore blue rather than red; many who rode in the remaining squadrons were Dutch. All the regiment wore the flat lancer cap with a square top, which looked like an exaggerated mortarboard. They wore short ankle boots, like the British, and carried their eight-foot-long lances about halfway along the shaft, first at the 'carry', with the foot in a bucket on their right stirrup, but in the charge swung it forward so that the steel point protruded well beyond their horses' heads. Below the point fluttered red and white pennants. Because it was only the front rank that would be able to use their lance in a charge, the rear ranks carried swords and carbines.

Beside Jerzmanowski's men came the first of the eight regiments of Milhaud's cuirassiers, the 9th with their dark blue uniform with primrose collars, tall black boots coming above the knee, brass-riveted cuirasses, tall steel helmets surmounted with a copper crest and horsehair plume. They carried their long sabres drawn, and their carbines slung on cross belts across their backs. Beyond the 9th came the 6th, with pale gold collars, then the 10th with their pink facings, then Marshal Ney and his small staff, then the 5th, the 12th, the 7th, the 4th and finally the 1st on the far right, their right-hand men on the Brussels road immediately south of the orchard at La Haie Sainte. The 1st and the 4th were much reduced, being the two regiments of Dubois' brigade who had been so cut up by the Household Brigade two hours before. It was a shocking, terrifying sight, line upon line of steel coated men, spread out across the corn, and with the very clear purpose of hacking the allied infantry to pieces.

This splendid preparation was very visible from the Allied positions, from where it was now clear that the weight of the assault would fall west of the road, on Edmund Wheatley standing in Ompteda's King's German Legion brigade, on Kielmansegge's Hanoverians, on Halkett's brigade, where Thomas Morris waited, and on the 1st Guards Brigade, to which Rees Gronow had attached himself. It would also fall on those battalions who had not yet been much engaged, except by artillery – on Mitchell's 4th Brigade, with Frank Tidy's 14th, the 23rd and William Wheeler with the 51st. The left-hand regiments of Ney's line would be riding directly at the Brunswickers, who had just been brought forward to the sunken lane where the banks and hedges became less of an obstacle and, if they crossed the Nivelles road, they would hit du Platt's King's German Legion and Adam's light infantry-men. The Allies' battalions were quickly drawn up in squares, 25 in total, occupying a chequerboard pattern just behind the ridge, and stretching out in depth beyond it. Eleven Allied artillery batteries, soon to be reinforced, were lined up actu-ally on the ridge itself so that they could fire over it. Although the gunners could see the French cavalry forming up, to most of the infantry, still hidden, the first they knew was the sudden increase in the intensity of the bombardment as the French gunners fired over the heads of their horsemen and discharged round after round onto the ridgeline.

As with the barrage from the Grand Battery earlier in the day, many of these rounds ploughed into the ridge itself, where they now did some damage to the artillery batteries, or bounced on it and passed over the heads of the waiting squares, but the sheer volume began to tell and Reille's guns, firing from the west of the road, had an easier shoot. The squares began to take severe casualties from both round shot and explosive shells from the French howitzers. Then the fire suddenly stopped and the men standing sweating in their squares heard a different roar. At first they were not sure what

it was. 'The very earth seemed to vibrate',[22] and then the
Allied guns started firing to their front. As Ney led his
squadrons forward, with his trumpeters ringing out first
'Walk', then 'Trot' and finally 'Charge', Wellington's batteries
began to rake them with canister, tearing huge holes in their
lines. Gunner John Edwards was with Hew Ross's troop, just
west of the crossroads and firing into the 1st Cuirassiers, who
were in the front right of Ney's lines. They waited until they
were 600 yards away then 'we fired case shot at them and
swept them off like a swathe of grass before a scythe. The
ground was covered with men and horses in 5 minutes.'[23]

Sir Augustus Frazer, the artillery commander, galloped over
to Mercer, still in position covering the Nivelles road. His face
as 'black as a chimney sweep's from the smoke, and the jacket-
sleeve of his right arm torn open by a musket ball'. Frazer
shouted at Mercer, 'left limber up, and as fast as you can'.
They followed him at the gallop onto the ridge, where the air
was suffocatingly hot and they were 'enveloped in thick
smoke' and 'cannon-shot ploughed and ground in all directions, and so thick was the hail of balls and bullets that it
seemed dangerous to extend the arm less it should be torn
off'. Arriving beside the Brunswickers formed into square
behind Hougoumont, Mercer saw the leading squadrons of
the advancing French cavalry 'coming on at a brisk trot, and
already not more than one hundred yards distant, if so much,
for I don't think we could have been so far. I immediately
ordered the line to be formed for action – case-shot! And the
leading gun was unlimbered and commenced firing almost as
soon as the word was given. The very first round brought
down several men and horses. They continued, however, to
advance.'

Mercer knew his orders were now to leave the guns and

withdraw his men to the safety of the squares but he thought if he did so the already shaky Brunswickers might break. His initial rounds had slowed the cuirassiers to a walk and he continued to fire case-shot after case-shot. 'Every discharge was followed by the fall of numbers, whilst the survivors struggled with each other, and I actually saw them using the pommels of their swords to fight their way out of the mêlée. Some, rendered desperate at finding themselves thus pent up at the muzzles of our guns and others carried away by their horses, maddened with wounds, dashed through our intervals – few thinking of using their swords, but pushing furiously onward, intent only on saving themselves.' But poor Gunner Butterworth, 'one of the greatest pickles of the troop' and a sponger, had just finished ramming and was stepping back when he got his foot trapped in the mud the moment the gun was fired. He threw his arms out to save himself from falling, and they were both blown off at the elbow. 'He raised himself a little on his two stumps, and looked up most piteously at my face.'[24]

Effective as the artillery fire was, and terrible as the casualties it caused, the cuirassiers and *chasseurs* were soon amongst the guns. The drill was for the gun crews to remove the left wheel of the gun and run back with it, taking refuge inside the infantry squares and then running forward to re-man their guns when the cavalry had gone. Generally few had time to remove their wheels, and realised that it would be very difficult for the cuirassiers to drag the guns away under fire from the infantry squares and through the still-cloying mud. John Edwards and his crew actually jumped on their gun-team horses, and rode them back, which many seem to have copied. They took refuge with some 'German Horse', probably the hussars of the King's German Legion, and subsequently charged with them four times. 'With a good horse and a sharp sword I caused five of them to fall to the ground, my horse received four cuts as I could not guard myself and my horse at the same time', he wrote to his brother, the village blacksmith in Newtown, Montgomeryshire.[25]

However, Ney's target was not so much the guns as the infantry squares behind, and as the squadrons breasted the ridge, now reduced – by heavy ground, their tired horses and the volleys of case-shot – to a walk, they were still a terrifying sight. Wheatley, above La Haie Sainte from where he could see over the ridge, saw them as they first moved off and was only exaggerating a bit when he wrote that 'No words can convey the sensation we felt on seeing these heavy-armed bodies advancing at full gallop against us, flourishing their sabres in the air, striking their armour with the handles, the sun gleaming on the steel. The long horse hair [referring to the long plumes the cuirassiers wore on their helmets], dishevelled in the wind, bore an appearance confounding the senses to astonishing disorder.'[26] And that, of course, was the point. The cuirassiers were meant to terrify their opponents, so that they had almost won their battle before they actually engaged; but it was not going to work on the British infantry on this occasion.

Gronow, with his battalion in one of the 1st Guards Brigade squares above Hougoumont, who could also see the whole charge, thought that 'not a man present who survived could have forgotten in after life the awful grandeur of that charge. You perceived at a distance what appeared to be an overwhelming, long moving line, which, ever advancing, glittered like a stormy wave of the sea when it catches the sunlight. On came the mounted host until they got near enough and one might suppose that nothing could have resisted the shock of this terrible moving mass. They were the famous Cuirassiers, almost all old soldiers, who had distinguished themselves on most of the battlefields of Europe. In an almost incredibly short period they were within twenty yards of us shouting "Vive L'Empereur!" The word of command "Prepare to receive cavalry" had been given, every man in the front ranks knelt, and a wall bristling with steel, held together by steady hands, presented itself to the infuriated Cuirassiers.'[27]

Nevertheless, the cuirassiers' appearance and reputation – it was the first time the infantry who hadn't been at Quatre Bras had seen them close up – caused something close to panic, even to more experienced men like Thomas Morris. 'None of them under six feet; defended by steel helmets and corslets, made pigeon-breasted to throw off the balls. Thus armed and accoutred they looked so truly formidable, that I thought we could not have the slightest chance with them. They came up rapidly until within about ten or twelve paces of the square, when our rear ranks poured into them a well-directed fire, which put them into confusion, and they retired; the two front ranks, kneeling, then discharged their pieces at them.'[28]

And that was the cuirassiers' problem, just as Delort had warned Ney. They had survived what was in effect a slow advance uphill, initially at a gallop but soon reducing to a trot and then a walk as they came over the ridge, been blown apart by the Allies' case-shot, and having reached the squares were unable to penetrate them so long as Wellington's young soldiers stayed steady. For those young soldiers those next few hours were the most frightening of their lives. Private John Lewis, standing with the 2nd Battalion of the 95th, summed it up. 'Boney's Imperial Horse Guards all clothed in armour made a charge at us, we saw them coming & we all closed in & formed a square just as they come within 10 yards of us &

they found they could do no good with us, they fired with their carbines on us & come to the right about directly & at that moment the man on my right hand was shot through the body & the blood run out of his belly & back like a pig stuck in the throat, he drop on his side, I spoke to him, he just said "Lewis I am done" & died directly.'[29]

Carbine fire from the saddle was notoriously inaccurate and Lewis's comrade was just unlucky. Otherwise the cuirassiers had to resort to riding round and round the squares, trying to break in so they could cut the infantrymen down, but being met everywhere by walls of bayonets. They would withdraw a short distance and then charge again, but with no more effect, and all the time they were being cut down by musket fire from the squares themselves, the chequerboard lay-out meaning that they could be shot at from several different directions so they were rarely out of range. The Allied infantry were told by their company commanders to fire low, and to hit the horses. There were two reasons for this. First, there was a rumour that musket balls would not penetrate a cuirass. This was not true. A well-rammed ball, fired straight on, would go straight through and kill the wearer. The issue was more that balls fired at an angle could glance off, and this seems to have made the Army think that the cuirassiers' armour made them somehow impregnable. Also men took shortcuts with their loading drills in the stress of continual action, just shaking the ball down the barrel rather than taking the time to ram it home, which meant their shots lost much of their penetrative power. Secondly, it was a deliberate tactic to render the cuirassiers useless, which they were, once dismounted, unable to do much in their heavy armour and boots.

There was much ribald laughter at those who had lost their

horses and were trying to run, in what the Brits called their 'chimney-armour', and being taken prisoner by the light-company skirmishers, who would raid out of their squares when it was safe to do so, running back in again as soon as the cavalry reappeared. The fallen horses also acted as a barricade that broke the impetus of future charges. The horses' suffering seemed, unsurprisingly, to affect the men more than that of their riders – 'many a time the heart sickened at the moaning tones of agony which came from man, and scarcely less intel-ligent horse, as they lay in fearful agony'.[30]

The decision on when to fire was strictly controlled by the officers from inside the square. The most effective tactic was to fire volleys when the cuirassiers were within about 30 yards. This would bring down so many horses and men that it effectively stopped anyone but the odd individual approaching nearer. But it could go wrong. There was a French tactic used by some squadrons to come near enough to be fired at, to wheel away and then to rush that side of the square whilst the men were unloaded. Strict fire control meant that it never succeeded. Just as at Quatre Bras, the most experienced cav-alry in Europe foundered on the bayonets of young British volunteers, held in formation by training and discipline but mostly by a desire not to let down those standing around them, whose respect mattered as much to them as injury or death.

Behind the Allied squares was the remnant of the Household Brigade, and 13 other cavalry regiments. As Ney had started his first attack, Piré's French light cavalry, who had so far spent the morning skirting around to the west of Hougoumont, made as if to attack the Allies' right flank. Grant's brigade, which had been waiting patiently astride the Nivelles road and behind the 1st Guards Brigade, moved off to intercept them. With three regiments, Standish O'Grady and the 7th Hussars, the 13th Light Dragoons and the 15th Hussars, Piré was over-faced and withdrew, but Grant's men then remained watching for any further movement. To their east, the Household Brigade, the Life Guards, the Blues and the King's Dragoon Guards, all those who had survived the earlier charge and struggled back to the ridge, mustered barely a full regiment between them. In front of them, and to their right, were the squares of the 33rd and 69th, still unsteady after their terrible experience at Quatre Bras, both of whom reeled at the cuirassiers' advance. Thomas Morris, standing near by, reckoned they were both penetrated and began to break up in disorder, closely pursued by the cuirassiers, who started to cut them down. At this point the wounded Samuel Ferrior of 2nd Life Guards ordered the men he had with him to charge. Wheeling into the cuirassiers' right flank, they scattered them and the squares were quickly reformed. The Household Brigade's horses were as spent as the cuirassiers, and rather than charging at the enemy it could be more accurately described as groups of as many men as could be gathered together trotting and then walking at each other, engaging in vicious hand-to-hand fighting.

Edward Kelly, with what was left of his squadron, attacked the 4th Cuirassiers at this point, the same regiment that the 1st Life Guards had charged in the freshness of their first attack earlier in the afternoon. He killed their commanding officer, Colonel Habert, and then claims to have dismounted to cut off his epaulettes as a trophy. This seems fairly unlikely, but whatever their origin, he certainly produced the epaulettes after the battle, when the unfortunate Haddy James was asked to keep them, covered in the Colonel's blood, in his suitcase. Kelly went on to kill a further ten men with his own sword, although again we have only his word for it. Private Samuel Godley of the Blues, who was completely bald and consequently nicknamed 'the Marquis of Granby' after the famous bald colonel of that regiment, and who had led the regiment in a charge at Warburg having lost his hat and wig, had his horse shot by a *tirailleur* and lost his helmet as he fell. Struggling to his feet, he attacked the nearest cuirassier, who gave him a terrific blow across his bare head. Godley collapsed, but as the cuirassier came in to finish him off, he struggled to one knee and managed to thrust his sword into the Frenchman as he raised his arm. He then remounted his horse and rejoined his squadron to shouts of 'Well done, the Marquis of Granby'. Thomas Morris also swears that at this point he saw a Life Guard, after fighting single-handed with a cuirassier for five minutes, 'struck his opponent a slashing back-handed stroke, and sent his helmet some distance with the head inside it. The horse galloped away with the headless rider sitting erect in the saddle, the blood spurting out of the arteries like so many fountains.'[31]

Once they had got over their initial terror at the sight of the massed ranks of horsemen, the infantry kneeling and standing in their squares began to realise that whilst the French were riding around them they were spared incoming artillery fire, which was far more frightening and considerably more dangerous. Eventually, furious and frustrated at meeting infantry who refused to break and run, the cuirassiers began to pull back, and as they did so the French guns again opened up. Fire from the Grand Battery was still mostly either hitting the ridge in front of the squares east of the crossroads, or bouncing over their heads, but on the west of the road Reille had deployed his batteries further forward, and as the enraged and wounded cuirassiers made their way back, they fired over their heads and started causing fresh chaos to the Allied squares. Added to this there were an increasing number of *tirailleurs* and sharpshooters firing from the hedges around La Haie Sainte – men left from d'Erlon's attack – and around Hougoumont.

At this point Wellington moved Adam's brigade forward, so that they could support the Brunswickers, and they ended up in front of the gun batteries, on the side of the ridge facing the French and alongside the hedge that formed the eastern boundary of Hougoumont orchard. He also deployed du Platt's King's German Legion brigade forward, but not so far, so that they were bolstering the Brunswickers from behind, and secured his right flank with Frank Tidy's 14th Foot. The 52nd, part of Adam's brigade, and about 200 yards behind Hougoumont, could therefore now see the French batteries very clearly, and as the French guns opened up they started to take significant casualties. They formed into two squares. 'The old officers, who had served during the whole of the Peninsular War, stated that they were never exposed to such a cannonade as that which the 52nd squares had to undergo on this occasion for two hours and a half, from the French artillery planted about half a mile to their front. There was one incessant roar of round-shot and shells passing over us or close to us on either flank. The standing to be cannonaded, and having nothing to do, is about the most unpleasant thing that can happen to soldiers in an engagement', wrote Ensign William Leeke.

He could see some brass guns which seemed to be nearer to them than others. 'I distinctly saw the French artilleryman go through the whole process of sponging out one of the guns and reloading it; I could see that it was pointed at our square, and when it was discharged I caught sight of the ball, which appeared to be in a direct line for me. I thought, Shall I move? No! I gathered myself up, and stood firm, with the Colour in my right hand. I do not exactly know the rapidity with which cannon-balls fly, but I think that two seconds elapsed from the time that I saw this shot leave the gun until it struck the front face of the square. It did not strike the four men in rear of where I was standing, but the four poor fellows on their right. It was fired at some elevation, and struck the front man about the knees, and coming to the ground under the feet of the rear man of the four, whom it most severely wounded, it rose and passing within an inch or two of the Colour pole, went over the rear face of the square without doing further injury. The two men in the first and second rank fell outward, I fear they did not survive long; the two others fell within the square. The rear man made a considerable outcry on being wounded, but one of the officers saying kindly to him "O man, don't make a noise", he instantly recollected himself and was quiet.'[32]

Hold as they did, as the artillery fire grew in intensity so the situation inside most of the Allied squares was becoming increasingly serious. The commanding officer would stand in the middle, with the ensigns holding the Colours, whilst his companies would line the surrounding faces, which became smaller and smaller as more men were hit. The wounded were manhandled inside to receive what rudimentary treatment they could spare, whilst the dead were chucked out once their cartouche box and ball had been taken off them.

Frank Tidy's 14th Foot was being particularly severely battered. They watched as the cuirassiers attacked a neighbouring square. Once they were clear they opened up a murderous fire on them, with which Bull's battery joined in. 'For a couple of minutes the smoke was so thick that it was impossible to see, but as it cleared the Cuirassiers lay strewn about in all directions, dead, dying and wounded. Horses running here and there without their riders; and the riders encumbered in heavy armour, scampered away as best they could.' Then the artillery fire started again. George Keppel, one of Tidy's 17 ensigns under the age of 21, was sitting on a drum just in front of him holding his horse. 'He was even stroking the poor things face at the time that the ball struck her down, broke the bit of the bridle and knocked her head over heels. The animal plunged in her agony, threw the square into great confusion, and her misery was speedily put an end to by the soldiers' bayonets.' Tidy, who had a strange way of cheering people up, was looking down at the inferno raging around Hougoumont, and said to the wounded Keppel, who was a younger son and therefore would not inherit and whose elder brother was serving in the Guards, 'I say, George, I hope your brother, the Lord, is there for your sake.'[33]

What Ney now did is difficult to understand. Having made no impression on the Allied squares with his first attack, he seemed determined to repeat the same tactic again. Napoleon was certainly aware of and must have been supportive of the first attack, although he would later deny it, as it is unlikely the light cavalry of the Imperial Guard would have been released without his authority. Now that he saw Ney was committed he took the definite decision to reinforce him with Kellerman's corps, and with Guyot's heavy cavalry of the Imperial Guard, a further eight regiments, mostly dragoons and Grenadiers à Cheval, totalling 4,000 men. Joining up with the survivors of Milhaud's first charge, this combined force, cajoled by Ney into some sort of order, and with Kellerman, another experienced cavalry commander, as reluctant as Milhaud had been, assembled at the bottom of the slope to assault the ridge once more. As Wellington and Uxbridge looked on in disbelief, the trumpets sounded and this second mass of horsemen began to move forward through the wreckage of their comrades.

As the French cavalry had pulled back, despite a large number of stragglers still riding about on the ridge, and the continuing rifle and musket fire from the French sharpshooters, the Allied gunners now raced forward to re-man their guns. Not a single one had been spiked or towed away, exactly as Wellington had predicted. Again they waited until the French were slowed to a trot, channelled by the carnage of their first charge, and as they started to climb the rise the British fired case-shot at a range at which they couldn't miss. Whole ranks of Napoleon's élite men were mown down, horses and men blown to pieces and their limbs scattered across the already bloody corn. Mercer's troop was in action again. This time he waited until the leading horsemen were within 50 yards before opening fire. 'The effect was terrible. Nearly the whole leading rank fell at once; the round shot penetrating the column carried confusion throughout its extent. The ground, already encumbered with the victims of the first struggle, became now almost impassable. Still, however, these devoted warriors struggled on.'[34]

Despite these casualties, the French cavalry gained the ridge for a second time, and the gunners again ran back for safety in the squares; but once amongst them there was no more that Kellerman's and Guyot's cavalry could do than their predecessors had achieved half an hour before. This time there is no record of them penetrating any of the squares, although Thomas Howell thought that his 71st, with Adam's brigade, only just made it in time after their move forward. 'Scarce had we time to form. The square was only complete in front when they were upon the points of our bayonets. Most of our men were out of place. There was a good deal of jostling for a minute or two, and a good deal of laughing. Our quartermaster lost his bonnet in riding into the square; got it up, put it on, back foremost, and wore it thus all day.'[35]

Some battalions were beginning to become concerned about their ammunition supply. Gronow thought the cavalry charges 'very formidable, but in reality a great relief, as the artillery could no longer fire on us: the very earth shook under the enormous mass of men and horses' but 'when they got within ten or fifteen yards they discharged their carbines, to the cry of "Vive L'Empereur!" but their fire produced little effect, as is generally the case with the fire of cavalry. Our men had orders not to fire unless they could do so on a near mass; the object being to conserve ammunition and not to waste it on scattered soldiers. The result was that when the cavalry had discharged their carbines, we occasionally stood face to face, looking at each other inactively, not knowing what the next move might be.'[36]

Slowly, unable to break in, Kellerman's squadrons were forced back, first in groups then individually, down the hill. Kellerman had, sensibly, kept one brigade, Blancard's carabiniers, about 800 men, in reserve, somehow managing to hide them from Ney's view. They were in a fold in the ground south of Hougoumont. Ney now saw them and, furious that they had not been committed, made them advance, which they did almost alongside the hedge that marked the eastern end of the Hougoumont orchard. Emerging, in their distinctive red headdress, at a gentle trot, 'they crossed the arena alone in column of troops, and rode all along the enemy batteries to attack the English right' but within minutes they had been blasted away by the Allied guns and those who survived were killed by volleys from the squares.[37] It was to be one of the most pointless French attacks of the day, one of their most poignant almost sacrificial losses, and one Ney would soon come very much to regret.

Behind them a large group of cuirassiers had re-formed, which now came on as well, and behind it a re-formed group of lancers. Major-General Sir Colquhoun Grant, commanding the 5th Cavalry Brigade, realising that Piré did not present a serious threat to the west of Hougoumont, had left a squadron of the 15th Hussars to watch them and returned to his position behind 1st Guards Brigade. He now saw this fresh threat developing. Forming the 13th Light Dragoons in line, with the half of the 15th Hussars he had with him on their left, they charged into the left flank of the cuirassiers as they came up to the ridgeline; behind them the 7th Light Dragoons rode into the *lanciers*. This unexpected charge drove the cuirassiers back to the bottom, and, unlike the Union Brigade, Grant called his men back.

As they withdrew, the cuirassiers rode past Thomas Howell and the 71st in their square, who 'gave the French a volley, which put them to the right-about; then the 13th at them again. They did this for some time; we cheering the 13th, and feeling every blow they received. When a Frenchman fell we shouted; and when one of the 13th we groaned. We wished to join them but were forced to stand in square.'[38] The light cavalrymen would charge repeatedly during the next two hours, taking terrible casualties, as light cavalry must do up against heavily armoured cuirassiers, but succeeded in driving away Ney's horsemen from the area around Hougoumont. Standish O'Grady made light of it when writing to his father. He thought they charged '12 or 14 times and once cut off a squadron of Cuirassiers every man of whom we killed on the spot except two officers', but otherwise he pretends to be more concerned at what happens to his baggage and with Kitty's latest letter. Others writing to his father afterwards speak of him 'gloriously contributing his personal exertions to victory'.[39]

The attack by Kellerman's carabiniers and the assorted groups of cuirassiers and *lanciers* constituted Ney's third major assault, but the Allies were past caring in what packages the French cavalry were despatched. For them it was a seemingly endless sequence of devastating and terrifying artillery fire interrupted by attacks by enemy horsemen. For most the events became blurred, and their concentration was more on the man next to them, on their ammunition, on keeping their musket firing or coaxing a last trot or even a canter out of an exhausted horse. Parched, blackened with powder, frequently unable to see due to the thick smoke from both their own muskets and the artillery, it was as if they were living in a netherworld of their square or their squadron. Gronow wrote that by now the 1st Guards' squares 'presented a shocking sight. Inside we were nearly suffocated by the smoke and smell from burnt cartridges. It was impossible to move a yard without treading upon a wounded comrade, or upon the bodies of the dead; and the loud groans of the wounded and dying was most appalling. The square was a perfect hospital, being full of dead, dying and mutilated soldiers.'[40]

During the third French attack, Ney finally did what many had supposed he might have done earlier, which was to advance his horse artillery and what infantry he could find with the cavalry. Thomas Morris had been getting increasingly irritated by the man kneeling next to him in the front rank of the 73rd Highlanders' square, who had a speech defect and kept saying 'Tom, Tom, here come the *calvary*'. Just as Morris was beginning to think that they had the cuirassiers 'baffled', he saw them bringing up artillery who 'turned the cannon in our front upon us, and fired into us with grape shot, which proved very destructive, making complete lanes through us; and then the horsemen came up to dash at the openings. But before they reached, we had closed our files, throwing the dead outside and taking the wounded inside the square, when they were again forced to retire.' They only rode back as far as their guns though, and Morris describes the terrifying moment when he saw the French gunners apply their match to the vent tube and the case-shot came 'as thick as hail upon us. On looking round I saw my left hand man falling backwards, the blood gushing from his left eye; my poor comrade on my right got a ball through his right thigh.' It stopped his annoying warnings, and he died a few days later.[41]

The 30th Foot suffered from the same experience. Macready saw two guns from the Horse Artillery of the Imperial Guard, which he recognised from their caps, unlimber at a 'cruelly short distance, down went the portfires and slap came their grape into the square. They immediately reloaded, and kept up a most destructive fire. It was noble to see our fellows fill up the gaps after each discharge. I had ordered up three of my light bobs [infantrymen] and they had hardly taken their places when two falling sadly wounded, one of them (named Anderson) looked up in my face, uttering a sort of reproachful groan, when I involuntarily said, "By God! I couldn't help it."'[42]

The Allied artillery was causing as many casualties to the French. Although Mercer was losing men and horses at an alarming rate, he was still able to sustain his fire on the advancing French squadrons. 'This time indeed it was child's play. They could not even approach us in any decent order, and we fired most deliberately; it was folly [for them] to have attempted the thing. I was sitting on my horse near the right of my battery as they turned and began to retire once more. Intoxicated with success, I was singing out "Beautiful! – Beautiful!"'[43]

At around six p.m. Foy's and Bachelu's infantry, who had been involved in the last attack on Hougoumont, were ordered to advance to the ridge and tackle the Allied squares. It was never going to work. They were badly outnumbered, and had already suffered significant casualties. It was too little and too late as by that stage Ney's cavalry charges had spent their impetus. They were met by Adam's brigade, who rapidly formed line and poured in a fire of 'extraordinary violence. Our soldiers fell by the hundred'. They also received 'very heavy case-shot. It was a hail of death',[44] wrote their commanders; Thomas Howell, who halted them with volleys, merely noted that we 'formed line, gave three cheers, charged the enemy and drove them back' but, as with Grant's cavalry, they did not pursue them, quickly re-forming square.[45]

Adam's brigade also routed a large number of French skirmishers who had made their way into the area immediately north and east of Hougoumont, and who were causing considerable casualties at this point, particularly to du Platt's King's German Legion brigade now positioned behind the Brunswickers. It was impossible for the Germans to form line and deal with them, given that they were being constantly charged by the cavalry, who would have liked nothing better than to have caught them in such a formation in the open, although Adam's light infantrymen seemed to have managed to achieve it. Private John Lewis, serving with one of the companies of the 95th detached to Adam's, reckoned there was rather more to it than Thomas Howell did. As they were advancing his 'front rank man was wounded by a part of a shell through the foot and dropt. I covered the next man I saw and had not walked twenty steps before a musket shot came sideways and took his nose clean off, & then I covered another man which was the third; just after that the man stood next to me on my left hand had his left arm shot off by a nine pound shot just above his elbow & turned round and caught hold of me with his right hand & the blood ran all over my trousers.'[46]

Things were as hellish for the French, those who were still alive and not trapped in the mud under the piles of wounded horses. Their commanders had suffered particularly badly, testament to their bravery in riding forward in front of their divisions and brigades. Ney, amazingly, was not hit but Kellerman was wounded and Milhaud had his horse killed from under him. Three of the four divisional commanders were wounded and seven of the eight brigade commanders. Total casualties were unknown, but gradually all the regiments who had charged became ineffective. A certain respect developed between the attacking cavalrymen and the men dying in the squares. Gronow had witnessed the Red Lancers of the Imperial Guard attacking one of the Brunswick squares. They had suffered severely and 'the ground was completely covered with those brave men, who lay in various positions, mutilated in every conceivable way. Among the fallen we perceived the gallant colonel lying under his horse which had been killed. All of a sudden two riflemen of the Brunswickers left their battalion and after taking from their helpless victim his purse, watch, and other articles of value, they deliberately put the colonel's pistols to the poor fellow's head and blew out his brains. "Shame! Shame!" was heard from our ranks, and the feeling of indignation ran through the whole line',[47] but then Gronow had never lived in a country under French occupation, and as he noted himself the French 'lanciers never failed to despatch our wounded, whenever they had the opportunity of doing so', which, riding around the battlefield, they frequently did, it being a simple matter to drive a lance through a body on the ground. The *lanciers'* reach also meant that they could cause casualties in the wall of a square in a way the cuirassiers could not, even with their longer swords. They were, it was generally agreed, the most daring and trouble-some of the enemy cavalry.[48] Overall the cavalry attacks earned more respect and pity than hatred. 'That man who brands our foe with cowardice deserves the lie; he advances to our cannon's mouth and seeks death from the destructive bay-onet', thought Thomas Anton at his most poetical.[49]

Ney's attacks had lasted two hours and the effect was begin-ning to tell. Mercer 'perceived the square next to me was broken, that there were gaps in every face, which the officers and sergeants were endeavouring to close by pushing the half stupefied boys together, scarcely any of them were above twenty years of age'.[50] 'Our situation now was truly awful', said Morris of the squares nearer the Brussels road, 'our men were falling by the dozens every fire'. One shell landed in their square with its fuse still burning. They wondered how many men it would kill when it went off, to which the answer was 17. Morris was hit by a lump of metal in his cheek. His 'poor old captain', whom he had long despised and who had never been in combat until Quatre Bras, was 'horribly frightened, and several times came to me for a drop of something to keep his spirits up. Towards the end of the day he was cut in two by a cannon-shot', Morris noted, with-out much regret.[51]

'The men were very tired and did begin to despair', remembered William Lawrence of the 40th, 'but the officers cheered them on: '"Keep your ground!" they cried. It was a mystery to me how it was accomplished, for there were scarcely enough of us left to form square. At 4 o'clock I was ordered to the Colours. Now I was as used to warfare as anyone but this was a job that I did not like at all. That day alone 14 sergeants and officers in proportion had been killed or wounded in the duty and the staff and Colours were almost cut to pieces.' No sooner had he taken up his post than 'I was with a captain and he was so close to me that his right side was touching my left. Within a quarter of an hour, a cannon-shot came and took his head clean off, spattering me all over with blood.'[52] Twenty-five more men would follow him before the day was done.

There was still room for some humour. George Keppel, one of Frank Tidy's cohort of very young officers, recalled that 'a young bugler of the 51st who had been out with skirmishers, and had mistaken our square for his own, exclaimed, "Here I am again, safe enough." The words were scarcely out of his mouth, when a round shot took off his head and spattered the whole battalion with his brains, the colours and the ensigns in charge of them coming in for an extra share. One of them, Charles Fraser, a fine gentleman in speech and manner, raised a laugh by drawling out, "How extremely disgusting!"'[53] In the 40th an old soldier called Marten shouted when a cannon ball took his platoon commander's head clean off, 'There goes my best friend.' 'Never mind,' said a lieutenant who quickly stepped forward to take his place, 'I'll be as good a friend to you as the captain.' 'I hope not, sir!' replied Marten, who was being sarcastic as the captain had frequently punished him with extra duties 'on account of the dirtiness of his person'. There was much laughter amongst those who could hear against the roar of the cannon. And there was some even blacker humour. One *lancier* officer was in the habit of riding out alone and firing his carbine, after which he would wave it around his head and shout, "'Come on, you English buggers!" This was several times repeated when some of our brave riflemen crawled upon their hands and knees until they were within easy reach of him, and when he came out again brought him down off his horse like a rook!'[54]

Between five and six p.m. the Allied cavalry charged repeatedly. The remnants of the Household Brigade charged eleven times, with Samuel Ferrior finally being killed towards the end of the day. Charge again remains an inaccurate description of engagements which were mostly at the walk, and involved bloody hand-to-hand fighting. Grant's 5th Light Cavalry Brigade was equally busy, and the burden increasingly fell on the Brunswick and King's German Legion regiments, and on the Netherlands cavalry. Uxbridge, to whom Wellington had delegated all cavalry operations, called forward Trip's Netherlands heavy-cavalry brigade, three strong regiments of carabiniers, over 1,200 strong. In the early part of the afternoon they behaved well, and took significant casualties, the 2nd Carbineers losing 156 men; but later, when Uxbridge led them personally to the sunken lane behind Hougoumont from where they would have been able to complete the work of Grant's brigade in clearing the remaining cuirassiers and *lanciers*, he appears to have been unable to persuade them to charge.

Uxbridge had even less luck with the Cumberland Hussars. They were a curious regiment, a sort of Hanoverian yeomanry made up of well-off volunteers, who dressed in rather elaborate green uniforms with much gold braid and fur-lined capes and rode their own horses. Initially positioned well in reserve behind the right wing, they had taken some losses from artillery, which seems to have unnerved them. Towards the end of Ney's mass charges, Uxbridge sent his ADC, Captain Horace Seymour, to tell their commanding officer, Colonel Hake, to bring them forward. To his disgust he found the regiment heading back to Brussels down the Nivelles road. Unable to turn them round, despite seizing hold of Hake's bridle, Seymour had to let them go, whereupon they broke into a gallop and didn't stop until they reached Brussels, where their sudden appearance and shouts that the French were coming caused understandable panic.

Whilst Ney's squadrons were wasting themselves on the Allied squares, and making no progress in Napoleon's overall objective of breaking Wellington's line, Bülow's Fourth Prussian Corps had been making steady progress through the Bois de Paris. Although initially rebuffed by Lobau, with his full corps now available, encouraged by Blücher, Bülow succeeded in driving the French out of Plancenoit and seizing the village amidst particularly fierce fighting. Rounds from his artillery started falling on the Brussels road. To the north Count Hans von Zieten's smaller First Prussian Corps, which had marched on the northern route from Wavre, was already at Smohain, with 5,000 men, meaning that the French now had two Prussian axes developing against their right flank. Napoleon's reaction was threefold. First, he ordered Durutte, with what was left of his division, which had attacked on the right of d'Erlon's corps, to attack Smohain to stop von Zieten and take the pressure off Lobau. He then sent Duhesme's division of the Young Guard to retake Plancenoit; and finally he told Ney come what may to take La Haie Sainte, which, immediately in front of his position at La Belle Alliance, he continued to see as the key to Wellington's fortunes. Ney placed himself at the head of 13th Légère, what was left of Donzelot's division, and advanced up the road once more.

Baring's men in La Haie Sainte had been pouring fire into the flanks of Ney's cavalry during their great assaults, the right-hand edge of which came up against the western wall of the farmyard.* It didn't seem to have much effect on them so Baring stopped as he was becoming increasingly concerned about how low his ammunition was getting. He sent back to Ompteda for a resupply. Ompteda sent forward Captain von Wurmb and the light company of the 5th Battalion King's German Legion, and then 200 Nassauers, but without extra ammunition, of which he was probably running short himself; so, as Baring's beleaguered garrison prepared to face Ney's fresh assault, they had very few cartridges left for their rifles. Baring sent yet another officer back asking for a resupply, but at that point the 13th Légère stormed the open entrance to the barn. They also got men onto the roof, which they managed to set on fire, and their engineers attacked the main gate off the road. Baring became seriously alarmed as, although there was water in the well in the yard, they had no means of drawing it. Luckily the Nassauers were carrying their 'large field cooking kettles'. Baring grabbed one, tearing it from the Nassauer's back, and his men all did the same. Soon not one of the Nassauers was left with his kettle, but the fire was extinguished – luckily much of the thatch had already been removed as bedding the previous night. However, it came at a terrible cost, with 'the blood of many a brave man' as every journey with the water had been in view of the French firing from the barn door and outside the walls.

The garrison was now concentrated in the farmyard itself, and in the farmhouse and the buildings alongside it on the northern

---

* You may find it helpful to refer to the map on p.230.

side. 'Many of the men, although covered with wounds, could not be brought to retire', Baring wrote. 'So long as our officers fight, and we can stand' was their constant reply, 'we will not stir from the spot.'[55] Lindau was one of the wounded, shot through the back of the head. Lieutenant Graeme ordered him to retire, but he refused. He took off his scarf, soaked it with rum, which somehow he still had in his flask, wound it round his wound and then rammed his shako back on to keep it in place. Reloading his rifle he took his place at the barn door again, just as the fire was taking hold. The French were firing back at them through the loopholes they had made in the wall. Lindau saw Baring, with Sergeants Reese and Poppe, running up with their kettles. Sergeant Reese was hit. Lindau put himself in front of a loophole and fired at a Frenchman taking aim on the other side. Just as he fired, the Frenchman seized his rifle through the hole. The man beside him shouted that he was loaded, and told him to hold on whilst he fired, which he did, killing the Frenchman. A second Frenchman then seized hold of Lindau's rifle, but the next man on Lindau's right stabbed him in the face through the wall. Lindau grabbed his rifle back, but as he did so 'a mass of bullets flew by me, rattling on the stone of the wall. One took the worsted tuft from my shoulder. Another shattered the cock on my rifle.' Hunting round for another he saw Sergeant Reese lying by the well, dying. He knew Reese's rifle was a good one so he grabbed it, but Reese pulled an angry face so he left it and found another. He went back to the barn door, but not without searching through the pockets of the fallen for ammunition, of which he was desperately low.

The French fire seemed to slacken, and they temporarily fell back. Baring took stock. 'With every new attack I became more convinced of the importance of holding the post. With every attack also the weight of the responsibility that devolved on me increased. This responsibility is never greater than when an officer is left to himself, and suddenly obliged to make a decision upon which, perhaps, his own as well as the life and honour of those under him may depend.'[56] And that was exactly what Baring now had to do. A quick count showed that his men were down to three of four cartridges each. At this point he saw two new columns forming up to attack and at that moment 'I would have blessed the ball that came to deprive me of life – but more than life was at stake'. His men shouted that 'No man will desert you – we will fight and die with you'. 'No one,' Baring later wrote, 'not even one that has experienced such moments, can describe the feeling which this excited in me.'

The French, urged on by Ney, attacked with 'renewed fury'. They concentrated on the barn door again, once more setting the roof on fire; it was extinguished in the same way, but now the defenders' fire was slackening as they ran out of cartridges. A group of his soldiers stood in the yard, bayonet-ing the French who were now breaking in through the barn, and swarming over the walls on either side. 'Inexpressibly painful as the decision was', Baring gave the order for the sur-vivors to fall back through a small door in the wall by the farmhouse which led to the kitchen garden. Lindau was not amongst them. He had bayoneted a French soldier who had jumped off the wall on top of him, but his bayonet had bent, which was not uncommon. As he tried to pull his rifle away from the now-useless bayonet embedded in the Frenchman's body, he found himself suddenly surrounded by the enemy. Using his rifle butt as a club he ran straight into them but was overpowered. He was now a prisoner and not at all sure what would happen to him.

Lieutenant Graeme rallied what was left of the rest of his

company and slowly they fought back, hand to hand, through the narrow passage into the kitchen garden. 'We wanted to halt and make one more charge but it was impossible', he wrote, as the French were firing down the passage at them at almost point–blank range. A French soldier levelled his musket at Graeme from five yards away. Ensign Frank shouted a warning at him, then stabbed the enemy soldier in the mouth with his sword. The point came out through the Frenchman's neck and he immediately fell dead. But there were more and more French piling up behind. Frank was hit by two shots but managed to get himself out of the passage and into an adjoining room which was full of wounded. He hid behind a bed. The French rushed in and shot the wounded, saying 'Take that for the fine defence you have made'. Frank remained hidden. A French officer and four soldiers now cornered Graeme. The officer, shouting 'C'est ce coquin' (*coquin*, literally 'shit', seems to have been the favoured French term for the Allied soldiers), grabbed him by the collar and the men with him levelled their bayonets to run him through. Graeme parried their points with his sword, and noticed that they all looked 'so frightened and pale as ashes'. He made a run for it and they fired two shots after him but missed. He ran out through the passage and the garden with 200 yards to run to reach the safety of the ridge. As he came into the field he saw his men forming square and cuirassiers charging them. By sheer good luck they were in a hollow and those with a cartridge left peppered the cuirassiers so that they fell back, and the very battered remnants of Baring's battalion struggled the last few yards into their own lines. Around 800 men had fought in the farm buildings; half were killed there. When Baring gathered his survivors together he counted 42 men, although more struggled in having made their way back in ones and twos over the next few hours. There is no record of French losses, but Baring's small force had held up a French division for the best part of five hours.

What happened now that the French had possession of the buildings showed just how important the German riflemen's action had been. Ney quickly did two things. First he brought up a troop of horse artillery that started a deadly fire on the crossroads, the sandpit with Simmons and the 95th Rifles, and also on Lambert's battalions, which had been brought up to reinforce Kempt's men just behind. Secondly, he had brought over Colonel Pégot's brigade from Durutte's division off on the right, to give himself more infantry; these men now started skirmishing forward from the kitchen garden, threatening Ompteda's brigade of the King's German Legion, who occupied the ridge just behind the farm and to whom Baring's decimated battalion belonged. Wellington had been emphatic about the importance of La Haie Sainte, and it was now the tactically confused Prince of Orange who took it upon himself both to recapture it and to see off Pégot's men.

Ompteda was an experienced officer, and even more so after what he had witnessed that day. He pointed out to the Prince that lurking behind Pégot's skirmishers were the remnants of the 1st and 4th Cuirassiers, who had already chopped up the Lüneburgers, then charged his squares, and who were still in significant numbers just to the west of the farmyard, and had just attacked Graeme's small band as they fell back. Any attack would, he suggested, likely be suicidal, and they should at least be supported by cavalry. Fully justifying all the concern his lack of judgement had caused in London back in March, the Prince of Orange, 'deaf to all protestations, peremptorily ordered Ompteda to deploy', saying, 'I must still repeat my order to attack the line with the bayonet, and I will listen to no further arguments.'[57] Ompteda could only obey. 'Then I will,'[58] he said, although he must have known he was going to his death.

Taking a horse that had belonged to his now-dead adjutant, Captain Schuck, Ompteda told Colonel Linsingen, who commanded the 5th Battalion, to try to save his two nephews, who were serving in it, and then placing himself at the head of that battalion, he breasted the ridge and started down the hill. He seemed determined to go out in style. Telling his men to walk forward until he gave the order to charge, he spurred his horse forward of their line and rode well in front. Pégot's first line levelled their muskets at him. Remarkably they held their fire, apparently 'astonished at the extraordinary calm approach of the solitary horseman, whose white plume showed him to be an officer of high rank'. Edmund Wheatley, who was in the line, said that the French just stood still until they reached them. Ompteda reached the garden hedge and jumped his horse clean over it and laid into the French infantry. Captain Berger of the 5th Battalion clearly saw his 'sword strokes smote the shakos off. The nearest French officer looked on in admiration without attempting to check the attack'. Berger turned round, and when he looked forward again 'I saw Colonel Ompteda, in the midmost of the throng of the enemy infantry and cavalry, sink from his horse and vanish'.[59]

Wheatley 'ran at a drummer, but he leaped over a ditch through a hedge in which he stuck fast. I heard a cry of "The Cavalry! The Cavalry!" But so eager was I that I did not mind it at the moment, and then on the eve of dragging the Frenchman back (his iron bound boots having saved him from a cut) I recollect no more.'[60] The cuirassiers then closed on the

5th Battalion and exercised their frustration at not having been able to break their square by slicing them up. Wheatley, on recovering his senses, found himself in a clay ditch with a violent headache. Close by him lay Colonel Ompteda on his back, his head stretched back with his mouth open, and a hole in his throat. A Frenchman's arm lay across Wheatley's leg. It was the second battalion the Prince of Orange had destroyed in two days. Very soon after this he was hit by a rifle bullet in the left shoulder and had to retire, an event which must have been as unpleasant for him as it was fortunate for the soldiers remaining east of the Brussels road; being forced to leave the battle undoubtedly did much to secure his legacy and his dynasty.

The battle now entered a second very dangerous phase while the Allies wondered whether they could hold on long enough for the Prussians to arrive in force. Edward Macready of the 30th, part of Halkett's brigade, wrote plaintively that 'the glow which sustains one upon entering into action had ceased'. He thought it was now a matter of which side had the 'most bottom and would stand the killing longest'.[61] The result of the Prince of Orange's débâcle was that what remained of Ompteda's King's German Legion and Kielmansegge's Hanoverians effectively broke. It was not so much Pégot's infantry as the terrible fire from the artillery of the Imperial Guard that Ney had finally brought forward and that was blasting men away every minute.

Halkett's men were suffering as badly. What remained of his brigade were coming under almost continual fire, being blasted by case-shot at about 300 yards, at which range it was at its most effective. Lieutenant Pontécoulant commanded some of the French guns. 'There was not another example of fire so lively and so accurate,' he recalled. 'All our gunners appeared to be galvanised by the danger of the crisis that we could see coming but could not prevent; each of our shots struck home, and we were so close to the enemy that we could distinctly hear the cries of the English officers, closing up the thinning ranks of their weakened battalions with strong curses and the flats of their swords.'[62] 'We would willingly have charged these guns', Macready continued, 'but, had we deployed, the cavalry that flanked them would have made an example of us', as indeed they just had of the 5th Battalion King's German Legion.

Wellington rode up at that point. He had spent much of the day near the 30th's position, it being roughly central. 'As he crossed the rear face of our square, a shell fell amongst our grenadiers, and he checked his horse to see its effect. Some men were blown to pieces by the explosion, and he merely stirred the reins of his charger, apparently as little concerned at their fate as at his own danger.' His presence steadied them. 'No leader ever possessed so fully the confidence of his soldiery', Macready thought, 'but none did love him. Wherever he appeared', even during the worst moments in the day, 'a murmur of "Silence – Stand to your front – here's the Duke" was heard through the columns and then all was steady as on a parade.' Two of his ADCs, Colonels Canning and Gordon, were wounded near the 30th's square and Colonel Canning actually died within it.

It took, though, rather more than the Duke's appearance to steady Ompteda's and Kielmansegge's bereaved men. They were falling back, partly due to the terrible artillery fire and partly because Pégot's men were skirmishing forward from La Haie Sainte and pressing them. Pégot also attacked the 30th and 1st Guards Brigade just beside them, but was pushed back. The poor Germans, though, having suffered so badly, losing effectively three battalions completely and the remainder being at best at half strength, started to falter. A dangerous gap was beginning to open up. If Ney could push through it, then he might finally shatter Wellington's line. 'Unfortunately, not having any infantry or cavalry, we were not able to advance or bring about a decisive result,' Pontécoulant lamented. Ney rode back to La Belle Alliance to argue with an increasingly fractious Emperor for more infantry. 'Where am I to get them?' Napoleon answered. 'Do you expect me to make them?' A mile away to his right the Young Guard had succeeded in driving the Prussians out of Plancenoit, but Bülow had regrouped his men, reinforced them as new formations came up, re-attacked and taken the village back.

What stopped the German withdrawal was the appearance of Hussey Vivian's 6th Light Cavalry Brigade, with the 10th Hussars and Henry Murray and his 18th Hussars. They had spent the whole day on the left of the line, complaining that they did not really know what was going on, which was fair; even Kempt, very much in the thick of things, said that Wellington concentrated on the west of the road and that he did not receive a single order from him during the battle.[63] The 10th Hussars had accomplished their mission of guiding in Zieten's Prussians to Smohain, and Vivian had moved his regiments, together with Vandeleur's 4th Brigade, over to their right and onto the Brussels road between the crossroads and Mont St Jean. Vivian's trumpeter – who was, unusually by 1815, still a black man, there having been an old but by then outdated British cavalry tradition of employing black trumpeters since the time of Charles II – sounded the advance, and, led by 10th Hussars, as they saw the King's German

Legion and Hanoverians falling back, they simply formed lines behind them and rode slowly forward.[64]

It was a grim situation. Murray noted that 'The air of ruin and destruction that met our view was calculated to inspire us with thoughts by no means akin to anticipation of victory, and many thought they had been brought from the left to cover another retreat'. It was a dangerous job for cavalry, and the artillery fire caused them as many casualties as it had the infantry. 'We remained in the rear of the Belgian troops (infantry)', wrote Sergeant Matthew Colgan from Henry Murray's regiment, mistaking the Germans for Belgians, 'with our horses' heads almost resting on their rear rank, during a most dreadful peal of musketry, which, had we not been thrown into open column at the time, would have placed us in the most destructive situation. However, the balls passed through our intervals.' Having slowly pushed the German infantry forward, they withdrew back 50 yards so they were less under the fall of shot, 'otherwise no cavalry could have remained motionless for any time under such a torrent of small arm fire'.[65] Wellington also moved up four Brunswick battalions whom he had held in reserve and the centre of the line west of the road was temporarily stabilised.

However, just in front of the light cavalry, to the east of the road, the guns of the Imperial Guard were causing equal chaos, firing into Lambert's battalions, those so recently arrived from America and whom Wellington had earlier moved up to reinforce Kempt's men. The battalion that suffered worst were the 27th Inniskilling Foot (not to be confused with the 6th Dragoons, confusingly also called Inniskillings). They were 698 men strong when they formed square, just behind the sunken lane and about 70 yards behind where George Simmons and his company of the 95th were

still occupying the sandpit. In the space of the next hour 480
of them were blown to pieces without being able to get to
grips with the enemy, the most terrible psychological as well
as physical suffering. They did not discharge one musket shot.
It had been a long journey to face sacrifice without account-
ing for any Frenchmen, especially for a warlike Irish battalion
as they were. Of 19 officers present, 16 were killed or
wounded. Only three lieutenants would emerge unscathed.
Sadly and unsurprisingly few first-hand accounts of this
slaughter remain.[66]

Pégot's infantry were also now able to pour fire across the
road and into the sandpit. Simmons was to begin with at his
most bullish and most irritating. He could see what was happening to the 27th, 'who literally fell as they stood by
hundreds'. At the same time, 'My young servant, a handsome
Englishman was struck by grape shot, close to me, just after he
had fired, his poor arm sadly shattered. He sung out lustily.
"My good fellow, giving tongue in that way will do you no
good, go off to the doctor,"' Simmons replied, demonstrating
his sang-froid and why he must have been such an annoying
company officer. The poor handsome young man set off but
was unsurprisingly immediately shot down. However, there is
no denying Simmons's bravery, and he led a party of men forward to the road to stop a group of French skirmishers who
were attempting to cross from the La Haie Sainte kitchen
garden. His friend Orlando Felix was hit, but Simmons felt
that 'he had a charmed life' and was feeling 'in the full vigour
of manhood', when he was hit by a musket ball which grazed
his arm, entered his side, broke two ribs, went through his
liver and lodged in his chest. He jumped 'as high as himself'
and fell near the hedge of La Haie Sainte.

Some remnants of the Life Guards, still just behind the

crossroads, mounted one of their many mini charges to help restore the situation, riding across Simmons's wounded body, but they drove the skirmishers back and Simmons's commanding officer, Andrew Barnard, organised his evacuation. The ever-patient Sergeant Fairfoot took him back to Mont St Jean. He was put in a cow yard, which was covered with the dying and wounded. 'Doctors were performing their evolutions with knife and saw in hand most vigorously'. He was put next to Lieutenant John Stillwell from his regiment and his body soon became so swollen that he had great difficulty in breathing, the warm blood oozing out of his side and the broken ends of his ribs giving him excruciating pain. He passed out.

At Hougoumont, now that La Haie Sainte had been taken, Reille's men made a renewed assault, attacking strongly through the orchard, but failing to make any progress, being cut down again by the Coldstream Guards firing on them from the garden. Mathew Clay, still manning the buildings in the farmyard, reported that the enemy's activity actually slackened, few of them now reaching as far as the château and its surrounding buildings.

It was now 7.30 p.m. and evening was coming on though few were inclined to check. Napoleon had sent two battalions of the Old Guard to retake Plancenoit. They had marched straight into the village, and had swept the Prussians out. The dangerous situation on his right flank seemed stable, and the Emperor was still of the opinion that the Prussians were a spent force after Ligny. In front of him the situation also seemed to be improving. Looking to the right-hand side of the Allied position he could see Durutte, with what troops Ney had left him, in possession of Papelotte. In the centre, La

Haie Sainte was in his hands, which meant he controlled the Brussels road as far as the ridgeline and from where his artillery were now dominating the centre of the battlefield. On the left Hougoumont was blazing and swarming with Reille's men.

What Napoleon could not see was the extent of the Prussian advance on their northern axis and that Zieten's corps was advancing in strength on Smohain; the fact that Wellington's light cavalry had been able to reinforce the Allied centre was because they felt confident that the Prussians had now secured the positions they had previously held. In fact the Prussians' advance had not been without problems. With Bülow's initial repulse from Plancenoit, Blücher had sent Captain von Scharnhorst, a name that would be often repeated in German military history, with an urgent message to Zieten to march south to his assistance, leaving Wellington's left flank open. Fortunately Müffling, Blücher's liaison officer to Wellington's headquarters, had already met up with Zieten's chief of staff, a Colonel Reiche, and impressed on him the greater importance of supporting Wellington. Scharnhorst and Reiche met near Smohain and a furious row ensued. Scharnhorst told Reiche that, unless he immediately turned Zieten's corps south, he, Reiche, would be held responsible for disobeying Blücher's orders, never an offence to be taken lightly in the Prussian army. But Reiche fully appreciated how critical it was to come to Wellington's assistance. Zieten was nowhere to be found. Poor Reiche was in as difficult a position as Baring had been. The head of the corps was already marching towards Wellington, when General Steinmetz, leading the column, 'charged at me, shouted at me, as was his custom, and without waiting to hear my explanation, ordered his advance guard to retrace their steps to the fork and head towards Plancenoit', Reiche later recorded. Just at that critical moment, both Zieten and Müffling appeared. There was a further heated argument. Müffling won, and Zieten's corps was committed to Wellington's assistance.

The smouldering Steinmetz was told to march on Smohain and came into action with Durutte's men soon after Napoleon had taken his last major decision of the day. This was to order Drouot, commanding the Imperial Guard, to take his only remaining battalions, many of them already committed at Plancenoit, and smash through the Allied centre. Wellington was alerted to this before he actually saw them by a French officer who deserted, although details of what he said are sketchy. Wellington had already deployed Chassé's Netherlands infantry forward, to the west of the road and behind the Brunswickers, about the only reserve he had left although he probably did not expect great things from them. They had until now been in the relatively undemanding job of holding Braine-l'Alleud, which had not been attacked. Wellington also pulled Adam's brigade back from beside Hougoumont and repositioned them behind the ridgeline, anticipating, correctly, that the Imperial Guard's attack would be preceded by another massive artillery bombardment. He had already pulled his light cavalry from the left wing into the centre. He now rode along the line, moving the battalions from squares into line, telling the commanding officers to lie their men down, partly as protection from the artillery but also so that the Imperial Guard would not know exactly where they were. There was little more that he could do. His artillery batteries were still in position along the ridge itself, but they were now severely reduced.

'Our gunners – the few left fit for duty of them – were so

exhausted that they were unable to run the guns up after firing, consequently every round they retreated nearer to the limbers; and as we pointed our two left guns towards the people who were annoying us so terribly, they soon came together in a confused heap, the trails crossing each other, and the whole dangerously near the limbers and ammunition wagons, some of which were totally unhorsed, and others in sad confusion from the loss of their drivers and horses, many of them lying dead in their harness attached to their carriages. I sighed for my poor troop – it was already but a wreck', wrote Mercer, although by that stage he was also conscious of fire coming from high ground to his front and left. At one point he was dismounted and helping to lay one of his guns when he was aware of a 'black speck' coming directly for him. He thought 'Here it is then!' assuming he was done for, but the round shot went 'whush' past his face, taking away part of his collar and killed a horse just behind him. Next a shell with a long fuse landed at his feet. He had rebuked his men earlier for throwing themselves flat, so he thought he couldn't and stayed standing for what seemed like eternity 'until the cursed thing burst – and strange to say without injuring me though so near'.[67]

The Middle Guard and Old Guard, apart from those who had been detached to drive the Prussians from Plancenoit, had spent the day in reserve, as they were normally deployed, behind Napoleon's centre, astride the road behind La Belle Alliance. The Imperial Guard were as much part of the Napoleonic legend as the man himself, who actively encouraged their reputation as the most feared infantry in Europe. They had been with him at his great victories, stood beside him at Borodino and on the retreat from Russia, guarded him in his palaces, protected him on campaign, and some had even been allowed to accompany him to Elba. They were an élite force, who owed their loyalty personally to the Emperor, whom they were allowed to address as 'Mon Empereur' rather than 'Your Majesty'. They were paid almost double what the line infantrymen received, had better food, their own medical service and hospitals. In terms of their unswerving devotion to a single individual and the cause he represented, they were not unlike the SS in Hitler's Wehrmacht, or the Revolutionary Guard Corps in modern Iran. Their distinctive blue uniforms were topped with tall bearskin caps, they were issued with superior equipment, their muskets had brass fittings and they had priority on the march. When the Guard passed, ordinary units had to stand aside and salute them, which they only sometimes bothered to acknowledge. They were not, unsurprisingly, that well liked throughout the rest of the army. What annoyed the line regiments most was that they were promoted to one rank above normal army rank, so that a corporal in the Imperial Guard ranked as a sergeant, and a Guard sergeant-major counted as an officer. There was nothing unusual in this throughout European armies; facing them across the valley at Waterloo were the British Foot Guards, whose officers also carried an army rank senior to their actual rank (which is why poor Mathew Clay found himself fighting alongside so many lieutenant-colonels at Hougoumont), and the Life Guards, the British Household Cavalry, were paid more than line cavalrymen, which caused similar resentment. It was only 25 years previously that Life Guards NCOs had stopped ranking as officers as well. What differentiated Napoleon's Imperial Guard from the French infantry of the line – apart from all their trappings of empire, their Napoleonic bees and their worship of their emperor, whose motto was wound into the badges on their tall caps – was their unique fighting ethos.

They were in effect a corps within themselves, with their own cavalry, Guyot's Grenadiers à Cheval and Empress's Dragoons, and Lefêbvre-Desnouëttes' *chasseurs* and *lanciers*. They had their own artillery, liberally equipped with the rare twelve-pounders, and highly effective horse artillery under Duchand. They had their own engineers, field hospital and even their own gendarmerie, responsible for looking after the Imperial baggage, and laughingly referred to as 'the Immortals' by the rest of the army, not because they had never been beaten but because they were supposed never to have been in action.[68] The idea behind the Imperial Guard was that they were a reserve, only committed at the end of a battle, when victory seemed assured, and then it was usually only the Young Guard who fought, the Middle and Old Guard being more there to parade behind their emperor past conquered foes. They were an integral part of Napoleon's charade of invincibility, albeit one that was wearing just a little thin after Russia and Leipzig. The British artist Benjamin Haydon, who enjoyed painting military types, had seen them at Fontainebleau in 1814 and thought he had never seen 'more dreadful looking fellows. They had the look of thoroughbred, veteran, disciplined banditti. Depravity, recklessness and blood thirstiness were burned into their faces ... Black mustachios, gigantic bearksins, and a ferocious expression were their characteristics.'[69] They went in for elaborate tattoos and earrings, but then earrings were common to all armies at the time and were also widely worn in the British ranks.

The Imperial Guard had, unsurprisingly, been disbanded by the Bourbons, apart from those few who had gone to Elba, and one of the first things Napoleon had done on his return was to recall them. Actually this was not a total success, large numbers choosing to stay away, and he had to resort to a draft of men from each line regiment to make up their numbers. There were not enough uniforms to go round either, so although the battalions who would shortly climb the ridge of Mont St Jean certainly contained many of the men who had served Napoleon for decades, they were not all smartly dressed veterans of 50 battles who had never known defeat. But for the young men facing them on the opposite hill they still represented something of an invincible force and they were frightened by them. When 17-year-old Ensign Edward Macready saw them he thought to himself 'Now for a clawing' and 'looked for nothing but a bayonet in my body, and I half breathed a confident sort of wish that it might not touch my vitals'.[70]

At this point in the battle it was not so much committing the Imperial Guard as a gesture to wrap up the remnants of Wellington's army before they marched triumphantly on to Brussels, more a realisation that they were all Napoleon had left at his disposal. Much of his cavalry and artillery had already been used up in Ney's prodigal charges, although Duchand's horse artillery was still uncommitted and they now joined the infantry. As they marched up the road from Rossomme, led by 150 bandsmen playing 'the triumphant marches of the Carousel as they went',[71] eight regiments filed past Napoleon, who placed himself at their head and led them as far as the corner of the orchard below La Haie Sainte where, conveniently out of shot, he handed over once more to Ney, who appears not to have known what was going on. 'A short time afterwards I saw four regiments of the Middle Guard, led by Napoleon, march in. With these men he wished me to renew the attack and break through the enemy's centre. He ordered me to lead them forward', he recalled.[72]

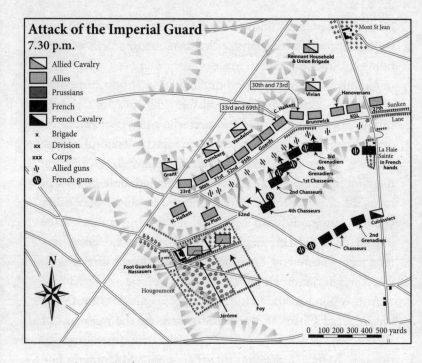

Attack of the Imperial Guard
7.30 p.m.

	Allied Cavalry
	Allies
	Prussians
	French
	French Cavalry
x	Brigade
xx	Division
xxx	Corps
⑂	Allied guns
⑩	French guns

Mont St Jean

Remnant Household & Union Brigade

30th and 73rd

Vivian

33rd and 69th

C. Halkett

Hanoverians

Sunken

Brunswick

KGL

27th

Lane

Vandeleur

Guards

La Haie Sainte in French hands

Dornberg

95th

3rd Grenadiers

Grant

52nd

71st

90th

4th Grenadiers

1st Chasseurs

23rd

2nd Chasseurs

4th Chasseurs

Cuirissiers

H. Halkett

du Platt

52nd

2nd Grenadiers

Chasseurs

Foot Guards & Nassauers

Hougoumont

Foy

Jérôme

N

0 100 200 300 400 500 yards

The Imperial Guard now divided into two lines. In the first were five battalions of the Middle Guard, two of grenadiers and three of *chasseurs*. In the second line, and kept well back in the dip between Hougoumont and La Haie Sainte, were the three battalions of the Old Guard. Three more battalions, the most senior ones, remained well behind them, the 1st and 2nd Grenadiers of the Old Guard at La Belle Alliance, and 1st Chasseurs way back at La Ferme du Caillou, where they were guarding the Imperial baggage and papers. All eight battalions committed to the attack formed into hollow square, only too aware of what the British heavy cavalry had done to d'Erlon's men when they had advanced earlier in column. Given that each battalion was about 600 strong, the face of each square, three men deep, would have been about 50 men wide, with their commanders riding in front and Duchand's horse-artillery teams deployed in between each square.

As they were forming into this attack formation from their columns, a cry had gone up that Grouchy was advancing to support them from the area of Papelotte, where large numbers of dark uniformed figures were beginning to become visible over the fields. It was, against stiff competition, probably one of Napoleon's greatest lies. He had instructed General Dejean to tell Ney, and Dejean had then ridden down the line, with his hat raised on the point of his sabre, shouting 'Vive L'Empereur! Soldats, voilà Grouchy!' and the soldiers had taken up his cry with 'En avant! En avant! Vive L'Empereur!' But he 'had hardly got to the end of the line when I heard cannon fire behind us'.[73] Enthusiasm gave way to a 'profound silence, to amazement, to anxiety'. The troops were in fact Zieten's 1st Corps, the irascible Steinmetz to the fore, and their artillery was already playing on the French lines. The commanders had realised that they had been deceived but the soldiers of the Imperial Guard perhaps did not and thus encouraged they stepped off, confident they were about to achieve final victory. Every man there must have realised that this was the decisive moment not just in the battle but for the campaign, and if the campaign was lost so was Napoleon, the Empire and everything that they had fought for in many cases for 20 long years. The Imperial Guard had not failed before and they had no intention of failing now.

What is difficult to understand is why the Imperial Guard was directed over the same ground as Ney's cavalry attacks had been, in other words the open fields between Hougoumont and La Haie Sainte, the one area Ney knew was dominated by Wellington's artillery, when he had a protected start line at La

Haie Sainte. It seems as if there was meant to be a supporting attack by what was left of d'Erlon's corps in parallel, and that would clear the area of the crossroads just as the Imperial Guard cleared the ridge to the west. There was such an attack, Donzelot's remnants attacking the Brunswickers and Nassauers beside La Haie Sainte, but it never came to anything.

As their drums beat the *pas de charge*, the two battalions of grenadiers of the Middle Guard stepped off, led by General Friant and General Harlet, aiming for the ridge just to the left of La Haie Sainte, where it was held by what was left of Halkett's battalions. Slightly after them the 1st and 2nd Battalions of the 3rd Chasseurs of the Middle Guard stepped off, heading roughly for the middle, to the area held by Maitland's 1st Guards Brigade. A little behind them came the 4th Chasseurs, who would hit the right-hand edge of the 1st Guards and Adam's brigade, now drawn up behind the ridge to their right.

The Imperial Guard would strike the Allied infantry as they began to collapse from exhaustion. John Kincaid, with the 95th in the sandpit, would never forget the scene on the battlefield just before they attacked. He 'felt weary and worn out', although 'less from fatigue than anxiety'. His division, the Third, which had started the day 5,000 strong, was reduced to 'a solitary line of skirmishers. The twenty-seventh regiment were lying literally dead, in square, a few yards behind us. My horse had received another shot through the leg, and one behind the flap of the saddle, which lodged in his body sending him a step beyond the pension list.' Kincaid walked 'a little way to each flank, to endeavour to get a glimpse of what was going on; but nothing met my eye except the mangled remains of men and horses'.[74] Away to his right, just where the 4th Chasseurs would strike, the 52nd had been pulled back 40 yards from the crest of the ridge so that they were 'nearly or quite out of fire'. It was just as well, as every available French gun opened up. 'The roar of roundshot still continued, many only just clearing our heads – others, striking the top of the position and rolling over us – others, again, almost spent and rolling down gently towards us like a cricketball, so slowly that I was putting out my foot to stop it, when my colour-serjeant quickly begged me not to do so, and told me it might have seriously injured my foot', remembered Ensign William Leeke. Whilst they were waiting he noticed a dead tortoiseshell kitten which he supposed had been frightened out of Hougoumont and which suddenly reminded him of his friends at home. Under the bank to his front were 20 of their badly wounded men, whom someone had covered with their blankets out of their knapsacks. To his left were several badly wounded horses, munching at the crushed corn despite having their legs shot off; as he was watching he saw them run over by a troop of horse artillery, dashing back to the ridge after replenishing their ammunition. That particular Waterloo smell, 'the smell of wheat trodden flat down with the smell of gunpowder', pervaded.[75]

Edward Macready stood with the 30th. They knew that they could take very little more and had, after much soul-searching, decided to send their Colours to the rear. It was an extreme measure which many of them didn't like. The Colours symbolised the heart of the battalion and should stay with it until the end, but Macready thought it was the right decision in case they should lose them and possibly because, as one of the few remaining ensigns, he would most likely end up carrying them in the line. 'Never in my life' had he 'felt such joy, or looked on danger with so light a heart, as when I saw our dear old rags in safety'.[76] Not long afterwards the

French artillery stopped, and all along the line the men lying in the trampled corn heard from over the crest to their front the shouts of 'Vive L'Empereur! Vive L'Empereur' and the constant beating of the *pas de charge*, relentless, urgent and menacing. The Imperial Guard was about to attack them.

From the Imperial Guards' perspective, they could see very little ahead of them except the Allied guns that were lining the ridge but not, Macready thought, firing as much as he expected; in fact he would complain that they had fired very little. This was partly because Macready, well behind the crest at this point, could not see what was happening to his front, but also because the Allied batteries had been much reduced by casualties, and two of them, Kuhlmann's and Cleeves', were replenishing their ammunition as the Imperial Guard attacked. Nevertheless the Imperial Guard reached the crest much less damaged than they might have been, and, to the waiting infantry, they appeared over it in seemingly perfect formation. They were, Macready thought, 'in as correct order as at a review. As they rose step by step before us, and crossed the ridge, their red epaulettes and cross-belts put on over their blue great-coats, gave them a gigantic appearance, which was increased by their high hairy caps and long red feathers, which waved with the nod of their heads as they kept time to a drum in the centre of their column.'[77]

The first of the Imperial Guard to breast the crest were the two leading grenadier battalions, coming directly for Halkett's brigade. Halkett rose in his stirrups and Macready remembers him shouting above the din 'My boys, you have done everything I could have wished, and more than I could expect, but much remains to be done; at this moment we have nothing for it but a charge'. It was, in the circumstances, probably something slightly snappier, but the effect was for the survivors of his three battalions to give three cheers and advance up the slope to meet the grenadiers head on. The grenadiers stopped when they were 40 yards away, brought their weapons from the shoulder, and fired a volley. Halkett went down wounded, a musket ball though his jaws. His men stopped, returned the volley and levelled their bayonets. The advance continued through the smoke. Some guns to their rear were firing grape into the grenadiers as they pushed on and, when the smoke cleared, Halkett's men saw the grenadiers' backs. They starred at each other, as if mistrusting their eyes. Their surprise was 'inexpressible'. The Imperial Guard had turned. The slaughter amongst them was dreadful and 'in no part of the field' did Macready 'see carcasses so heaped upon each other'.

But their moment of excitement was short-lived. They pushed on, now breasting the ridge themselves, where they immediately became a target for Duchand's horse artillery, which had advanced interspersed with the Imperial Guard battalions. Duchand had placed two of his guns in between each battalion square, and now they poured fire into Halkett's brigade, which paused. 'The cries from the men struck down, as well as from the numerous wounded on all sides of us, was terrible. An extraordinary number of men and officers went down almost in no time. Prendergast was shattered to pieces by a shell; MacNab killed by grape-shot, and James and Bullen lost all their legs by round shot.' They fell back, initially in good order but then in a jumbled mass, the battalions all becoming mixed up with each other, and threw themselves under the hedge lining the sunken lane to find what shelter they could. Macready fell as he reached it. Struggling to his feet a 'friend knocked up against me, screaming, half maddened by his five wounds and the sad scene going on, "Is it deep, Mac, is it deep?"'

The men began to lose any sense of order. Officers and
NCOs trying to stop them stampeding, 'cursing and crying
with rage and shame, seized individuals to halt them' but
were carried away in the stampede. Someone at this 'infernal
crisis' had the good sense to cheer. They all joined in and
everyone suddenly halted, 'as if coming back to their senses'.
They quickly sorted themselves out. Thomas Morris, whose
73rd were in similar straits, threw himself down under the
bank only to find his brother, who served in a different company; he had gone missing earlier in the day. He had been
taken prisoner, escaped, hid in one of the Guards squares and
had only just rejoined his own battalion. Captain Garland,
now the senior officer left in the 73rd, gathered what men he
could to get the advance going again. About twelve of them
followed him, including both Morris and his brother. They
only made six yards before every man was hit, apart from the
Morrises, who dragged the unfortunate Garland back to the
bank. The 73rd were now down to 3 officers and 70 men,
having started the day respectively with 29 and 550.

Beside them Major Chambers got the light company of the
30th together and turned them round, sending them back
down the hill as skirmishers. The line companies formed
themselves into a line four deep, and the 33rd and 69th did
the same. They whole fiasco had lasted just minutes, and
luckily the French had not been able to take advantage of it,
although Macready thought that if 50 cuirassiers had appeared
they would all have been finished off. Looking to their left
they saw the Brunswickers, who had reeled under Donzelot's
supporting attack, steady themselves and drive the French off.
Minutes later they saw a battalion of Netherlands infantry
pass them, shouting like mad and with their shakos on the tips
of their bayonets.

The next two battalions of the Imperial Guard to hit the crest were the 1st and 2nd Chasseurs, who marched in equally perfect formation, albeit having been hit harder by the Allied artillery, which was now increasing its fire. These battalions breasted the crest directly in front of Maitland's 1st Guards Brigade, which was still lying down. Gronow exaggerated quite a bit with the benefit of hindsight when he wrote 'We now had before us probably about 20,000 of the best soldiers in France, the heroes of many memorable victories; we saw their bear-skin caps rising higher and higher, as they ascended the ridge of ground which separated us and advanced nearer and nearer to our lines'.[78] Actually both battalions of the *chasseurs* numbered nearer 1,500 men, but the psychological effect of the Imperial Guard was such that they seemed to him many more. 'They continued to advance till within fifty or sixty paces of our front, when the Brigade were ordered to stand up. Whether it was from the sudden and unexpected appearance of a corps so near them, which must have seemed as starting from the ground, or the tremendously heavy fire we threw into them, La Garde, who had never before failed in an attack, *suddenly* stopped. Those who, from a distance and more on the flank, could see the affair, tell us that the effect of our fire seemed to force the head of the column bodily back. In less than a minute 300 were down. They now wavered, and several of the rear divisions began to draw out as if to deploy, whilst some of the men in their rear began to fire over the heads of those in front', wrote Harry Powell of 1st Foot Guards.[79] Digby Mackworth, ADC to Lord Hill, was one of those observers. In poetic if sombre mood after the battle he recalled 'a peal of ten thousand thunders burst at once on their devoted heads, the storm swept them down as a whirlwind which rushes over ripe corn'.

As the Chasseurs of the Middle Guard faltered, Wellington, who was behind Maitland's line, lifted his hat and shouted, 'Get up and charge!' The order was shouted down the line. 'Now's the time, my boys!' Saltoun yelled at the remaining men of his light companies, and 'immediately the Brigade sprang forward'. 'We were instantly on our legs, and after so many hours of inaction and irritation all the time suffering the loss of comrades and friends, the spirit which animated officers and men can easily be imagined'.[80] They rushed down the hill, bayonets levelled, and cheering. They caught the *chasseurs* opposite the end of the Hougoumont orchard. The charge now developed into a series of individual fights, for which the élite of Napoleon's army appeared to have little stomach. 'La Garde turned and gave us little opportunity of trying the steel', Powell wrote. Gronow saw several run through the body by his men's bayonets without offering any resistance. A Welshman in his company, called Hughes, six foot seven inches tall, killed twelve men with his bayonet or by smashing their heads with the butt of his musket.

But 1st Guards Brigade had overreached themselves. As they were battling with the 1st and 2nd Chasseurs, the 4th Chasseurs, numerically the strongest of the Imperial Guard battalions, and who had moved off in square a little behind them, had been making steady progress to their left. They were now coming up on 1st Guards Brigade, which had of course lost formation as they fought hand to hand. Maitland tried unsuccessfully to re-form his men into squares, but his orders were not heard amidst the noise. Instead they slowly peeled off and withdrew to the ridge in small groups and singly. The 4th Chasseurs had advanced without taking significant casualties. They had been fired on by the right-hand Allied batteries, and had been close enough to kill many of the gunners. They were now coming up on Maitland's two battalions just when they were split up and at their most vulnerable. Maitland's men were in imminent danger of being taken in the flank and wiped out. It was now that Adam moved his brigade – it had been forward but Wellington had pulled it back behind the ridge before the Imperial Guard's advance began – forward of the ridge again and wheeled them into line at right angles to the Imperial Guard's advance, thus with their backs to Hougoumont orchard.

As 4th Chasseurs closed with 1st Guards Brigade, the left-hand face of their square came into contact with the company of skirmishers that the charismatic Sir John Colborne, commanding the 52nd in Adam's brigade, had thrown out to cover his advance. The 4th Chasseurs' square stopped, and their flank facing the 52nd fired several accurate volleys into them. The 52nd's skirmish line faltered. Two of its officers fell severely wounded. The line fell back, but the main body of the battalion was coming up close behind them. The *chasseurs* fired again; 140 of the 52nd fell, including the ensign carrying the Colour. The 52nd returned fire, and now the *chasseurs* wavered. Their commanding officer Agnès fell. The exchange of volleys continued but it was the *chasseurs* who faltered. 'As we closed they did not wait for our charge, but the leading column at first somewhat receded from us, and then broke and fled.'[81]

All along the ridgeline the Imperial Guard had been halted, had faltered, and had broken. Ney's horse was killed under him, and he had to seek refuge in the 3rd Chasseurs' square. General Friant was wounded and General Michel, the overall second-in-command of the *chasseurs*, killed. All the *chasseurs'* battalion commanders were dead. To the left Zieten had forced back Durutte from Papelotte, and his infantry could now clearly be seen moving across the open fields to the east of the Brussels road. Invisible from the ridgeline, but Blücher, now that Bülow's corps had been joined by Pirch's corps, had just ordered a renewed assault on Plancenoit. Everywhere the French line was on the point of breaking. Adam's brigade, pursuing the 4th Chasseurs, paused; they saw cavalry and fired at it, but it turned out to be the 23rd Light Dragoons, in their blue uniforms, part of Dörnberg's 3rd Cavalry Brigade, coming up alongside Vivian and Vandeleur. Wellington shouted at them to go on. The Duke then lifted his hat and waved forward Maitland's Guards and Halkett's brigades to move as well, so that the whole British line advanced. On Halkett's left, the Brunswickers and Hanoverians sprang forward, including the Osnabrück Battalion in the brigade commanded by his brother Hew. The whole line cheered as they surged forward.

Sergeant Robinson of the 92nd was to the east of the Brussels road. He had been watching something very odd to his front: crossfire into the French lines from the area of Papelotte. 'Troops in the same dress had turned the extremity of their line and were advancing rapidly.' They thought perhaps it was a French mutiny, but just then an ADC galloped up shouting that the Prussians had arrived. Kincaid, listening from the sandpit, heard the cheering off to his west. They knew it was British. 'It gradually approached, growing louder as it drew near; we took it up by instinct, charged through the hedge down upon the old knoll, sending our adversaries flying at the point of the bayonet. Lord Wellington galloped up to us at the instant, and our men began to cheer him; but he called "No cheering, my lads, but forward, and complete your victory".'[82]

It was after eight p.m. as the line moved forward, resem-

Ensign William Leeke, 52nd Foot, Light Infantry. Joining the army aged seventeen in the weeks before the battle, his subsequent account would ignite one of its most longstanding controversies.

Lieutenant Colonel Frank Tidy, commanding 14th Foot. His battalion was the youngest in the army, with fourteen officers and three hundred soldiers under twenty.

Lieutenant Colonel Sir Henry Ellis, commanding 23rd Foot. Feared, but very well liked, he was considered the ideal model of an infantry battalion commander.

The tactically challenged Prince of Orange, who the British thought had cost the 69th their Colour and Colonel Ompteda his life.

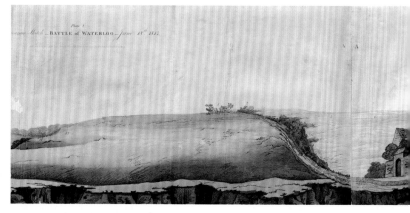

A contemporary panorama of Waterloo, drawn just after the battle, showing how pronounced the ridge was before it was excavated. La Haie Sainte and the sandpit can be clearly seen on the left.

Repelling the French at the North Gate of Hougoumont, one of the critical points in the whole battle.

An idealised but contemporary drawing of Wellington and his staff by the elm at the cross roads, which shows the height of the ridge above La Haie Sainte.

A French attack on the South Gate of Hougoumont. Mathew Clay would fire from the window above, using the bodies of his dead comrades as a barricade.

general scene showing just how crowded and confused the battle was. Two hundred thousand
en would fight in an area barely two miles wide and a mile deep.

ench cavalry attacking the Allied squares. The British infantry were most afraid of the French lancers.

Ney leads the French cavalry charges, which were as magnificent and terrifying to watch as they were tactically doubtful.

Captain Edward Kelly, 1st Life Guards, cutting off the epaulettes of Colonel Habert. Poor Haddy James was asked to keep these bloody trophies in his baggage.

...antry advancing. The pursuit after the Imperial Guard were repulsed was one of the few occasions ...t the soldiers trusted their bayonets.

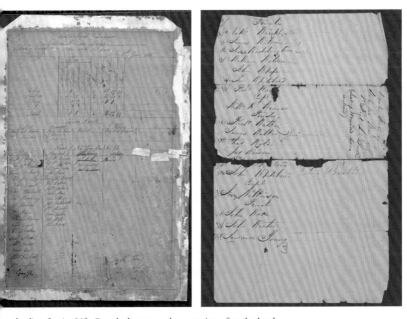

...sualty lists for 1st Life Guards drawn up the morning after the battle.

Burying the dead, whose bodies, stripped naked by the local Belgians, were tossed into enormous pits, which remain unmarked to this day. British soldiers would have to wait sixty years for the privilege of individual graves. Hougoumont can be seen in the background of the second watercolour.

bling 'the curvature of the surf on the shore'.[83] The infantry stopped loading, a welcome relief, having been tearing cartridges in their teeth for eight hours, and relied on their bayonets. The 73rd had no ensigns left to carry their Colours, so they were wrapped round the torso of a sergeant who was told to take them back to Brussels for safe keeping. With the line of infantry battalions rode Vivian's, Vandeleur's and Dörnberg's brigades of light cavalry, now in their element in the pursuit, a task for which they were ideally suited. On their right came what was left of Grant's brigade. Yet it was far from being a victory march. The first five battalions of the Imperial Guard may have broken, but the three battalions behind them remained impassively in their squares forward of the Brussels road – the 1st Chasseurs à Pied under their famous commander Cambronne, who had been wounded at Ligny and turned down promotion so that he could stay with his beloved Imperial Guard, the 2nd Chasseurs and 2nd Grenadiers. 'They were standing in a line of contiguous squares with very short intervals, a small body of Cuirassiers on their right, while the guns took post on their left. They were standing in perfect order and steadiness.'[84]

The 52nd paused. The French guns were trained on them and fired, but the case-shot went high and missed. The cuirassiers did nothing, as if transfixed, and, slowly and deliberately, the three squares of the Imperial Guard, keeping perfect formation, moved slowly back. The light cavalry tried to attack them, but, keeping in squares as they moved, they could not be touched and it was the Allied artillery who raked them with case-shot as they slowly retraced their steps back down the road to La Belle Alliance. The Imperial Guard ignored all calls to surrender. Cambronne had somehow got himself outside his square of *chasseurs* with his staff. They were spotted by Hew Halkett and his Hanoverians. Hew Halkett pursued him, cutting at him with his sword, at which point Cambronne shouted he would surrender. Just then Hew Halkett's horse was shot and fell. He managed to get it on its feet again, and remounted, catching Cambronne by his shoulder cords as he was running back. It was Cambronne who is supposed to have said at this point, 'La Garde meurt, elle ne se rend pas!', which means 'The Guard dies but it never surrenders', although he would always deny that he did. A 'desperate uneducated ruffian who was a drummer in Egypt',[85] he is perhaps more likely simply to have said 'Merde' or 'Shit', which became known in France as 'le mot Cambronne', his more heroic utterance being, as with so much afterwards written about the Imperial Guard, designed to promote their legacy and Cambronne's future career.

The sight of the Imperial Guard variously breaking and retreating, the arrival of the Prussians, and the Allied advance now reduced Napoleon's army from a state of some disorder to one of chaos. The remaining Imperial Guard battalions were being whittled away by artillery so that by the time the grenadiers reached La Belle Alliance they were reduced to a triangle, at which point they dispersed, each man taking his own chances; the rest of the army was in flight. Napoleon himself had moved back to his command post at La Belle Alliance after he had witnessed the failure of the Imperial Guard's attack. Colonel Crabbé, one of Ney's ADCs, remembered Napoleon sitting in front of his table, strewn with maps, 'Slumped in his chair, exhausted and angry' and complaining that Ney had acted stupidly again. 'He has cost us the day! He has destroyed my cavalry and is ready to destroy my Guard! He manoeuvres like a good-for-nothing!'[86]

As the Imperial Guard streamed back, Napoleon had to

take refuge within one of two squares of the grenadiers of the Old Guard, which remained unmovable either side of the Genappe road. Under Maréchal de Camp Petit, they acted, to quote Adkin, as 'two rocks upon which the chaos, confusion, panic and tide of fugitives could make no impression'.[87] It was Petit who had received the singular honour of Napoleon's final farewell kiss as he had left Fontainebleau for his first exile, and he provided a refuge for him now. With 'the whole army in the most appalling disorder — infantry, cavalry, artillery — everybody was fleeing in all directions'; but Petit's men stood firm. They had the Eagle of the grenadiers with them, and they sounded the 'Grenadière' to rally any Guards who had been caught up in the torrent of fugitives. With 'the enemy close at our heels, and, fearing that he might penetrate the squares, we were obliged to fire at the men who were being pursued and who threw themselves wildly at the squares',[88] Petit wrote. All around, as Napoleon stood in a square which was firing at his own soldiers, shouts of 'La Garde recule' and 'Sauve qui peut' showed that the Army of the North, which had so confidently crossed the frontier only four days before, was disintegrating.

Private John Smith, advancing with the 71st, said they 'heaved their knapsacks and arms from them in all directions and run, our brigade cheered and charged them as long as we seed a mass of them for dark night'.[89] Some did rally, and the 71st were charged several times, but they were now futile gestures and Thomas Howell felt nothing could impede their advance. As they neared La Belle Alliance, the French army was in universal retreat. They 'moved on towards a village and charged right through, killing great numbers, the village was so crowded'.[90] It's not clear whether he meant La Belle Alliance or Rossomme but by the time they reached the former they were becoming mixed up with the Prussians.

At around 8.30 p.m. Blücher had finally driven the Imperial Guard out of Plancenoit, and men from Bülow's and Pirch's corps were now pursuing the retreating French on their right. At the same time Zieten's troops were streaming in from the area of Papelotte. There was, inevitably, some of what armies call 'blue on blue', or in this case 'red on black and grey' as the Allies fired on the Prussians by mistake. Mercer had engaged an unidentified battery that was firing at him, fairly accurately, and so not unreasonably he returned fire. Soon after, a lugubrious Brunswicker came galloping up, shouting, 'Ah! Mine Gott! De English kills dere friends de Proosiens!' Mercer pointed out that if it was the Prussians he was firing at then they were making quite a decent job of trying to kill him, but the Brunswicker was unmoved and insisted he stop. Mercer did so, at which point three rounds landed beside them, one very near the Brunswicker, who shouted 'dis is terreebly to see de Proosien and de English kill vonanoder' and galloped off. Mercer never saw him again.[91] More usually there were warm greetings. William Leeke, pausing with his exhausted men on the Brussels road, met a Prussian regiment coming up. They broke into slow time, by way of salute, and their band struck up 'God Save the King'. Leeke was carrying the tattered remnants of their Colour. A mounted Prussian officer came up to him, asked whether it was an English Colour and then 'pressed it to his bosom, and patted me on the back, exclaiming, "*Brave Anglais*".'[92]

It was something of a relief for the infantry battalions to see that the Prussians were able to take over the pursuit. Few had reached further than La Belle Alliance when they stopped. The light-cavalry regiments, however, were still fresh enough to

venture much further and found that they still had to do plenty
of fighting. They didn't really know what was happening, and
although they could tell things were temporarily going rather
better, they were largely 'ignorant of our success'; as they rode
down the slope from the ridge, past the wreckage of Ney's
cavalry charges and the bodies of the Imperial Guard piled
high below the crest, they were not sure whether they were
going to 'charge a successful column of the enemy or pursue a
beaten one'.[93] The 16th Light Dragoons, in Vandeleur's
brigade, took the right-hand side. They soon encountered two
French guns still firing, which aimed case-shot at them but
missed, and then saw about 1,000 French infantry in column,
probably behind the wood at Hougoumont. They charged
them, but the French fired back, before trying to form square.
Many threw down their muskets and fled, but a few did form
makeshift square, and Tomkinson's horse charged straight into
them, something the cuirassiers had not achieved all afternoon.
Tomkinson confided that this was because his horse was blind
in one eye and couldn't see what it was doing; it was, predictably, called Cyclops. In the charge Lieutenant-Colonel
James Hay was hit in the chest by a musket ball; he fell, so seriously wounded that he could not be moved for eight days. No
other troops they came across actually stood, and by ten p.m.,
when it was completely dark, they stopped. They were at the
rear of the original French battle position and found a surprising amount of raw meat and brandy. The meat had been badly
butchered and was full of hair and gristle, too unappetising
even for starving men like them, so they left it, but the brandy
was more appealing.

George Farmer, with his 11th Light Dragoons in
Vandeleur's brigade, fared worse, the French guns causing significant casualties as they rode down the slope. Sergeant

Emmet was hit in the groin and reeled in his saddle. Farmer was riding beside him and caught him just before he fell. The ball also hit Farmer on the knee, but the bone was saved by his cloak, which he was carrying in folds in front of him because he had not found time to roll it away behind his saddle as he should have done. However, once the brigade had halted, his wound did not stop him from going to see what he could find lying around the battlefield. It would turn out to be a terrible experience.

Alongside them, Henry Murray had led his 18th Hussars forward and Private John Marshall had ridden with the 10th Hussars. Marshall was feeling every bit as nervous in that final hour as he had in the morning. Vivian, their brigade commander, was equally unclear as to what they would find as they crossed the ridge. He gave them all a short talk, telling them that he was sure they would do their duty, the sort of thing that soldiers usually find rather irritating. Marshall 'well knowing what we was going to do offered up a prayer to the Almighty that for the sake of my children and the partner of my bosom, he would protect me'.[94] His wife was pregnant at the time and he hadn't heard from her for some weeks. They trotted over the crest, with much cheering. Whilst the French seemed to have favoured set cries such as 'Vive L'Empereur!' and 'En avance', the British were more given to 'huzzaing', which was more of a general cheer. They much enjoyed 'huzzaing' Wellington, who usually reacted with just a curt nod, and during the battle there had been much cheering, although there had, until the last half an hour, been little to occasion it.

One hundred yards down the far side of the crest, the 10th broke into a charge as they fell amongst the retreating Imperial Guard whom 'they slew and overthrew like so many children'. They also attacked and overran the remnants of Reille's artillery, and Duchand's horse-artillery teams, taking 16 guns and killing the gunners. They then came up against Cambronne's *chasseurs*, who gave them volleys as they re-formed and they took several casualties. Marshall claims that they got inside the *chasseurs*' squares as they fell back, but it is likely that he became confused as most accounts say that the *chasseurs* held together until they reached La Belle Alliance. Beside them the 18th Hussars 'cut away all through till we came to the reserve', by which they also meant the *chasseurs*, 'when we was saluted by a volley at the length of two swords' and took several casualties.[95] Sergeant Matthew Colgan tried to be merciful. When attacking the French guns he 'galloped to the outrider or driver on the foremost horse, and he was only a "boy" ... I knocked him off his horse with the flat of my sword (the poor fellow looked so sheepish ... here I con-fess I regret him tumbling under the leader's [leading horse's] feet.' He tried to get another man to surrender, showing 'him mercy as long as I considered my life safe, and when not I gave him the fatal blow'.[96] He was more merciful than a soldier of the 52nd who encountered the commander of a French artillery battery, a veteran Napoleonista, wearing the Légion d'honneur, who refused to surrender. He stood defiant, sword in hand, amidst the ruin of his guns. The soldier of the 52nd 'threw him on the ground, and keeping him down with his foot, reversed his musket to bayonet him. The repugnance to the shedding of human blood unnecessarily ... burst forth in a groan of displeasure from his comrades. It came too late; the fatal thrust had passed.'[97]

The remnants of the Household Brigade also moved for-ward. Richard Coulter had survived the main charge earlier in the day and had charged repeatedly during the afternoon. 'Towards night', he had his 'horse shot in a Charge against a solid column of infantry. I found he was shot I endeavour'd to get to the rear but before I had got him twenty yards he received another Ball he tumbled over another horse which dropit before me. I had my legs out of the stirrups to quite [quit] but another horse came upon me and dropt dead upon my legs this was about 20 yards from the face of the column of 1500 or 2000 men', he wrote to his cousin, exaggerating French strengths. 'I struggled to get clear. They saw me and sent some musket shot at me but they struck in the Horses. I squatted down with my head but I was almost breathless my poor Horse had a great many balls in him but struggled to extricate himself by this means I got my legs clear, looked over his neck and saw more approaching to bayonet me. I mustered all my strength and run of faster than I ever to school in my life their flankers fired after me. I tumbled down but now with their shot I was spent.' He ended up 'fell down upon the road covered with dead men and dead horses'. He took a cloak from one, being all he now had in the world apart from his sword belt that 'was all blood from the horses and my own wound in the hand'. Whilst he was lying there, which was probably on the road between La Haie Sainte and La Belle Alliance, as the Imperial Guard retreated, he was shot in the left arm. Just then 'Blücher gave them such a salute with his cannon that they never looked back'.[98]

The light-cavalry brigades, and what was left of the heavy cavalry, had been operating on the right of the Allied line, to the west of the Brussels road. As the left-hand side of Wellington's line swept forward they came back through the bloody remnants of La Haie Sainte. They found it crammed with dead and wounded. Frederick Lindau was not there. After he had been overpowered he had been taken onto the road outside the farmyard and systematically robbed. There is something a little ironic in his indignation at the injustice of two French soldiers grabbing the bag of gold coins he had so recently stolen from the French officer he had shot. Others took his supply of watches – he had one gold and two silver, which were also looted. He was perhaps more justified in his anger that his pack was torn off and plundered, and that Captain Holtzermann's sash and scabbard were torn off. He and his comrades grabbed stones and 'wanted to avenge such offensive behaviour on the part of the hated French' but Holtzermann calmed them down, and two Allied cannonballs landed near by, killing quite a few of the French, which cheered Lindau up. They were then taken to the rear by a group of cuirassiers, being forced to run beside their horses; one man who couldn't keep up was killed with a sword through his back. Shut in a barn, probably around Rossomme, they realised that the French army was disintegrating. Another mob of French infantry came in and robbed them again. Lindau escaped in the confusion. Stopping for a drink at a well he found it surrounded by more French soldiers. He asked one in French for water; the man replied in German. He was a Hanoverian who had been captured several years before but could not stand captivity so had entered French service. Lucky to escape Lindau's fury, he gave him water and bread and told him how to avoid being retaken.[99]

Edmund Wheatley had also been taken prisoner in La Haie Sainte, having been knocked unconscious beside Colonel Ompteda. When he came to, he was dragged into the farmhouse by the French. The inside he found 'completely destroyed, nothing but the rafters and props remaining. The floor was strewed with bodies of the German infantry and French Tirailleurs.' Wheatley, as a lieutenant, wore epaulettes on his uniform jacket which made him stand out as an officer and therefore as a prisoner of some importance. He tried to pass himself off as a private in the grenadier company, who also wore a sort of epaulette, but the French were not convinced and interrogated him. Like Lindau he was sent to the rear, along the Genappe road, passing ditches 'crammed with groaning wounded'. In his group was a foot soldier on horseback, 'his right leg shattered at the knee that his leg hung down by one single piece of sinew', and his 'stomach sickened as it dangled backwards and forwards splashing his horse with gore and marrow'. Against the wall of a garden he saw 'a foot soldier sitting with his head back and both his eyeballs hanging on his cheeks, a ball having entered the side of his head and passed out at the other. His mouth was open, stiff and clotted, clear blood oozed out of his ears and the purulent matter from his empty sockets emitted a pale steam from the vital heat opposed to the evening cold'. But Wheatley was more closely guarded, and even in the chaos of the French collapse he was unable to escape.[100]

Lindau and Wheatley were lucky to be alive. Many prisoners were not so fortunate. The French murdered many prisoners as did the Germans, and particularly the Prussians. There was a rumour in the British ranks that the French had been seen flying a black flag, signifying that no quarter would be given, a sort of skull-and-crossbones idea. John Marshall said that the light cavalry certainly believed that 'if [they] had beat us I dare say they would have showed us none [mercy], and I myself am witness to it, that many of them was laid to the ground which would not have been but for that',[101] which would seem to be a different take to that of the 52nd, upset at the bayoneting of the French artillery officer.

By the time the Prussians were in full pursuit it was dark. Napoleon had left the grenadiers' square and made his way back to La Ferme du Caillou, where the remaining battalion of *chasseurs à pied* were still guarding his baggage, and his coach. He was not in time to enjoy it, having to abandon it amongst the crush of his fleeing soldiers and escaping on horseback with what was left of the cavalry of the Imperial Guard. Wellington had ridden forward past La Haie Sainte and La Belle Alliance to Rossomme and conferred there with Vivian and the cavalry commanders. Afterwards he rode back towards Waterloo, intent as much on chasing up the commissariat for supplies as on sending word to London.

In a scene soon to be made well known by war artists, Wellington met Blücher and his staff as he retraced his steps past La Belle Alliance and quickly conferred. The exhausted British and Allies would rest whilst Bülow's corps would lead the pursuit. Wellington was without Uxbridge. He had been hit on his right knee by one of the last case-shot the French fired that day and had lost his leg. It allegedly prompted that since well known exchange, with Uxbridge saying, 'By God, sir! I've lost my leg,' to which Wellington is supposed to have replied, 'By God, sir! So you have.' Some said Wellington's lack of sympathy was because he was still in a rage about the lack of control of the heavy brigades; others that he could never forgive Uxbridge for using influence in London to get command of the cavalry over Wellington's preferred candidate, Stapleton Cotton, and because he had eloped with Wellington's sister-in-law. More likely it was just the reaction of a tired man with much on his mind.

Adam's, Halkett's and Maitland's brigades stopped where the Imperial Guard had bivouacked the night before. In the conflict between exhaustion and hunger, exhaustion won and most fell asleep where they stood. There was little elation. Mercer had been ecstatic when the artillery had finally

stopped firing. He would never forget that 'moment of exul-
tation' but for him, as for most, it was short-lived. He was
congratulating himself on the 'happy results of the day' when
an ADC rode up urging him to get his guns forward. Mercer
looked round at the remains of his troop. 'How, sir?' he
replied. He had just enough men left to man four guns with
skeleton crews and about 60 horses from the 200 he had
started the day with. He remained where he was on the ridgeline.[102] William Lawrence was so hungry he decided to try to
cook. He sent a man called Rouse, who had survived unhurt
all day, in search of sticks. He came across a French artillery
ammunition wagon and started cutting up the cover for fuel.
His hook came into contact with a nail and created a spark.
The powder in the wagon exploded. Remarkably Rouse was
still just alive when his body came down. He had everything
blown off him except his shoes. He said what 'a fool he was
and cursed his eyes, even though they were both gone'. He
survived long enough to be taken back to Brussels, where he
died a few days later 'raving mad'.[103]

Lawrence was then told he had to act as orderly sergeant to
General Adam. He was asked to find some food for the general's horse. Whilst searching he came across a sack which
not only contained corn but also two chickens and a ham.
Adam gratefully accepted the corn but told Lawrence to keep
the food, warning him to watch out for the Prussians, 'who
he said were a slippery set of men and might steal it'. They
finally got the fire going, without poor Rouse, and 'enjoyed
their mess as never before' when some Prussians came along.
Lawrence thought it wise to offer them some food, and they
went away content. He was then too tired to sleep and lay
awake by the fire, thinking about the day. All he had suffered
was a scratch on the face, aggravated by a private who was

standing next to him overpriming the pan on his musket. When he fired, the powder had 'flown up and caught the wound' making him 'dance without a fiddle for a while'. But he knew there were over 300 of his regiment missing and he had heard that the regiment on their right, which would have been the 52nd, had lost 600.

At Hougoumont, things became eerily quiet after Mathew Clay and the survivors of the 2nd Guards Brigade heard the cheering as the Allied line advanced. He looked round and 'saw the sad havoc the enemy had made of our fortress'. The fire had destroyed much of the farmyard. The wounded who had not been burned alive were laid out in the château kitchen. Some Netherlands soldiers came in looking for wounded comrades and tried to bayonet the wounded French but the 3rd Foot Guards stopped them. Clay had some pork in his haversack which he started to cook over a fire, until he realised that the fire was being fuelled by a 'half consumed body'. Lieutenant-Colonel Francis Home saw the pigeons coming home to roost in their house, which stood in the middle of the farmyard and had miraculously survived untouched. The pigeons did not, making 'an excellent supper roasted on ramrods over the burning rafters' and being the first food many of them had tasted for two days.[104]

Once the 11th Light Dragoons had 'gone firm' for the night, George Farmer stole out 'upon a cruise' with a comrade. He would admit that his intention was to see what loot he could find. He would never forget the extraordinary sights as he rode over the battlefield. 'Arms of every kind – cuirasses, muskets, cannon, tumbrils, and drums, which seemed innumerable, encumbered the very face of the earth. Intermingled with these were the carcases of the slain, not lying about in groups of four or six but so wedged together, that we found it, in many instances, impossible to avoid tramping them. Then again the knapsacks ... were countless ... but not one I examined contained more than coarse shirts and shoes that belonged to the dead owners with here and there a little package of tobacco and a bag of salt.' He had spotted a man killed in their final charge who had been wearing a gold watch. He had memorised where it was and now retraced his steps. He found the poor man all right but he was already completely naked, stripped to the skin and no sign of his watch. Farmer could see where the ball had entered exactly in the middle of his chest. They got lost trying to find their way back and stopped, exhausted. When they woke they found they were near Plancenoit. There was a terrible smell coming from a nearby farmyard, which they found to be crammed with wounded and dying French. Many of them had been bayoneted *in situ* by the Prussians.

6

19 JUNE AND AFTERWARDS

Mrs Edmund Boehm was greatly looking forward to the evening of Wednesday 21 June. Her husband had made a great deal of money over the previous decade; he was one of those people who had done very well out of the war, and the sort of person the Secretary and the Club in the Royals thought had grown fat on the back of their efforts in Portugal and Spain. His wealth had bought Number 16, St James's Square, a very fine house, and Mrs Boehm was determined that she should be accorded the corresponding position in society that such an address demanded. She had realised that there was no better way to accomplish her ambition than to persuade the Prince Regent to attend a ball. The intelligence and planning that such an event demanded would not have disgraced Wellington and De Lancey, and His Royal Highness had finally accepted her invitation for that Wednesday night. The preparations were immense and Mrs Boehm had 'spared no expense to render it the most brilliant party of the season'.[1] This was Mrs Boehm's opportunity to arrive and nothing was going to stand in her way.

After dinner, 'the ladies had gone upstairs, and the gentlemen had joined them' and 'the ball guests began to arrive. They came with unusual punctuality, out of deference to the Regent's presence.' Mrs Boehm walked up to the Prince and asked whether it was his pleasure that the ball should open. 'The first quadrille was in the act of forming, and the Prince was walking up to the dais on which his seat was placed, when I saw everyone without the slightest sense of decorum rush to the windows which had been left wide open because of the excessive sultriness of the weather. The music ceased and the dance was stopped.' Outside was a post-chaise and four, out of whose windows were hanging 'three nasty French eagles'. Without a moment's thought for poor Mrs Boehm's feelings, out jumped Major Henry Percy, such a dusty, dirty figure, and 'pushing aside every one who happened to be in his way, darting upstairs, into the ball room, stepping hastily up to the Regent, dropping on one knee, laying the flags at his feet, and pronouncing the words "Victory, Sir! Victory!"' He then undid a large purple handkerchief, which he had been given by a partner at the Duchess of Richmond's ball, and handed over Wellington's despatch, which he had brought directly from Waterloo.

It was too bad. The party was ruined. 'Never did a party promising so much terminate so disastrously! All our trouble, anxiety and expense were utterly thrown away in consequence of – what shall I say? Well, I must say it, the unseasonable declaration of the Waterloo victory! Of course one was glad to think one had beaten those horrid French, and all that sort of thing; but still, I always shall think it would have been far better if Henry Percy had waited quietly till the morning instead of bursting in on us, as he did, in such indecent haste,' complained Mrs Boehm.

The despatch that Percy handed over, which had been

written by Wellington the night of the battle, carried news of the victory, and singled out some regiments – such as the Guards – and individuals for praise, but not others. This was to prove divisive. It was also accompanied both by the enticing Eagles and by an initial but incomplete casualty list. The immediate reaction in London was one of almost delirious celebration and relief. Had Wellington and Blücher failed, and were Napoleon to be occupying the Grand Palais in Brussels, then all the royal families, politicians, bankers and businessmen not just in London but also in Berlin, Vienna and Moscow, would have been waking up to a very different Europe and an uncertain future.

The concerns of those waking up on the battlefield on Monday 19 June were more immediate. Thomas Morris had fallen asleep where he stopped, but woke at midnight, 'almost mad for want of water'. He picked his 'way among the bodies of his sleeping as well as dead comrades; but the horrors of the scene created such a terror' in his mind that he could not go on. He went to wake his brother so that they could go together, and passed a dead horse lying on its side and noticed a man sitting upright with his back against the horse's body. He thought the man called out to him and 'the hope that I could render some assistance overcame my terror'. Attempting to lift him to make him more comfortable, his hand passed straight through his body and he realised that a round shot had gone through both man and horse. He now ran back as fast as he could to get his brother. He was so desperate for water that he risked his fury on waking him. They came across a man called 'Cossack' Smith, so called because of his violent temper, who was sleeping with his head on a full canteen, with the strap passed around his body. They gingerly raised his head, took the full canteen and replaced it with an empty one. They quickly downed the delicious water, threw away the canteen and then slept till sunrise, when they were woken by Smith shouting that when he found who had taken his water he would run them through. They knew him sufficiently well to believe that he might, so they kept well away. Morris then went in search of Jack Parsons. There was no sign of him and when the 73rd held their roll call no one answered to Private Parsons, J. Poor Thérèse was distraught, but stayed with the battalion when they marched.[2]

Normally after a battle the talk around the bivouac fires was of who had been hit; the morning after Waterloo it was rather of who had survived. 'I had never heard of a battle where everyone was killed', recorded John Kincaid, 'but this seemed to be the exception.'[3] Colonel Felton Hervey, a staff officer, riding around the position very early, found his horse up to its fetlocks in blood. There is no absolutely accurate number for those killed, particularly as with the French army falling apart by the end of the day it is not clear how many of them fell and how many ran away; the same problem applies to estimating the Netherlands' casualties. Wellington lost about 17,000, of whom 3,300 were listed as 'missing', which means that a number of Netherlanders and a few Hanoverians ran away. The remainder lay either dead or wounded on the field. Alongside them lay around 31,000 French and 7,000 Prussians; thus in the confined space between Hougoumont and Papelotte, and between La Belle Alliance and Mont St Jean, 55,000 mangled bodies or parts of bodies were strewn amongst the corn and the grass.[4] They were laid in lines where the squares had been, or where d'Erlon's battalions had attacked, or were in heaps where the artillery had mown down whole ranks in one shot. Around Hougoumont the

French infantry were in mounds, as were the cuirassiers near La Haie Sainte. No one knew who was dead and who simply wounded, the latter often trapped under piles of bodies of men and horses.

Gronow took himself down to Hougoumont early. He went first into the orchard, where there were 'heaps of dead men in various uniforms; those of the Guards in their usual red jackets, the German Legion in green, and the French dressed in blue, mingled together. The dead and wounded positively covered the whole area of the orchard; not less than two thousand men had fallen there. Every tree was riddled and smashed in a manner which told that the showers of shot had been incessant. On this spot I lost some of my dearest and bravest friends, and the country had to mourn many of its most heroic sons.'[5] Mathew Clay looked out on 'the heaps of the enemy's slain about the exterior of the farm'. The haystack by the south gate, behind which he had sheltered to fire at the French the previous morning, had burned with such ferocity that the bodies of his light-company comrades lying near by were already desiccated. The wood was equally full of bodies; he tried to help a wounded Frenchman who was propped up against a tree but the man refused and, with so many other wounded about, Clay left him to his fate.[6]

Mercer's troop was also awake early. They had been told to replenish their ammunition supply from a dump near Waterloo, but they were so short of horses that it took several journeys. Whilst his men were thus engaged, Mercer wandered down towards Hougoumont as well. The first thing that surprised him was that the ground was covered in books and papers, until he realised that they were the French soldiers' pay books that they all carried and which had been tossed away by the looters. Numerous groups of peasants were wandering around, stripping the dead and 'finishing those not quite so. Some of these men I met fairly staggering under enormous loads of clothes etc. Some had firearms, swords etc. and many had large bunches of crosses and decorations; all seemed in high glee and professed unbounded hatred of the French.'

Mercer went into the orchard. The Guards had collected most of their wounded in, but the place was full of wounded French. Mercer gathered some of his men and they took them water from the well near by. They found them particularly grateful and those who were strong enough were happy to talk. Mercer was a bit taken aback that 'all the non-commissioned officers and privates agreed in asserting that they had been deceived by their officers and betrayed; and, to my surprise, almost all of them reviled Bonaparte as the cause of their misery'. Many of them begged Mercer's men to kill them rather than leave them to be sliced up by the marauding peasants. They also found a desperately wounded lancer officer, a strong-built square man with reddish hair. Evidently an arch-Bonapartist, he refused all assistance, knocking aside the proffered water canteen.[7]

Bodies were hard to identify and finding dead friends was difficult as overnight most had been stripped. William Tomkinson went early in search of Lieutenant Alexander Hay of 16th Light Dragoons, but although he knew roughly where he had fallen 'no search could ever discover him. He probably fell in the corn, and was stripped early by the peasants'. The same happened to many of the Household Brigade who had fallen on the great charge. John Hibbert complained that it was 'the Belgic troops, who were without exception the greatest set of cowards and rascals in the world' who 'stripped them of everything but their shirts and left them in this miserable way all night. Our officers were only known by the

name on the shirts; I daresay many died of cold in the night.'[8]
He was unfair in blaming the Netherlands army, it being the
local civilians who were the main culprits, and he did record
that 'the peasants for miles around assembled the following
morning on the field'. Tomkinson saw them pulling the boots
off a badly wounded Guards officer before he was dead.
Tomkinson tried to stop them, but the local Belgians clearly
couldn't see what all the fuss was about. One of the looters'
less attractive habits was to chisel out teeth from the dead and
almost dead. They would also eat well for several weeks on
the thousands of horses whose bodies lay all around.

Tomkinson found another Guards officer who had been
shot in the hip. He told one of his dragoons to take him to the
field hospital but the man could not bear being moved. They
had to leave him where he was. Near by they found Colonel
Canning, one of Wellington's ADCs. He shouted at them
not to ride over him, which they were about to do. He had
been hit in the body with case-shot and was determined that
he was done for. Tomkinson tried to get him to a surgeon but
he refused. Cheered up by the news of the victory, he handed
Tomkinson his sword and watch to pass to his relations, and
died soon afterwards.[9]

The worst casualties percentage-wise were in the 2nd Life
Guards, who lost 155 men out of the 235 who had waited
nervously behind the ridge that morning, or two-thirds of
their strength. Playford went off searching for any survivors.
He and Corporal William Webster found Shaw. At first they
only saw the back of a Life Guards uniform, but rolling the
body over they recognised him. He had a deep wound in his
side, near his heart, which they thought had been inflicted by
a bayonet or lance. There were several bodies of French soldiers lying around him. There were few other English bodies

round about, and the legend would grow that Shaw, having been knocked off his horse for the second time, took off his helmet and whirled it round his head as a club until he was finally overpowered. He now lay beside the wall at La Haie Sainte, and Playford thought he must have been killed there during their initial charge. When the remnants of the regiment were gathered together they 'looked a strange medley, some on French horses and some on foot, and from time to time they picked up one of their own horses whose rider had been killed'.[10] When the Squadron Corporal Majors called out the roll they marked off those who did not reply either in red pencil or, if no pencil was to hand, by pricking the paper; no one answered when John Bingley's name was called in H Troop of the Blues.

The King's Dragoon Guards had lost 275 men, almost exactly half the number they had started with. Private Charles Stanley had his 'rap' with 'Mr Boney Part Harmey' but would never see his large family at Edwinston again. The Royals lost nearly half as well. The Club would now be much smaller. 'Windsor, Forster, Magniac, Sykes and Shipley bit the dust', the Secretary recorded of the five officers killed. 'Radcliffe, Clarke, Gunning, Kiely, Trafford [the Secretary himself], Windowe, Omaney, Blois and Goodenough were wounded. Perhaps the one most seriously wounded was old Gubbins', the 'Man of Kent' as the Secretary always referred to George Gunning, as he came from Frindsbury, and who had 'behaved nobly in the charge'. Even Ben the Ruler was reckoned to have led the regiment rather well, but two officers had incurred the Club's displeasure – Mr Bridges, who had been observed 'going to the rear at a famous rate' and Heathcote. They would soon have to account for themselves.[11]

The Scots Greys mustered three officers, two sergeants and

16 privates, although some of their men were away escorting prisoners. The light cavalry, later to feel their part in the battle had been rather overlooked, suffered heavily as well. O'Grady's 7th Hussars also lost nearly half their men, 155 out of 362, whilst Hay's 12th Light Dragoons lost a quarter. Both O'Grady and Hay survived unhurt.

The worst casualties by number were in the 27th, the Inniskillings, the Irish infantry battalion who had been smashed by artillery fire from the guns Ney had brought forward to La Haie Sainte. They lost 478 men. Next worst hit were 1st Guards, who lost 342, then Thomas Morris's 73rd, who lost 280. Baring's 2nd Light Battalion of the King's German Legion had lost 202, again nearly half its strength whilst the 5th Battalion of the King's German Legion, who had so bravely charged with Ompteda, lost 162. The 95th, the Rifles, had lost a total of 403 split between their two battalions. The 33rd had 185 casualties. Captain John Haigh had already been killed at Quatre Bras. He had, as we have seen, been hit by a cannonball. His brother Thomas, also an officer in the battalion, 'saw him fall and his bowels all gush out' and said, 'Oh kill me with him!' 'He has since had his wish fulfilled', noted their regimental surgeon, 'being shot through the neck'. Their father, also John Haigh, was serving in the battalion as their quartermaster, having risen from the ranks. He was reputed to have been a great favourite with Wellington, who was said to have helped him get his commission. One of the many commanding officers to fall had been Arthur Heyland, just as he had so sadly predicted in that last letter home, which would arrive after news of his death.

The artillery had lost a quarter of their officers. Major Norman Ramsay was killed commanding his eponymous troop; he was the third member of his family to be lost in the recent war. His brother, also a gunner, had been killed in America a few months before, and the only other surviving brother, a naval officer, had just died in the West Indies. It was a bitter summer for their retired naval officer father, who lived in Edinburgh. Ramsay was famous throughout the Army, having led his troop in a very brave dash to bring his guns into action at Fuentes de Oñoro, and having been put under arrest by Wellington – everyone agreed, most unfairly – for allegedly disobeying an order at Vitoria. The staff, the gilded staff, had suffered equally. Famously Wellington finished the day without an ADC, and De Lancey was badly wounded. Four generals had been killed, including Picton and Ponsonby, and seven wounded. There had been the odd field burial after Quatre Bras, during those clammy hours of waiting for the French advance, but now there was little time. There were no formal prayers, and it was not until some time afterwards that Edward Frith, the fighting padre, and one of the very few men of the cloth to put in a forward appearance, managed to hold a service for the Fifth Division. He used as his text 'Rejoice and return thanks to the Lord for his mercies He has granted you'. 'There was hardly a dry eye in the whole division, and it had an excellent effect on the men.'[12]

But the Army had little time to recover. Although they all knew that they had won a great victory, and that they had chased the French from the field in pieces, they also thought that they might well have to fight again. The Prussians had taken over the chase the evening before, and were in relentless and merciless pursuit, but Wellington and what was left of his staff were not sure where Grouchy was nor whether Napoleon had plans to regroup and to make a stand in France. There was an urgency in following him up to frustrate this, and to take Paris before he was able to reorganise the French army. Napoleon was very much of that mind. He wrote to his brother Joseph in Paris on 19 June that 'All is not lost. I suppose that, when I reassemble my forces, I shall have 150,000 men.' These were supposedly coming from the National Guard, the training depots and 100,000 from conscription. 'I shall use carriage horses to drag the guns', the Emperor continued. Grouchy should be able to give him 50,000 men within three days, he reasoned, 'plenty to keep the enemy occupied, and to allow time for Paris and France to do their duty. The Austrians are slow marchers; the Prussians fear the peasantry and dare not advance too far. There is still time to retrieve the situation.'[13]

It is hard to read this letter without wondering whether Napoleon was losing his grip on reality. Nowhere does he mention any regret at the enormous loss he had just suffered, not even for the Imperial Guard, and all around him his army was disintegrating. 'Not only the main road', noted a Prussian prisoner who was with the French army that Monday, 'but also every side road and footpath was covered with soldiers of every rank, of every arm of the service, in the most complete and utter confusion. Generals, officers, wounded men – and these included some who had just had limbs amputated; everyone walked or rode in disorder.'[14] People would later question why Napoleon had not sought a soldier's death on the battlefield, leading his Imperial Guard in their final attack, instead of handing over to Ney and withdrawing to La Belle Alliance. The answer must be that he thought he was far from finished, and his mind was on how to fight back rather than on a second lonely exile, or worse.

Soon after daybreak on Monday 19 June, ADCs came round the waking British brigades with orders to move. There was to be no time to bring up their baggage, still mostly in Brussels or where they had been billeted, and it would be several days before those who were lucky enough not to have had theirs plundered would see it again. The Netherlands army were again widely accused of being the worst looters. For men who had just been through the last three days, losing their baggage, and in many cases most of what they possessed in the world, was nevertheless one of the low points. Ensign John Howard, in Thomas Morrris's 73rd, noted almost prosaically that he had been wounded at Quatre Bras, and that on the morning of 19 June only 72 men answered their names on parade. A bullet had passed through his cap which 'must have been within an eighth of an inch of my head', but 'the most melancholy part' of his tale was that 'our baggage which had been sent [to Brussels] for safety was plundered and destroyed, they say by Belgic troops, but so it was in our regiment. We had not a second shirt or blanket to cover us from wet weather. Think of a man being wet and dry in the same clothes for ten days; no halting days.'[15]

As distasteful to Mercer was when a carriage arrived beside his position, 'the inmates of which, alighting, proceeded to examine the field'. They were very smartly dressed, and a middle-aged man in a cocked hat approached Mercer with a low bow, holding 'a delicately white perfumed handkerchief to his nose'. He asked Mercer, his hands and face 'begrimed and blackened with blood and smoke', for an account of the battle to entertain his sightseers, but Mercer felt unwilling to oblige![16]

Many would agree that the ten days to come, the time it took them to reach the outskirts of Paris, were amongst the worst of the whole campaign. There was little time to give thanks for having survived the battle, and more would fall before the French capital finally surrendered, but it was the exhaustion, the lack of food in the first few days of marching, and having no kit that concerned them as much. Ensign Thomas Wedgwood of 3rd Foot Guards wrote to his mother that after the battle he had dutifully thanked God, who had been pleased to spare him, for which he hoped he 'was as thankful as I ought', but then complained that they were five days without anything other than what they stood up in. 'You have no idea what we underwent during that time, sleeping in the fields without even a hedge to cover us, generally raining the whole night and the ground ankle deep in mud. I was 48 hours without eating anything, even a bit of biscuit.'[17]

Lieutenant George Horton, marching with Thomas Howell and the 71st, felt much the same. He had lost all his kit, and had just one shirt, which he had been wearing for eight days. 'I am quite at a loss to know what to do, and I am in a most miserable state, obliged to let the clothes dry on my back, and lying out in the rain, as we have very wet weather almost every night. We never had such long marches, ten or twelve leagues without halting and I am obliged to walk all the way', he lamented to his mother, followed by a demand for money![18] There was little hope of getting any replacement kit without paying for it, and the loss of their baggage cost many of them dearly.

There were lighter moments. Mathew Clay would always remember the time when the 3rd Foot Guards marched into Nivelles. They camped by a stream and 'cleansed ourselves from our uncomfortable state, caused by excessive perspiration; marching through the clouds of dust bespattered with dirt, laying on the wet ground by night, biting off the ends of cartridges, and being for many hours warmly engaged amongst burning fragments of destruction in the Chateau of

Hougoumont. Now came the time for the distribution of rations, camp kettles all in requisition, and a general cooking along the hedge rows, the issue of rations liquor, and a buzz of congratulating interchanges, sitting or reclining on the ground, each listening to the narrative of his comrade.'[19]

By the time they marched on 19 June, the majority of the French army had gone. They had not wanted to wait to surrender to the Prussians, who routinely killed all prisoners. 'They treated the wretches they overtook with unparalleled barbarity. Except for a few imperturbable veterans, most of the soldiers had thrown away their weapons and now found themselves defenceless. They were nonetheless massacred without mercy', complained Fleury de Chaboulon, Napoleon's secretary, who was trying to get to Paris with the Imperial treasure and papers before Blücher's men got him too.[20] The British regiments were not above 'living off the land' a bit as well. Private John Lewis told his mother that 'wine was more plenty than water for all their cellars was full of wine, the same as Squire Tucker's is full of cider and that was the first place all the soldiers broke open'.[21] Wellington got the commissariat to come up behind them as soon as he could so that after the first five days they were finally being fed.

There does not seem to have been any great desire for revenge on the French but there were isolated incidents of bad behaviour. Playford, ever the moralist, was cutting forage one evening when they surprised a French soldier hiding in the corn. They took him to their bivouac and told him to sit down under a tree. One of their farriers saw him and said, 'That fellow shot at me yesterday and now I will have my revenge.' He drew his sword, and advanced on the prisoner muttering, 'I'll cut him to pieces.' Playford stepped in front of him. The farrier cursed him but threw down his sword. What surprised Playford is that several of his troop 'hinted their disappointment at my conduct; and yet these men had formerly been as kind and humane as the generality of mankind. But shedding blood had deadened their sensibilities, and it required time for them to regain their former principles and tenderness.'[22]

The Prussians however behaved considerably worse. In a hurry to get to Paris, they not only lived by taking what they wanted but also used their march as an opportunity to avenge Davout's appalling conduct in Berlin after Jena. George Farmer and the 11th Light Dragoons were deeply shocked when they passed a large château 'with village attached'. He and his men were sent, as a matter of course, to protect it but came too late. 'The Prussians had been here before us and the skill and industry with which they seemed to have carried on the work of devastation I have no language to describe.' Everything in the château had been wantonly smashed. The mill had been ransacked and all the flour sacks slit and the flour scattered over the road. All the stables, cowsheds, poultry houses and gardens were destroyed, and the doors, windows and roofs of every dwelling in the village smashed in so that it was uninhabitable.[23] Gronow, who witnessed similar destruction as the Coldstream Guards marched through a village, added that any of the locals who remonstrated were either severely beaten or more likely shot.[24] As the Prussians neared Paris a false rumour circulated that they had burned the porcelain factory at Sèvres. Blücher was reported as being set on putting all Paris to the torch and hanging Napoleon publicly in the ashes.

The retreating French were not above plundering their own people, particularly those near the border they considered

Belgian. Privates Murphy and Power, two of William Hay's dragoons, both 'Irish lads, sharp, active, brave soldiers to a fault, but both great scamps and up to any lark', were on a reconnaissance patrol when they saw four cuirassiers sneak into an already plundered farmhouse to take what the poor farmer had left. Picking up a stray German dragoon, whom they placed on sentry duty at the door, the Irish pair rushed the place. 'One Frenchman was in the act of stooping to drink, when at one cut' Murphy severed his neck. The other three immediately surrendered, and the grateful farmer came to thank Hay.[25]

The British Army marched first by Nivelles, then Valenciennes, to Cambrai with little fighting. On 23 June they stormed Cambrai, where eight men were killed and 29 wounded before the town capitulated. The same thing happened at Péronne, but the Governor there surrendered before any fighting took place. On 27 June Grouchy finally made his reappearance, engaging the Prussians at Compiègne but never pressing his attack. There was ragged fighting between his army and Blücher over the next three days whilst Napoleon tried to save his regime. He failed, leaving Paris on 29 June and heading for the west coast, where he seemed to have some idea of getting a ship to America. It was not until four days later that the provisional government that replaced him agreed terms, and on 6 July the Prussians entered Paris, with Blücher intent on extracting huge reparations and blowing up the Pont d'Jena, commissioned by Napoleon to celebrate their terrible defeat. At one point it was feared that the rumours might have been true and that Blücher might torch the whole city.

To begin with, Wellington's men stayed outside the capital, most of the regiments finally entering on 7 July. Ensign

William Leeke thought it was the proudest moment of his life, when he found himself 'riding down the centre of the avenue of the Champ Elysées, bearing in triumph into the enemy's capital that same 52nd regimental colour which I had the honour of carrying to victory on the eventful and glorious day of Waterloo'. Finally the Army could relax, at least a bit, and although they now had tiresome guard duties to perform, such as acting as sentry on the Pont d'Jena to stop Blücher blowing it up (it didn't stop him trying) they could now reflect at least a little on what they had achieved.

Edward Heeley, his father, their horses, the mule and Sir George Scovell's entourage, along with many others who had been left in Brussels, set out on Tuesday 20 June. They rode first to Waterloo, the road being above their horses' knees in mud. As they entered the village Edward's horse shied at a hand sticking up through the mud, 'the body being buried in it'. They found the place deserted and the houses 'full of dead men'. Continuing south they came onto the battlefield. 'Nothing but dead bodies presented themselves to our view, as far as the eye could reach. We noticed what a great number of dead men lay close to every dead horse, or broken carriage, the poor creatures had crawled there for shelter when first wounded.' They wanted to stop and pick up a souvenir but had been told by Scovell not to as they might find themselves drafted into service by the burial parties. Each of these consisted of five or six men and an NCO. The bodies were being gathered on carts, then thrown into 'great holes, like gravel holes'. Heeley found it odd how little effect it had on him. 'The faces of the dead were very much disfigured and ghastly, but the parties who were burying them seemed to be joking as if at any other ordinary employment', he wrote, and he was surprised to see groups of farriers going round removing the shoes off the horses so that nothing was wasted. A country boy, he was shocked by the devastation to the countryside and the crops, which he reckoned would have been enough to feed both the armies for a year, and 'all this misery', he reflected, 'brought about by the ambition of one man'. They laughed at being told by one of the burial parties that they had scooped up the body of a light dragoon who immediately sat up and reached for his sword, demanding to know if that was how they 'treated a fellow after fighting for three days and nights'. He had been sent to the rear on some detail and on his return had made free with all the spirits he could find in discarded canteens so that he had lain there drunk since Sunday night.

They continued by way of Nivelles and thence to Mons. Coming up with a column of infantry, the wretched mule, who was carrying their supplies, bolted and knocked down several soldiers with her load. They attacked her with the butt end of their muskets and Edward reckoned he was lucky to get her back alive. By 22 June they were in Le Cateau, where they saw Louis XVIII and his scruffy Royal Guard en route back to Paris from Ghent. Edward's father was, as he admitted, a 'desperate thief' and he took Edward, whom he called Ned, off to see what they could find. As they were helping themselves to forage, the mule bolted again, taking their horses with her, and Ned had to run all the way back to the town, chased by an irate French farmer. From Le Cateau they went to Péronne, passing some Prussian infantry on the road. It was intensely hot and some of the men fell out from the ranks to drink from puddles by the roadside, only to be beaten back by their NCOs with canes. Edward thought these 'coups de cannes' were a 'scandalous thing' and heard a Frenchman say that Napoleon 'always said it was the "coups

de cannes" that caused him to lose so many officers in action'.
On 6 July they entered Paris.[26]

Those who reached Paris were the lucky ones. Well over
10,000 Allied soldiers remained wounded on or around the
battlefield and many were still prisoners, never a good position
to be in but even more dangerous when your captors are
vengeful and unpredictable. The French units who were still
together enough to do so held on to those they could as they
fled; taking prisoners not only denied combat power to the
enemy but they were also a useful bargaining chip. Frederick
Lindau had slipped away from the barn in Rossomme with
Corporal Fastermann from his battalion, who had been taken
at the same time. It was about midnight by the time they got
away and they were not sure where they were, although there
was a bright moon. In fact they ended up walking the wrong
way, moving with the retreating French rather than back
towards their own lines. They walked on through the wood
where the German in the French army had given them water,
driven on by the cold. They could hear shouts of 'Vive
L'Empereur' and sporadic firing but it gradually died out.
They came to a dip in the wood but immediately heard 'Halt
la, qui vit?' and saw a French soldier fixing his bayonet.
Fastermann rushed him and managed to seize him by the
throat, pushing him up against a bank. Lindau tried to seize
his rifle but couldn't get it away from him. As Fastermann
held him, Lindau got the bayonet off the rifle and stabbed him
twice through the body. Fastermann took the rifle and Lindau
kept the bayonet and they moved on.

Shortly they came to a barn. The door was open and creeping up to it they heard French cursing coming from inside.
They saw a smaller barn near by and sneaked inside. They

thought they might be safe, but suddenly heard a 'rustling and banging and a high pitched cry' above their heads. Jumping up in alarm, they were greeted by a large cock, and realised that they were in a hen house. They moved on again just as it began to get light. They saw a peasant, who ran from them. Fastermann shouted at him to stop but he ran on so Fastermann 'threatened him with a shot'. He stood, and said that he was on his way to fetch the Prussians who were camped near by as the French troops were plundering his village and threatening to burn it. They stayed with him and came into the Prussian camp, where they found a squadron of lancers. Whilst they galloped off to deal with the French, one man was detailed to take them into the nearby village, which was Genappe.

There were Prussians everywhere, even 'looking in the dirt for valuables'. Napoleon's carriage had been plundered in the village overnight. It had been abandoned when the *chasseurs* had failed to clear a passage for the Emperor and he had been forced to flee on a horse. It was now sitting rather forlornly in the street. Lindau thought it very luxurious: 'lined with velvet, a sofa was in it and behind that was a kitchenette'. They were taken into a house and given bread and meat and a bucket so they could get some water. They lay down, and Lindau realised just how painful his wound had become. A Prussian doctor came and washed away the congealed blood and dressed it with an adhesive plaster. Later they were evacuated on a wagon and taken back towards Brussels, but finding the 2nd Battalion King's German Legion was not easy. They resorted to lying in the ditch beside the road until Baring came past but 'in what formation!' Lindau exclaimed in horror, 'there were perhaps only one hundred men'. Lindau wanted to stay with them but was ordered back to hospital in Brussels. The hospitals were all full so he was put in a private house, where he was well treated but bored until Lieutenant Graeme was brought in. Lindau's wound took a long time to heal and it was not until mid July that he was allowed to move on to join the battalion in Paris.[27]

Edmund Wheatley had not managed to slip away and, being an officer, was closely guarded. He was taken from the garden where he had been allowed to rest alongside some terribly wounded men. Two foot soldiers escorted him and forced him over the fields, away from the sound of artillery, which grew 'fainter and fainter'. A drunken cuirassier passed, shouting he would do for him, and advanced with his sword until he was stopped by an officer. A woman in a farmhouse they passed shouted at him, 'Ah, dog! You are the cause of this bloodshed.' 'One may fancy the respect paid to a trudging, skulking, unhappy Englishman', he wryly noted. A passing soldier tried to make him carry his rucksack, but Wheatley bravely threw it down in the mud and was lucky that the soldier scrabbled to retrieve it or he felt he would have 'paid dearly'.

It began to get dark, and Wheatley wondered how he could escape. He still didn't know the outcome of the battle, and it was not until they reached a main road that 'was choked up with hurry and disorder' that he realised that the French had been defeated. Escape was not going to be easy. One of his escorts told him to dip his cap in a barrel standing beside a house they passed. He did, and found it was brandy. Having eaten and drunk nothing he 'became stupid'. The road in front became more and more impassable, jammed up with the rabble of the French army. His two escorts stopped and took him into a small farmyard, where they rested on a dungheap. Here, 'free from observation', they demanded his epaulettes.

Still drunk, he 'foolishly refused' whereupon they threw him on the ground and ripped off not only his epaulettes but all the silver lace from his coat, and pulled off his boots and stockings, which one of them then put on.

Now barefoot, they prodded him with a bayonet and told him to walk on. 'Every stone I trod on lacerated the bottom of my feet and the torture was acute', he remembered. They 'suddenly came to a plain strewed with naked bodies. The multitude was so thronged I felt a temporary relief to my feet in treading on through soft jellied lumps of inanimate flesh.' They were the Prussian dead from Ligny. They stopped because it was dark, and poor Wheatley found himself in a bad state. His wound was pounding, his feet shredded, and the brandy was making him feel sick. He was also parched with thirst; as they threw themselves down in a field he saw a puddle beside the road. Desperately scooping it up in his hand he 'found it was horse's urine. So nauseous and disgusting was the taste it produced an instantaneous nausea with a violent reaching.' The only antidote he could think of was to suck the sweaty lining of his cap, which was still infused with brandy.

In the morning they reached Charleroi. A grenadier of the Imperial Guard approached him and asked him what was written in the pocketbook of a German officer he had killed. It was only the names of the dead officer's company, but the grenadier demanded that Wheatley write 'some recommendation of him that it might be of use if ever he fell into our hands'. He duly did so, scrawling, 'I Edmund Wheatley, Lieutenant in the German Legion, write this on a bundle of bricks in the middle of the retreating French army. Cold, wounded, barefooted, bareheaded, like a dog in a fair, every one buffets me ad libitum.' The grenadier tried to persuade

Wheatley to come with him but he refused, thinking he might now be able to get away. Suddenly he heard cheering and saw Napoleon dash by, a strong guard with drawn swords clearing the way for him.

Moved on, as they left Charleroi they came across a group of Belgian prisoners dragging a cannon through the mud and being beaten by their French escort with the flats of their swords. They seized Wheatley, but he refused to help, despite being repeatedly hit on his neck and back, so they tied his wrists together and then dragged him behind their horses as they trotted away. He endured it for so long, then collapsed. When he came to, he found himself lying surrounded by a large group of men, with an officer. They left him, and he was now unguarded but in a pretty desperate state. A cuirassier came past, and this one actually put him behind him on his horse for a couple of hours until he told him to get off, although he did hand him a two-franc piece.

Wheatley trudged on for hours, until he met a group of French cavalry in a wood. They amused themselves by riding over him. Wheatley shouted at them and one then tried to trample him. He summoned up the energy to run, chased by the cavalryman intent on cutting him down. Seeing one of his tormentors was drunk, Wheatley reasoned that he might be able to get him to help, which he did, drawing his sabre and waving it at the man who was riding at him. His saviour then allowed him to hold on to his stirrup and dragged him into Beaumont. He was seized as they came into the town and shut in a cellar where he found two fat Prussians, three British infantrymen, a 7th Hussar and a Scots Grey who had been shot through the hand. They were taken out as a group and made to march on, Wheatley pretending the Prussians were Hanoverian to stop them being murdered.

They stopped again, and Wheatley now refused to move. His escort seemed to lose interest and left him, and he made his way into a house. He was just entering when he saw it was full of quarrelling French soldiers. He managed to slip upstairs and then drew himself up into a chimney to hide. Sadly he didn't fit and, suffocated with soot and dust, he realised that not only had he had got himself stuck but his feet were hanging down over the fire. Three soldiers who were looting the house came in and yanked his feet down, but luckily they were so amused that they didn't kill him and he walked on with them.

Slipping away from them, Wheatley hid in a garden and slept until morning. It was now 20 June. He woke and crept down to a brook to drink, only to be fired at by a party of French infantry. Cowering in a hedge, two peasants told him to turn his coat round and run into a nearby wood, which he duly did, hiding there until Thursday 22 June, by which time he reasoned most of the French army would have gone. Binding up his feet as best he could, starving, cold, lost, his mind filled with images of Eliza, he made his way out onto the road and eventually back into Beaumont, which he now found full of Prussians. He eventually made it back to his battalion on 29 June.[28] At least he was alive; many others who had been taken prisoner were simply killed, and there was little quarter given between French and Prussian.

For many of the wounded there would be no such respite. By the evening of 18 June, there were over 10,000 Allied wounded either lying on the battlefield or in various stages of treatment between Waterloo and Antwerp, together with an unknown number of French, probably about 15,000–20,000. Once they were evacuated, and under medical care, the British wounded had a good chance of survival. Only 11.1

per cent of those who reached a hospital died.[29] Basic as we may consider the treatment today, it was, by contemporary standards, very good and far better than would have been available to the majority of soldiers had they been badly injured at home. As soon as news of the battle reached London, eminent surgeons flocked to Brussels to take over the care of not only the British but also the French. Men like Sir Charles Bell, consulting surgeon at the Middlesex, and George Guthrie, the youngest man ever to have been elected to the Royal College of Surgeons,[30] had arrived by 29 June; they and many others would work without pay, despite Guthrie's financial problems, until the wounded were stabilised.

The selfless reaction of the medical profession to the needs of the soldiers at Waterloo is in marked contrast to the lamentable lack of concern shown by the Church; eventually there was one surgeon for every 45 casualties.[31] However, what was less good was the immediate evacuation and care, which meant that many of the wounded had died or deteriorated to an inoperable state by the time they reached hospital. The overall organisation of the medical services was poor, despite the improvements that had been made during the Peninsular campaign, and it does not seem as if anyone such as McGrigor, who should have done so, really gripped it in the days of waiting. What was especially bad was that there was no pre-agreed method of evacuation. That is why so many died lying on the battlefield when they could have been saved if they had been found and recovered in time.

The presence of regimental surgeons, men like Haddy James, did however mean that, where a plan was operating, life-saving surgery could be carried out near the front line, and generally speaking the regimental surgical teams did a

very good job. Most regiments and battalions operated a
system whereby the regimental surgeon set up behind the
lines, and all wounded who could walk or ride and who were
'sent to the rear' went to them first. George Steed, for example, the respected surgeon of the Royals, established an aid
post near Mount St Jean and kept a record of all the wounded
who passed through it, as the wretched Bridges would later
discover.

Haddy James, having spent the night before the battle forward with 1st Life Guards in their lines, established his aid post
in Mont St Jean farmyard as did many other regimental surgeons' teams. He did not see much of the battle itself.
'Indeed,' he remarked, 'had I been at the front I should have
seen little enough, as by now the smoke lay thick and dark
over the field, restricting the visibility to a few yards.' But the
noise, even behind the lines at Mont St Jean, was still deafen-
ing. His work was 'grim in the extreme, and continued far
into the night. It was all too horrible to commit to paper', he
wrote, 'but this I will say, that the silent heroism of the greater
part of the sufferers was a thing I shall not forget. When one
considers the hasty surgery performed on such an occasion,
the awful sights the men are witness to, knowing that their
turn on that blood soaked operating table is next, seeing the
agony of an amputation, however swiftly performed, and the
longer torture of a probing, then one realises fully of what our
soldiers are made.'[32] He was rather surprised that the old
woman who owned the farm stayed in Mont St Jean all
through the battle, 'while cannon balls were breaking through
the wooden gates into the farm yard and striking against the
walls of the house'. Captain John Whale, who had lost two
horses shot under him and was having his wounds dressed,
asked her what she was up to, and was told that all she had in

the world were the 'poultry, cows, calves and pigs and that if she did not stay to take care of them they would all be destroyed or carried off', which was undeniably true.[33]

The need to move early on 19 June to pursue the French was the reason that many battalions could not organise a comprehensive search for their wounded and James, as with most of the regimental surgical teams, had to move with his regiment. This meant he had little choice but to patch up the men as best he could and then evacuate them back to Brussels. It was that journey, on unsprung carts and wagons, that many found the hardest part. 'One's mind shrinks at imagining the sufferings they must have endured on that jolting ride, or that weary tramp, and then only to face in so many cases the pain and disgust of a spreading gangrene', James wrote. Actually his survival rates were remarkably good, with only 11 out of the 45 injured in 1st Life Guards dying; for the 2nd Life Guards their surgeon Samuel Broughton did even better, only losing 4 out of 63 wounded, but then of course those figures only relate to those who were brought back, many others bleeding to death, dying of exposure or being sliced up by the local Belgians on the battlefield.

Those who got back to Brussels found it in chaos. Edward Costello of the 95th, who was wounded early in the day at Quatre Bras when his finger was torn off by a musket ball, found the city so crowded with Netherlands officers and men that no one could see him. The square was covered with straw and hundreds of wounded. No sooner had he arrived than an alarm was given that the French were coming and a general panic ensued. They were indeed coming, '1700 or 1800 French prisoners, under escort of some of our dragoons'. Costello slept on the straw in the open. In the morning the scene 'surpassed all imagination and baffles description; carts, wagons, and every other attainable vehicle, were continually arriving heaped with sufferers. The wounded were laid, friends and foes indiscriminately, on straw, with avenues between them, in every part of the city, and nearly destitute of surgical attendance.'[34] He did though have kind words for 'fair ladies of Brussels' who moved amongst them, strapping and bandaging wounds, serving tea, coffee and soups, and stripping off the gory bloody uniforms to replace them with clean shirts. He was equally amused to see a Highlander distinctly uncomfortable to find a particularly attractive young lady moving his bloodstained kilt from 'a severe wound in the thick part of the thigh'.[35]

Costello stayed in Brussels for three days, and had ample opportunity for 'witnessing the cutting off of legs and arms'. He thought the French were distinctly wet about undergoing such operations when compared to the stoical British. He recorded a private of the Royals, whom George Steed had sent back, having his arm amputated under the elbow, quietly holding 'the injured limb with his other hand without betraying the slightest emotion, save occasionally helping out his pain by spirting forth the proceeds of a large plug of tobacco, which he chewed most unmercifully while under the operation'. Near by, a French soldier was bellowing his heart out as a surgeon probed for a ball in his shoulder. This seemed to annoy the Royal Dragoon, as, once his arm was off, he 'struck the Frenchman a smart blow across the breech with the severed limb, holding it at the hand-wrist, saying, "Here take that, and stuff it down your throat, and stop your damn bellowing."' Costello was more sympathetic to a 19-year-old German gunner who had lost both his legs to a cannonball. Whilst lying on the ground a cuirassier had slashed one of his arms whilst a musket ball had hit the other. Both had now to be amputated so he 'lay a branchless trunk'. Costello was treated, recovered quickly, and was put to work helping the Provost staff, who were rounding up plundering Netherlands troops. They brought in 16 of them one morning and Costello, irritated at their behaviour both on and off the battlefield, enjoyed seeing them flogged.

The annoyingly hearty George Simmons, who had been treated initially in the farmyard at Mont St Jean, also made it back. He was seriously injured and would not be able to rejoin his battalion until the following January. He found his treatment actually worse than being wounded. His liver had become horribly enlarged, and the only remedy was bleeding. He endured this for seven days, but when his surgeon took two large basins of blood from his arm, he fainted and they thought they should try something else. The surgeon reverted to applying leeches, and Simmons suffered from having 25 on him at a time, which bit him raw. The surgeon then insisted on putting fresh leeches on his raw side, and despite him kicking, roaring and swearing, his arms were held whilst they were applied. 'Such torture', he recalled, 'I never experienced.' Like many, Simmons was nursed by a combination of men from his battalion and the local family on whom he had previously been billeted, who, as in so many cases, treated him as one of their own. He was well enough to travel back to England in October, 'his riddled body held together by a pair of stays'.[36]

By the end of the week there were six hospitals operating in Brussels, treating 2,500 British soldiers, and a seventh, in the gendarmerie, treating the French. A further 2,500 wounded were being treated in Antwerp, and men like Bell made a point of ensuring that the French were equally well cared for. Many were still being brought in days after the battle, 'many dying, many in agony, many miserable racked with pain and spasms'.[37] He found that he had to work flat out. Whilst he amputated one man's thigh, 'there lay at one time thirteen, all beseeching to be taken next. It was a strange thing to feel my clothes stiff with blood, and my arms powerless with the exertion of using the knife.' Later going round the wards he noted there was 'a resentful, sullen rigidness of face, a fierceness in their dark eyes as they lay half covered in the sheets', young men contemplating what Napoleon's last spurt of ambition had done to their now-wrecked bodies.

The majority of wounds were caused by artillery fire, from both round and case-shot, and by musket balls. Most of the artillery wounds on both sides were 'in the lower extremities'. In the 33rd Foot there were 'perhaps 15 or 16 legs taken off for one arm'. There were not many bayonet wounds, but a lot from sabres and lances, the latter being deep and particularly harmful if not fatal.[38] The lack of bayonet wounds in the French was because the British infantry did not trust their flimsy bayonets not to bend, and, once inserted, they could get stuck and leave the soldier vulnerable as he struggled to extract it; in hand-to-hand fighting most had preferred to use their musket as a club.

Of those who suffered leg amputations, generally those below the knee were successful, whilst those above, around the thigh, were less successful (as they still are) and caused complications, particularly if near the groin.[39] Charles Radclyffe of the Royals had been hit by a musket ball in his knee quite early on. He duly went back via George Steed, who was all for immediate amputation above the knee. He had Mr Gunning, Wellington's surgeon with him, and poor Radclyffe was really in no position to argue his case. The 'instruments were out and in a few minutes the limb would have been off' but a renewed French attack resulted in an order for Steed to pull further back. Radclyffe's operation was forgotten about. He made a fairly full recovery, and regained partial use of the leg, although the ball was never actually extracted. Uxbridge, whose leg had been smashed by a case-shot at the very end of the day, had it taken off well above the knee by John Hume, using a knife that he borrowed from an artillery surgeon and which had already been used in a good many amputations that day. Cutting round the flesh and muscle, he exposed the bone which he quickly sawed through. The only comment Uxbridge made was to say 'Damn the saw' and he made a full recovery.

Those left lying on the battlefield fared worst of all. What happened to James Carruthers of the Scots Greys was typical. His horse had been shot in the Union Brigade charge, and although unwounded, he had been trapped underneath it. Left that evening, a French soldier had robbed him, then stuck a lance into his side. He was still alive when Sergeant Archibald Johnston and a party from the regiment found him, but he died as they were recovering him.

Poor Magdalene De Lancey had an especially difficult week. So very much in love with her husband, and so taken with the exotic world which she had so recently entered, the reality of war had come even harder to her than it did to most. Evacuated to Antwerp, she received a message on Monday morning that William was safe. Her host, Lady Hamilton, had seen the casualty list of senior officers and his name had not been on it. Magdalene was in such a 'fever of happiness' that she had to walk up and down for two hours. Later that morning she was called down to see Lady Hamilton, who confessed that she had written the list she had shown Magdalene and had left William's name out; she had not wanted her to be shocked so suddenly. She now assured Magdalene that William was alive but seriously wounded; he had in fact been listed in Wellington's despatch as 'severely wounded'. Magdalene now wanted to rush to find him, but rushing anywhere from Antwerp along roads thronged with refugees and wounded was not easy. She set off at one p.m. in a coach that had to battle its way through the surly crowds. Two men hijacked a ride on the back and they dared not ask them to get off. At Malines they met a Captain Hay, who told Magdalene the sad news that it was too late and William had died. She sank back in the carriage seat and returned to Antwerp unable to collect her thoughts at all.

That night she collapsed in her room and refused to see anyone, wandering 'around the room incessantly beseeching for mercy'. It took violent knocking for anyone to get in but the next day her maid managed to tell her that General Mackenzie was downstairs and had good news. Now not sure who or what to believe, poor Magdalene came down to be told that William was alive and would recover. She now became panicked about getting to him and 'lost all self command'. With Mackenzie's help she set off for Brussels at eight p.m. on the Tuesday. The road was less busy but they got stuck behind a Prussian wagon moving agonisingly slowly and which refused to let them pass. They came into Brussels where the 'smell of gunpowder was very perceptible' and the 'heat was oppressive'. They met George Scovell, Edward Heeley's boss, who told them De Lancey was at Waterloo. Nine miles and three and a half hours later she finally found him, lying very badly wounded in a house in the village. He greeted her with the words 'Come, Magdalene, this is a sad business, is it not?' which, in the circumstances, shows remarkable sang-froid.

De Lancey had been riding beside Wellington when he had been hit by a cannonball. It had struck him behind his right shoulder and thrown him off his horse. Wellington had thought he was dead, saying goodbye to him and leaving him on the field. A cousin of his had seen what had happened and realised that he was only badly wounded and had him removed in a blanket, probably to Mont St Jean, from where he had been recovered to Waterloo. His wound was very serious but the doctors told Magdalene that there was a good chance of his recovering and she spent the next week by his side, appalled at the bleeding by the surgeons, especially when they used leeches, and seeing him gradually deteriorate as the pain in his chest grew intolerable. She was at least with him when he died, writing afterwards that 'the violence of grief is more like delirium than the sorrow of a Christian'. She buried him in the Reformed Church on the Louvain road out of Brussels, 'a sweet, quiet, retired spot'. She visited his grave on 4 July and then set out for England, back to the quiet life she had left. 'That day', she noted sadly, 'three months before, I was married.'[40]

Magdalene De Lancey was not alone in getting false information, and the business of notifying families was haphazard. There was no proper notification system in place, which, combined with there being no comprehensive list of killed and wounded, meant that there was a painful degree of delay and confusion. Wellington's despatch, which was published in full in *The Times* on Thursday 22 June, listed all the officers he thought had been killed and wounded, but it was far from complete and, having been made in a hurry so soon after the battle, was inevitably inaccurate. It also, as was the convention, made no mention of the more junior officers nor of any non-commissioned officers or private soldiers. Their families were left to discover what had happened largely by word of mouth or from letters from friends in their regiment.

John Bingley's parents received the sad news that Private Bingley of H Troop of the Blues had been killed, from seeing a list in the *Field*. He was the second son they had lost, and they spent a wretched few weeks wondering not only what had happened to him but what would become of the family farm at Littlethorpe. Then in late July they suddenly received news that John was alive and recovering from his wounds near Brussels. He was well enough to write to them on 13 August, explaining that he had been so severely wounded that on the evening of the battle he did not think he would survive. His left arm and right knee remained very weak but otherwise the letter came with 'his sincere love to you and all my friends hoping that you are in good health as I am at this time and I thank God for it'. He became even more religious now, ending up by thanking 'God in His great and boundless mercy' and hoping that he would soon be home and able to 'give you comfort in your old age before you depart this mortal life'.[41]

At least their news arrived the right way round. Major Isaac Clarke had taken over command of the Scots Greys after Colonel Hamilton was killed. On 19 June he wrote to Lieutenant James Carruthers's father, explaining about his son's injuries but concluding that his wound was not dangerous and that he should speedily recover. Five days later his poor father received a letter from John Sadler, James's great friend, telling how he had been killed outright by a cannonball and buried. Two weeks after that Edward Payne, another friend, wrote to give the true version, that James had been wounded, then robbed and stuck with a lance as he lay unable to move. He had subsequently died.

There was meant to be a ban on letters home that was not lifted until 6 July, although this was more practical than anything else as the post could not keep up with the Army marching on Paris. It did not, however, stop people writing from Brussels and some incoming post had arrived during the three days of fighting. Private Joseph Lord of 2nd Life Guards had the difficult job of passing on the news that his brother had been killed. He wrote sadly to his own wife on 3 July from outside Brussels, where he was recovering from a slight hand wound and looking after injured horses, that 'I must inform you and my mother and sister in law that I have lost the best of brothers, and they have lost in him an affectionate son and tender and loving husband'. He promised to return home and to spend the remainder of his days looking after them all. Courtney Ilbert seems to have ignored all bans and continued to write to his dearest Anne every day. He never did get up to the battlefield, but remained organising the resupply of the artillery until 27 June when he left to join the Army in France.

Another man who wrote regularly from Brussels in the week after the battle was Edward Kelly. He had fought as bravely at Waterloo as he had at Genappe, having three horses shot under him, including his favourite bay mare, who had carried him to safety from the lancers, and whose rather mouldy tail is still in the Household Cavalry Museum. At about seven p.m. on 18 June he had been wounded in the leg, but not seriously, by a cannon shot. 'Our friend Kelly was particularly distinguished', wrote Lord Greenock, who was an assistant quartermaster general, 'and was not a little proud of his own performance.'[42] Kelly wrote to Maria and the girls in Marlow almost daily from his hospital bed, describing his own role in the battle in some detail. 'The officers and men of my Regiment are all pleased to bestow kind praises upon me and I consider myself fortunate in having been the first man in with the enemy in every attack we made', he told them, and Uxbridge had said, 'I have marked your conduct and shall mention you particularly to the Duke of Wellington.' Kelly also wrote to his brother-in-law, speculating as to what his reward might be. He thought a peerage possible, and certainly a brevet promotion, there being no way he could afford to purchase a majority. Maria still didn't answer, not even demanding money, and poor Kelly's letters became more and more aggrieved as he was disappointed by every incoming post.[43]

On 25 June, Standish O'Grady received a letter from Kitty as he was sitting on his horse awaiting the possible attack on Cambrai. 'She never expected to find her letter in such an honourable situation', he joked to his mother, who was still pressing him to accept her. Otherwise he was more concerned with complaining about the Belgians plundering their baggage, leaving him, like many, with only the clothes he was wearing. He had, though, seen a list of killed and wounded. 'There never was such a bill of fare presented to John Bull before; I wonder how he likes it. I never was so glad to find my name unimmortalised.'[44] Sergeant Billy Tennant wrote directly to his Anne the morning after the battle, sitting on the ridge where his 1st Foot Guards had spent the night. 'This was the hardest battle that ever was fought', he concluded, 'but it was a glorious victory. We have give them a complete drubbing and I think about another month the war will be over and then my love I shall embrace you in my arms once more.'[45] Three days later he received a crossing letter from Anne telling him that he now had a son.

*

Once they were settled in Paris, the British Army found the first few weeks of occupation to be rather agreeable. They enjoyed being in the famous city, seeing the sights, and there was something exciting in being the victors in the enemy's capital. There was also much occasion, with the arrival of the Tsar and the Austrian emperor, parades and the chance of female company. They were amused at how quickly the tricolour cockades, which 'were universally worn in Paris at 11 o'clock', on 6 July, disappeared and 'at 3 the white [of the Bourbons] had universally replaced it, what an extraordinary weather cock nation',[46] Arthur Kennedy wrote to his mother. Edward Heeley enjoyed it all immensely. 'The Austrian army had a very grand appearance nearly all dressed in white, some of the cavalry were splendid regiments, particularly the Hungarian Hussars. Prince Schwartgenberg was their commander in chief. He was billeted in the same house as Sir George, he was a fine looking man, but very fat. Old Blucher got much cheered at the head of the Prussians, though the French mortally hated him and his army but the French were regular gluttons at this moment giving vent to their loyal feelings.' He thought they liked cheering the Tsar with 'Vive L'Empereur!' as they really meant Napoleon.[47]

The British contingents in these parades looked rather less impressive. They 'appeared in the same clothes in which they had marched, slept and fought for months. The colour had faded to a dusky brick-dust hue; their coats, originally not very smartly made, had acquired by constant wearing that loose, easy set so characteristic of old clothes, comfortable to the wearer, but not calculated to grace his appearance. *Par surcroit de laideur*, their cap is perhaps the meanest, ugliest thing ever invented. For all these causes it arose that our infantry appeared to the utmost disadvantage – dirty, shabby, mean and very small.'[48] They lived, however, in some comfort, and although many were in tents in the nearby suburbs, the weather was fine and there was enough to eat. Napoleon and the French army had gone, and everywhere they seemed to be welcome as liberators, which many found as ironic as young Heeley; but they were not complaining.

Those that had not yet written home, now did so. Some wrote very much in the stiff-upper-lip style like William Pritchard, who had been at Hougoumont with Mathew Clay, and wrote affectionately 'Dear Wife, I take this opportunity of addressing you these few lines'. He went on to say that during the battle he 'thought of nothing but fighting and gaining victory and it pleased the Almighty to grant my request and keep me from being injured, thanks to Him for His preservation' and signed off with a loving poem:

> Dear girl the drum it beats to arms
> And we must make for wars alarms
> Pray for my safety while I go
> To meet my country's haughty foe

Others thought that having survived such a battle would improve their chances with the girls they fancied. Captain Philip Wodehouse tried it on with Miss Parry, writing 'Though I cannot persuade myself that the cuish that you once so kindly expressed is still as lively as then, yet not to use you as you appear to use me, I write to say that I suffered no harm from the Affair. I only send these few lines written according to your desire in hurry and confusion to assure you that in spite of your forgetfulness, my affection for you is as strong as ever.'[49] Private John Abbott of the 51st wrote to Anne Bank that 'there's a young man in our company declare that if you remain single until we return as he is a Yorkshireman he will come down with us on furlough and according to our recommendation he will make you his bride', adding 'that is if you are agreeable'.[50]

The normal pattern of army life was re-established remarkably soon. Wellington sent out a short 'General Order' on 20 June, taking 'this opportunity of returning to the Army his thanks for their conduct in the glorious action on the 18th instant and he will not fail to report this sense of their conduct, in the terms which it deserves, to their several Sovereigns'.[51] The same day he confirmed a sentence of 1,000 lashes on Private William Montgomery of the 52nd for having deserted in Spain in 1813, despite what he had just gone through.

There were, inevitably, long discussions as to what had happened at Waterloo. There was much praise, and mutual congratulation, but there were also recriminations. The Secretary and the Club were incensed by the behaviour of Charles Bridges, who had taken himself to the rear before the great charge but who did not appear to have been wounded and did not pass through the regimental aid post, where Surgeon George Steed had kept a careful list. Ben the Ruler convened a meeting of the officers and Bridges was sent for to explain his conduct. His defence did not find much favour. First he maintained that his saddle had slipped, then that his horse had bolted and that he had found himself in the Prussian camp, which was highly unlikely given that their leading troops had still been several miles away at midday. The officers were unsympathetic. He was given two choices. He could either immediately send in his resignation or he could choose to be tried by a court martial. Unsurprisingly he chose to resign, and infuriated the regiment by 'carrying the whole thing off with a very high hand; forsooth he was sick of the old Royals; he should now go into the Hussars, a life more suitable to his inclinations; he returned to England, strutted about town as if he was the most meritorious officer' and 'said that he had resigned as he was denied the medals he had most certainly deserved'. Trafford was furious that 'in the neighbourhood of his father's seat in Hampshire he is considered a most gallant, meritorious, ill-used young officer'.[52]

A second tribunal of officers was altogether less satisfactory. Ben the Ruler had never liked poor Heathcote, and he now summoned him to explain why he had 'gone to the rear' as well, something which no one else seemed to have noticed. Heathcote gave the perfectly decent explanation that he had taken part in the charge, his mare had been shot under him, giving him the most severe fall. He had got on a troop horse 'which was unable to move' and had gone back to find his famous brown horse, which he had bought off Windsor, and which he had asked to be held in the rear as a spare but that the dragoon looking after it had panicked and let it go. Heathcote had then been carried along in the stream of fugitives. It was clear that the Secretary and the Club believed him and were sympathetic, but Ben the Ruler was determined to get rid of him and vindictively gave him the same options as Bridges. Poor Heathcote! He had fought bravely throughout the Peninsular campaign, and although he may have not been quite the sporting type the Ruler liked, he was a decent and respected young officer. Naturally he also resigned, but left very bitter, and the Club did not forgive the Ruler lightly. Trafford was indignant. 'For years', he fumed, 'had the regiment tolerated Mr Jones who was not only a coward and a villain but a thief, yes, a thief. For years was Mr Benjamin Cook, who was everything that was bad; for years was Paddy

Knipe supported, who ran away at Fuentes D'Onor and at Guinaldo. Bagwell, ousted coward, left the regiment in a manner most disgraceful after having a few days previously deserted his post at a certain bridge in the retreat from Madrid. Yet all these gentry remained as long as they pleased, and nothing was said.'[53] The row was nothing to that which would soon engulf the Royals.

Private Bertram, the man who had said he was ill and refused to go on as William Lawrence tried to push him back into place, eventually turned up after six months. He was given 300 lashes. It was a harsh punishment, Lawrence agreed, but 'if there had been many like Bertram, the battle of Waterloo would have ended in favour of the French'. He was sent to hospital to recover and on his return it was found that most of his equipment was missing, so he was sentenced to another 300 lashes. The drummers did not spare him as 'there is no one they felt more strongly about than a coward'. He spent another three weeks in hospital and was put under 'stoppages of pay' to make good the cost of his lost equipment. This left him short of funds, so he took himself into Paris and sold his new kit, for which he was given a third set of 300 lashes. Later, once the regiment had been sent to Scotland, he transgressed a fourth time, was flogged once more and then turned out of the regiment. 'The Colonel ordered his coat to be turned, and a large sheet of paper pinned on it with the words 'This is a coward, and a very bad soldier, and one who has been whipped four times' and he was sent on his way.[54] He was not much missed.

The physical and mental intensity of battle, particularly one as violent and destructive as Waterloo, and the thrill of surviving it, creates in the soldier's mind an expectation that what follows will be proportionately as rewarding. A small part of this is physical, the thought of beer and food and home and hearth that has sustained men in combat for generations, but much more of it is in the heart and the head, a desire for some sort of fulfilment to compensate for the often extreme emotions they have suffered. This is difficult to quantify and consequently often impossible to find. It is one of the reasons that ex-servicemen can find it difficult to settle into civilian life. The sentiments expressed by Bingley and Tennant, of coming home to a hero's welcome and then living well provided for lives in domestic bliss are as common in this century as they were in 1815. Sadly the reality was as different then as it is now, and although the nation was to be more grateful to the men who fought at Waterloo than it habitually was, individuals' circumstances were actually no different on 19 June to what they had been three days earlier.

Once the excitement of occupying Paris had subsided, the reality for most was that they faced a long stay in less glamorous towns throughout France as part of the Allied army of occupation. Even the Household Cavalry and Foot Guards, traditionally the first to be returned home so they could resume their duties in London, were to remain until 1816. In June 1816, a year after the battle, Billy Tennant, now with 1st Foot Guards in Cambrai, had still not seen his beloved Anne or their new son, and he was getting desperate. The rules over soldiers being accompanied had been relaxed, and he was now urging her to join him but the French were being difficult about issuing passports. He told her to get to London, dress up in her best clothes, and present herself at the French embassy, being 'sure not to tell [them] that you are a soldier's wife'. By August she still had not arrived, it was as wet a summer as 1815 had been, and Tennant was getting depressed.

Actually Anne had been ill, as had their little boy, but they recovered and she finally reached France, which was fortunate as Billy's battalion was to stay until 1818.[55]

There was a certain amount of sympathy for the French people. In November 1815, William Wheeler and the 51st found themselves in Verriers, where he was billeted with an old couple who were 'far advanced in years, have seen better days, seventy winters have passed over their heads and now their life is one continued round of toil and sorrow'. They had lost six sons to Napoleon's ambition – one in Italy, one in Spain, three in Russia and one at Waterloo. Their only daughter had been 'victim to a pretended lover and shortly after died of a broken heart'. They had just had the Russians billeted on them, who had commandeered their bed. They thought Wheeler would do the same but, as he said, 'I then told the old man that we were British soldiers' and the old couple slept in their bed once more whilst Wheeler and his section slept on straw.[56]

The Royals quite enjoyed life in Rouen, where the Union Brigade was despatched in late July, and they had a pleasant four-day march through the Normandy countryside to get there.[57] The regiment was quartered in an old cavalry barracks, whilst the officers were billeted in the town. There was female company, 'little black eyed Norman damsels', and rather too much gambling. Ben the Ruler 'behaved tolerably well' but lodged near the barracks, which gave him 'the opportunity of frequently being troublesome'. He decided he would inspect all the officers' horses and saddlery, much to their annoyance as many had lost all their spare sets with their baggage. Every officer had to pass their horses in front of him, to be greeted by 'I am well aware that you cannot be expected to be all of you mounted as I am; it is not every officer who can ride such horses as I do; such a thing as that I do not expect, but then you may ride better horses than you do. Mr Saunders thought proper the other day to buy a long tailed French horse; he never asked my leave, I'll not pass it, no I won't.' His rage increased when he found the Secretary imitating him by conducting a mock kit inspection, riding a mule and with a fool's cap on his head. This resulted in extra riding-school drills for the officers. Sergeant Major Smyth, the senior 'rough rider', was asked how everyone was riding. He said they were all riding too long except for Ben the Ruler, whose stirrup length was of course perfect. All the officers were made to take their stirrups up two holes and to do two hours mounted drill. Luckily the Ruler's father died in August and he went home on leave. Phil Dorville assumed temporary command, which was much more civilised, but, as the Allied zones of occupation were reassigned, they moved to Montvillers near Harfleur, which they found 'provokingly quiet'.

With autumn in Normandy approaching, a sadder note comes into the Secretary's writing. The mess at Montvillers is rather soulless. There 'was no Heathcote to argue that black was white, nor Barwell to act a boisterous joke'. Even Phil Dorville 'was generally low spirited and no longer sang "Sweet Kitty". Upon the whole all was very flat.' Relations between the Royals and the Scots Greys were very good and they saw a lot of each other, but they both found the Inniskillings, the third regiment in the Union Brigade and the only one not to take an Eagle at Waterloo, unfriendly. This 'Eagle jealousy' came to a head when the Secretary saw an article which appeared in the *Globe* on 23 August and which read 'The gallant Eniskilleners, a regiment entirely Irish, had proved themselves at the memorable battle of Waterloo, not merely the most undaunted but efficient regiment on the entire field'. The article went on to say that Napoleon himself had acknowledged that he made his most determined effort against the Inniskillings and that if the Russians had fought as they had then history would have been very different. There was no mention of the Royals or Greys at all. Apart from 'little Watson', whom they liked, the Club, the younger officers of the Royals, refused to speak to the Inniskillings from then on.

Standish O'Grady seemed to manage to spend most of his time in Paris, which he much enjoyed, and he became even braver in teasing his mother. She was enquiring why he had not been back to see Kitty. O'Grady explained that 'orders here are uncommonly severe with respect to going to England and no officer is allowed to do so except he is ordered by a Medical Board, which considering the plumpness of my present condition I have no chance of prevailing on'. Anyway, he continued, 'this frivolous country completely dissipates all inclination to Ennui and has had the wonderful effect of driving all manner of serious thought out of my head; even that malady called love, on which you are so amusingly pathetic. I however regret', he continued, rather naughtily, 'not being in London that I might have the satisfaction of introducing you to the little show girl that frequents watering places that you might be convinced that there does not exist as much deception in the set as you give credit for.'[58] Courtney Ilbert, who took love rather more seriously, kept writing to Anne every few days, his letters becoming increasingly affectionate. He wrote from La Chapelle on 18 July, signing off 'God bless you all my darlings with kindest love . . . and blessings to my dear boys, believe me ever affectionately your own husband'. It is the last surviving letter he wrote. He died early the next year at Valenciennes, never having seen his beloved Anne or the children again.[59]

Napoleon had reached the west coast of France on 3 July. On 13 July he wrote to the Prince Regent, possibly overestimating both the Regent's capacity for forgiveness and his knowledge of the classics, saying that he came, 'like Themistocles to throw myself on the hospitality of the British people'. On 15 July he was instead transferred onto HMS *Bellerophon*, a British warship, which anchored off Torbay. He came on board from a French brig, wearing the green uniform of the *chasseurs à cheval*, and cheered by the French sailors, but not greeted with any honours by the Royal Navy. Word soon spread that he was off Torbay, and even now he exercised his extraordinary fascination. Lady Charlotte Fitzgerald was furious that the traditional chants of 'Monster', 'Rascal' and 'Roast him alive' were replaced by 'Poor fellow, I do pity him', and 'his appearance seems to have effaced the recollections of British blood he has spilt'.[60] He was transferred to HMS *Northumberland*, which set sail for St Helena, where he landed on 16 October. This time he was guarded not by his own Imperial Guard but by British soldiers. The commanding officer of one of the battalions allotted this task was Samuel South of the 20th Foot. He had started his military career as a private soldier, become a sergeant-major and was subsequently commissioned and made a lieutenant-colonel in 1818. It is a nice irony that the defeated emperor of Revolutionary France should have been guarded by a man who had benefited so directly from a system which was supposedly only favourable to privilege.

Napoleon died on St Helena in 1821. The Allies concluded a peace treaty with France on 20 November 1815.

France lost much of her eastern territory, as she traditionally does when she has lost a war with Germany, and agreed to pay an indemnity of £28m, or about £2 billion today. The army of occupation, 150,000 Allied soldiers, was to remain in France for five years at French expense. Slowly, as the occupation zones were sorted out, some British regiments started to go home, but by the time they got there the excitement at their victory was fading. As Thomas Morris and the 73rd approached their new barracks in Colchester they thought they had better make something of a show and stopped to pick some laurel from a gentleman's park so that they could decorate their caps. The gentleman was not amused, and 'not only gave a peremptory refusal but also applied to us the term "vagabonds"',[61] wrote the offended Morris, although the townspeople were more welcoming and came out in their hundreds to cheer as they marched in, their tattered Colours bearing the new honour of Waterloo in gold.

They fared rather better than the poor 42nd, whose only welcome as they entered Edinburgh were the words 'Welcome, gallant heroes' written on a pocket handkerchief and hung from an axe handle.[62] However, the inhabitants did make it up to them, Anton recording that they paraded into Edinburgh Castle, were given two nights' free admission to the theatre, two to the circus and two days to the newly constructed panorama of Waterloo, which must have been an interesting experience for them. There was then a civic reception in the Assembly Rooms, where 'the drink was of the best, and fame tells a lie if the beer was not mixed with strong-ale or spirits' and they all enjoyed it so much that they staggered out, 'bonnets falling in all directions'. Quite a few fell over, causing 'the loose folds of the kilt' to lap upwards, and 'leaving their thighs uncurtained to the view of the numerous spectators'. Luckily, Anton noted, 'Some ladies endeavoured to withdraw from this indelicate situation' but not very hard so that they 'rendered themselves more prominent by their ineffectual struggles to retire'.[63]

It is perhaps not surprising that some homecomings were rather muted, it being in most cases over a year since the bells had rung out in celebration. However, although the excitement may not have been quite so fresh, the deeper significance of what they had achieved was becoming apparent and there was, within contemporary parameters, a genuine attempt to recognise their extraordinary achievement. Everyone who fought in the battle was awarded two years' seniority for pay and pension, which was known as the Prince Regent's bounty and meant that someone like William Ingilby of the artillery could write that 'it brings me within the list for a shilling a day for five years service'.[64] It also meant that men could retire two years earlier with their full pension. They were also to have their names marked out in red on the regimental rolls, a slightly less obvious honour which many thought was a device so that the clerks could ensure others did not claim their extra privileges.

The Prince Regent gave a personal lead to this mood of national recognition. Very soon after the battle he had started to focus on its legacy, and what may unkindly be called its propaganda value, as well as on the minutiae of the victory. One of his first orders to the War Office after the battle was that they should collect all the Napoleonic paraphernalia from the battlefield and from soldiers who had acquired it. Whilst Wellington was closing on Paris, and negotiating the delicate matter of the French surrender, his staff were rather surprised to receive a letter from Torrens in the War Office telling them that 'The Prince Regent wants all French cuirasses left on the ground – or that may have been taken possession of by the troops in the late battle may be collected and sent over here'.[65] He claimed all trophies for the Crown, which is still the cause of some sharp debates between individual regiments and various government bodies to this day.[66]

Eighteen sixteen saw a plethora of celebratory dinners. On the first anniversary the Duke of York came to Windsor, where both the Blues and one of the battalions of 1st Foot Guards, of which he was Colonel, were stationed; the other 1st Foot Guards battalion with lonely Billy Tennant was still in Cambrai. The Duke presided over three days of celebrations, during which the 1st Foot Guards were renamed the Grenadier Guards in honour of their defeat of the Old Guard in those final bloody stages of the battle, and on the last day of which he gave a dinner for both regiments at tables laid out on the Long Walk in Windsor Park. The pleasure of his hospitality was slightly diminished by the men having to wear their full dress uniform in the summer heat, and by having to listen to a very lengthy sermon by Mr Roper, the garrison chaplain, before the roast beef was served, but they were no doubt appreciative of His Royal Highness's good intentions.

On the second anniversary the 2nd Life Guards formed a special escort for the formal opening of the new Waterloo Bridge, formed entirely by men who had fought. The event was commemorated in a special dinner service presented to Wellington by a grateful King of Prussia. When new Standards and Guidons were presented to the Life Guards and the Blues they only carried the battle honours 'Waterloo' and 'Peninsula' above and below the Royal Arms, almost as if all their previous battles now counted for nothing. The Blues were formally made part of the Household Cavalry, and the Prince Regent paid them the particular honour of making himself their Colonel-in-Chief, a position previously held by Wellington, who had been conspicuously bad at visiting the regiment.[67]

In Brighton, where the 10th Hussars and 51st Foot were both stationed, they had a massive celebration on 18 June 1816. It started with a parade and a 'feu de joi', after which the battalion formed square and were mock charged by the cavalry to show the thousands of onlookers and holidaymakers what it was like. A gentleman standing near by told Wheeler it was 'one of the most sublime sights he ever saw'. Afterwards tables were placed in the barrack yard, festooned with laurels and flowers and groaning 'under the weight of roast beef and plumb pudding'. A barrel of beer was placed at the end of each table, which was consumed fairly quickly, after which the 51st carried Corporal Adam, known in the battalion as Old Father Adam, a simple but brave soldier who was felt to have particularly distinguished himself in the battle, around the town on their shoulders. There was then a cricket match against the Hussars, which the 10th won, followed by a ball for all the officers at the Steine Hotel and one for the sergeants at the King and Queen Inn, which cost what Wheeler thought was the enormous sum of £32, or £2,500 today. At five o'clock in the morning, as they were going home, they all met up and, no doubt to the great joy of the sleeping residents, with the band and Colours and the whole corps of the 51st's buglers, they marched home together.

There were two other major departures to benefit the soldiers. On Lady Day, 25 March 1816, everyone who had fought was presented with a silver medal with a red and blue ribbon, the first campaign medal to be issued by the British Army since Cromwell had similarly rewarded his men for their victory at Dunbar. Each individual recipient's name was inscribed around the base, and it also went to the King's German Legion. Its issue caused real annoyance amongst the Peninsular regiments who had not been present at Waterloo, and who felt aggrieved that such recognition was being given in many cases to raw recruits and militiamen who had survived one battle whilst they had received scant reward for years of very hard campaigning.

Secondly, in April 1817, there was an issue of prize money, a bounty more normally awarded to the Navy. Generals received £1,274 10s. 4d., or about £95,000 today, down to sergeants, who got £19 (about £1,425 today), and corporals and below, who got £2 11s. 4d. (about £200), although, in the way that only the British government knows how, its issue was slightly marred by being subject to Stamp Duty of a shilling. However, it also went to next of kin and a real effort was made during that summer to track them down. Importantly for many there was also an amnesty on missing equipment and as late as 1817 men were still claiming that deficient items had been lost in the battle, what is known in the contemporary British Army as the '*Atlantic Conveyor*' syndrome due to the vast amount of lost equipment that supposedly went down when that supply ship was sunk off the Falkland Islands in 1982.

Another, slightly double-edged, way of rewarding those who fought was the more liberal awarding of commissions. One brevet promotion was given to each regiment, to be awarded on merit, very difficult to judge and inevitably the cause of much jealousy. Men who had particularly distinguished themselves were given individual commissions, such as Sergeant Ewart of the Scots Greys, who had captured the Eagle of the 45th. He became an ensign in the 5th Veteran Battalion, which he was not at all certain was what he wanted.

First, although he now had an ensign's pay, he lost his 24 years' service (26, with the Prince Regent's bounty) pension as a sergeant, and, as he pointed out, Corporal Styles in the Royals had also been commissioned and was now paid the same despite having served for considerably less time. Secondly, they tended to be commissioned into battalions which had boring or unattractive roles. Styles became an ensign in the 6th West Indian Regiment and was predictably sent to serve in the West Indies, then considered most unhealthy; he had had enough after two years and went on half pay. Ewart's battalion, which was a home-based garrison unit, was in fact disbanded in 1821 but he was retired on an ensign's full pay and went to live near Salford.

There was also a feeling that junior officers had been overlooked, as it was customary only to mention the conduct of officers down to the rank of captain, and there was much annoyance, particularly in the Foot Guards,[68] that the very brave actions of many of their lieutenants and ensigns had been ignored. George Gunning, the Warrior Gubbins or the Man of Kent as the Secretary called him, was more explicit. 'It was not all gold that glittered at Waterloo, and that the Duke of Wellington knows as well as I do. Had justice been distributed fairly in the army, and not court influence and favour shown to a select few, many old British subaltern officers would have been promoted. The subalterns of the army are its mainspring, and I hope to see their services more justly rewarded. Like the working clergy, they want their merits brought fairly before the public.'[69]

There was also considerable, and probably inevitable, jealousy between regiments as to how their role in the battle came to be regarded. Wellington had famously not mentioned the role of Adam's light infantrymen in defeating the

Imperial Guard in his despatch, concentrating instead on the
Foot Guards. He was known throughout the Army for
favouring the Foot Guards, and men like Sir John Colborne,
who commanded the 52nd, were indignant that their
undoubtedly critical action in wheeling through 90 degrees
to pour volleys into the 4th Chasseurs had not been acknowledged. There was a growing resentment, as Gunning hinted,
that Wellington had singled out the titled and well-connected
people whose names would find favour at court and in the
War Office and had ignored many of the real heroes. This
feeling would not go away. Even James Kempt, who had
commanded his brigade with such distinction throughout
the three days, and who received endless honours, ending
up knighted, a full general and Governor-General of Canada,
felt that Wellington's accounts did 'not do justice to himself
or the army that fought under his orders in the field of
Waterloo'.[70]

A rumour also developed that the cavalry had not done
very well, attributed partly to remarks allegedly made by
Wellington about the Household and Union Brigades' lack of
control, and more insidious comments that the light-cavalry
brigades had not really contributed as they could have done.
Wellington's comments about the heavy cavalry were almost
certainly misrepresented by Gronow, who was an inveterate
gossip. He reports Wellington saying in Paris in July, on hearing the news that the Prince Regent had made himself
Colonel of both the Life Guards and the Blues, 'His Royal
Highness is our sovereign and can do what he pleases; but this
will I say, the cavalry of other European armies have won
victories for their generals, but mine have invariably got me
into scrapes.' Gronow also related that whilst Wellington was
standing in one of the squares of Foot Guards during the

afternoon of the battle he kept asking, 'Where are our cavalry? Why don't they come and pitch into those French fellows?'[71]

Yet much of this seems to have been just low-level regimental complaining, common between units on operations, and certainly in London both the Household and Union regiments were very much the heroes of the day. More damaging were the comments made by senior officers about the light cavalry. Lieutenant-Colonel James Stanhope, who fought at Waterloo with the Foot Guards and who was an influential figure, having previously been on Wellington's staff, wrote that 'The heavy cavalry did wonders, but our light cavalry partly from being brought up in small isolated attacks instead of a great mass, in this part of the battle, near us, did very little'.[72] These sort of comments became more commonplace, and, particularly given the very heavy casualties in the 7th and 12th Light Dragoons, caused much resentment. In a long letter to his parents on 11 July, the first he had ever written to them, Private John Marshall of the 10th Hussars complained that he had seen in 'an English newspaper that the Life Guards were the only cavalry to have been of any service' and that he did not want 'to show his vanity' but he was incensed at such allegations.[73]

Wellington himself was directly critical, many thought most unfairly, of the artillery. Much as he was known for favouring the Foot Guards, he was equally renowned for disliking the gunners, but his remarks after the battle were harsh and led to life-long resentment. He complained that they had run too far back during the French cavalry attacks, instead of taking refuge in the infantry squares as he and his staff had. This, he alleged, meant that, once the French cavalry had been driven off, there were no gunners available to fire at them. 'In fact', he continued, 'I should have had no artillery during the whole of the latter part of the action, if I had not kept a reserve in the commencement.'[74] Although he wrote in his despatch that the artillery was conducted 'much to his satisfaction',[75] few gunners received much reward. Mercer was especially angry. As late as 1859, by which time he was a retired major-general, he was still writing that 'You perhaps may be aware that I never got anything, and probably am now the only instance of one holding a command on that day who has never been noticed in any way, nay more, who has invariably been refused everything, brevet rank, the CB [Companion of the Order of the Bath] etc.'. He seems to have been singled out as one of the culprits for not taking his men to seek refuge in the squares, although he maintained that instead of running too far back they stayed manning their guns.

Perhaps one of the bitterest arguments that developed was an internal one in the Royals as to who actually took the Eagle. Alexander Clark (he later added a Kennedy to his surname) maintained that he had taken it and handed it to Corporal Styles to take to the rear. The Secretary, and his friend George Gunning, to whose troop Styles belonged, would always claim that Styles had taken it directly and that Clark was merely in the vicinity. The argument became so heated that at some stage the pages that covered the incident in the Club Book were ripped out, probably by Clark, given that they were written by Trafford, who was very much in the Styles camp. In the end both were rewarded, Styles by his commission, even if it was in the West Indies, and Clark was given a CB. He left the regiment, though, rather bitter, transferring to the Scots Greys and went on to enjoy a successful Army career, finishing as colonel of the Inniskilling Dragoons, alongside whom he had charged, and whom the Secretary thought so unfriendly. He had the Eagle incorporated in his coat of arms when he assumed his additional surname.

The disputes about who did exactly what at Waterloo would drag on for decades. They are testament partly to its significance, and the importance it assumed in the nation's conscience, but mostly to the fact that with so many men engaged in a confined space no one had an overall view of what happened. Wellington, in his rare more generous moments, would admit that 'Some individuals may recollect all the little events of which the great result is the battle won or lost; but no individual can recollect the order in which, or the exact moment at which, they occurred, which makes all the difference as to their value or importance'.[76] However much he may have been accused of favouring one regiment over another, he could do little for any of them in the longer term and, as the country settled down to enjoy the peace, it set once more to reducing the Army that had secured it.

The Army reductions that came in late 1818, once the government was confident that Napoleon was finally unable to stage another comeback, were severe and went much further than those of four years earlier. The instruction was once again to 'select for discharge such of the men who are least efficient either to stature or bodily strength'.[77] The cavalry were reduced by about one-third within their regiments, whilst the infantry were reduced to just one battalion per regiment, except for the Guards and Rifle regiments. There were some reforms too, with cuirasses being reissued to the Household Cavalry and some heavy-cavalry regiments, whilst two light-dragoon regiments were equipped with lances, but most of the 'improvements' were merely cosmetic. There was a drive by the Prince Regent to adopt the heavy French bearskin caps, made famous by the Imperial Guard. They were adopted by the Foot Guards, who still wear them today, and by the Household Cavalry, who found them impractical on horses and got rid of them as soon as they tactfully could. Although most were happy to find an alternative to the uncomfortable shako, there were some reservations at copying too much from the French. Arthur Kennedy grumbled that he supposed they would soon be told 'to fight like the French'[78] as well and there was no doubt but that the Prince Regent was as fascinated by Napoleon as everyone else.

The long-term effect was to be serious. With the final defeat of France, and the end of a war that had been going on intermittently since the 1690s, there was no other potential enemy in Europe against which to judge and match the British Army. It entered a long period of peacetime service, always bad for armies, and all it could do was to compare itself to how it had fought in 1815. With Wellington and Hill at Horse Guards, and with a whole generation of generals taking their inspiration from Waterloo, there was little attempt to modernise. Consequently the next time it fought in a European War, nearly 40 years later in the Crimea, it was essentially the same Waterloo army with a few Napoleonic additions. This almost had disastrous consequences.

The human impact was more immediate. 'The reduction that was soon to take place, would soon render the Royals a regiment only in name', lamented the Secretary. Many left because they had to, but others, like Sigismund Trafford, sensing that flatness he had noticed develop during 1816 become more permanent, decided to go voluntarily. It was becoming clear that there would be little need for the Army and that few of his friends would stay. The decision that many of them had put off in 1814 now became more straightforward. A 'few old officers that were doomed to remain' would, he thought, think back on those happier times in Spain and after Waterloo when the regiment was alive and full of purpose and 'while taking their solitary ride on the turn-pike road in some remote or outlandish quarter in Yorkshire or in Ireland would be but too happy to remember the days gone by'.[79]

Rees Gronow and Standish O'Grady left as well. Gronow was never going to stay, regarding the Army as a natural extension of his social life and which he was happy to drift in and out of. Had there been another war he would certainly have joined up again as he would not have wanted to miss out. As it was he enjoyed his society life, flitting between London, Paris and the country until his money was all gone. O'Grady was rather different. Like Trafford he saw no future in the Army. He also went on half pay, returning to Cahir in Co. Limerick, for where he became MP in 1820. And he decided not to marry Kitty. Taking his time, much to his mother's frustration, he finally settled on Gertrude Paget, niece of Uxbridge (now promoted to Marquess of Anglesey). They had lots of children and lived happily in Ireland, where he succeeded his father as Viscount Guillamore in 1840. He died in 1848, much agitated at the extreme suffering caused to his locality by the great famine resulting from the failure of the Irish potato crop.

Young William Leeke stayed for a few years, becoming a lieutenant in 1823, but leaving soon afterwards to join the Church. He served as Rural Dean of Duffield for 25 years, but in 1866 published his own account of Waterloo, which reignited the controversy as to who had really defeated the Imperial Guard – the Foot Guards or the 52nd! It raged for years. He only died in 1879, 'a much loved pastor deeply admired by all who knew him'.[80] Edward Macready, on the other hand, having finally got his commission, held on to it, making the Army his career, and serving for a long time in India. He left as a major and wrote military history, dying in

1848. Mercer also stayed on, having a very successful career and ending up as a major-general, but nothing he achieved in his subsequent long life would ever compensate for his deep feeling of hurt that the achievements of his troop at Waterloo had been ignored. He died in Exeter in 1868 at the age of 85, still troubled by the wound that had originally been caused by his bloodsoaked overalls drying hard and cutting into his perineum as he rode to Paris.

Of the Household Cavalrymen, life actually worked out rather as John Bingley had planned it from his hospital bed. He recovered, left the Army in 1817, and went home to Littlethorpe. In October 1818 he married Ann Spence. He still seems to have been racked by guilt, writing to ask Ann's parents for her hand and declaring that 'I have been a back sliding and ungrateful youth'. Littlethorpe is now part of Leicester itself, just beside the M1; there is still a Bingley road there and the Bingley descendants may have done rather well out of the farm after all. Thomas Playford had an unhappier time. He returned to London in 1816, married, and stayed on in the Life Guards, settling down to a life of fairly dull ceremonial duty. But the loneliness he had felt as a child, his bookishness, the uncomfortable feeling he had experienced at the privilege he had seen in London in 1814, and the difficulty he found in despatching Frenchmen on the battlefield, emerged in 1824 as a deep religious belief. He took his wife and family, and his pension of 1s. 10½d. per day (or a bit under £3,000 per annum today) and went off to Canada as a Methodist minister. It did not work out, and on the return journey his wife and children died. He was a widower for twelve years, remarrying his landlord's daughter in 1836 and eventually settling as a minister in Australia. Both Bingley and Playford lived on, wearing their medals on Waterloo Day but otherwise forgotten, whilst John Shaw's legacy thrived. He became a national hero, the modern-day Achilles who had represented all the toughness and phlegm so admired by men like Walter Scott. The legends about his exploits on the battlefield grew, until he came to epitomise everything that the British public believed the British soldier to have been.

Many of those who had joined the infantry from the volunteers or the militia went back to their civilian lives. Thomas Morris left in 1817, his seven years being up. His captain at the time, Captain Cohen, attempted to get him to sign on again and engaged the services of the bottle to do so. Morris drank him under the table, picked up his kit and returned to London. He published his memoirs in 1845, part fascinating historical record and part diatribe against military discipline. Mathew Clay on the other hand decided to stay. He did predictably well in the 3rd Foot Guards, who became the Scots Guards, rising to be a drill sergeant, one of the most senior NCO ranks. He married in 1823, had twelve children, of whom only three survived infancy, served in Portugal in 1828, retired in 1833 and returned to the militia as sergeant-major of the Bedfordshire Militia until 1852. He died in 1873, aged 78.

William Wheeler stayed too, rationalising that – as he now had seven years' service since he volunteered from the militia, which had been increased to nine with the Regent's bounty – he was a long way towards qualifying for a full pension. He determined to 'follow the fortunes of my old corps as long as I am fit for service'. He finally left, aged 43, in 1828, devoting his remaining years to making a fair copy of his many spidery letters home. James Anton also stayed on, becoming a quartermaster sergeant, serving in Ireland, Gibraltar and Malta and not leaving until 1832. He became a Chelsea pensioner, publishing his memoirs in 1841, and no doubt telling many a tale in the Royal Hospital. There were other happy stories. Billy and Ann Tennant eventually met up and went on to have three more children, and William Hay finally got away from Dorchester, to which his regiment had returned, ending up as Commissioner of the Metropolitan Police.

William Lawrence had a more adventurous time. Towards the end of 1815, and whilst the Allies were working out who was going to occupy which part of France, the 40th had been billeted in St Germain, outside Paris. Outside their barracks was a small stall which sold fruit, spirits and tobacco. It was owned by a local gardener and run by his daughter, Clotilde. Lawrence struck up a friendship with her. One day a soldier of the 27th tried to make off with some tobacco without paying for it. Lawrence chased him and got it back. Clotilde was most grateful. Friendship turned to love and they decided to marry. Lawrence had to get permission from his colonel, who thought it quite extraordinary to marry a Frenchwoman, but consented, and they were duly married, Lawrence, always careful about money, noting cheerfully that 'It cost us nothing'.

The 40th were then sent to Cambrai and the newly-weds went with them, and then back to Glasgow in 1817. The boat to which they were assigned should have taken three days to sail from Calais to Leith but there was no wind and the journey took seven weeks. Clotilde, who spoke not a word of English, seems to have adapted remarkably well to her new circumstances and settled quickly into Glasgow life. They had a bit of money, as Lawrence received his Waterloo prize-money. In the autumn of 1817 he received a letter saying that his father was dangerously ill, and they set off for Briantspuddle to see him before it was too late. Their plan was to go by ship to London and then walk to Dorset, Lawrence wearing his uniform with his Waterloo medal, which would open many doors on their journey. Clotilde does not appear to have baulked at the prospect of walking halfway across England in the winter, and off they went.

Lawrence had last seen his family twelve years before, when he had run away from the builder he was apprenticed to, and it was an emotional reunion. First they met his sister, who shaved off his long thick beard and moustache, and he was waiting for his parents as they emerged from Sunday service, his father hobbling across the churchyard on two sticks, his mother wearing the same 'old black bonnet and red cloak that she had worn when I left'. She half fainted on seeing him, leaning against a wall and none of them able to speak for a long time. At last his father said, 'My child, I did not expect to see you again.' They stayed nearly three weeks, being celebrated by all the family, and then walked back to Glasgow, arriving within one day of Lawrence's leave running out.

The 1818 reductions hit the 40th hard, losing 400 men from 1,000. Once the 'old and disabled' were discharged, their commanding officer decided the fairest way to determine who else had to go would be to draw lots, and Lawrence was unlucky. He was sent down to London to undergo a medical assessment. He was asked his length of service. 'One of the gentlemen called out "Seven!" but the doctor immediately said "Nine!" because of the wound on my knee. This meant that I should receive a pension of ninepence a day for that what was settled on me for life.' They then walked back to Briantspuddle, where Lawrence took a job as a farm labourer. He didn't like it much, and when there was a call to join the veteran battalions in 1819 for service in Ireland he re-enlisted and spent two years chasing smugglers around Cork.

Discharged again in 1821, he returned to Dorset, where he and Clotilde started running a pub in Studland, which they called the Wellington Inn. It seems to have thrived until Clotilde died in 1853, after which Lawrence negotiated an extra threepence a day for his pension, retired and wrote his memoirs. It is also rumoured that he learned quite a bit about smuggling whilst in Cork and may have been tempted to indulge in a little illicit trade on the Dorset coast, but there is no hard evidence for this.[81]

The King's German Legion was disbanded in 1816, ahead of the reductions that were made to the rest of the Army. Edmund Wheatley was put on half pay of 4s. a day in April that year (so about £5,500 per annum today) on which he found it difficult to survive. He finished his diary in May 1817, ending it with the words 'Good bye, dear. God bless you my dear Eliza. Remember I swear to be yours only, only Eliza's. Never think I have forgotten you'.[82] And he did not, reconciling himself to her family and marrying her in 1820, their first child being born rather under nine months later. They travelled to Belgium, and had three more children. It is not clear what Wheatley did but he lived until 1848 at Trèves. His diary was not published until 1964 when his great-great-grandson handed the manuscript to a publisher. Frederick Lindau did have his contribution recognised, being awarded the Guelphic Medal, which carried a pension. Predictably he quickly tired of peacetime soldiering and asked to be discharged in October 1815, taking advantage of the Regent's Bounty, which applied equally to the King's German Legion, and ahead of his battalion's disbandment. He went back to Hameln where, surprisingly, he settled down to become a shoemaker, the trade to which he had originally been apprenticed. He married soon after, his wife dying in 1827, after which he married again. Between his two families he ended up with nine children, and when his memoirs were published in 1847 he was struggling financially. It is not clear when he died. Several King's German Legion units were transferred to the Hanoverian army. From there, two cavalry regiments and two infantry regiments became part of the German army after 1871, and would fight in 1914 and again in 1939. It was not until 1945, when the old German regimental linkages were destroyed, that the King's German Legion finally ceased to exist.

Those who still sought active service, like Macready, had to go to India to find it. Edward Kelly did the same. Nothing came his way after the battle except for a presentation sword from his own regiment, a very nice acknowledgement which would mean a great deal to most soldiers (and which still hangs in the Household Cavalry museum) and the Order of St Anne of Russia, dished out by a relieved Tsar to those Allies who had distinguished themselves. Uxbridge may have said something to Wellington but if so no CB and certainly no peerage resulted. Maria's demands for money grew more insatiable and he sadly decided he could no longer afford to remain in the Life Guards. Selling his commission, he purchased one in the cheaper 23rd Light Dragoons, going with them to India. Debts and the cost of his family caught up with him once more and he sold again, transferring now to the 6th Foot. He joined the staff of Stapleton Cotton (now Lord Combermere), was present at the Siege of Bhurtpore and died of disease in India in 1828. It was a sad end to a frustrated life, although one cannot help but wonder just how many Indians found an excuse to leave the campfire when the Waterloo stories started.

Henry Murray also served on. A younger son of the Earl of

Mansfield, he had no estate to inherit, but, unlike Kelly, he had ample private means. He ended up a general and knighted, having had an agreeable if unexciting career after Waterloo, serving in England and Ireland. He and Emily continued to move house, and she bore a much-adored son, Arthur, whilst they were stationed in Cork in 1820. Arthur followed his father into the Army, dying of wounds he received at Bloem Plaats in South Africa in 1848 whilst serving with the Rifle Brigade. His father published an unsurprisingly sad memoir of Arthur's life, and Henry's and Emily's final years, when they finally settled in Wimbledon, must have been difficult and empty.

As the peace became established, and as the true significance of Napoleon's defeat became apparent, Waterloo veterans began to acquire an almost cult-like status. As late as 1846, when Private William Westwood, who had charged with 1st Life Guards, died, his funeral made the front page of *The Times*.[83] Waterloo men would parade on 18 June every year, wearing their medals. Back home in Lancashire James Smithies of the Royals, who described the sound of the regiment clashing with the cuirassiers so vividly, wore his rather more often, pinning them to his coat whenever he attended church; he said that whilst he was on active service he would always imagine that he heard his local church bells. He continued to do so until he was run over by a colliery wagon in his eighty-first year. There were many reunions too, William Bentinck of the 23rd beating the assembly at the Rochdale gathering with the same drumsticks that he had used to sound the call to battle.[84] Men like Charles Ewart were in constant demand to speak at dinners and open fêtes, something Ewart thought was far worse than having to charge the French.

This cult of celebrity masked the fact that, for many, life did not work out quite as tidily as it did for John Bingley or William Lawrence. Thomas Howell initially went home to Edinburgh but found his mother dead and lived with his married sister, to whom he felt he was a burden. He found that he could not even get labouring work. 'I would be useful but can get nothing to do.'[85] He determined to go to South America and wrote sadly to a friend that he would never come back and that he wished he was a soldier again. He was last seen working as a road mender, although his memoirs were probably first published in 1819.

Edward Costello was another who found himself discharged in 1818 as he was wounded and therefore counted as 'disabled'. With a wife and a new child, he found he was trying to live on 6d. a day (about £1.50 today), and became near destitute. He applied to the Patriotic Fund for support, but the secretary, a Mr Woodford, helpfully told him, 'Damn it Sir! Did you expect to fight with puddings or Norfolk dumplings? If men go into battle what else can they expect but wounds! I am now busy and cannot be troubled with you.' Costello and his wife had to part, she returning to France and her family with the baby whilst he tried his luck elsewhere. Having given all his money to her, he found himself in Dover, literally without a farthing and determined to rob the first man who came along. Bizarrely that happened to be Jem Conner, with whom he had served in the 95th. Staying with him, he managed to approach Andrew Barnard, and got himself re-enlisted in the Army to serve in Spain. In the meantime his wife died in France, Costello thought 'most likely owing to her father', who had never approved of him, and he set out for a new, lonely life, soldiering in Spain once more.[86]

There was no safety net. Men were given what money

they were owed, which was not very much, and then left to their own devices. The Royal Hospital took those it could who were recommended to it on discharge, but it could never hope to accommodate all those who fell on hard times. Others turned to crime more seriously than Costello. William Hay recorded that Private Power, the dragoon who had saved the local farmer from the marauding cuirassiers just after Waterloo, took to highway robbery. He was caught and sentenced to a thousand lashes, which he took 'without uttering a word, except desiring the farrier to strike him fair'. On being 'taken down' from the halberds, he looked around, saw Hay, and 'his back lacerated and covered in blood, requested that I bear witness to his having on many occasions acted as a brave soldier'.[87]

There was also the inevitable shell shock, the mental wounds of battle, or post-traumatic stress disorder as it is now known. It was not readily acknowledged at the time, and it was only in the twentieth century that it was truly recognised and diagnosed. Consequently much of it must have gone unobserved, masked in some cases by veterans living in village communities where care of the old and occasionally odd was accepted as part of everyday life, particularly if they could tell their stories over and over again. Some veterans became very odd indeed. A journalist recorded visiting Lord Saltoun late in his life, to be greeted by a 'very queer-looking person, short of figure, round as a ball, his head shrunk between very high and rounded shoulders and with short stumpy legs. He was curiously attired in a whole-coloured suit of gray; droll-shaped jacket the great collar of which reached far up the back of his head, surmounted by a pair of voluminous breeches which suddenly tightened at the knee.'[88]

Care of orphans was more haphazard. The traditional

British Army way of looking after them was to keep them with the regiment, their mother often remarrying into it, and for them to live in that rather loose and curiously tolerant social community. However, with the 1818 reductions, the increasing use of barracks and the coming sense of public priggishness, that became increasingly difficult. Some children did very well. The poor Heyland family did as their father Arthur had bidden in his last letter. Two sons duly joined the Army, and both fought in the Crimea, their mother having to cope with yet more anxiety as her youngest lost an arm at the Battle of the Alma. Others had to rely more on regimental and family charity. Edward Serjeant, a sergeant in the 51st, died on 1 September from a fever he had contracted from a cold that had started on the night before the battle. His friend Private Richard Armstrong wrote to his mother and sister saying that he 'departed leaving behind him a poor amount and a faithful widow and a charming fatherless boy whom we all consider the very model of his father'. The poor widow is 'in such a state of present grieving that she can cannot be spoke to in any reason' so Armstrong and his friends are writing in her stead to entreat them to look after her and her son, not something that they necessarily took for granted.[89]

England being as muddled and sentimental in the early nineteenth century as it is today about prioritising animals over people, there was sometimes more fuss made about the horses who survived than the soldiers. Not many came home, as the parsimonious War Office would not pay to ship them back from France, and the Royals sadly said goodbye to theirs in Calais. However, the Household Cavalry horses were returned as they were needed for ceremonial duties, although the wounded ones were sold off at auction. Twelve of the most seriously injured were bought by Sir Astley Cooper, a famous surgeon, who operated on them, removed their bullets and grapeshot, and then took them to his estate to convalesce. To his great delight, one day when they were all healed, he saw them 'form line, charge, and then retreat, and afterwards gallop about'. They obligingly repeated these manoeuvres each morning.[90]

The story of what happened to Napoleon's marshals and colonels is a book in its own right. A few, like Ney, were court-martialled and shot, much to the chagrin of many of the Allies, who admired Ney's personal bravery. Eighteen others were sentenced to death *in absentia*, one of whom was the Bonapartist diehard Lallemand, the Royals' old antagonist from Maguilla. He fled with Napoleon and was taken with him onto HMS *Bellephoron*. He wrote to General Slade from Plymouth on 2 August, saying he had been told that he was being sent home rather than accompanying Napoleon to St Helena and he begged Slade to intervene, citing the fact that he had cared well for the Royals prisoners from Maguilla and saying that he could not believe 'that the British government would violate in such a palpable and in such an odious manner the right of men against us'.[91] He was not handed over to the Bourbons, but instead sent to prison in Malta, from where he was eventually released and spent the remainder of his life travelling the globe, from Persia to Egypt and the USA, offering his military services and trying to start revolts to restore the Bonapartes. After the 1830 revolution he returned to France, and ended his days back in Napoleonic service, acting as a courier for Joseph Bonaparte. This arch-Napoleonic adventurer, and highly capable cavalry general, died in Paris in 1839.

Lefèbvre-Desnöettes, that dashing commander of light cavalry, had a sadder life. Also sentenced to death, he escaped to the USA, where he became a travelling brush salesman. His devoted wife lobbied for him in Paris and in 1821 he was pardoned. On his return voyage to be reunited with her and his daughter, whom he had never seen as she had been born shortly after Waterloo, his ship sank off Kinsale and he was drowned.

A surprising number of Napoleon's marshals ended their days restored to favour. Grouchy fled to the USA but returned to France in 1820, and had his marshal's baton restored in 1831. D'Erlon fled to Germany, where he ran a pub, but again was eventually pardoned and became a Marshal of France in 1843. Reille also became a marshal, in 1847, and was eventually a senator, whilst Lobau, initially sentenced to death, escaped because he was captured by the British and in exile. He returned to France in 1818. In the strange way of coincidence, many of those who had fought met again in very different circumstances. In 1832 the gallant Marquis de Cubières, who had been felled from his horse at Hougoumont by Sergeant Fraser, was Governor of Ancona, where he chanced upon Colonel Woodford. They predictably spent long hours talking about the battle, and Cubières maintained that he enjoyed many more happy years because the Foot Guards would not fire on him as he lay wounded.

And what happened to the Royals? Ben the Ruler remained terrorising the regiment as commanding officer until 1829. He then got promoted, did other Army jobs, became a general and returned, knighted, as Colonel of the Regiment, which post he occupied for a further 27 years. He died, unmarried and reputedly as grumpy as ever, in 1869. The Secretary went on half pay soon after the Royals landed in England on 4 January 1816. They had a rather sad farewell dinner at Wright's in Canterbury at which only 15 officers sat down, all that was left of the determined band who had set out from Exeter nine months before. Trafford then divided his time between Wroxham Hall, his house in Norfolk, and rue de Lille in Paris, where he died on 14 February 1852. Did he ever recover that sense of comradeship and common purpose that he so enjoyed with the regiment between landing in Lisbon in 1809 and returning from France seven years later? It is doubtful. His life seemed rather sad, with all his children dying before him except one daughter. He would always miss that time when 'all were in the heyday of life and spirit. The present time was sufficient for their enjoyment. The morrow provided for itself.'[92]

There were brief moments when the old Waterloo spirit could come flooding back. In 1838, at one of the many parades for Queen Victoria's accession, the regiment were amused to see Marshal Soult, now French Ambassador in London, showing off by riding in Napoleon's old stirrups and leathers. One of those revered items broke, his horse bucked and he was thrown clean off. Only military discipline prevented an outbreak of cheering. But that spirit could never really be re-created. Trafford would always regret its passing. There is something very sad about the parting of that close-knit group of officers and their soldiers, who had fought together for seven years, got to know each other so well, suffered together, both from the enemy and their commanding officer, lost friends and favourite horses, and who had given so much to 'the regiment'. For the rest of their lives they would miss the comradeship, the humour, the intuitive understanding and appreciation of one another. Generations of regimental officers have shared that same spirit, albeit few tested as severely as the Club were. It was a spirit that existed because there was a war to be fought; it passed because the war was done, and regiments are there to fight. Then, as now, that is what the British Army is for.

> Trodden and bruised to a miry tomb
> Are ears that have greened but will never be gold,
> And flowers in the bud that will never bloom.

THOMAS HARDY,
The Dynasts

THE BATTLEFIELD TODAY

The Waterloo battlefields are remarkably well preserved. They are also easy to reach, being just a two-and-a-half-hour drive from Calais, or even less if you take a ferry to Ostend, which would be more in keeping with the voyage Wellington's soldiers made. The best way to see the battlefields is by car. Start at Quatre Bras, still the crossroads where the old Nivelles–Namur road, the N93, dissects the Charleroi–Brussels N5. The extensive motorway network has relegated the N93 to what passes for a country road in modern Belgium, which means it is only moderately suicidal. The N5, by contrast, is horribly busy and this makes it difficult to get an overall view of the action on 16 June. The ground is also, unsurprisingly, still undulating and heavily cropped, just as it was two centuries ago.

The main features and buildings are still there. Frasnes has become something of an indeterminate sprawl, but the N5 still rises across the ridge where Ney made his dispositions. Grand Pierrepoint, the right-hand end of the line Perponcher's men held on the night of 15 June, is signposted off to the left as you leave the village and is now a smart golf club. Gemioncourt is hardly changed, being the very obvious farm buildings of dark Brabant brick in the dip to the right. There are endless signs forbidding entry, but you can get a good view from the main road. The main action took place in the fields between Gemioncourt and the Quatre Bras crossroads. Bossu Wood, to the left of the N5, has virtually disappeared. It was gifted to Wellington by a grateful Netherlands government after the battle and he is reputed to have had the timber cut down and sold.

As you approach the Quatre Bras crossroads from the south, in other words the direction in which the French advanced, there is a rather heavy memorial to the Duke of Brunswick, marking the point where he was shot. It is also near where the 69th lost their Colour. Turn right at the crossroads, leaving the original farm buildings on your left, and drive slowly east along the N93. To the right, along the ditch, is where Picton's men first deployed. They formed their squares in the open fields a few hundred yards further south towards Gemioncourt, which you can see in the distance. The 95th's original positions were in the woods and farm buildings as the road starts to dip.

Retrace your steps and, taking care at the traffic lights, cross back over Quatre Bras towards Nivelles. Just on your left is the ditch Wellington jumped as he sought cover with the 92nd. Immediately after the crossroads on the left is a modern memorial to the British and Hanoverian units that fought there. It is a good place to park, and it also marks the spot from which the Guards Division set off on their evening mission to clear Bossu Wood. Opposite is a modern memorial to the Netherlands cavalry, shaped like a sword.

From Quatre Bras, drive north along the N5, remembering that the manic lorry drivers are probably more interested in getting home for dinner than sharing your fascination with the battle, and turn off into the centre of Genappe. This is the route of the old road along which the British withdrew on 17 June. Stop in the centre of the town and walk across the bridge over the Dyle. This is where the 7th Light Dragoons made their escape, and where the French bunched to make them such a tempting target for Kelly's Life Guards. It is also where poor Mercer just managed to save his guns after being deployed by Uxbridge in the northern outskirts.

From Genappe, stop at La Ferme du Caillou, about ten minutes further on and where Napoleon retired to on the evening of 17 June, having realised that he would have to fight the next day. It was in the small yard and garden here that the Chasseurs à Cheval waited, where they tried to extricate the Emperor and his portable paraphernalia of government as the French army collapsed, and where the Napoleonic dream – or nightmare, depending on your perspective – can be said to have finally ended. It is now an excellent small museum. In the garden is a sombre ossuary built in 1912, containing the bones of soldiers gathered from the battlefield; supposedly all French, although quite how that was achieved is not recorded. It is inscribed 'For the Emperor often; for the Fatherland always'.

Drive on north towards Brussels. You are now passing through where the rear elements of Napoleon's army arrived – wet, hungry and pretty disgruntled – on that soaking Saturday evening. Pass slowly though Rossomme. Here the Imperial Guard bivouacked either side of the road. The road rises, and you emerge onto open fields. On your left is a small white house, La Belle Alliance, near where Napoleon had his headquarters on 18 June. To the right, a lane leads down to Plancenoit, where the fighting with the Prussians was at its most intense. Stop by La Belle Alliance, and look north. You are now on the French front line, where Reille's and d'Erlon's men formed up. You may be forgiven for thinking that the Allied ridge, about 900 yards away, doesn't really look like a ridge at all. That is a fair point, as large parts of it were shovelled away by armies of Belgian labourers in the 1820s to construct the Lion Mound, the conical artificial hill you can see to your left. It marks the spot where the Prince of Orange was wounded, to the greater advantage of the Allied cause, and is a monument to the unity of the Netherlands! Wellington was caustic enough about it; imagine what Ompteda's reaction might have been.

Drive on along the main road. Almost immediately on your right you will see a flattish high area in the cornfields; this is where the Grand Battery was drawn up. As the road dips, you will notice two things. First, the ridge is actually more of a ridge than you realized; and, secondly, on the left is the remarkably well preserved La Haie Sainte, whose patient owners (descendants of the family who lived there in 1815) put up with a stream of visitors as they try to run a modern farm. The road climbs to the crossroads where the Ohain lane, the sunken lane, still crosses the main road and which marked almost the centre of the Allied line. There is a small car park on the right. Stop here and look and think. You are standing on one of the several mass graves on which the municipality has thoughtfully sited a picnic area. The trees just south of the picnic tables are where the 95th's sandpit was.

Turn to look back the way you have just come, and face the French positions. Remember that most Allied soldiers spent the battle behind the ridge and few actually saw the field as you now can. Look to your left. There is a modern red-brick building in some trees about 300 yards away across a cornfield.

In this field, north of the lane, was Picton's Fifth Division; and behind them the Union Brigade, drawn up in the lower ground in the dip. The lane divides by the red-brick building, which is a convent. The modern branch curves southwards, whilst the original heads slightly north, brushing the convent and then deteriorating into a farm track. It was behind this track that the light-cavalry brigades were placed. It is only here that it looks much as it did 200 years ago. It is well worth the short walk to see it. Retrace your steps to the car park at the crossroads. Keep looking left, and now south back towards the French positions, and you can see Papelotte and La Haie, the farm complexes which formed the far left of the Allies' positions and where the northern of the two Prussian columns started to arrive in the evening. The country is still wooded and broken unlike the open plough or corn of the centre and right.

Now walk from the picnic tables, skirting the cornfield, and a path will lead you back down to La Haie Sainte, emerging opposite the kitchen garden, where Ompteda was killed and Wheatley wounded. There is a monument opposite to Gordon, Wellington's ADC, who fell wounded in the nearby square of the 30th Foot. On the sandpit side of the road is a sizeable monument to the Hanoverian soldiers who fell. You will realise from here just why La Haie Sainte was so important and how, once in possession, Ney could shell the left-hand side of the Allied line with impunity. Walk back to the picnic spot. Just across the road are two memorials – a small one to Picton, who was shot here as he countered d'Erlon's initial attack, and a sad one to the 27th Foot, the poor Inniskillings, who suffered the worst casualties of the battle, massacred by the Imperial Guard artillery firing from La Haie Sainte.

Now, taking your life in your hands once again, cross the main road, heading west. This part of the battlefield is very changed. Much of the earth from here ended up in the Lion Mound and all traces of the high banks and hedges that once bordered the sunken lane have disappeared. On your right are some modern buildings, including the 1815 Hotel. This is where the King's German Legion was drawn up. Behind the hotel, between its garden and the wood, was the Household Brigade. Most of the fighting with the cuirassiers took place between the road and La Haie Sainte, a few hundred yards on your left. There is a track through the field on your left which leads down to La Haie Sainte itself. Sometimes it has a 'Route Interdit' sign on it, understandable given the number of visitors, but you can walk down and look at the farm buildings close up; they are remarkably little changed and you can follow every action of Baring's men, although the orchard to the south, through which the French first attacked, is now part of the ploughed field.

Walk back to the road and on towards the Lion Mound. You are passing through the Third Division's positions. There is a café below the mound, the Wellington Café, and a visitor centre which has been much reworked for the bicentenary. Part of this is the Panorama, built in 1910, which has an excellent round painting of the French cavalry charges. Stand in the middle and you get an exciting impression of what it must have been like to wait in those squares. You can then climb the Lion Mound, the Butte de Lion, should you be so inclined. It has 226 steps, so you will feel quite pleased with yourself when you reach the top, from where you get a good but not exceptional view of the centre and right parts of the battlefield. Remember that no one could have enjoyed such a view in 1815.

Beyond the Lion Mound, the lane continues south-east. It still has no hedges but it does still accurately mark the top of the ridgeline. In the fields on your right, between the lane and the motorway embankment, is where most of the Allied squares were formed, and the French cavalry charges took place over the open fields between La Haie Sainte and Hougoumont, whose trees you will now see emerging ahead of you. The lane was roughly where the French breasted the ridge. Halfway between the mound and Hougoumont is a small stone memorial to Mercer's Troop and it marks the spot to which he galloped to stop Ney's first charge. Beyond Mercer's monument you come to the area in which the Guards Division and the 52nd finally routed the Imperial Guard.

The lane now enters a small wood behind Hougoumont. Continue down it and branch off left towards the north gate of the château yard. A lot of work has recently been done to the Hougoumont buildings, to which the British government contributed generously. Whilst it was undoubtedly necessary to stop them falling down, it has slightly spoiled its previously melancholy atmosphere. Nonetheless, apart from the past demolition of the château itself, the rest of the complex is as it was and you can still follow the fighting in detail. The chapel and barns in the yard are now a visitor centre. Having looked at them, and seen the half-burned crucifix, leave by the south gate. Just ahead of you and to your right is another mass grave, under where the haystack behind which Mathew Clay sheltered, once stood. The wood in front of the walls has long gone, but you can see the holes left by musket balls in the few old trees that remain. Walk around the walled garden; the orchard beyond it is now part of the plough field, but the covered way, by which the Guards came and went from the ridge, is clearly visible beyond the northern garden wall. Spend time at Hougoumont. There are several memorials in the garden and it is still the one place on the battlefield where the fighting feels at its most immediate. Think also of the many men of all nationalities who fell there, and of Mercer's description of the sight the morning after. Although the motorway now runs very close behind, the noise is muted by the embankment and the dead rest in at least comparative peace.

There are numerous other monuments around the battlefield, both at Quatre Bras and at Waterloo itself. They are a reminder of the human cost. You may though be forgiven, having completed your tour, for coming away with the odd sense that the battle was a French victory over the Dutch and Belgians. Such is the continuing obsession with Napoleon and everything Bonapartist that much of the emphasis in the local memorabilia is on the Emperor. Wellington gets only the odd mention and Blücher hardly features at all. There is a touching monument in Plancenoit, but otherwise twentieth-century embarrassment at German militarism seems to have precluded commemorating the vital service performed by the Prussian army.

Other places worth a visit are the Wellington Museum in Waterloo village, about two miles north up the Brussels road and at the end of the now very busy high street. This is where he spent the nights before and after the battle and it has some interesting material. Mont St Jean, which housed the Allied dressing station, is on the side of the Waterloo road as you drive north, just behind the crossroads, but is not open to the public. If you are staying in Brussels then visit the splendidly unmodernised Royal Museum of the Armed Forces in Parc du Cinquantenaire, which has a very good collection, particularly of French uniforms and weapons.

For me, the most moving memorials are not, though, those on the battlefields or in the capitals. Rather they are the many plaques and tombstones that adorn our local churches across the United Kingdom and Ireland, and on which families have proudly recorded the contribution of a loved father or grand-father to this greatest of victories – honouring the soldiers of Waterloo within the communities from which they came.

NOTES

Abbreviations

NAM	National Army Museum
PRO WO	Public Records Office War Office
SAHR	The Society for Army Historical Research
WA	*The Waterloo Archive*

Prologue: The Day After

1 Quoted in Haythornthwaite *Redcoats* p.166
2 Mercer *Journal of the Waterloo Campaign* p.185
3 Hope Pattison *Horror Recollected in Tranquillity* p.72
4 Brett-James *The Hundred Days* p.185
5 These two stories come from *The Waterloo Roll Call* pp.277–8; Elizabeth Watkins's story originally appeared in the *Sphere* but I don't have the date; Thérèse Roland's story featured in the *Pall Mall Gazette* of 18 June 1904
6 It is, of course, impossible to arrive at an absolutely accurate number for both military and civilian casualties and estimates vary widely. I have used Esdaile's figures and those given by Dr Michael Rapport of Glasgow University in *Interpretations of the French Wars and Their Legacy*, a lecture given at King's College London in September 2013

1: January–March 1815

1 See Burnham & McGuigan *The British Army Against Napoleon* p.2 and Fortescue *The Campaign of Waterloo* p.20 for full details
2 See J. Steven Watson *The Reign of George III* (Oxford History of

England) Chapter XX for a good survey of wages and conditions in
   1814–15

3 These quotes, and the majority of the quotes about the Royals that
   follow, come from the Club Book; see note 9 below

4 Ibid. p.198

5 This had been reduced from 33,667 in 1809 to 15,858 to furnish
   troops for the Peninsula but was now increased again. Burnham &
   McGuigan p.5

6 Club Book p.200

7 Lord Macaulay, quoted by Hilton *A Mad, Bad and Dangerous People*
   p.112

8 White-Spunner *Horse Guards* p.273

9 Trafford was 'The Secretary' who wrote the Club Book, an informal
   journal of the Royals' experiences in the Peninsula and at Waterloo,
   which is in the Household Cavalry archive: Accession No. 682. The
   page numbers used in these notes are from the copy produced in 1904

10 Ibid. p.197

11 Captain William Hay *Reminiscences 1808–1815 Under Wellington*
   p.157

12 Ibid. p.200

13 Club Book p.203

14 Ibid. p.208

15 Ibid. p.210

16 Ibid. p.203

17 Ibid. p.154

18 Brigades had been used in the British Army since James II's army
   reforms of 1686 but were not formalised until much later. The rank
   of brigadier was, until 1788, held by corporals in the Life Guards,
   and only later became the senior rank given to colonels who commanded brigades

19 For all currency conversions I have used the Bank of England's equiv-
   alent-rate calculator and have applied a factor of 75 to 1815 prices

20 Francis Kinchant's letters are reproduced in WA3 pp.26–33

21 The recruiting poster is in the National Army Museum and is reproduced in Divall *Napoleonic Lives* p.97

22 O'Grady's letters are in the National Army Museum (NAM 9008-
   140-16-1)

23   Gronow *The Reminiscences & Recollections of Captain Gronow* p.43

24   Ibid. p.28

25   See note 19 above

26   For a table of the cost of commissions, see Burnham & McGuigan p.140.

27   Ibid. p.153

28   Mercer *Journal of the Waterloo Campaign* p.xiii

29   Ibid. p.15

30   PRO WO 3/609 Folio 149

31   Well explained by Gareth Glover in WA1 p.173

32   Edward Macready's journal, which has become well known, is in the NAM 6807-209. I draw on it for his vivid description of the fighting

33   White-Spunner *Horse Guards* p.277

34   PRO WO 3/609 Folio 141

35   Philip Haythornthwaite covers this very well in *Redcoats* p.106

36   Ibid. p.110. Macbride is an assumed name

37   Morris *Recollections of Military Service* p.92

38   *Letters of Private Wheeler* p.40

39   Ibid. This quote is from Coss *All for the King's Shilling* p.201

40   Cockerill *Sons of the Brave* p.73

41   White-Spunner *Horse Guards* p.278 explains how the attestation process worked

42   Thomas Playford's diary is AB2999 in the Household Cavalry Museum Archive in Windsor

43   Knollys *Shaw the Life Guardsman* p.2

44   Thomas Playford's diary; see note 42 above

45   John Bingley's correspondence is AB2989 Item 29 in the Household Cavalry Museum Archive; it includes the poignant letter he wrote to his father after being reported killed, but in fact badly wounded, at Waterloo

46   Eileen Hathaway (ed.) *A Dorset Soldier: The Autobiography of Sergeant William Lawrence 1790–1869*

47   These figures, and those that follow, come from the British Soldier Compendium, an analysis of the detailed data from 21 regiments whose records are in the PRO and which are quoted by Coss in the appendices to *All for the King's Shilling*

48   Ibid. p.63

49   Thomas Morris *Recollections of Military Service in 1813–1815* p.3

50   There is an excellent article about the Dorset Volunteer Rangers in *Journal of the Society for Army Historical Research* Winter 2012 Vol. 90 Number 362 by David Clammer which gives a very good example of how a Volunteer Force operated. For a more in-depth study see Austin Gee's *The British Volunteer Movement 1794–1814*

51   Hope Pattison *Horror Recollected in Tranquillity* ed. S. Monick has some very good notes on the militia system and the various acts that governed it, see pp.36–7

52   James Anton *Retrospect of a Military Life* p.39

53   Edward Costello *Rifleman Costello: The Adventures of a Soldier of the 95th (Rifles)*

54   Mrs Ward's *Recollections of an Old Soldier* is a biography of Colonel Tidy by his daughter. She clearly adored him, hence she may have portrayed him a touch too favourably. But his regiment's high opinion of him is supported in other accounts

55   The full career and foibles of Ben the Ruler are covered in detail, if somewhat libellously, by Trafford in the Club Book

56   WA4 p.175 from a letter written by an unknown officer in 23rd Foot

57   For a good detailed survey of economic conditions in 1815, see Steven Watson, Chapter XXI

58   Steven Watson p.xx

59   Household Cavalry Museum Archive AB2999

60   Hay p.157

61   Gronow p.45

62   Hilton p.249

63   Byron *Childe Harold's Pilgrimage* Canto III

64   Hilton p.210

65   Hilton p.103

66   Club Book p.210

67   Brett-James p.21

68   Hathaway *A Dorset Soldier* p.105

69   Hay p.158

70   The correspondence between Lieutenant James Gairdner, 95th Regiment, and his father in America is 1971-01-20 in the National Army Museum

71   The mobilisation correspondence from the War Office is contained in several different files in the Public Record Office (National

Archives). Torrens's correspondence for Bathurst is in PRO W.O. 3/609. This quote is from Folio 72

72　PRO W.O. 3/609 Folio 75

73　Ibid. Folio 85

74　Andrew Bamford covers this problem well in the *SAHR Journal* No. 90 (2012) pp.25–43

75　For an exact breakdown of where each infantry battalion was posted in early 1815, see Burnham & McGuigan pp.69–74

76　Hibbert *A Soldier of the 71st* p.104

77　Wheeler p.158

78　Gairdner Letters NAM 1971-01-20

79　William Leeke's *The History of Lord Seaton's Regiment*, published in 1866, contains a valuable account of Waterloo and the role played by the 52nd. I make extensive use of it

80　All the details and quotes in this paragraph are taken from PRO W.O. 1/660, folios 72 through to 815 of which deal with the mobilisation and establishments of the various regiments. I have spared the general reader the precise detail of all but a few, although the more interested military historian would find the whole file an educational read. Sadler's letter regarding his balloon project is Folio 733

81　PRO WO 3/609 Folio 132. Torrens to Wellington 16 April 1815

82　Friedrich Lindau *The Reminiscences of Friedrich Lindau* ed. Bogle & Uffindell, Frontline Press 2009

83　Club Book pp.211–12

84　Ibid. p.213 and quotes which follow are all from the Club Book

85　Gronow p.65

86　Knollys p.3

87　Lindau p.155

88　Wheatley p.57

89　The story of the De Lanceys is told by Magdalene in *A Week at Waterloo* (Reportage Press, 2008) with an excellent introduction by Andrew Roberts

90　Crumplin's *Guthrie's War* (Pen & Sword, 2010) has an excellent account of Guthrie's service after Waterloo; from it I have drawn this material

91　Haddy James *Surgeon James's Journal 1815* ed. Jane Vansittart (Cassell, 1964) is Haddy James's own very vivid account of Waterloo

92 Edward Heeley kept a remarkable journal during the Waterloo campaign which is now in the National Army Museum

93 Mercer p.2

94 Johnston's correspondence is reproduced in *The Waterloo Archive* ed. Gareth Glover, WA3 p.39

95 Schofield p.343

2: April–June 1815

1 WA4 p.98

2 PRO WO 3/609 Folio 85

3 Quoted in Brett James *The 100 Days* p.20

4 *Wellington at War: Letters* ed. Antony Brett-James p.306

5 Brett-James p.20

6 General Mathieu Dumas quoted by Andrew Roberts *Napoleon & Wellington* p.147

7 WA3 p.20

8 WA4 p.179

9 Mercer p.47

10 WA3 p.125

11 WA4 p.204

12 Haythornthwaite has a good piece on this system in *Redcoats* p.114

13 WA3 p.24

14 O'Grady letters NAM 1990-08-140-23-2

15 Ilbert's extensive correspondence with his wife is reproduced in WA3

16 Quoted in Haythornthwaite *Redcoats* p.127

17 WA3 p.30

18 WA4 p.10

19 Lieutenant-Colonel the Hon. Henry Murray 18th Hussars/Light Dragoons; his correspondence is in the NAM: 7406-34. His writing is very difficult to read

20 The Tennant correspondence is reproduced in full in WA3 pp.89–108

21 Murray correspondence NAM 7406-34

22 WA4 p.101

23 Based on an exchange rate of 14 franks to £1 in May 1815; this rose

to 19 franks after Napoleon invaded. See Hussey Packe's correspondence in WA4

24 O'Grady Letters NAM 9008-140-32-1

25 WA4 p.205

26 WA3 p.42

27 WA4 p.60

28 Club Book quoted by White-Spunner *Horse Guards* p.296.

29 WA3 p.41

30 The correspondence between Wellington and the Duke of York is in the PRO WO 3/609. Although it is not immediately relevant to this book, I spent an enjoyable few hours reading through it. It dispels a few established myths and I would recommend that file as required reading for anyone embarking on a study of the Allied high command in the Waterloo campaign

31 WA4 p.180

32 Trafford's description is from the Club Book p.217 and also covered in detail in White-Spunner *Horse Guards* pp.315–16

33 Mercer p.118

34 Club Book, p.217

35 Murray's correspondence NAM 7406-34; letter to his wife dated 7 June 1815

36 The issue of at what level of tactical unit to mix nationalities has exercised armies for centuries. Most modern commanders would agree with Wellington that even today it is inadvisable to mix nationalities within a brigade for demanding tactical actions. That said, politics plays as much a part in these decisions as military common sense, and the author commanded a brigade in Macedonia with 21 different nationalities and one in Kabul of 16. Neither mission was, understandably, as taxing as Waterloo!

37 We have very exact figures for each formation at Waterloo thanks to the extensive and forensic interest taken in the battle immediately afterwards. Mark Adkin's *The Waterloo Companion* has an excellent wiring diagram of the Allied order of battle, with exact figures, and *The Waterloo Roll Call* tells us who the individual officers were. The First Guards numbered 4,266; the Second Division, 7,992; the Third Division, 8,091; the Fourth Division, 2,245; the Fifth Division, 6,724; and the Sixth, 5,158,

although this last formation was not actually present at the battle. For details of numbers in each brigade and battalion, see Adkin pp.39–50

38 I am indebted to my friend and black-powder expert Brian Gibbs for taking me through the musketry drills and describing the process and effect of firing a Waterloo Brown Bess

39 Mark Adkin's *The Waterloo Companion* gives an excellent and comprehensive breakdown of both musketry drills and infantry tactics. See also Haythornthwaite p.52

40 See Hibbert *Waterloo* p.117

41 Anton p.184

42 Mercer p.91

43 Mercer p.83. Mercer gives a complete description of the organisation of a British artillery battery/troop on pp.87–9

44 Haythornthwaite p.124

45 Ibid. p.99

46 The individual incidences are recorded by Burnham & McGuigan p.233; those who would lose their Colours in the Waterloo campaign were 2nd Battalion 69th Foot (at Quatre Bras), and 5th & 8th Battalions of the King's German Legion at Waterloo itself

47 Morris p.133

48 WA4 p.178

49 Hilton p.179

50 From the portrait of Colonel Frank Tidy by his daughter which appears in several sources; WA1 p.169 has a full extract, as does *100 Days*

51 Harris p.93

52 Oman p.249

53 Ibid. Burnham & McGuigan have useful statistics on the number of floggings ordered by regimental courts pp.204–8 and Coss has a good general description pp.140–2

54 Costello p.163

55 Described by Private O'Neil of 8th Foot, who received 300 lashes for refusing to attend church parade and quoted by Coss p.139

56 Ibid. Coss gives a good analysis of the utility and effects of flogging

57 Wheeler p.15

58 Morris p.93.

59 WA4 pp.182–3
60 Zamoyski has comprehensive coverage of French use of corporal punishment on their own troops in the 1812 campaign
61 Household Cavalry Museum Archive AB2989 Item 29
62 Wheeler p.153
63 Burnham & McGuigan p.14
64 Haythornthwaite pp.68–70 is a good survey of chaplaincy cover in the Peninsula
65 Divall *Inside the Regiment* p.188; Divall gives a useful survey of regimental and army medical arrangements in Chapter 8
66 Oman has a good piece on the Brunswickers in the Peninsula (p.224) and Adkin has an excellent synopsis of their Waterloo order of battle on p.181
67 This story is reproduced by Adkin p.181 but I cannot find it in Costello's original diary
68 Household Cavalry Museum Archive AB2999.
69 Quoted in Mann p.5; for a more polished version see WA3 p.25
70 NAM 1971-01-20
71 Morris p.130
72 Heeley Manuscript NAM p.12

3: 12–17 June 1815

1 Fortescue p.63. Fortescue has the best summary of the preliminary strategic moves in the Waterloo campaign
2 Morgan Crofton *The Household Cavalry Brigade in the Waterloo Campaign* p.9
3 William O'Connor Morris *The Campaign of 1815* p.67
4 I have taken these figures partly from Fortescue and partly from Adkin p. 285
5 O'Connor Morris p.67
6 Fortescue p.62
7 O'Connor Morris p.67
8 Lady Georgiana Lennox's memoirs quoted by Brett-James p.41
9 Heeley p.12
10 Ross-Lewin p.176
11 Heeley pp.12–13

12 WA4 p.33
13 White-Spunner p.318
14 Farmer p.138
15 Brett-James p.50
16 Mercer p.127
17 Lawrence p.107
18 Morris p.130
19 Heeley p.12
20 Brett-James p.47
21 De Lancey p.4
22 Staveley letters NAM 1999-06-149-10
23 WA4 p.133
24 WA3 p.194
25 Costello p.210
26 WA4 p.33
27 Haddy James p.16
28 Farmer p.139
29 Wheatley p.60
30 Costello p.211
31 Gardiner recovered, went on to half pay in 1819 and finally retired from the Army in 1827
32 Simmons's correspondence is reproduced in WA4 pp.201–23
33 Anton p.193
34 The full text of Soult's message is reproduced in the correspondence of Captain Bourdon de Vatry, an ADC to Jérôme Bonaparte, and quoted by Brett-James p.65
35 Fortescue p.100; Fortescue has the best description of this part of the battle and I have made considerable use of his account
36 WA3 p.137
37 Stanhope p.172
38 Captain Frederick Pattison, of the 33rd, saw the engagement and wrote about it in his account. Hope Pattison p.50
39 See *Waterloo Roll Call* p.143 and Brett-James p. 63
40 Private George Hemingway to his mother 14 August 1815; reproduced in WA1 p.167
41 Pattison's account of Quatre Bras is contained in the first letter of his Memoirs; pp. 47–53

42 Hope Pattison p.51
43 Ensign Robert Batty, 1st Guards, quoted by Brett-James p.56
44 Ibid.
45 Fortescue p.108
46 Clay p.7
47 Ibid. p.10
48 The correspondence about Barrington's death is reproduced in WA4 p.135 onwards
49 Fortescue p.125 quoting Houssaye's *Waterloo* p.80
50 Account of Major Lemonnier-Delafosse, ADC to Foy, quoted by Brett-James p.65
51 Malcolm's correspondence is reproduced in WA3 p.137
52 He survived his wound, became a major and lived until 1829. See *Waterloo Roll Call* p.159
53 Clay p.10
54 WA4 pp.211–12
55 Clay p.7
56 Morris p.135.
57 Clay p.12
58 WA4 p.214
59 Morris p.139
60 Mercer p.146
61 Standish O'Grady's correspondence NAM 9008-140-32-1
62 Haddy James p.23
63 Ibid. p.24
64 White-Spunner *Horse Guards* p.322
65 Much of this detail and Kincaid's quote is from Morgan Crofton p.30
66 Mercer p.148
67 Mercer's long and exciting account of his withdrawal on 17 June is pp.139–56 in his journal

4: 18 June 1815: Morning and Afternoon

1 Wheeler p.169
2 Haddy James p.27
3 Fortescue p.128

4 Wheatley p.63
5 Quoted by Brett-James p.100
6 Clay p.14
7 Haddy James p.28
8 Club Book p.218
9 Hay p.174
10 WA4 p.184
11 WA1 p.111
12 Wheeler p.170
13 Private George Hemingway in a letter to his mother; WA1 p.167
14 2nd Lieutenant Richard Eyre to his mother; WA3 p.115
15 Playford's diary; Household Cavalry Museum Archive AB2999.
16 Described by Anton p.209 and Ross-Lewin p.184
17 Mercer pp.157–9
18 Mann p.28
19 Hibbert p.106
20 Morris p.145
21 Professor Laurent Bock of the University of Gembloux has done much work on the topography of the battlefield, some of which was broadcast on the History Channel on 28 December 2008
22 Anton p.206
23 Private John Smith to his brother 14 July 1815; WA3 p.113
24 Heyland's letter is reproduced in WA3 p.139
25 One could write a book in itself on the numbers present on the battlefield; there is no absolutely accurate count. I have used Adkin's figures over Siborne's and Fortescue's as he seems to have done the maths more thoroughly
26 Lieutenant-Colonel Ponsonby's record of the battle, reproduced in WA4 p.57
27 This conversation is taken from *La Vie Militaire du Général Foy* and is quoted at length by Fortescue p.137. It is not clear whether Foy witnessed this exchange or whether Reille told him about it afterwards
28 Anglesey *One Leg: The Life & Letters of Henry William Paget, First Marquess of Anglesey* p.132
29 Gronow p.68
30 Hay pp.163–4
31 Wheatley p.64

32 Ibid. p.64
33 Brett-James p.105
34 Lindau p.163
35 Murray's journal NAM 7406-34, and also quoted in Andrew Uffindell *National Army Museum Book of Wellington's Armies* p.291
36 Ibid. p.291
37 Both quoted by Field p.55
38 Haddy James p.32
39 Napoleon *Memoirs* (Soho Books, 1986) p.522 and quoted by Field *Waterloo: The French Perspective* (Pen & Sword, 2012) p.53
40 Letter from Ensign Short to his mother dated 19 June 1815. In possession of the author
41 Field p.70
42 Clay p.26
43 Gronow p.68
44 Wheatley p.64
45 I have taken these figures from Adkin's analysis of the Grand Battery, which is the most detailed available; *Waterloo Companion* p.301
46 John Grant to his father; original in Hart papers in Northumberland Record Office. Copy in NAM 8111-802
47 *A Soldier of the 71st* p.107
48 Lawrence p.109
49 WA1 pp.13–14
50 WA3 p.113
51 Morris p.147
52 Mercer p.165
53 Ibid.
54 This story appears in *A Memoir of Charles Mayne Young* (1871) Chapter VII pp.168–72, where it is considerably elaborated, and also in G. R. Gleig *The Life of Arthur Duke of Wellington* (1909) Chapter XXVII p.230, but I am not sure it really happened
55 Related by Ensign George Keppel and quoted by Adkin p.159
56 Playford Diary
57 Heeley pp.20–1
58 Corporal Canler, 28th Ligne, quoted in Field p.99
59 Captain Duthilt, ADC to General Bourgeois, and quoted by Brett-James p.115
60 Lieutenant Jacques Martin, 45th Ligne, quoted in Field p.98

61 Adkin p.346
62 Field p.99
63 Captain Duthilt, 45th Regiment, quoted by Brett-James p.115
64 Lieutenant Martin quoted by Field p.99
65 Quoted by Brett-James p.114
66 The 7th Battalion, which held its position in the line, was later publicly congratulated by Wellington
67 Duthilt, for one
68 Diary of an unknown officer of 95th Rifles quoted in WA4 p.199
69 Brett-James p.115
70 Elton's letters are in the NAM 1963-10-36. This is from his of 15 July to the Colonel of the King's Dragoon Guards
71 Playford manuscript
72 Ibid.
73 Ibid.
74 Taken from interviews conducted by the artist Benjamin Haydon after the battle and reproduced in WA1 p.232
75 Richard Coulter 1st Life Guards to his cousin 20 July 1815; Household Cavalry Museum Archive Box 42
76 The individual stories recounted here are mostly from White-Spunner *Horse Guards* pp.329–35
77 Playford manuscript
78 Kennedy Clark's extensive correspondence is in the Household Cavalry Museum Archive
79 *Waterloo Roll Call* p.57. She was later granted a pension of £50 per annum in recognition of her son's service
80 White-Spunner *Horse Guards* p.334
81 Ibid. p.333
82 The best description of the Scots Greys' charge is given by Corporal John Dickson and reproduced by Brett-James p.117
83 WA3 p.31. Unnamed source
84 Ewart's account has been published in many sources; Brett-James p.119
85 Anton pp.210–11
86 Brett-James p.115
87 Hay p.183
88 The British Army is sometimes absurdly oversentimental about dogs. When the author was commanding 16 Air Assault Brigade in Kabul

in 2001, the Brigade Signal Squadron adopted an Afghan stray called Tiger. Despite very strict orders that he was to stay in Kabul, I discovered him about a year later living happily in the squadron accommodation in Colchester, having been smuggled back, no doubt to the horror of every Health & Safety official in the land

89   Ponsonby told his story when he had eventually recovered; his story became very well known. It is reproduced in WA4 p.57
90   Brett-James p.119
91   Captain Chapuis, 85th Ligne, quoted by Field p.113
92   Adkin p.352
93   Private Thomas Hasker's story is from WA1 p.18
94   Hibbert's letters p.10
95   Playford Diary
96   Lieutenant-Colonel Wyndham quoted by Field p.115
97   Fortescue p.159, as is the quote above
98   Field p.119
99   Brett-James p.114

5: 18 June 1815: Afternoon and Evening

1   Clay p.25
2   Brett-James p.111
3   Ibid. p.112; the original is in Apsley House
4   Paget & Saunders p.64
5   Ibid.
6   WA1 p.137
7   Clay p.27
8   Quoted by Paget & Saunders p.63.
9   Ibid. p.111
10   Field p.128
11   Paget & Saunders p.58.
12   Ibid. p.59
13   Home's views are given in a letter to Mr Mudford. He was equally critical of Wellington on other matters. Quoted in WA1 p.142
14   There is some controversy about this as Colonel Trefcon, who was Bachelu's chief of staff, later stated that they did not move until much later in the day. As always during the battle it is impossible to reconcile

timings accurately as everyone seems to have had his own idea as to
what happened when. If these troops were not from Bachelu's division, then it is hard to identify where Reille found them

15 Hepburn quoted by Paget & Saunders p.68
16 Ibid.
17 Mercer p.167
18 Brett-James p.141
19 Ibid. p.145
20 Lindau pp.168–70
21 Field p.139
22 Gronow p.69
23 Gunner John Edwards to his brother, quoted in WAI p.102
24 Mercer pp.172–3
25 Gunner Edwards, op. cit.
26 Wheatley p.65
27 Gronow p.69
28 Morris p.148
29 WA1 p.158
30 Gronow p.71
31 Morris p.152
32 Quoted by Brett-James p.132
33 Lieutenant-Colonel F. S. Tidy by his daughter. Reproduced several
   times and partly in WA1 pp.169–76
34 Mercer p.175
35 *A Soldier of the Seventy-First* p.108
36 Gronow quoted by Brett-James p.135
37 Field p.158 quoting Captain de Brack
38 *A Soldier of the Seventy-First* p.108
39 NAM 9008-140-27-2
40 Gronow p.70
41 Morris p.149
42 Quoted by Adkin p.361
43 Mercer p.176
44 Field p.156 quoting Colonel Trefcon and General Foy
45 *A Soldier of the Seventy-First* p.108
46 WA1 p.159
47 Gronow p.70

48 Ibid.

49 Anton p.213

50 Mercer p.177

51 Morris p.149

52 Lawrence p.110

53 Quoted by Brett-James p.147

54 Story told by Sergeant Archibald Johnston, Scots Greys, and quoted in WA1 p.52

55 Brett-James p.143

56 Ibid.

57 Beamish *Journal of 5th Line Battalion King's German Legion* quoted in Wheatley p.69

58 Fortescue p.175

59 Captain Berger, 5th Line Battalion King's German Legion, quoted by Summerville p.377

60 Wheatley p.70

61 Brett-James p.154

62 Field p.173

63 See Kempt's correspondence, reproduced in WA4 p.196

64 This record of Vivian's trumpeter is from the account of Sergeant Matthew Colgan and reproduced in WA4 p.93

65 Sergeant Matthew Colgan's correspondence quoted in WA4 p.94

66 Although there are several descriptions from officers of the 95th who saw what happened to them from the sandpit; see Simmons and also WA4 p.200 for an account by an unknown officer

67 Mercer pp.177–9

68 Actually they did go into action in 1807 and performed rather well

69 From John R. Elting *Swords Around a Throne* p.183

70 Brett-James p.155

71 Colonel Octave Levasseur's memoirs, quoted by Brett-James p.158

72 Ney to Joseph Fouché, President of the Provisional Government in Paris. Brett-James p.159

73 Ibid. note 67

74 Ibid. p.162

75 Ibid. p.156; the 52nd spelled serjeant with a 'j' rather than a 'g', as the Rifles still do in the British Army today

76 Ibid. p.154

77   Ibid. pp.154-5

78   Gronow p.70

79   Brett-James p.160

80   Gronow p.71

81   Leeke, quoted in Field p.202

82   Captain John Kincaid quoted in Brett-James p.163

83   Captain William Clayton of the Blues quoted in Brett-James p.164

84   Gambier, an officer of the 52nd, quoted in Adkin

85   Summerville p.63 quoting Colonel Campbell

86   Field p.216

87   Adkin p.399

88   Field p.225

89   WA3 p.113

90   *A Soldier of the Seventy-First* p.109

91   Mercer p.179

92   Leeke quoted by Brett-James p.169

93   William Tomkinson *With Wellington's Light Cavalry* p.312

94   Private John Marshall's letter to his parents quoted in WA1 p.90

95   Lieutenant Henry Duperieur WA3 p.80

96   Quoted by Haythornthwaite p.139

97   Edward Cotton *A Voice from Waterloo* p.127

98   Private Richard Coulter to his brother 20 July 1815, Household
     Cavalry Museum Archive

99   Lindau's account of his escape, which is an exciting story in itself, is
     told in full in *A Waterloo Hero* pp.174–80

100 Wheatley pp.72–4

101 WA1 p.91

102 Mercer p.181

103 Wheeler p.112

104 WA1 p.143

6: 19 June and Afterwards

1   This account is as told by the actor Julian Young and is from Brett-
    James p.190

2   Morris p.161

3   Brett-James p.163

4 I have used the figures worked out by Adkin (p.73) as they seem to be the most accurate available
5 Gronow p.72
6 Clay p.30
7 Mercer p.187
8 Hibbert's letters p.10
9 Tomkinson p.315
10 Playford's Journal, Household Cavalry Museum Archive
11 Club Book p.211
12 Haythornthwaite *Redcoats* p.70
13 Brett-James p.179
14 Ibid.
15 Ensign James Howard to his brother from Paris 8 July; reproduced in WA1 p.164–6
16 Mercer p.189
17 Ensign Thomas Wedgwood to Mrs John Wedgwood 24 June 1815; reproduced in WA1 p.148
18 Lieutenant George Horton to Lady Mary Horton 23 June; WA1 p.154
19 Clay p.31
20 Brett-James p.177
21 WA1 p.161
22 Playford Manuscript, Household Cavalry Museum Archive
23 Farmer p.157
24 Gronow p.75
25 Hay p.193
26 Edward Heeley's Journal, NAM
27 Lindau pp.176–80
28 Wheatley pp.73–85
29 Adjutant General's Report April 1816 quoted in Haythornthwaite p.167
30 Crumplin's biography of Guthrie covers his whole military career from Canada through to Waterloo
31 Haythornthwaite p.162
32 Haddy James p.35
33 Captain John Whale, 1st Life Guards, quoted in WA4 p.33–4
34 Costello pp.214–15
35 Ibid. p.216

36 Simmons pp.369–79

37 Sir Charles Bell quoted in Brett-James p.202

38 Assistant Surgeon Donald Finlayson, 33rd Foot; WA3 p.217

39 John Davy quoted in WA1 p.221

40 Magdalene De Lancey *A Week at Waterloo* tells the full, sad story

41 Bingley's letters are in the Household Cavalry Museum Archive AB2989

42 Greenock's letter from Roissy 1 July 1815 quoted in WA4 p.4

43 Kelly's letters are in The Household Cavalry Archive Box 42.

44 Standish O'Grady to his mother 25 June 1815

45 Sergeant William Tennant to his wife 19 June 1815; WA3 pp.94–5

46 Arthur Kennedy to his mother 8 July 1815, quoted in WA4 p.84

47 Heeley's Journal, NAM

48 Mercer p.271

49 NAM 1988-04-32; Philip Wodehouse to Miss Parry

50 NAM 7607-34; Private John Abbott to Anne Bank from Vervier 12 November 1815

51 Army General Order No. 2 and No. 4 Nivelles 20 June 1815; General Orders 1810–18 Vol. VII

52 Club Book pp.212–13

53 Ibid.

54 Lawrence p.115

55 WA3 p.105

56 Wheeler p.187

57 All the descriptions of the Royals in Normandy come from the Club Book pp.221–4

58 NAM 9008-140-32-1 O'Grady to his mother 7 September 1815

59 WA3 p.214

60 Brett-James p.221

61 Morris p.200

62 Haythornthwaite p.170

63 Anton p.253

64 WA1 p.105

65 PRO WO 3/609 Folio 297 War Office letter 28 June 1815

66 For example, the Eagle of the 105th, captured by the Royal Dragoons, is claimed by The Blues & Royals although it is on display in the National Army Museum, which maintains that, because of the Regent's order, it belongs to the nation rather than to the regiment.

The author, as an officer of The Blues and Royals and a trustee of both the Household Cavalry and the National Army Museum, finds his loyalties somewhat divided. The regiment currently has a replica

67　For more detail see White-Spunner pp.346–9

68　Gronow p.73

69　Household Cavalry Museum Archive AB2385 Item 42; George Gunning's account of Waterloo

70　Kempt to Major-General Sir James Willoughby Gordon 3 July 1815; quoted in WA4 p.195

71　Gronow p.74

72　Stanhope p.177

73　Private John Marshall to his parents 11 July 1815 WA1 p.91

74　Wellington to Lord Mulgrave, Paris, 21 December 1815. From *Wellington at War* p.322

75　*The Times* Thursday 22 June 1815

76　Wellington to John Wilson Croker from Paris 17 August 1815. *Wellington at War* p.320

77　White-Spunner p.349

78　WA4 p.118

79　Club Book p.216

80　NAM 2002-02-910-4, which includes his obituary from the Derby *Mercury*

81　Lawrence pp.114–28

82　Wheatley p.88

83　White-Spunner p.366

84　Haythornthwaite pp.175–7

85　*A Soldier of the Seventy-First* p.112

86　Costello pp.228–34

87　Hay p.194

88　Quoted unsourced by Adkin p.340

89　NAM 1974-12-129; Private Richard Armstrong letter 1 September 1815

90　Gronow p.358

91　His letter is with Slade's papers in the Household Cavalry Museum Archive AB2997 Item 46

92　Club Book p.217

BIBLIOGRAPHY

So much has been published about Waterloo, both by people who were there and subsequent historians, that anyone writing about the battle now has to be selective. There is also much unpublished material, and I am sure more lurking in regimental archives or family attics that we still have the pleasure of discovering. I have concentrated on first-hand accounts, preferably by the more junior ranks, as it is their story I want to tell. I have listed a short bibliography below. The best collection of original manuscripts is in the National Army Museum archive, on which I have drawn extensively. The Public Record Office files in the National Archive have added some useful factual background and the odd touch of colour, whilst our own Household Cavalry Museum Archive remains one of the finest collections military of documents, much of it still to be properly studied. I am particularly indebted to Gareth Glover, the doyen of Waterloo researchers, for his most excellent series *The Waterloo Archive*, which is invaluable for anyone now studying the battle. Published in six volumes, the *Archive* is an anthology of original letters and diaries from British and German sources, most of which are previously unpublished. Another book I have found particularly useful is Mark Adkin's

The Waterloo Companion, a complete factual guide to the battle with well researched facts and figures and excellent plans. These two authors' work has helped me considerably.

Otherwise I have consulted:

Unpublished Sources

National Archive

W.O.1/660: War Office Correspondence 1815
W.O. 1/205: Regimental Correspondence
W.O. 44/730: 1818 Reductions
W.O. 1/160: Various War Office Correspondence
W.O. 3/609 War Office Out Book February to August 1815
W.O. 3.610: War Office Out Book August 1815 to February 1816
W.O. 4/427: Miscellaneous Correspondence
W.O. 1/1136: Miscellaneous Correspondence

Household Cavalry Museum Archive

Club Book: The unofficial diary of the subalterns of 1st Royal Dragoons in the Peninsular and Waterloo. AB2566

Correspondence in Box 42:

Bingley, Private John, RHG: AB2989
Casualty Returns: AB3145, 2370, 2963 and 2989 Items 25 & 26
Coulter, Private Richard, 1LG: Box 42 unnumbered letter
Elley, Sir John, RHG: AB2197
Equipment Losses: AB2989 Item 27
Gill, Private: AB2997
Gunning, Captain George: AB2385
Kelly, Captain (later Colonel) Edward: AB2193
Kennedy, Captain Alexander Clark, 1RD: AB2392
Kershaw, Private Hartley, 1LG: AB2161
Lallemand, Lieutenant-general (French Army): Correspondence with General Slade AB2997

Playford, Corporal of Horse Thomas, 2LG: Diary. AB2999
Prize Money Recipients: AB2989 Item 28
Regimental Orders: 1 LG: 2LG: AB2545 RHG: 1RD:
Richmond, Duchess of: AB2989
Somerset, Major-General Lord Edward: AB2997
Tathwell, Lieutenant Tathwell Baker, RHG: AB2989

Makins, Major (later Colonel) Douglas, *Cavalry & their Leaders in the Peninsula*, Staff College Lecture 1906

National Army Museum

Some National Army Museum sources have been compiled and published by Andrew Uffindell in his *National Army Museum Book of Wellington's Armies* (Pan 2005).

Others consulted with accession numbers from the Templer Study Centre archive are:

Abbott, Private John, 51st Light Infantry, 7607-34
Armstrong, Private Richard, 51st Light Infantry, 1974-12-129
Bingham, Private Thomas, Royal Horse Guards, 1990-08-79
Boulter, Private Samuel, Scots Greys, 9501-118
Churchill, Major Chatham, 1st Guards, 1990-12-38
Colborne, Colonel Sir John, 52nd Light Infantry, 1968-07-452-10
Elton, Captain William, 1st Dragoon Guards, 1963-10-36
Evelyn, Captain G, 3rd Guards, 1993-10-134
Gairdner, Lieutenant James Penman, 95th Rifles, 1971-01-20
General Orders 1810–1818 Vol. VII 11 April – 31 December 1815
Gomm, Lieutenant-General Sir William, 1989-02-199
Grove, Captain Henry, 23rd Light Dragoons, 1978-05-74
Gubbins, Captain James, 13th Light Dragoons, 1992-12-138
Hamilton, Lieutenant James, KGL, 2002-02-1352
Hart, Lieutenant John, 52nd Light Infantry, 8011-802
Heeley, Edward, 1984-09-98
Kelly, Captain Edward, 1st Life Guards, 2002-01-254 (but the complete set of Kelly's letters are in the Household Cavalry Museum Archive)

Murray, Lieutenant-Colonel Hon. Henry, 18th Light Dragoons, 7406-34

O'Grady, Lieutenant Standish, 7th Hussars, 9008-140-32-1

Pritchard, Private William, 3rd Guards, 1968-07-157-17

Simmonds, Sergeant William, 7th Hussars, 1997-04-51

Slow, Surgeon-Major David, Royal Horse Guards, 1992-07-77

Staveley, Lieutenant William, Staff, 1999-06-149

Tellier, Pierre-Joseph, 1990-06-169

Turner, Lieutenant William, 13th Light Dragoons, 7509-62

Tyrwhitt-Drake, Captain William, Royal Horse Guards, 2001-06-27
(contains full details of heavy cavalry saddlery, equipment, saddling
instructions and costs)

Walton, Ensign William, Coldstream Guards, 1976-08-14

Wodehouse, Captain Philip, 1988-04-32

Other Unpublished Sources

Bowlby, Captain Peter, 4th (Kings Own), King's Own Royal Regiment
Museum archive, KO0949/02

Clark, Trooper James, 2nd Life Guards: Correspondence with his parents
12 February to 4 June 1815. In possession of Valerie Lanceley

Short, Ensign C.W., Coldstream Guards: Letter of 19 June 1815 to his
mother. In possession of Gary Barnshaw

Published Primary Sources

A British Officer on the Staff, *An Account of the Battle of Waterloo* (Gosling
Press, 1993)

Aitchinson, John, *The Letters of John Aitchinson,* ed. W. F. K. Thompson
(Michael Joseph, 1981)

Anton, Quartermaster Sergeant James, *Retrospect of a Military Life of the
Last War* (Edinburgh, 1841; reproduced Ken Trotman, 1991)

Army List: *A List of all the Officers of the Army and Royal Marines on Full and
Half Pay* (War Office, 13 March 1815)

Army List 1815 (reprinted by Naval & Military Press)

Bell, Major-General Sir George, *Soldier's Glory* (Spellmount, 1991)

Blathwayt, Colonel George, *Recollections of My Life including Military Service
at Waterloo* (Ken Trotman, 2004)

Clay, Private Matthew, *A Narrative of the Battles of Quatre Bras and Waterloo, with the Defence of Hougoumont*, ed. Gareth Glover (Ken Trotman Publishing, 2008)

Coignet, Captain Jean-Roche, *The Note-Books of Captain Coignet: Soldier of the Empire, 1799–1816* (Greenhill Books, 1985)

Costello, Rifleman Edward, *The Adventures of a Soldier of the 95th (Rifles) in the Peninsular & Waterloo Campaigns of the Napoleonic Wars* (Leonaur, 2005)

Cotton, Edward, *A Voice From Waterloo* (EP Publishing, 1974)

De Lancey, Magdalen, *A Week at Waterloo* (Reportage Press Despatches, 2008)

Douglas, Sergeant John, *Douglas's Tale of the Peninsula and Waterloo*, ed. Stanley Monick (Leo Cooper, 1997)

Eaton, Charlotte Anne, *The Days of Battle; or, Quatre Bras and Waterloo* (Elibron Classics, 2005)

Facey, Sergeant Peter, *The Diary of a Veteran: The Diary of Sergeant Peter Facey, 28th (North Gloucester) Regiment of Foot 1803–1819*, ed. Gareth Glover (Ken Trotman, 2007)

Farmer, George, *The Adventures of a Light Dragoon in the Napoleonic Wars*, narrated to G. R. Gleig (Leonaur, 2006)

Glover, Gareth, *Letters from the Battle of Waterloo* (Greenhill Books, 2004)
———, *The Waterloo Archive:* Volume One: British Sources (Frontline Books, 2010); Volume Three: British Sources (Frontline Press, 2011); Volume Four: British Sources (Frontline Press, 2012); Volume Five: German Sources (Frontline Press, 2013)
———, *From Corunna to Waterloo: The Letters and Journals of Two Napoleonic Hussars 1801–1816* (Greenhill Books, 2007)
——— (ed.), *Eyewitness to the Peninsular War and the Battle of Waterloo: The Letters and Journals of Lieutenant Colonel James Stanhope* (Pen & Sword, 2010)

Gronow, Captain Rees, *The Reminiscences and Recollections of Captain Gronow*, ed. John Raymond (Bodley Head, 1964)

Hay, Captain William, *Reminiscences 1808–1815 Under Wellington* (Ken Trotman, 1992)

Hibbert, Christopher (ed.), *A Soldier of the Seventy-First: The Journal of a Soldier in the Peninsular War* (Leo Cooper, 1976)
———, *The Wheatley Diary: a journal and sketchbook kept during the*

Peninsular War and Waterloo Capaign by Edmund Wheatley (Longmans, 1964)

Hibbert, Lieutenant John, *Waterloo Letters: The 1815 Letters of Lieutenant John Hibbert, 1st King's Dragoon Guards,* (Ken Trotman, 2007)

Hope Pattison, Frederick, *Horror Recollected in Tranquillity: Memories of the Waterloo Campaign*, ed. S. Monick (Naval & Military Press, 2001)

James, Dr Haddy, *Surgeon James's Journal 1815*, ed. Jane Vansittart (Cassell, 1964)

Jones, George, *The Battle of Waterloo, also of Ligny, and Quatre Bras . . . published by authority, with circumstantial details. By a near observer . . .* (John Booth, London, 1817)

Keppel, George, Earl of Albermarle, *50 Years of My Life* (Macmillan 1876)

Lawrence, Sergeant William, *A Dorset Soldier: The Autobiography of Sergeant William Lawrence 1790–1869*, ed. Eileen Hathaway (Spellmount, 1993)

Leeke, William, *The History of Lord Seaton's Regiment* (Author, 1866; reproduced Kessinger Publishing)

Lindau, Friedrich, *A Waterloo Hero: The Adventures of Friedrich Lindau* (Hameln, 1846. English edn. ed. Bogle and Uffindell, Frontline Press, 2009)

Mercer, General Cavalié, *Journal of the Waterloo Campaign* (Da Capo Press, 1995)

Morris, Thomas, *Recollections of Military Service in 1813–1815, Through Germany, Holland, and France* (Author, 1845; reproduced Kessinger Publishing)

Patterson, Major John, *Camps And Quarters: Scenes and Impressions of Military Life* (London, 1840. This edn., Kessinger Publishing)

Richardson, Ethel M., *Long Forgotten Days* (Heath Cranton, 1928)

Ross-Lewin, Major Harry, *With 'the Thirty-Second' in the Peninsular and Other Campaigns* (Leonaur, 2010)

Shaw Kennedy, General Sir James, *Notes on the Battle of Waterloo* (Spellmount, 2003)

Siborne, Major-General H.T. *Waterloo Letters* (Greenhill Books, 1993)

Simmons, Major George, *A British Rifleman: Journals and Correspondence during the Peninsular War and the Campaign of Wellington* (Greenhill Books, 1986)

Taylor, Captain Thomas, *Letters of Captain Thomas William Taylor of the*

10th Hussars, during the Waterloo Campaign from April 20th to August 2nd, 1815 (Ken Trotman Military Monograph 4, 2002)

Tomkinson, William, *With Wellington's Light Cavalry: The Experiences of an Officer of the 16th Light Dragoons in the Peninsular and Waterloo Campaigns of the Napoleonic Wars* (first published 1894; Leonaur, 2006)

Uffindell, Andrew, *National Army Museum Book of Wellington's Armies* (Pan, 2005)

Walter, Jakob, *The Diary of a Napoleonic Foot Soldier,* (Windrush Press, 1997)

Wheeler, Private William, *The Letters of Private Wheeler 1809–1828*, ed. B. H. Liddell-Hart (Michael Joseph, 1951)

Published Secondary Sources

Adkin, Mark, *The Waterloo Companion* (Aurum Press, 2001)

Alsop, Susan Mary, *The Congress Dances* (Weidenfeld & Nicolson, 1984)

Barbero, Alessandro, *The Battle* (Atlantic Books, 2005)

Black, Jeremy, *Waterloo: The Battle That Brought Down Napoleon* (Icon Books, 2010)

Brett-James, Antony, *The Hundred Days: Napoleon's Last Campaign from Eye Witness Accounts* (Macmillan, 1964)

———, *Wellington at War 1794–1815* (Macmillan, 1961)

Bromley, Janet & David, *Wellington's Men Remembered: Volume 1 A–L* (Pen & Sword, 2012)

Bruce, Evangeline, *Napoleon and Josephine: An Improbable Marriage* (Phoenix, 1985)

Burnham, Robert & McGuigan, Ron, *The British Army Against Napoleon: Facts, Lists and Trivia 1805–1815* (Frontline Books, 2010)

Buttery, David, *Waterloo Battlefield Guide* (Pen & Sword, 2013)

Cannon, R., *Historical Record of the First, or King's, Regiment of Dragoon Guards* (London, 1837)

Chesney, Colonel Charles, *Waterloo Lectures* (Greenhill Books, 1997)

Cockerill, A. W., *Sons of the Brave: The Story of Boy Soldiers* (Leo Cooper, 1984)

Coss, Edward J., *All for the King's Shilling: The British Soldier under Wellington, 1808–1814* (University of Oklahoma Press, 2010)

Crofton, Captain Sir Morgan, *The Household Brigade in the Waterloo Campaign* (Sifton, Praed & Co. Ltd, London, 1912)

Crumplin, Michael, *Guthrie's War: A Surgeon of the Peninsula & Waterloo* (Pen & Sword, 2010)

Cusack, Ray, *Wellington's Rifles* (Pen & Sword, 2013)

Dalton, Charles, *The Waterloo Roll Call* (London, 1904. This edn. Arms & Armour Press, 1978)

Divall, Carole, *Inside the Regiment: The Officers and Men of the 30th Regiment during the Revolutionary and Napoleonic Wars* (Pen & Sword, 2011)

———, *Napoleonic Lives: Researching The British Soldiers of the Napoleonic Wars* (Pen & Sword 2012)

———, *Redcoats Against Napoleon; The 30th Regiment During the Revolutionary & Napoleonic Wars* (Pen & Sword, 2009)

Elting, John R., *Swords Around a Throne: Napoleon's Grande Armee* (Weidenfeld & Nicolson, 1988)

Esdaile, Charles, *The Peninsular War* (Penguin, 2002)

Field, Andrew W., *Waterloo: The French Perspective* (Pen & Sword, 2012)

Fisher, John, *1815* (Cassell, 1962)

Fortescue, Sir John, *The Campaign of Waterloo* (Greenhill Books, 1987)

Foulkes, Nick, *Dancing Into Battle: A Social History of the Battle of Waterloo* (Phoenix, 2006)

Gee, Austin, *The British Volunteer Movement 1794–1814* (OUP, 2003)

Gillespie–Payne, Jonathan, *Waterloo: In the Footsteps of the Commanders* (Pen & Sword, 2004)

Gleig, G. R, *The Life of Arthur Duke of Wellington* (Dent, 1909)

Graves, Donald, *Dragon Rampant: The Royal Welch Fusiliers at War: 1793-1815* (Pen & Sword, 2010)

Guy, Alan, *The Road to Waterloo: The British Army and the Struggle Against Revolutionary and Napoleonic France, 1793–1815* (Alan Sutton, National Army Museum, 1990)

Haythornthwaite, Philip, *The Waterloo Armies: Men, Organisation and Tactics* (Pen & Sword, 2007)

———, *British Infantry of the Napoleonic Wars* (Arms & Armour, 1987)

———, *Redcoats: The British Soldiers of the Napoleonic Wars* (Pen & Sword, 2012)

Hibbert, Christopher, *Waterloo* (Wordsworth, 1967)

————, *The Court at Windsor* (Longmans, 1964)

————, *Wellington: A Personal History* (Harper Collins, 1998)

Hill, Joanna, *Wellington's Right Hand: Rowland, Viscount Hill* (Spellmount Press, 2011)

Hilton, Boyd, *A Mad, Bad and Dangerous People: England 1783–1846* (Clarendon 2006)

Hofschroer, Peter, *Waterloo 1815 Series: Quatre Bras & Ligny* (Pen & Sword, 2005)

————, *Waterloo 1815 Series: Wavre, Plancenoit & the Race to Paris* (Pen & Sword, 2006)

Holmes, Richard, *Wellington: The Iron Duke* (Harper Collins, 2003)

Keegan, John, *Intelligence In War* (Pimlico, 2004)

————, *The Face of Battle* (republished Bodley Head, 2014)

Knight, Roger, *Britain Against Napoleon: The Organisation of Victory 1793–1815* (Allen Lane, 2013)

Knollys, William Wallingford, & Shaw, John, *Shaw the Life Guardsman* (originally published by Dean and Sons; this edition, Rare Books Club, 2012)

Mann, Michael, *And They Rode On* (Michael Russell, 1984)

McNish, Robin, *Iron Division: The History of the 3rd Division 1809–2000* (Ian Allan, 3rd edn., 2000)

Mileham, Patrick, *The Yeomanry Regiments* (Canongate, 1985)

Muir, Rory, *Wellington: The Path to Victory* (Yale, 2013)

O'Connor Morris, William, *The Campaign of 1815* (Grant Richards, 1900)

Oman, Sir Charles, *Wellington's Army 1809–1814* (Oxford 1912; this edn., Greenhill Books, 2006)

Paget, Sir Julian, & Saunders, Derek, *Hougoumont* (Leo Cooper, 2001)

Palmer, Alan, *Metternich: Councillor of Europe* (Phoenix, 1972)

Prince, Andrew, *Then Came a Voice He Knew: An Account of the Extraordinary Number of Related British Officers Engaged in the Waterloo Campaign of June 1815* (Ken Trotman, 2007)

Roberts, Andrew, *Napoleon & Wellington* (Phoenix, 2001)

————, *Waterloo: Napoleon's Last Gamble* (Harper Collins, 2005)

Schofield, Victoria *The Highland Furies: The Black Watch 1739–1899* (Quercus, 2013)

Steven Watson, J., *The Reign of George III, 1760–1815* (Oxford History of England) (Clarendon, 1960)

Summerville, Christopher, *Who Was Who At Waterloo* (Pearson, 2007)

Tyler, R. A. J., *Bloody Provost* (Phillimore, 1980)

White-Spunner, Barney, *Horse Guards* (Macmillan, 2006)

Wood, Field Marshal Sir Evelyn, *Cavalry at Waterloo* (Pall Mall Magazine, 1895; republished by Leonaur Books, 2009)

Young, Charles Mayne, *A Memoir* (Macmillan 1871)

Zamoyski, Adam, *1812: Napoleon's Fatal March on Moscow* (Harper Collins, 2004)

Journals, Pamphlets and Newspapers

Journal of the Society for Army Historical Research

Bamford, Andrew, *Finding Manpower for Northern Europe 1813 & 1814*, Volume 90, Number 361, Spring 2012

Clammer, David, *Pride of Service: The Dorset Volunteer Rangers 1794–1802*, Volume 90, Number 364, Winter 2012

The Times Thursday 22 June 1815

ACKNOWLEDGEMENTS

I started this book about six years ago and it has consequently taken me rather longer to prepare it for publication than I originally intended. During that period, countless kind people have both directed me to sources and patiently answered my endless and persistent queries. It is thus somewhat difficult to single out whom to thank in particular. However, I must start with Michael Sissons, my long-suffering friend and agent at PFD, who has been his usual tireless source of encouragement and advice, and Fiona Petherham, who works with him. Without Michael this book would not have happened. I am also much indebted to Mike Jones, head of non-fiction at Simon & Schuster when the manuscript was submitted, who kindly and sympathetically advised on how to improve it! Jo Whitford at Simon & Schuster has taken the project forward and has been a patient and helpful sub-editor whilst my old friend Hugo de Klee has been a painstaking copy editor.

I am also much indebted to my daughter Letty, who conducted much of the research of original sources and illustrations. I am very grateful to her for putting up with my often vague direction and frequent grumpiness. John Lloyd and Ted Land at the Household Cavalry Museum Archive in

Windsor have also been a huge help, not just for the work they have done to make that priceless collection accessible but also for their detailed help on individual documents. Colonel Stuart Cowen, Commander Household Cavalry, has kindly allowed me to quote from the Club Book, that unique manuscript which in fact is only briefly about Waterloo, mostly covering the Peninsular campaign, and which we hope soon to publish in its own right. Harry Bucknall and Valerie Lanceley have very kindly allowed me to use previously unpublished family letters and David Lyon has lent me the *Waterloo Book*, a valuable collection of letters and memoirs published very soon after the battle. Gareth Glover has kindly pointed me to other original sources and I am also most grateful to him for all the work he has done to publish his six-volume *Waterloo Archive*.

Many thanks also to my friend and black powder expert Brian Gibbs, who has educated me in the niceties of firing the Indian Pattern Brown Bess.

Mark Adkin generously allowed me to reproduce photographs from his excellent *Waterloo Companion* and Viscountess Stormont has gone to great trouble to acquire good copies of her portrait of Henry Murray and of the Raeburn of Emily Murray which hangs in the dining room at Scone Palace. Lastly many thanks to Ed Kneale, a devotee of Byron, who came up with the name *Of Living Valour* during a long lunch in Turkey, and to whom I am also indebted for pointing me towards the Hardy quote I have used as a postscript.

To them and everyone else who has helped I remain most grateful. As with anyone writing a book, I must thank my wife, Moo, our children and our dogs for putting up with me during its period of gestation.

INDEX